Oxford IB Course Preparation

MATHEMATICS

FOR IB DIPLOMA COURSE PREPARATION

Jim Fensom

Great Clarendon Street, Oxford, OX2 6DP, United Kingdom

Oxford University Press is a department of the University of Oxford.

It furthers the University's objective of excellence in research, scholarship, and education by publishing worldwide. Oxford is a registered trade mark of Oxford University Press in the UK and in certain other countries

© Oxford University Press 2020

The moral rights of the author[s] have been asserted

First published in 2020

All rights reserved. No part of this publication may be reproduced, stored in a retrieval system, or transmitted, in any form or by any means, without the prior permission in writing of Oxford University Press, or as expressly permitted by law, by licence or under terms agreed with the appropriate reprographics rights organization. Enquiries concerning reproduction outside the scope of the above should be sent to the Rights Department, Oxford University Press, at the address above.

You must not circulate this work in any other form and you must impose this same condition on any acquirer

British Library Cataloguing in Publication Data

Data available

978-1-38-200492-3

10 9 8 7 6 5 4 3 2

Paper used in the production of this book is a natural, recyclable product made from wood grown in sustainable forests.

The manufacturing process conforms to the environmental regulations of the country of origin.

Printed and bound by CPI Group UK Ltd, Croydon, CR0 4YY

Acknowledgements

The publisher would like to thank Peter Gray for authoring the DP-style questions.

Although we have made every effort to trace and contact all copyright holders before publication this has not been possible in all cases. If notified, the publisher will rectify any errors or omissions at the earliest opportunity.

Links to third party websites are provided by Oxford in good faith and for information only. Oxford disclaims any responsibility for the materials contained in any third party website referenced in this work.

The manufacturer's authorised representative in the EU for product safety is Oxford University Press España S.A. of El Parque Empresarial San Fernando de Henares, Avenida de Castilla, 2 – 28830 Madrid (www.oup.es/en or product.safety@oup.com).
OUP España S.A. also acts as importer into Spain of products made by the manufacturer.

Contents

Introduction	iv
1 Number	
1.1 Number systems	1
1.2 Sets	2
1.3 Approximations and rounding	4
1.4 Modulus (or absolute value)	6
1.5 Operations with numbers	8
1.6 Prime numbers	9
1.7 Greatest common factor and least common multiple	11
1.8 Fractions	13
1.9 Exponential expressions	15
1.10 Surds (radicals)	19
1.11 Standard form	20
Chapter 1 test	23
2 Algebra	
2.1 Manipulation of algebraic expressions	26
2.2 Calculating the numerical value by substitution	29
2.3 Addition and subtraction of algebraic fractions	31
2.4 Use of inequalities	33
2.5 Solutions to linear equations	34
2.6 Solutions to linear inequalities	39
2.7 Factorizing quadratics	41
2.8 Solutions to quadratic equations and inequalities	43
2.9 Linear equations in two variables	46
Chapter 2 test	50
3 Units and ratio	
3.1 Système international	53
3.2 Units of area and volume	54
3.3 Ratio	56
3.4 Percentages	60
3.5 Direct proportion	65
3.6 Currency	66
Chapter 3 test	69
4 Graphing functions	
4.1 Mappings	71
4.2 Graphing linear functions using technology	75
4.3 Graphing quadratic functions using technology	80
4.4 Linear and quadratic models	82
4.5 Finding the equation for a linear model	85
Chapter 4 test	87
5 Geometry	
5.1 Points, lines, planes and angles	89
5.2 The triangle sum theorem	93
5.3 Properties of triangles and quadrilaterals	94
5.4 Compass directions and bearings	99
5.5 Geometric transformations	101
Chapter 5 test	117
6 Right-angled triangles	
6.1 Pythagoras' theorem	121
6.2 Mid-point of a line segments and the distance between two points	126
6.3 Right-angle trigonometry	128
6.4 Problem solving with right-angle triangles	135
Chapter 6 test	137
7 Volumes and areas of 2- and 3-dimensional shapes	
7.1 Perimeter and area of plane figures	141
7.2 The circle	144
7.3 Three-dimensional shapes	147
Chapter 7 test	154
8 Statistics	
8.1 Collection and representation of data	158
8.2 Simple statistics	166
Chapter 8 test	173
9 Probability	
9.1 Calculating probabilities of simple events	176
9.2 Sorting data	179
9.3 Tree diagrams	184
Chapter 9 test	189
10 Speed, distance and time	
10.1 Speed, distance and time	192
10.2 Rates of change	198
Chapter 10 test	200

 Worked solutions can be found at www.oxfordsecondary.com/9781382004923

Introduction

The Diploma Programme (DP) is a two-year pre-university course for students in the 16–19 age group. In addition to offering a broad-based education and in-depth understanding of selected subjects, the course has a strong emphasis on developing intercultural competence, open-mindedness, communication skills and the ability to respect diverse points of view.

You may be reading this book during the first few months of the Diploma Programme or working through the book as a preparation for the course. You could be reading it to help you decide whether the Maths course is for you. Whatever your reasons, the book acts as a bridge from your earlier studies to DP Maths, to support your learning as you take on the challenge of the last stage of your school education.

DP course structure

The DP covers six academic areas, including languages and literature, humanities and social sciences, mathematics, natural sciences and creative arts. Within each area, you can choose one or two disciplines that are of particular interest to you and that you intend to study further at the university level. Typically, three subjects are studied at higher level (HL, 240 teaching hours per subject) and the other three at standard level (SL, 150 hours).

In addition to the selected subjects, all DP students must complete three core elements of the course: theory of knowledge, extended essay, and creativity, action, service.

Theory of knowledge (approximately 100 teaching hours) is focused on critical thinking and introduces you to the nature, structure and limitations of knowledge. An important goal of theory of knowledge is to establish links between different areas of shared and personal knowledge and make you more aware of how your own perspective might differ from those of others.

The **extended essay** is a structured and formally presented piece of writing of you to 4,000 words based on independent research in one of the approved DP disciplines. It is also possible to write an interdisciplinary extended essay that covers two DP subjects. One purpose of the extended essay activity is to develop the high-level research and writing skills expected at university.

Creativity, action, service involves a broad range of activities (typically 3–4 hours per week) that help you discover your own identity, adopt the ethical principles of the IB and become a responsible member of your community. These goals are achieved through participation in arts and creative thinking (creativity), physical exercises (activity) and voluntary work (service).

DP Mathematics syllabus

Basics

Two Mathematics subjects are offered in Group 5 of the IB Diploma: Mathematics: analysis and approaches (MAA) and Mathematics: applications and interpretation (MAI). For your IB Diploma course you will need to select one Mathematics course from:

- Mathematics: Analysis and Approaches (MAA) Standard Level (SL)
- Mathematics: Analysis and Approaches (MAA) Higher Level (HL)
- Mathematics: Applications and Interpretation (MAI) Standard Level (SL)
- Mathematics: Applications and Interpretation (MAI) Higher Level (HL)

The whole content of each SL course forms part of the corresponding HL course. There is also considerable overlap in the content of MAA and MAI and, indeed, 60 teaching hours is common to all four syllabuses.

One of the purposes of this book is to help guide you to the most appropriate course for you.

The courses

The MAA course follows a traditional approach to High School mathematics. The course guide describes a typical MAA student as one who "should be comfortable in the manipulation of algebraic expressions and enjoys the recognition of patterns and understands the mathematical generalization of these patterns … and (will have) the ability to understand simple proof." (IB Mathematics course guide 2019)

The MAI course puts more emphasis on the mathematics used in the workplace or in those other academic disciplines which increasingly rely on mathematics to underpin the work they do – for example, Biology, Environmental science, Economics, Medicine, Sociology. The course guide describes a typical MAI student as one who "should enjoy seeing mathematics used in real-world contexts and being used to solve real-world problems." (IB Mathematics course guide 2019)

How the book will help you to choose a course

This book covers the prior learning required for all the courses and the questions will help you develop the necessary skills and techniques for whichever course you do. There are a few sections in the book that are based on prior learning required for the HL courses. These are clearly labeled as "Higher level". You do not need to cover these sections if you are preparing for an SL course.

To help you decide which of the two subjects – MAA or MAI – might suit you best, some questions are labeled as **DP Style: Analysis and approaches** or **DP Style: Applications and interpretation**. There is a lot of overlap in the style as well as the content of the two courses, but the questions here focus on the differences.

The DP style: MAA questions will often allow you to work at a slightly more abstract level, to use algebra to generalize results, to make conjectures and devise simple proofs.

The DP style: MAI questions are mainly set in a real-world context. You will need to decide how to use the mathematics you have learned to solve the real-world problem. Then, when you have worked out the mathematics, you will need interpret your answer within the context given in the question.

Both of the higher level courses, and both of the standard level courses, are seen by the IB as equally challenging. There is, however, a considerable increase in difficulty between each standard level course and the corresponding higher level course. This is an increase in the difficulty of the concepts covered, as well as in the complexity of the mathematics and the depth of understanding required to succeed on the course.

In order to help you to decide whether or not a higher level course is for you, the DP-style questions are labeled as either SL or HL. These are questions based on the work within the prior learning section of the syllabus, but they are also designed to help you to develop these ideas and allow you to explore some of the consequences of the mathematics.

A potential higher level candidate is not expected to complete all of these DP style HL questions easily, but they should enjoy trying them. The IB guide describes a potential higher level student as someone who "enjoys spending time with problems and who gets pleasure and satisfaction from (their solution)".

Each chapter ends with a test. The test includes a DP-style question for both of the courses and for each of the levels.

Your experience of tackling the different types of question will indicate which course would be the most rewarding for you. This though is only one of several factors in deciding. You also need to consider which courses are offered by your school, which other diploma courses you are taking and any entry requirements for particular universities.

Internal Assessment

All DP subjects have an Internal Assessment (IA) component. This assessment allows students to demonstrate their knowledge and to apply skills in a topic of choice often linked to personal interest. The exploration is a piece of work that involves in-depth investigation in a chosen area of mathematics and/or its application to a real-world problem.

Although the IA has no time limitation like externally-assessed components, schools will have a timeline and internal deadlines for submission of a draft and the final submission after written feedback has been given on the draft. It is internally assessed by the teacher against five criteria, but like all DP internal assessment components it is subject to external moderation.

Introduction

Using this book effectively

Throughout this book you will encounter separate text boxes to alert you to ideas and concepts. Here is an overview of these features and their icons:

Icon	Feature	Description of feature
🔑	Key terms	Mathematical terms that you need to learn to prepare you for the DP Mathematics course.
◉	Key point	Definition or rule.
🔍	Investigation	A mathematical investigation, with step-by-step instructions. This will help develop your mathematical understanding of a topic and your inquiry skills. It also prepares you for your DP Mathematics course, which is taught through investigations.
✏️	Worked example	A question with a full worked solution. The working and answer are in the left-hand column. Notes in the right-hand column explain the steps in the working.
✏️	Exercise	Questions for you to answer, to practise what you have learned.
→	Note	Extra information to help you understand a worked example or an explanation.
Hint	Hint	A hint to help you answer a mathematics question.
＞	Command term	Explanation of a command term — a word that tells you what you need to do in a question, for example **identify**, or **describe**.
DP style	DP style question	A question based on the mathematics in this book, written in the style of DP questions. Labelled MAI or MAA, SL or HL, to help you get an idea of the type and difficulty of questions you will be working on in each course.
Higher Level	Higher level content	Mathematics that is only required for the Higher level DP Mathematics courses.
∞	Internal link	Reference to another section in this book, where there is more information on a topic.
🔗	DP link	Explanation of how this topic will be used or developed further in the DP courses.
🌐	DP ready: International-mindedness	Description of the use of mathematics around the world.
🧠	DP ready: Theory of knowledge	Ideas or concepts in mathematics that prompt wider discussions about the different ways of knowing.
🎓	DP ready: Approaches to learning	Lists the skills you need to be an effective DP Mathematics learner, and that you will develop as you work through the activity.

You may have covered some of the mathematics in this book before, so you may find you do not need to spend equal amounts of time on each of the chapters.

A good place to start is the first page of each chapter where the learning outcomes and key terms to be covered are listed. You can also check the chapter summary, which comes immediately before the end-of-chapter test.

NUMBER AND ALGEBRA

1 Number

Learning outcomes

In this chapter you will learn about:
- → Number systems
- → Sets
- → Approximation and rounding
- → Absolute value
- → Operations with numbers
- → Prime numbers, factors and multiples
- → Greatest common factor and least common multiple (HL only)
- → Exponential expressions
- → Exponential expressions with rational indices (HL only for MAI, SL for MAA)
- → Surds (radicals)
- → Rationalising the denominator (HL only)
- → Standard form

Key terms
- → Set
- → Approximate
- → Modulus
- → Prime number
- → Multiple
- → Factor (divisor)
- → Fraction
- → Exponent (also called power or index)
- → Surd (radical)
- → Standard form

1.1 Number systems

Key point

The natural numbers, $\mathbb{N}$, are the counting numbers (including the number 0): 0, 1, 2, 3, 4, 5, …

The integers, $\mathbb{Z}$, include all the natural numbers and their negative values too: … −2, −1, 0, 1, 2, …

The rational numbers, $\mathbb{Q}$, include all the integers and numbers in the form $\frac{a}{b}$, $b \neq 0$, where a and b are integers. Examples of rational numbers are $\frac{5}{6}, -\frac{1}{2}, \frac{20}{7}, 3\frac{1}{2}, …$

Terminating decimals like 0.5, 175, and −7.396 and recurring decimals like 0.333… and 1.7272… are also examples of rational numbers, since they can be written in the form $\frac{a}{b}$, $b \neq 0$.

The real numbers, $\mathbb{R}$, contain both the rational and irrational numbers. Irrational numbers include $\pi, \sqrt{2}, \sqrt[3]{10}$ and any non-terminating, non-recurring decimals.

DP ready | International-mindedness

Most early number systems, such as the Babylonian, Egyptian and Roman systems, had no symbol for zero. There is evidence that the Mayan civilisation in Central America had a zero symbol in the first century BCE, the Khmer civilisation in Cambodia used a zero symbol in the 6th century CE and the Hindu number system in India used a symbol for zero in the 9th century CE.

The Western number system, based on the Hindu-Arabic system, was only introduced in the 13th century CE.

1

NUMBER AND ALGEBRA

> **DP link**
>
> In Mathematics DP, HL students also learn about a set of numbers called the complex numbers, $\mathbb{C}$.

These groups of numbers can be organised in sequence, where each group contains all of the numbers from the previous group(s): natural numbers ($\mathbb{N}$); integers ($\mathbb{Z}$); rationals ($\mathbb{Q}$) and irrationals; real numbers ($\mathbb{R}$). For example, the rational numbers contain all of the integers and all of the natural numbers.

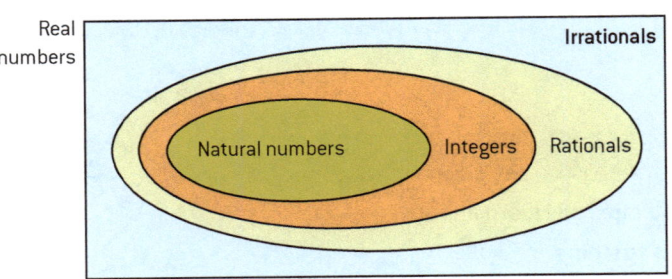

> **Command term**
>
> **Identify** means you should choose an answer from a number of possibilities.
>
> **Describe** means you should give a detailed account.

Exercise 1.1

1 **Identify** which is the *smallest* set ($\mathbb{N}, \mathbb{Z}, \mathbb{Q}$ or $\mathbb{R}$) each number belongs to.

  1 12
  2 -4
  3 0
  4 $\sqrt{5}$
  5 $\sqrt{16}$
  6 $\dfrac{5}{7}$
  7 $-\dfrac{12}{4}$

1.2 Sets

> **Key point**
>
> A **set** is a collection of objects: for example, a collection of numbers, letters, geometrical objects or anything else.

As you saw in 1.1, $\mathbb{N}, \mathbb{Z}, \mathbb{Q}$ and $\mathbb{R}$ are sets of numbers.

You **describe** a set by writing a list of everything in it, or by writing a description of what is contained in the set, written inside curly brackets (or braces) {}.

For example:

$A = \{1, 2, 3, 4\}$
$B = \{a, e, i, o, u\}$
$C = \{red, green, blue\}$
$D = \{English, Chinese, History, Physics, Mathematics, Art\}$
$E = \{\text{Integers between 1 and 10}\}$
$F = \{\text{Countries in the EU}\}$
$G = \{\text{Planets in the Solar System}\}$
$H = \{\text{Irrational numbers}\}$

You call individual items in a set **elements**.

> **Key point**
>
> The number of elements in a set A is its **cardinality**, $n(A)$.
>
> The set that contains no elements at all is the **empty set**, $\varnothing$. $n(\varnothing) = 0$.
>
> The set of all the elements you are considering is the **universal set**, U.

> **Key point**
>
> The symbol $\in$ means 'is an element of' and $\notin$ means 'is not an element of'.

For example:

$2 \in \{1, 2, 3, 4\}$ Jupiter $\in \{\text{Planets in the Solar System}\}$

You can also describe sets using **set-builder notation**.

For example, you can write the set $\{2, 3, 4, 5\}$ as $\{x \mid x \in \mathbb{N}, 2 \leq x \leq 5\}$.

| the set of values of x | such that | x is a natural number | x is between 2 and 5 inclusive |

> **Internal link**
>
> $2 \leq x \leq 5$ is an example of an inequality. You will study these in chapter 2.

1 Number

A **Venn diagram** is a way of representing sets:

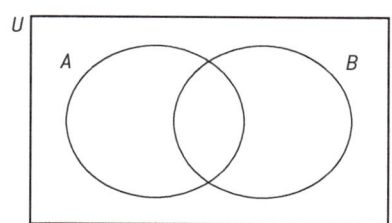

Key point

The set of elements that are in both A and B is the **intersection** of A and B, $A \cap B$.

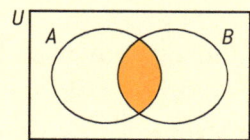

The set of elements that are either in A or B or both is the **union** of A and B, $A \cup B$.

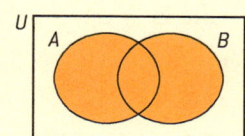

The set of elements of U that are not in A is the **complement** of A, that is, A'. $A' = \{x \mid x \in U, x \notin A\}$.

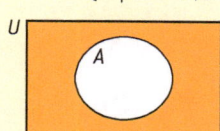

Example 1

$U = \{1, 2, 3, 4, 5, 6, 7, 8, 9\}$, $A = \{2, 4, 6, 8\}$ and $B = \{3, 6, 9\}$.
Draw a Venn diagram to represent these sets.

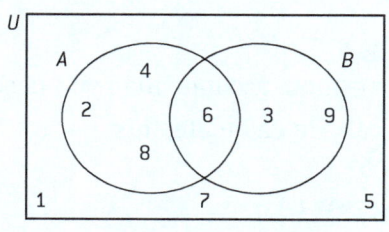

6 is in both A and B so write it in the intersection.

The other elements of A are 2, 4 and 8. Write these in the outer part of A.

The other elements of B are 3 and 9. Write these in the outer part of B.

The other elements of U are 1, 5 and 7. Write these outside of A and B.

Exercise 1.2

1 **Write down** the set of natural numbers that are less than 6:
   a as a list inside braces
   b using set-builder notation.

2 Consider the sets $P = \{2, 4, 6, 8\}$, $Q = \{1, 3, 5, 7\}$, $S = \{x \mid x \in \mathbb{Z}, 2 < x \leq 6\}$.
   Determine which of the following statements are true and which are false. Where a statement is false, re-write and correct it so that it is true.
   a $4 \in P$ b $5 \notin Q$ c $P \cap Q = \emptyset$ d $n(P) = 4$ e $n(P) = n(S)$

DP style   Analysis and Approaches HL

3 $U = \{n \mid n \in \mathbb{N}, n \leq 10\}$, $M = \{1, 2, 3, 5, 8\}$ and $N = \{3, 6, 8\}$
   a Draw a Venn diagram to show sets U, M and N. Write the numbers 0 to 10 in the appropriate section of the diagram.
   Write down each set as a list:
   b M' c N' d $M \cap N$ e $M \cup N$

DP link

DP students use Venn diagrams to tackle problems in probability in MAI and MAA at HL and SL.

Command term

Write down means you should obtain the answer without any calculations. You do not need to show any working.

Determine means you should obtain the only possible answer.

Note

To help you decide which of the two routes — Analysis and approaches or Applications and interpretation — might suit you best, questions have been labelled throughout. You are not expected to complete all of these DP-style questions easily, but working through them should help you to decide where your interests lie!

3

NUMBER AND ALGEBRA

4 Write down the definition of rational numbers in 1.1 using set-builder notation.

DP style — Analysis and Approaches HL

5 Given that $n(A) = 6$, $n(B) = 12$, $n(A' \cap B) = 9$ and the universal set has 24 elements, write down:

a $n(A \cap B)$ b $n(A' \cap B')$ c $n(A' \cup B')$.

DP style — Applications and Interpretation HL

6 A student conducts a survey of cars that pass the school. She notes the colour and the make of the cars. When looking at the data she notices the most common colour is silver and the most common make is Peugeot.

Of the 100 cars she surveyed, 38 were silver and 22 were made by Peugeot.

Given 48 were either made by Peugeot or were silver, use a Venn diagram to find:

a the number of cars that were neither made by Peugeot, nor were silver

b the number of silver Peugeots.

1.3 Approximations and rounding

When you use a calculator, the result may be more accurate than you need.

For example, Adam earns € 35 023 per year. He calculates his monthly salary:

$$35\,023 \div 12 = 2918.58333\ldots$$

He can round this to the nearest whole number of euros or he can round to 2 decimal places (d.p.) so it is in euros and cents.

Key point

When rounding, consider the figure immediately to the right of the last digit you are rounding to. If the next figure is 0, 1, 2, 3, or 4, round down. If the next figure is 5, 6, 7, 8, or 9, round up.

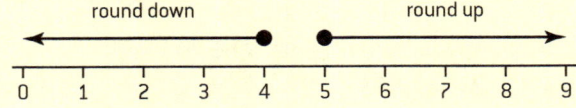

For Adam,

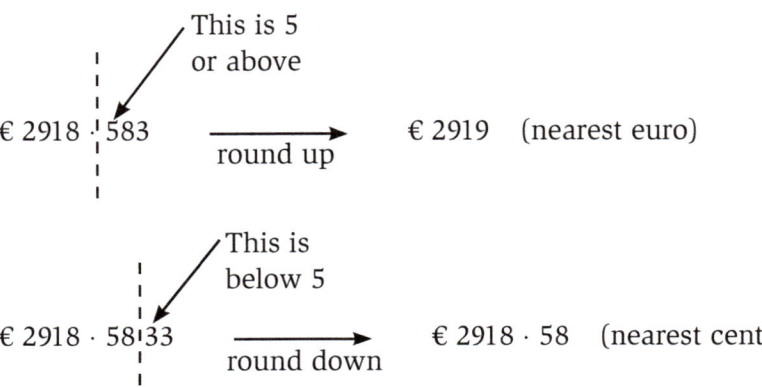

1 Number

Example 2
1 Rahul earns € 35 060 per year.
   a **Calculate** his monthly salary.
   b Calculate his weekly pay.

2 Write down the value of 456.8 to the nearest whole number.

1	a 35 060 ÷ 12 = 2921.666… Rounding to 2 d.p. Rahul's monthly salary is € 2921.67	Round the amount in euros to the nearest cent. Look at the 3rd decimal place. Since it is 6, you round up the 2nd decimal place.
	b 35 060 ÷ 52 = 674.2307… Rounding to 2 d.p. Rahul's weekly salary is € 674.23	There are 52 weeks in a year, so divide by 52. Round the amount in euros to the nearest cent. Look at the 3rd decimal place. Since it is 0, you round down the 2nd decimal place.
2	456.8 is 457 to the nearest whole number.	Look at the 1st decimal place. Since it is 8, you round the number in the units column from 6 up to 7.

> **Command term**
> **Calculate** means you should obtain a numerical answer showing the relevant stages in your working.

In IB examinations you should give numerical answers exactly or to three significant figures.

The first significant figure is the first non-zero digit from the left.

For example, 2.1538461538 = 2.15 to 3 s.f., 0.0215386 = 0.0215 to 3 s.f. and 40.52 = 40.5 to 3 s.f.

Example 3
Round these numbers to 3 s.f.
a 12.72   b 10 730   c 0.02646   d 34.65   e 7895

a 12.72 = 12.7 to 3 s.f.	Look at the 4th figure. Since it is 2, you round the 3rd figure down.
b 10 730 = 10 700 to 3 s.f.	The 4th figure is 3, so you round the 3rd figure down. Insert a zero to keep the place value.
c 0.02646 = 0.0265 to 3 s.f.	Begin counting from the first non-zero figure. The 4th figure is 6, so you round the 3rd figure up.
d 34.65 = 34.7 to 3 s.f.	The 4th figure is 5, so you round the 3rd figure up.
e 7895 = 7900 to 3 s.f.	The 4th figure is 5 so you would round the 3rd figure up, but since it is 9, you round up by 'adding 1' to the 3rd digit, which makes it ten.

Hint
If you are continuing a calculation and using an answer further, do not round your first answer. Only when you reach the final answer should you round to an appropriate degree of accuracy.

NUMBER AND ALGEBRA

DP link

Consideration of errors and the effect they have on real-life situations is one of the themes of the MAI course.

Command term

Comment means you should make an observation based on the result of your calculation.

Calculator hint

Your calculator has a key marked Ans. You can press this to use the most recently calculated value to the full accuracy of your calculator. As a shortcut, for example, instead of pressing the Ans key and typing × 5, you can type × 5 and the calculator will insert Ans for you. Some calculators also let you copy and paste answers. All calculators let you store values to use later in a calculation.

Using the value to the full accuracy of your calculator makes sure that your final answer is as accurate as possible.

Exercise 1.3

1 Round each of the following numbers given in parts **a – i** to
   i   2 d.p.
   ii the nearest whole number
   iii 3 s.f.

   a 764.382   b 234.368   c 0.02379
   d 0.005456   e 15.098   f 86.798
   g 178867.352   h 0.5798   i 29.891

DP style | **Applications and Interpretation HL**

2 A box contains 13 nails and costs $2.90.
   a The cost of the box goes up by $0.50. Calculate the new price of one nail. Write down the answer given by your calculator and then round it to 3 s.f.
   b The shopkeeper decides to put 15 nails in each box instead of 13. Use the new price of one nail from part **a** which is
      i   given unrounded by your calculator
      ii rounded to 3 s.f.
      to calculate the price of a box of 15 nails, correct to 2 d.p.
      Comment on what your answers to part **b** tell you about rounding before the final answer.

1.4 Modulus (or absolute value)

The modulus tells you how far away a number is from zero. It does not matter whether the number is positive or negative, so (for example) $|-6| = 6$ and $|6| = 6$.

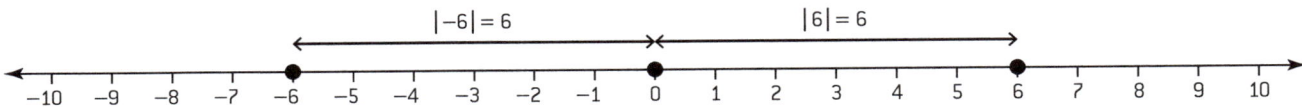

Key point

The **modulus** or absolute value $|x|$ of x is $\begin{cases} x \text{ for } x \geq 0 \\ -x \text{ for } x < 0 \end{cases}$.

Investigation 1.1

Copy and complete the table.

a	b	$\|a+b\|$	$\|a\|+\|b\|$	$\|a-b\|$	$\|b-a\|$	$\|a\|-\|b\|$	$\|\|a\|-\|b\|\|$	$\|a \times b\|$	$\|a\| \times \|b\|$
2	5								
−3	4								
1	−2								
−5	−4								

1 Number

1. Look at the results for $|a+b|$ and $|a|+|b|$. What do you notice?

   Use one of the symbols =, ≥ or ≤ (where ≤ means *less than or equal to*, and ≥ means *greater than or equal to*) to replace □ and complete the following conjecture.

   $|a+b| \,\square\, |a|+|b|$

2. Look at the results for $|a-b|$ and $|b-a|$. What do you notice?

   Use one of the symbols =, ≤ or ≥ to replace □ and complete the following conjecture.

   $|a-b| \,\square\, |b-a|$

   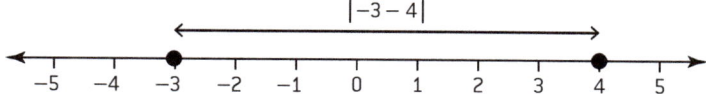

   This distance is called the **absolute difference** of the two numbers.

3. Look at the results for $|a-b|$ and $||a|-|b||$. What do you notice?

   Use one of the symbols =, ≤ or ≥ to replace □ and complete the following conjecture.

   $|a-b| \,\square\, ||a|-|b||$

4. Look at the results for $|a \times b|$ and $|a| \times |b|$. What do you notice?

   Use one of the symbols =, ≤ or ≥ to replace □ and complete the following conjecture.

   $|a \times b| \,\square\, |a| \times |b|$

Exercise 1.4

1. If $a = -5$, $b = 3$ and $c = -2$, **find**:

   a $|ab|$ **b** $|bc|$ **c** $|abc|$ **d** $|a| \times |bc|$ **e** $|a|+|b|-|c|$ **f** $|ab|-|bc|$

2. If $p = 4$ and $q = -10$, find:

   a $\left|\dfrac{p}{q}\right|$ **b** $\dfrac{|q|}{|p|}$ **c** $\dfrac{|p|}{|q|}$ **d** $\dfrac{|q|}{|p|}$ **e** $|pq^2|$ **f** $\dfrac{p}{|q^2|}$

> **Command term**
>
> **Find** means you should obtain an answer, showing relevant stages in the working.

DP style   MAA and MAI HL

3. The symbol $|a|$ is a measure of the shortest distance from a to zero.

   Imagine a city built on a grid, with roads running north–south and east–west along every unit square. To get from one place to another, you can only travel along the roads; you cannot travel through the middle of a square. The point O is at the centre of the grid.

   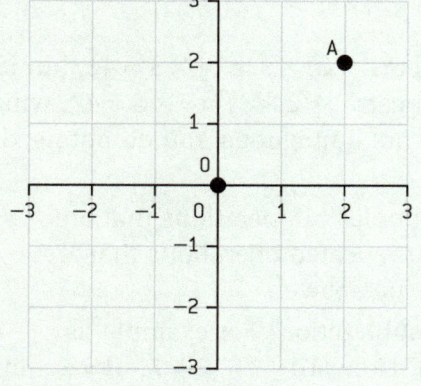

> **DP link**
>
> The MAA course will look at a range of proofs in mathematics. A result that has been proved is stronger than a conjecture as you are showing that the result is true in all cases, rather than just the specific examples from your investigation. Those at HL are more rigorous than at SL. Conjecture and proof are part of MAA HL paper 3 in particular.

NUMBER AND ALGEBRA

 Command term

Verify means

 DP link

This question follows the HL paper 3 idea (for both the MAA and MAI courses) of taking an idea and extending it with further questions.

If A is a point on the grid, let |OA| be the shortest distance of travelling from O to A.
  a If A is at (2,2), find |OA|.
  b Conjecture a formula for |OA| if A is at the point (a,b).
  c **Verify** your formula is true for the point A $(-2,1)$.

In this system we define a **circle** with radius of 4 and centre (0,0) as the set of points which are a distance of 4 units from (O,O). Using this definition, a circle of radius 4 on the grid is the set of all points, A, for which |OA| = 4.

  d Draw the circle of radius 4 on graph paper. Note: this will be a series of points rather than a continuous curve.

The diameter of a circle is defined as the longest distance between any two points on the circle.

  e Verify that the diameter (d) of the circle is 2 times the radius.

The circumference (C) of the circle is the distance around all the points in the circle.

  f Given that $C = pd$, find the value of p and verify this value is the same when considering a circle of a different radius.

DP ready | Theory of knowledge

In investigations you look at a range of specific examples and then, from these examples, you try to deduce a general result. This result is called a **conjecture**.

How do you know that a conjecture is always true?

Mathematicians try to **prove** a conjecture. In the 17th century, Pierre de Fermat made a conjecture that $x^n + y^n = z^n$ has no solutions where x, y and z are all integers for values of $n \geq 3$. For three centuries, mathematicians tried to prove or disprove this. Finally, in 1993, Andrew Wiles presented a proof of the theorem at a conference in Cambridge.

 Key point

You can summarize the rules for the order of operations as:
1. **Brackets** (or parentheses),
2. **Orders** (indices or exponents),
3. **Multiplication/Division**,
4. **Addition/Subtraction**,

You can remember this using the mnemonic **BOMDAS**

1.5 Operations with numbers

How can you find the value of $2 + 3 \times 4$?

Either: step (1): $2 + 3 = 5$ or   step(1): $3 \times 4 = 12$
        step (2): $5 \times 4 = 20$ step(2): $2 + 12 = 14$

Is the answer 20 or 14? It depends which order you carry out the operations.

The correct answer is 14. You get this when you carry out operations in the following way:

What happens when you add three numbers together? For example, $2 + 3 + 4$.

If you add 2 and 3 first, you get $(2 + 3) + 4 = 5 + 4 = 9$, but if you add 3 and 4 first then you get $2 + (3 + 4) = 2 + 7 = 9$, which is the same answer. So $2 + 3 + 4$ is not ambiguous. You do not need any parentheses to make it clear.

What happens when you multiply three numbers together? For example, $7 \times 2 \times 3$.

If you multiply 7 and 2 first, you get $(7 \times 2) \times 3 = 14 \times 3 = 42$, but if you multiply 2 and 3 first then you get $7 \times (2 \times 3) = 7 \times 6 = 42$, which is the same answer. So $7 \times 2 \times 3$ is not ambiguous. You do not need any parentheses to make it clear.

Multiplication and addition are examples of operations that are **associative**. The order you perform repeated operations that are associative makes no difference to the answer.

Does the same thing happen with subtraction? For example, is $(10 - 3) - 2$ the same as $10 - (3 - 2)$? Here $(10 - 3) - 2 = 7 - 2 = 5$ and $10 - (3 - 2) = 10 - 1 = 9$, so the answers are not the same.

Subtraction is not associative, so $10 - 3 - 2$ *is* ambiguous. Here you should work from left to right, but to make the calculation clear you should also include parentheses.

Division is not associative either. $(12 \div 6) \div 2 = 2 \div 2 = 1$ and $12 \div (6 \div 2) = 12 \div 3 = 4$. These answers are not equal, so you should use parentheses to make repeated division clear.

Example 4

Calculate **a** $3 + 6 + 12$ **b** $2 + 4 - 3$ **c** $8 + 2 \times 3$ **d** $13 - (5 - 2)$ **e** $5 \times 2 \times 7$ **f** $18 \div (2 \times 3)$

a $3 + 6 + 12 = 9 + 12$ $= 21$	Since $+$ is associative you can also calculate $3 + 6 + 12 = 3 + 18 = 21$
b $2 + 4 - 3 = 6 - 3$ $= 3$	The correct order is from left to right.
c $8 + 2 \times 3 = 8 + 6$ $= 14$	You should multiply before you add.
d $13 - (5 - 2) = 13 - 3$ $= 10$	Calculate the subtraction inside the parentheses first.
e $5 \times 2 \times 7 = 10 \times 7$ $= 70$	Since $\times$ is associative the order of calculation makes no difference to the answer. It is slightly easier to multiply $5 \times 2 = 10$ first because it is easier to multiply by 10 than it would be to multiply by 14 if you had multiplied 2×7 first.
f $18 \div (2 \times 3) = 18 \div 6$ $= 3$	You can write a division using a fraction line. $18 \div (2 \times 3)$ is the same as $\dfrac{18}{2 \times 3}$. The fraction line takes the place of the parentheses. Take care with calculations like this.

Exercise 1.5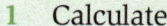

1 Calculate
   a $3 + 4 - 2$ **b** $10 - 5 - 2$ **c** $30 \div 6 \times 2$ **d** $36 \div 4 \div 3$

2 Find
   a $8 - 4 \div 2$ **b** $15 \times 2 + 4$ **c** $7 - 2 \times 3$ **d** $9 - 10 \div 5 + 2$

3 Calculate
   a $6 \times (5 - 3)$ **b** $3(4 + 2) \div 2$ **c** $\dfrac{24}{3 \times 4}$ **d** $\dfrac{5 - 2 \times 3}{3 \times 2 - 7}$

When you use your calculator, entering calculations in the same way as you would write them on paper can help a lot. Your GDC will then use the correct order of operations.

Use the fraction template that looks like to enter a fraction line. Find out how to do this with your GDC.

> **Internal link**
>
> Return to **Exercise 1.5** and calculate each of the answers with a GDC. Check that you get the same results as when you calculated them by hand.

1.6 Prime numbers

When you learned multiplication tables, $1 \times 2 = 2$, $2 \times 2 = 4$, $3 \times 2 = 6$,... you were learning about multiples. The result of multiplying one positive integer by another is its **multiple**. So, the multiples of 2 are $2, 4, 6, \ldots$

The number 12 is a multiple of 1, 2, 3, 4, 6 and 12.

A **factor** (or **divisor**) is a positive integer that will divide exactly into another integer. So, 1, 2, 3, 4, 6 and 12 are all **factors** of 12.

NUMBER AND ALGEBRA

Command term

List means you should give a sequence of brief answers with no explanation.

Key point

A **prime number** is a positive integer, greater than 1, that has exactly two factors. It is not a multiple of any other number apart from 1 and itself. Numbers that have more than two factors are composite. The number 1 is neither prime nor composite.

Example 5
a List the first 8 multiples of 3.
b Find all the factors of 48.

a The multiples of 3 are:
   3, 6, 9, 12, 15, 18, 21, 24.
b $48 = 1 \times 48, 2 \times 24, 3 \times 16, 4 \times 12, 6 \times 8$
   The factors of 48 are:
   1, 2, 3, 4, 6, 8, 12, 16, 24, 48

Example 6
Which of these numbers is prime?
a 17   b 9   c 51   d −11   e 0

17 is prime	$17 = 17 \times 1$ are the only two factors
9 is not prime	$9 = 9 \times 1$ $9 = 3 \times 3$. It has more than two factors
51 is not prime	$51 = 51 \times 1$ $51 = 17 \times 3$
−11 is not prime	−11 is not positive
0 is not prime	0 is not a positive integer

Investigation 1.2

In this investigation, you will find all the prime numbers between 1 and 100.

1	2	3	4	5	6	7	8	9	10
11	12	13	14	15	16	17	18	19	20
21	22	23	24	25	26	27	28	29	30
31	32	33	34	35	36	37	38	39	40
41	42	43	44	45	46	47	48	49	50
51	52	53	54	55	56	57	58	59	60
61	62	63	64	65	66	67	68	69	70
71	72	73	74	75	76	77	78	79	80
81	82	83	84	85	86	87	88	89	90
91	92	93	94	95	96	97	98	99	100

1 Draw a circle around 2. Cross through all multiples of 2 (such as 4, 6, 8, 10,…).
2 3 is the next number that you have not marked. Draw a circle around 3 and cross through all of its multiples. You have already crossed some of these.
3 Continue through the table, circling the first unmarked number and crossing through all its multiples.
4 What is the largest circled number that has a multiple in the square?
5 Circle the remaining unmarked numbers that are greater than 1.
6 List all the circled numbers: 2, 3, … etc. These are the prime numbers.

1 Number

The number 1 is still unmarked. It is neither a prime nor a composite number.

7 Find the values of $x^2 + x + 11$ when $x = 0, 1, 2, \ldots$ to complete this table

x	0	1	2	3	4	5	6	7	8	9	10
$x^2 + x + 11$	11	13									

8 The values when $x = 0$ and when $x = 1$ are both prime numbers. Which other values of x give prime values? Which is the smallest composite number?

9 Does the formula $x^2 + x + 11$ find all the prime numbers up to the first composite number?

Exercise 1.6

1 Are these numbers prime or composite?
   a 113   b 251   c 119   d 173   e 169

DP style — Analysis and Approaches

2 The operation $\cdot$ is defined for $a, b \in \mathbb{Z}$ by $a \cdot b = a + b - 2$.
   a By considering $a \cdot b \cdot c$ show that $\cdot$ is associative.
      The identity element e is such that $a \cdot e = a$.
   b Find the value of e.
   c Find   i $a \cdot a$ ii $a \cdot a \cdot a$ iii $a \cdot a \cdot a \cdot a$
   d Suggest an expression for $\underbrace{a \cdot a \cdot a \cdot \ldots \cdot a \cdot a \cdot a}_{n \text{ terms}}$
   e Hence, find $a \cdot 2 \cdot a \cdot 2 \cdot a \cdot 2 \cdot a \cdot 2 \cdot a$

DP link

This investigation is similar to the style of investigation which you will encounter if you study the MAA course. You will look at a variety of specific examples and then try to use these to suggest a generalization or rule.

Higher Level

1.7 Greatest common factor and least common multiple

Example 7

Find the greatest common factor of 54 and 36.

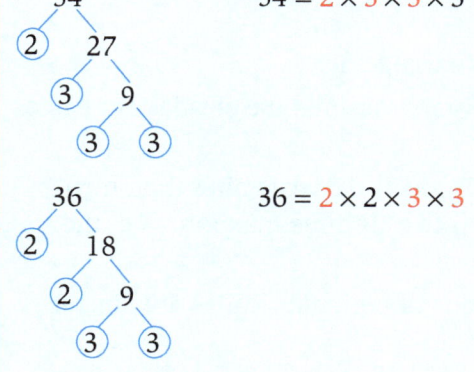

$54 = 2 \times 3 \times 3 \times 3$

$36 = 2 \times 2 \times 3 \times 3$

Begin dividing each number by the smallest prime number which is a factor. Here, divide by each of the prime numbers 2, 3, … in turn until you reach an answer 1.

Write each number as a **product** of the divisors.

$2 \times 3 \times 3 = 18$

The greatest common factor of 54 and 36 is 18.

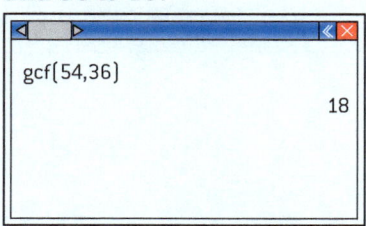

Find the product of all the factors that are common to both numbers.

Most GDCs have a function that will find the greatest common factor.

Key point

The **greatest common factor** (divisor) of two (or more) numbers is the largest number that will divide into them both.

Note

A **product** is two or more numbers multiplied together.

11

NUMBER AND ALGEBRA

 Key point

The **least common multiple** of two (or more) numbers is the smallest number that both (or all) the numbers will divide into.

 DP link

In Maths DP, HL students also learn to generalize results of greatest common factor and least common multiple in algebra and use them for factorization and combining algebraic fractions.

Example 8

Find the least common multiple of 15 and 25.

The multiples of 15 are: 15, 30, 45, 60, 75, 90, 105, 120, 135, 150, 165, 180, 195, 210, 225, 240, …	List multiples of each number
The multiples of 25 are: 25, 50, 75, 100, 125, 150, 175, 200, 225, 250, …	
The least common multiple of 15 and 25 is 75.	Find the smallest number that is in each list.
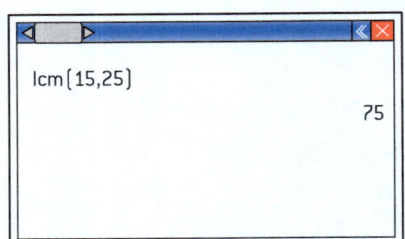	Most GDCs have a function that will find the least common multiple.

Exercise 1.7

1 Find the greatest common factor of
   a 36 and 20   b 6 and 12   c 18 and 42   d 36, 54 and 90.

2 Find the least common multiple of
   a 6 and 12   b 8 and 20   c 15 and 40   d 4, 6 and 21.

DP style | **Applications and Interpretation HL**

3 The size of populations of different species often follows a periodic cycle. Often the population will increase to a certain level and then decrease due to competition. The length of the cycle will be the time between successive maximums.

Suppose three species have cycles of length 4, 6 and 9 years respectively, and suppose all populations are at their maximum at year 0.
   a Find when the populations will again all be at their maximum together.

Periodical cicadas emerge in a swarm after a fixed number of years. Assume the cicadas are eaten by all three of the species above.
   b If a population of cicadas emerged in year 0 and periodically every 12 years after that, how many of the next ten emergences would match with **i** one **ii** two **iii** three maximums of the predator populations.

In fact, the number of years between emergences for populations of periodic cicadas are almost always prime numbers.
   c Repeat part **b** given that the population emerges every 13 years.
   d Two species of periodic cicadas share the same territory. The periods of the two groups are 13 and 17 years. Explain why these numbers will provide an evolutionary advantage over the similar length cycles of 12 and 18 years.

1 Number

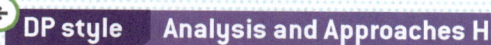 **DP style**   Analysis and Approaches HL

4 a i Write 30 and 135 as products of their prime factors.
   ii By consideration of the factors, show that the product of 30 and 135 is equal to the product of their highest common factor and least common multiple.

Consider two numbers $m, n \in \mathbb{Z}$. Let h be the highest common factor of m and n and l be the least common multiple of m and n.

b Show that $m \times n = h \times l$

1.8 Fractions

Although you can perform these numerical calculations with a calculator, your GDC cannot perform operations with algebraic fractions in the same way. It is therefore important that you understand how to perform these operations without your GDC so you know the methods required if you start calculating with algebraic fractions.

The way you write a fraction is not unique. For every fraction there are **equivalent fractions**. Equivalent fractions have the same value but have different denominators, such as $\frac{1}{2}, \frac{2}{4}, \frac{3}{6}, \ldots$. The fraction you should use is one that is in its **simplest terms**, that is, a fraction that you have cancelled as far as you can.

 DP link

In Maths DP, HL students also learn to manipulate algebraic fractions.

Example 9

a Find fractions that are equivalent to $\frac{2}{3}$.

b Write $\frac{60}{108}$ in its simplest terms.

a $\frac{2}{3} = \frac{2 \times 2}{3 \times 2} = \frac{4}{6} = \frac{2 \times 3}{3 \times 3} = \frac{6}{9} = \frac{2 \times 4}{3 \times 4} = \frac{8}{12}$

Multiply the numerator and denominator by the same number to find an equivalent fraction.

b $\frac{60}{108} = \frac{60 \div 2}{108 \div 2} = \frac{30}{54} = \frac{30 \div 2}{54 \div 2} = \frac{15}{27} = \frac{15 \div 3}{27 \div 3} = \frac{5}{9}$

write this as $\frac{\cancel{60}}{\cancel{108}} = \frac{\cancel{30}}{\cancel{54}} = \frac{\cancel{15}}{\cancel{27}} = \frac{5}{9}$

Divide by common factors until no more dividing is possible. This is called 'cancelling'.

When you add (or subtract) fractions, they must have the same denominator. You should write any answer in its simplest terms.

For example: $\frac{2}{10} + \frac{3}{10} = \frac{5}{10} = \frac{1}{2}$

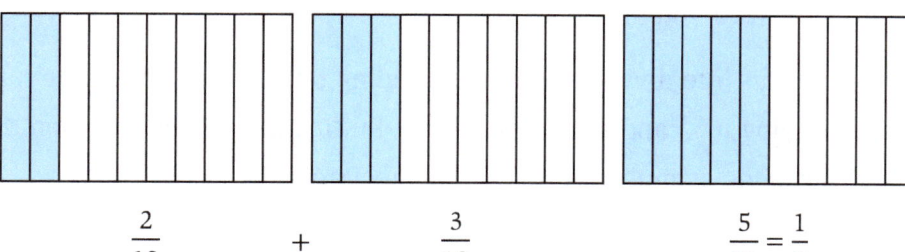

13

NUMBER AND ALGEBRA

DP ready | International-mindedness

The Egyptians wrote fractions as a sum of fractions which all had a numerator of 1. For example, you can write $\frac{2}{3}$ as $\frac{1}{3}+\frac{1}{4}+\frac{1}{12}$. The Babylonians, who lived in present-day Iraq, used a sexagesimal system based on 60. They had a method similar to our decimal system. $0.11 = \frac{1}{10}+\frac{1}{100}$ is equivalent to $\frac{6}{60}+\frac{36}{60^2}$. The present-day system of writing fractions was not introduced in Europe until the 17th century.

If you are adding fractions that do not have the same denominator, you must first find equivalent fractions with a common denominator.

For example, $\frac{1}{6}+\frac{3}{4}=\frac{2}{12}+\frac{9}{12}=\frac{11}{12}$.

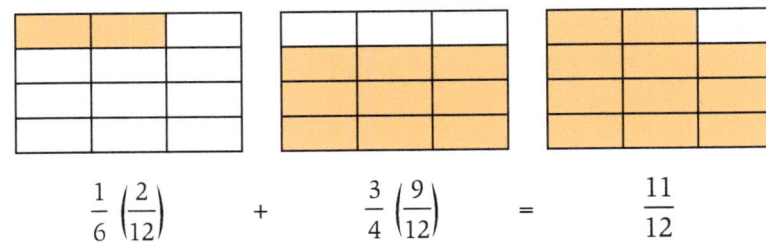

Multiplication of fractions is the process of finding one fraction of another. For example, to find $\frac{3}{4}\times\frac{5}{8}$ you have to find $\frac{3}{4}$ of $\frac{5}{8}$.

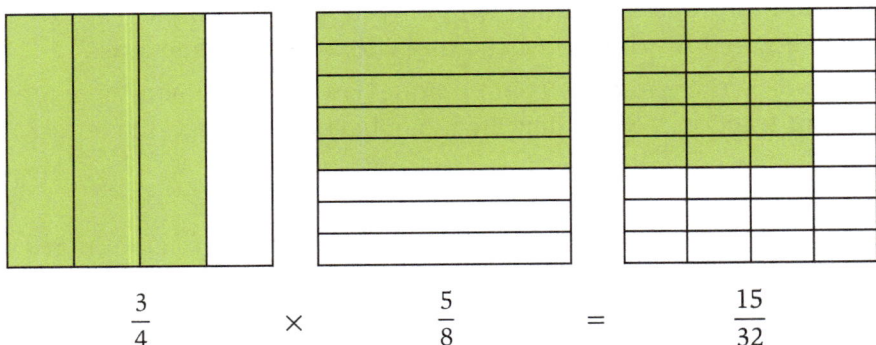

You can see in the diagram above that you multiply fractions by multiplying the numerators together and multiplying the denominators together.

For example, $\frac{3}{4}\times\frac{5}{8}=\frac{3\times 5}{4\times 8}=\frac{15}{32}$.

Because numerators are multiplied, and denominators are multiplied, you can cancel fractions 'diagonally' before multiplication in order to make the calculation simpler.

Find $\frac{1}{6}\times\frac{4}{5}$.

Dividing top and bottom by 2 gives $\frac{1}{\cancel{6}_3}\times\frac{\cancel{4}^2}{5}=\frac{1\times 2}{3\times 5}=\frac{2}{15}$.

Dividing by 2 is the same as multiplying by $\frac{1}{2}$ and dividing by 4 is the same as multiplying by $\frac{1}{4}$. It follows that dividing by $\frac{1}{2}$ is the same as multiplying by 2 and dividing by $\frac{1}{4}$ is the same as multiplying by 4. $\frac{1}{2}$ is called the **reciprocal** of 2 and $\frac{1}{4}$ is the reciprocal of 4.

What happens if you divide by $\frac{3}{4}$?

First, split this into dividing by 3 and dividing by $\frac{1}{4}$. This is the same as multiplying by $\frac{1}{3}$ and multiplying by 4. Putting these back together, this is the same as multiplying by $\frac{4}{3}$; the reciprocal of $\frac{3}{4}$.

For example, $\frac{7}{8}\div\frac{3}{4}=\frac{7}{\cancel{8}_2}\times\frac{\cancel{4}^1}{3}=\frac{7\times 1}{2\times 3}=\frac{7}{6}$.

Key point

Division is equivalent to multiplication by a reciprocal.

The answer to this example is what is known as an **improper fraction** as the numerator is greater than the denominator. You can write the answer as a **mixed number**, $\frac{7}{6} = 1\frac{1}{6}$.

Exercise 1.8

1. Write in simplest terms

   a $\frac{12}{28}$ b $\frac{15}{40}$ c $\frac{18}{54}$ d $\frac{125}{1000}$

2. Calculate

   a $\frac{3}{11} + \frac{5}{11}$ b $\frac{1}{3} + \frac{1}{6}$ c $\frac{3}{5} - \frac{1}{4}$ d $\frac{3}{8} + \frac{5}{12}$

3. Calculate

   a $\frac{1}{2} \times \frac{3}{5}$ b $\frac{2}{3} \times \frac{9}{16}$ c $\frac{3}{4} \div \frac{5}{8}$ d $\frac{1}{2} \div \frac{1}{8}$

1.9 Exponential expressions

An **exponent** (or **index**) is a **power** of a number.

$$8^3 = \underbrace{8 \times 8 \times 8}_{3 \text{ times}}.$$

3 is the exponent

The exponent is the number of times you multiply the number by itself.

You can write:

$2 \times 2 \times 2 \times 2$ as 2^4

3×3 as 3^2

$10 \times 10 \times 10 \times 10 \times 10 \times 10$ as 10^6.

You can also write 2 as 2^1 or 4 as 4^1.

> **Key point**
>
> $a^1 = a$
>
> $a^n = \underbrace{a \times a \times \cdots \times a}_{n \text{ times}}$

Investigation 1.3

1. $2^1 \times 2^2 = (2) \times (2 \times 2) = 2 \times 2 \times 2 = 2^3$

   Multiply $2^2 \times 2^3$, $2^1 \times 2^4$, $2^2 \times 2^2$, $2^3 \times 2^4$ writing your answers as powers of 2.

   Do you notice a pattern? Can you generalize and find a rule for combining the powers of 2 when you multiply?

   Multiply $3^2 \times 3^3$ and $5^1 \times 5^2$.

   Does your rule apply to these multiplications as well?

2. $2^5 \div 2^2 = \dfrac{2 \times 2 \times 2 \times \cancel{2} \times \cancel{2}}{\cancel{2} \times \cancel{2}} = 2 \times 2 \times 2 = 2^3$

   Divide $2^4 \div 2^3$, $2^6 \div 2^4$, $2^3 \div 2^2$, $2^5 \div 2^1$ writing your answers as powers of 2.

   Is there a pattern? Can you find a rule for division with powers of 2?

   Try dividing some powers of 3 and 5. Does this rule apply to division with powers of these numbers too?

NUMBER AND ALGEBRA

Key point

You can combine indices according to these rules:

$a^m \times a^n = a^{m+n}$

$a^m \div a^n = a^{m-n}$

$(a^m)^n = a^{m \times n}$

$a^n \times b^n = (a \times b)^n$

DP link

In DP Maths, HL and SL students learn about logarithms, which rely on these laws of indices.

3 $(2^2)^3 = (2 \times 2) \times (2 \times 2) \times (2 \times 2) = 2 \times 2 \times 2 \times 2 \times 2 \times 2 = 2^6$

Calculate these powers of powers: $(2^1)^4$, $(2^2)^2$, $(2^3)^2$, writing your answers as powers of 2.

Is there a pattern? Can you generalize and find a rule for powers of powers of 2?

Try this with powers of other numbers. Does the rule you found apply to these numbers too?

4 $2^3 \times 3^3 = (2 \times 2 \times 2) \times (3 \times 3 \times 3)$
   $= 2 \times 2 \times 2 \times 3 \times 3 \times 3$
   $= 2 \times 3 \times 2 \times 3 \times 2 \times 3$
   $= (2 \times 3) \times (2 \times 3) \times (2 \times 3)$
   $= 6 \times 6 \times 6$
   $= 6^3$

Calculate $2^2 \times 4^2$, $3^2 \times 4^2$, $2^4 \times 5^4$

Is there a pattern? Can you generalize and find a rule for multiplying the same power of two numbers?

Example 10

Find the value of each expression. Where possible, use the laws of indices to first simplify the expression.

a $2^3 \times 2^4$ b $3^2 \times 4^2$ c $2^2 \times 3^2 \times 2^3 \times 3^3 \times 5^2$ d $6^5 \div 6^3$

e $\dfrac{2^4 \times 3^2 \times 3^3}{2^2 \times 3^4}$ f $(3^2)^2$ g $\sqrt{225}$ h $\sqrt[3]{27}$

a	$2^3 \times 2^4 = 2^{3+4} = 2^7 = 128$	Add indices when multiplying.
b	$3^2 \times 4^2 = (3 \times 4)^2 = 12^2 = 144$	Same index.
c	$2^2 \times 3^2 \times 2^3 \times 3^3 \times 5^2 = 2^{2+3} \times 3^{2+3} \times 5^2$ $= 2^5 \times 3^5 \times 5^2$ $= (2 \times 3)^5 \times 25$ $= 6^5 \times 25$ $= 7776 \times 25$ $= 194\,400$	Deal with powers of different numbers separately.
d	$6^5 \div 6^3 = 6^{5-3} = 6^2 = 36$	Subtract indices when dividing.
e	$\dfrac{2^4 \times 3^2 \times 3^3}{2^2 \times 3^4} = 2^{4-2} \times 3^{2+3-4} = 2^2 \times 3^1 = 4 \times 3 = 12$	A fraction line implies division.
f	$(3^2)^2 = 3^{2 \times 2} = 3^4 = 81$	Multiply the indices.
g	$\sqrt{225} = 15$	$\sqrt{225}$ is the number which when squared gives 225. The value can be found using the GDC.
h	$\sqrt[3]{27} = 3$	$\sqrt[3]{27}$ is the number which when cubed gives 27. Again, the value can be found using the GDC.

16

1 Number

Exercise 1.9a

1 Find:
  a 2^5
  b 3^3
  c 10^6
  d $(-3)^5$
  e -4^2

2 Calculate:
  a $5^2 \times 5^2$
  b $4^6 \div 4^4$
  c $2^3 \times 5^2 \times 2^2 \times 5^3$
  d $(2^3)^4$
  e $\dfrac{3^2 \times 3^4}{3^3}$
  f $\dfrac{2^2 \times 3^3}{2 \times 3}$
  g $\dfrac{4^3 \times 5^4}{4^4 \times 2 \times 5^2}$
  h $(7^2)^3 \div 7^4$

3 Use a calculator to find:
  a 1.4^6
  b 2.53^5
  c 1.025^{14}
  d $(-0.3)^5$
  e $(-2.5)^4$

> **DP link**
>
> DP students will study the laws of exponents in greater detail in both MAA and MAI at SL and HL

Higher Level

So far in section **1.9**, you have only dealt with indices that are positive integers.
Look at 2^0. Applying the rules of indices, $2^2 \div 2^2 = 2^{2-2} = 2^0$. **Compare** this to $4 \div 4 = 1$. It follows that $2^0 = 1$.
What does 2^{-1} mean? Applying the rules of indices,
$2^1 \div 2^2 = 2^{1-2}$.
    $= 2^{-1}$
Compare this to $2 \div 4 = \dfrac{1}{2}$.

You can **deduce** that $2^{-1} = \dfrac{1}{2}$.

Now look at $2^{\frac{1}{2}}$. What does this mean? Applying the rules of indices,
$2^{\frac{1}{2}} \times 2^{\frac{1}{2}} = 2^{\frac{1}{2}+\frac{1}{2}}$
       $= 2^1$
       $= 2$
Compare this to $\sqrt{2} \times \sqrt{2} = 2$.

You can deduce that $2^{\frac{1}{2}} = \sqrt{2}$.

Similarly $2^{\frac{1}{3}} = \sqrt[3]{2}$

Generalizing from these results:

> **Command term**
>
> **Compare** means you should give an account of the similarities between two items, referring to both of them throughout.
>
> **Deduce** means you should reach a conclusion from the information given.

> **Internal link**
>
> You use this result to express numbers in standard form.

Example 11

Find:
  a 10^{-3}
  b $4^{-2} \times 4^3$
  c $3^{\frac{1}{2}} \times 2^{\frac{1}{2}}$
  d $\dfrac{2^3 \times 2^{-4}}{2^{-1}}$

  a $10^{-3} = \dfrac{1}{10^3} = \dfrac{1}{1000} = 0.001$

  b $4^{-2} \times 4^3 = 4^{-2+3} = 4^1 = 4$

> **Key point**
>
> $a^0 = 1$
>
> $a^{-n} = \dfrac{1}{a^n}$
>
> $a^{\frac{1}{n}} = \sqrt[n]{a}$

17

NUMBER AND ALGEBRA

c $3^{\frac{1}{2}} \times 2^{\frac{1}{2}} = (3 \times 2)^{\frac{1}{2}} = \sqrt{6}$	Both numbers are to the same power.
d $\dfrac{2^3 \times 2^{-4}}{2^{-1}} = 2^{3-4-(-1)} = 2^0 = 1$	Subtract the negative index to divide.

Look at $2^{\frac{3}{2}}$. Since you can write $\dfrac{3}{2} = \dfrac{1}{2} \times 3$

$$2^{\frac{3}{2}} = 2^{\frac{1}{2} \cdot 3} \quad \text{or} \quad 2^{\frac{3}{2}} = (2^3)^{\frac{1}{2}}$$
$$= (\sqrt{2})^3 \qquad\qquad = \sqrt{2^3}$$

Generalizing from this result we get the key point here.

> **Key point**
>
> $a^{\frac{m}{n}} = a^{\frac{1}{n} \cdot m} = (\sqrt[n]{a})^m$
>
> $= (a^m)^{\frac{1}{n}} = \sqrt[n]{a^m}$

Example 12

Find $8^{\frac{4}{3}}$

$8^{\frac{4}{3}} = (\sqrt[3]{8})^4 = 2^4 = 16$	Notice that it is easier to calculate $(\sqrt[3]{8})^4$ than $\sqrt[3]{8^4} = \sqrt[3]{4096}$

Exercise 1.9b

1. Calculate:
   a 3^{-2}
   b 5^{-1}
   c 4^{-3}
   d $\left(\dfrac{1}{2}\right)^{-1}$
   e $\left(\dfrac{2}{3}\right)^{-2}$

2. Find:
   a $5^{-2} \times 2^4$
   b $3^{-1} \times 3$
   c $12 \times 3^{-1} \times 2^{-2}$
   d $\dfrac{5^2}{5^4}$
   e $\dfrac{2^3 \times 3^2}{2^5 \times 3^3}$

3. Calculate:
   a $27^{\frac{1}{3}}$
   b $\left(\dfrac{16}{9}\right)^{\frac{1}{2}}$
   c $4^{\frac{5}{2}}$
   d $32^{\frac{3}{5}}$
   e $9^{-\frac{1}{2}}$

DP style — Analysis and Approaches HL

4. a i Find the greatest common factor of 90 and 135.
     ii Hence prove $3^{135} > 5^{90}$
   b Find a counter example to show that the statement $(a^n)^{\frac{1}{n}} = a$ is not always true.

DP style — Applications and Interpretation HL

5. Kepler's third law of planetary motion states that the average distance of a planet from the sun (R), where R is measured in astronomical units (AU), is related to the period (T) of its orbit by the equation
   $$R^3 = kT^2$$
   where T is time in days, and k is a constant.
   a Given that the average distance of the earth from the sun is one astronomical unit (AU) and that the earth takes 365.25 days to orbit the sun, find the value of k.
   b The orbital period of Jupiter is 4333 days. Find its average distance from the sun in astronomical units.
   c Rewrite the equation in the form $T = k_1 R^a$
   d Hence find the orbital period of Neptune given its average distance from the sun is 30.07 AU.

1 Number

1.10 Surds (radicals)

Numbers like $\sqrt{2}, \sqrt{3}$ and $\sqrt{7}$ are **surds** (or **radicals**). Surds are irrational numbers.

> **Note**
> Square numbers, such as $\sqrt{4}$, are not surds as, for example, $\sqrt{4} = 2$.

Key point

$\sqrt{a} \times \sqrt{b} = \sqrt{ab}$ and $\dfrac{\sqrt{a}}{\sqrt{b}} = \sqrt{\dfrac{a}{b}}$

Investigation 1.4
Look at these expressions:

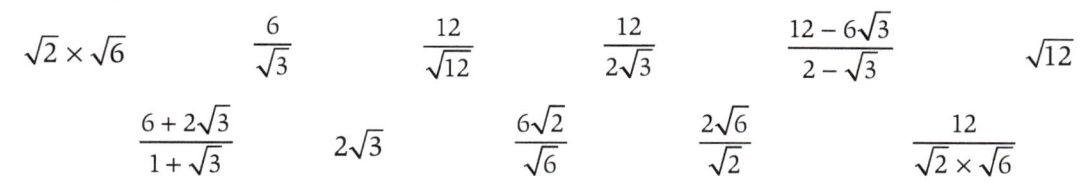

$$\sqrt{2} \times \sqrt{6} \qquad \dfrac{6}{\sqrt{3}} \qquad \dfrac{12}{\sqrt{12}} \qquad \dfrac{12}{2\sqrt{3}} \qquad \dfrac{12 - 6\sqrt{3}}{2 - \sqrt{3}} \qquad \sqrt{12}$$

$$\dfrac{6 + 2\sqrt{3}}{1 + \sqrt{3}} \qquad 2\sqrt{3} \qquad \dfrac{6\sqrt{2}}{\sqrt{6}} \qquad \dfrac{2\sqrt{6}}{\sqrt{2}} \qquad \dfrac{12}{\sqrt{2} \times \sqrt{6}}$$

1. Can you find any that are equal? If necessary, use your calculator to evaluate them.
   (Some GDCs will evaluate the expressions as decimals while others will express them in terms of surds unless you use the keypress that gives a decimal answer).
2. Which of the expressions that are equal do you think are the simplest?
3. Calculate $2\sqrt{3}$ to 3 s.f. and square your answer. Calculate $\left(2\sqrt{3}\right)^2$. Compare your answers. Which is the most accurate?

You should write expressions containing surds so that you cannot simplify them any further.

> **DP link**
> This style of investigation is similar to those contained in both the MAI and MAA courses.

Example 14
Simplify:
a $\sqrt{18}$ b $\sqrt{6} \times \sqrt{8}$

a $\sqrt{18} = \sqrt{2 \times 9} = \sqrt{2} \times \sqrt{9} = \sqrt{2} \times 3 = 3\sqrt{2}$	Look for factors that are square numbers
b $\sqrt{6} \times \sqrt{8} = \sqrt{6 \times 8} = \sqrt{48} =$ $= \sqrt{16 \times 3} = \sqrt{16} \times \sqrt{3} = 4\sqrt{3}$	Combine terms and then look for square factors

Exercise 1.10a
1. Simplify:
   a $\sqrt{32}$ b $\sqrt{12} \times \sqrt{10}$
2. Simplify:
   a $\sqrt{2}\left(3 + \sqrt{2}\right)$ b $3\sqrt{2} + \sqrt{8} - \sqrt{18}$

> **DP link**
> DP students taking MAA at SL and HL will study exact values of trigonometric ratios using surds.

Higher Level

Rationalizing the denominator

An expression is simpler if it has a rational denominator.

To rationalize the denominator in an expression like $\dfrac{1}{\sqrt{2}}$ you multiply the numerator and denominator by $\sqrt{2}$.

You can also simplify more complicated expressions like $\dfrac{1}{1 + \sqrt{2}}$ by multiplying top and bottom by the equivalent expression with opposite sign in the middle, e.g. $1 - \sqrt{2}$

19

NUMBER AND ALGEBRA

Example 14

Simplify a $\dfrac{1}{\sqrt{2}}$ b $\dfrac{6}{5\sqrt{3}}$ c $\dfrac{1}{1+\sqrt{2}}$

a $\dfrac{1}{\sqrt{2}} = \dfrac{1 \times \sqrt{2}}{\sqrt{2} \times \sqrt{2}} = \dfrac{\sqrt{2}}{2}$

Multiply numerator and denominator by $\sqrt{2}$

b $\dfrac{6}{5\sqrt{3}} = \dfrac{6 \times \sqrt{3}}{5\sqrt{3} \times \sqrt{3}} = \dfrac{6\sqrt{3}}{15} = \dfrac{2\sqrt{3}}{5}$

Multiply numerator and denominator by $\sqrt{3}$

Multiply numerator and denominator by $1 - \sqrt{2}$.
If $1 + \sqrt{2}$ is $a + b$ then $1 - \sqrt{2}$ is $a - b$.

c $\dfrac{1}{1+\sqrt{2}} = \dfrac{1}{1+\sqrt{2}} \times \dfrac{1-\sqrt{2}}{1-\sqrt{2}}$

$= \dfrac{1-\sqrt{2}}{1^2 - (\sqrt{2})^2}$

$= \dfrac{1-\sqrt{2}}{1-2}$

$= \dfrac{1-\sqrt{2}}{-1}$

$= \sqrt{2} - 1$

Use the difference of 2 squares result
(see Internal link box below)

simplify

divide by -1

Note
The rationalized form is simpler because its relative size can easily be seen and it can then be used to add surds.

Internal link

Multiplying top and bottom by the equivalent expression with opposite sign in the middle comes from a result called the difference of two squares: $(a+b)(a-b) = a^2 - b^2$. You will learn about this in chapter 2.

Key point

To rationalize the denominator when it is $\sqrt{a} \pm \sqrt{b}$ you multiply the numerator and denominator of the fraction by $\sqrt{a} \mp \sqrt{b}$.

Exercise 1.10b

1 Simplify

a $\dfrac{2}{\sqrt{6}}$ b $\dfrac{\sqrt{24}}{2\sqrt{3}}$ c $\dfrac{\sqrt{3} \times \sqrt{10}}{\sqrt{12} \times \sqrt{5}}$

2 Simplify

a $\dfrac{1}{2+\sqrt{3}}$ b $\dfrac{9}{\sqrt{5}-\sqrt{2}}$ c $\dfrac{6}{3\sqrt{2}+2}$

d $\dfrac{\sqrt{2}+1}{\sqrt{2}-1}$ e $\dfrac{\sqrt{3}-\sqrt{2}}{\sqrt{8}+2\sqrt{3}}$

Did you know

For example, the average distance from the Earth to the Sun is about 149 598 000 000 m, one atomic weight unit is 0.000 000 000 000 000 000 000 000 001 66 kg and the surface area of the earth is 453 000 000 000 000 m².

1.11 Standard form

In science, you often have to deal with very large and very small numbers.

To help make large and small numbers more comprehensible, you can use **standard form** (or **scientific notation**).

Key point

In standard form you write numbers in the form $a \times 10^n$ where $1 \le a < 10$ and $n \in \mathbb{Z}$.

To be able to use standard form, you need to use powers of 10. Remember that $10^1 = 10$, $10^3 = 1000$, etc. You will also need to know that $10^0 = 1$ and that $10^{-n} = \dfrac{1}{10^n}$, for example $10^{-3} = \dfrac{1}{10^3} = 0.001$.

> **Internal link**
>
> Section 1.9 explained indices or powers.

Numbers written in standard form are easier to compare and easier to calculate with.

> **Example 15**
>
> 1 Write these numbers in standard form.
>
>   a 149 598 000 000   b 0.000 000 000 000 000 000 000 001 66
>
>   c 453 000 000 000 000

> **DP link**
>
> In DP HL students will learn more about indices that are not positive integers.

> a $149\,598\,000\,000 = 1.496 \times 100\,000\,000\,000$
> $= 1.496 \times 10^{11}$
>
> b $0.000\,000\,000\,000\,000\,000\,000\,001\,66$
> $= 1.66 \times 0.000\,000\,000\,000\,000\,000\,000\,001$
> $= 1.66 \times 10^{-27}$
>
> c $453\,000\,000\,000\,000$
> $= 4.53 \times 100\,000\,000\,000\,000$
> $= 4.53 \times 10^{14}$

> **DP link**
>
> DP students will study operations with numbers in standard form in MAA and MAI at SL and HL.

Your calculator will express answers that are very large or very small in standard form. Some calculators use a recognizable index notation, but others use the symbol E. This form of calculator notation (seen in some computer applications too) is **not** acceptable in the DP course. For example, you should write 3.4×10^3 and **not** 3.4E3.

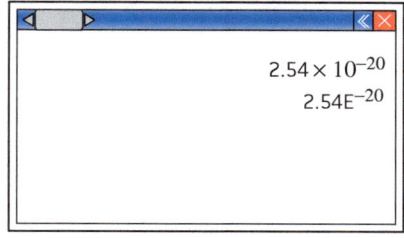

You cannot always give an answer in standard form, so you will need to know how to write it as a decimal number.

> **Example 16**
>
> Write these numbers as decimal numbers.
>
>   a 2.12×10^2 b 3.58×10^4 c 8.05×10^{-1} d 6.95×10^{-5}

> a $2.12 \times 10^2 = 212$ — Move the point two places to the right.
>
> b $3.58 \times 10^4 = 35\,800$ — Move the point four places to the right.
>
> c $8.05 \times 10^{-1} = 0.805$ — Move the decimal point one place to the left.
>
> d $6.95 \times 10^{-5} = 0.0000695$ — Move the point 5 places to the left and fill extra places with zeros.

The way you enter numbers in standard form also depends on the GDC you have. To enter the number 2.54×10^{-20} you should type either $2.54 \times \boxed{10^x}\ -20$ or $2.54\ \boxed{E}\ -20$, depending on which GDC you are using. You could use the 10^x key and type $2.54 \times 10^x\ -20$ or you could use the ^ key and type $2.54 \times 10\ \wedge\ -20$, but the standard form key E requires only one keypress and is easier to use.

NUMBER AND ALGEBRA

Exercise 1.11

1. Jupiter's diameter is 1.43×10^5 km and its mean distance from the Sun is 7.78×10^8 km. Saturn's diameter is 1.21×10^5 km and its mean distance from the Sun is 1.43×10^9 km. State which of the two planets is farthest from the Sun and which is the largest.

2. Write these numbers in standard form.
   a 324 000 000
   b 456 000
   c 0.000 128
   d 0.000 006 21

3. Write these numbers as decimal numbers.
   a 2.50×10^3
   b 4.81×10^1
   c 2.85×10^{-2}
   d 3.07×10^{-4}

DP style — Applications and Interpretation SL

4. Protons and neutrons have a mass of 1.67×10^{-27} kg and the mass of an electron is 9.11×10^{-31} kg.
   a Calculate how many times more massive a proton or neutron is than an electron.
   b An oxygen atom has 8 protons, 8 neutrons and 8 electrons. Calculate how much it weighs.

Chapter summary

- **Numbers:**
  - The natural numbers, $\mathbb{N}$, are the counting numbers (including the number 0): 0, 1, 2, 3, 4, 5, …
  - The integers, $\mathbb{Z}$, include all the natural numbers and their negative values too: … −2, −1, 0, 1, 2, …
  - The rational numbers, $\mathbb{Q}$, include all the integers and numbers in the form $\frac{a}{b}$, $b \neq 0$, where a and b are integers. Examples of rational numbers are $\frac{5}{6}, -\frac{1}{2}, \frac{20}{7}, 3\frac{1}{2}, \ldots$, terminating decimals like 0.5, 1.75, −7.396, and recurring decimals like 0.333… and 1.7272….
  - The real numbers, $\mathbb{R}$, contain both the rational and irrational numbers. Irrational numbers include $\pi, \sqrt{2}, \sqrt[3]{10}$ and any non-terminating, non-recurring decimals.

- **Sets:**
  - A **set** is a collection of objects, for example a collection of numbers, letters, geometrical objects or anything else.
  - The number of elements in a set A is its **cardinality**, $n(A)$.
  - The set that contains no elements at all is the **empty set**, $\varnothing$. $n(\varnothing) = 0$.
  - The set of all the elements you are considering is the **universal set**, U.
  - The set of elements of U that are not in A is its **complement**, A'. $A' = \{x \mid x \in U, x \notin A\}$.
  - The set of elements that are either in A or B or both is the **union** of A and B, $A \cup B$.
  - The set of elements that are in both A and B is the **intersection** of A and B, $A \cap B$.

- When rounding, consider the figure immediately to the right of the last digit you are rounding to. If the next figure is 0, 1, 2, 3, or 4, round down. If the next figure is 5, 6, 7, 8, or 9, round up.

- The **modulus** or absolute value $|x|$ of x is
$$\begin{cases} x & \text{for } x \geq 0 \\ -x & \text{for } x < 0 \end{cases}$$

- You can summarize the rules for the order of operations as:
  1. **B**rackets (or parentheses),
  2. **O**rders (indices or exponents),
  3. **M**ultiplication/**D**ivision,
  4. **A**ddition/**S**ubtraction,

  You can remember this using the mnemonic **BOMDAS**

- A **prime number** is a positive integer, greater than 1 that has exactly two factors. It is not a multiple of any other number apart from 1 and itself. Numbers that have more than two factors are composite. The number 1 is neither prime nor composite.

- The **greatest common factor** (divisor) of two (or more) numbers is the largest number that will divide into them both.

1 Number

- ☐ The **least common multiple** of two (or more) numbers is the smallest number that the numbers will divide into.
- ☐ Fractions:
  - ☐ Equivalent fractions have the same value
  - ☐ If you are adding fractions that do not have the same denominator, you must first find equivalent fractions in order to write them with a **common denominator**
  - ☐ When multiplying fractions, multiply the numerators and multiply the denominators
  - ☐ Division is equivalent to multiplication by a reciprocal
- ☐ Rules of indices:
  - ☐ $a^1 = a$

    $a^n = \underbrace{a \times a \times \cdots \times a}_{n \text{ times}}$
  - ☐ $a^m \times a^n = a^{m+n}$

    $a^m \div a^n = a^{m-n}$

    $(a^m)^n = a^{m \times n}$

    $a^n \times b^n = (a \times b)^n$

- ☐ $a^0 = 1$ (HL)
- ☐ $a^{-n} = \dfrac{1}{a^n}$ (HL)
- ☐ $a^{\frac{1}{n}} = \sqrt[n]{a}$ (HL)
- ☐ $a^{\frac{m}{n}} = a^{\frac{1}{n} \cdot m} = \left(\sqrt[n]{a}\right)^m$ (HL)

  $= (a^m)^{\frac{1}{n}} = \sqrt[n]{a^m}$

- ☐ $\sqrt{a} \times \sqrt{b} = \sqrt{ab}$ and $\dfrac{\sqrt{a}}{\sqrt{b}} = \sqrt{\dfrac{a}{b}}$
- ☐ To rationalize the denominator when it is $\sqrt{a} \pm \sqrt{b}$ you multiply the numerator and denominator of the fraction by $\sqrt{a} \mp \sqrt{b}$.
- ☐ In standard form you write numbers in the form $a \times 10^n$ where $1 \leq a < 10$ and $n \in \mathbb{Z}$.

Chapter 1 test

DP style — Analysis and Approaches SL

1 $P = \{p \mid p \in \mathbb{Z}, 4 \leq p < 10\}$ and $Q = \{q \mid q \in \mathbb{N}, q \leq 7\}$, where $U = \mathbb{Z}$

  a Write the sets P and Q as lists inside curly brackets $\{\}$.
  b Determine which of these statements are true and which are false:
   i $8 \in P \cap Q$ **ii** $-2 \in P \cap Q$ **iii** $10 \in P'$ **iv** $0 \in P \cup Q$
  c Write the set $P \cap Q$ using set builder notation.

2 Calculate 2.84×37.6, giving your answer to:
  a 3 s.f.
  b 2 d.p.

3 Find
  a $|3 \times (-4)| - |3| \times |-4|$
  b $|3 - (-2)| - |3| - |-2|$
  c $|(-4)^3| + |-4|^3$

4 Determine which of these statements are true and which are false:
  a $2 + (4 - 5) = (2 + 4) - 5$
  b $(3 \times 4) \div 2 = 3 \times (4 \div 2)$
  c $6 - (2 - 3) = (6 - 2) - 3$
  d $24 \div (6 \div 2) = (24 \div 6) \div 2$

5 State which of these numbers is prime. If a number is composite, write it as a product of prime factors.
  a 57   **b** 73   **c** 97   **d** 143   **e** 133

NUMBER AND ALGEBRA

6 Simplify each of the following expressions:
  a $\dfrac{3}{4} - \dfrac{1}{8}$
  b $\dfrac{1}{2} \times \dfrac{5}{8}$
  c $\dfrac{10}{27} \div \dfrac{5}{12}$
  d $\dfrac{2}{5} + \dfrac{1}{10} \times \dfrac{3}{4}$

7 Simplify each expression.
  a $10^3 \times 10^2$ **b** $8^5 \div 8^3$ **c** $\dfrac{2^4 \times 10^2}{5^3}$

8 Simplify each of the following expressions:
  a $\sqrt{18}$
  b $\sqrt{24} \div \dfrac{\sqrt{2}}{2}$
  c $\dfrac{\sqrt{2}}{2} \times \sqrt{24} \times \sqrt{3}$

9 a Write these numbers in standard form:
  i 123 580 000   **ii** 0.00127
  b Write these numbers in decimal form:
  i 2.54×10^5 **ii** 7.68×10^{-2}

DP style — Analysis and Approaches SL

10 All numbers in this question are written in standard form.
  a Given that
  $$\dfrac{1.5 \times 10^p}{2 \times 10^q} = a \times 10^r$$
    i find the value of a
    ii find an expression for r in terms of p and q
  b **i** find an expression for d in terms of b and c given that $b \times 10^6 + c \times 10^7 = d \times 10^7$
    ii state an additional constraint that must be satisfied by b and c and justify your answer.

DP style — Applications and Interpretation SL

11 Under certain conditions the size of a population of fruit flies can be modelled by the equation
$$N = a2^{bt}$$
where N is the size of the population and t is the time in weeks from a fixed point.
A population of fruit flies in a large container initially (at $t = 0$) has just 5 fruit flies. After 2 weeks there are 320 fruit flies.
Assuming the equation is a good model for the population:
  a find the values of a and b
  b find the size of the population after 3 weeks.
The equation is rewritten in the form $N = ac^t$.
  c Write down the value of c.
  d Find the first week on which the population exceeds 1000.

Higher Level

12 a Find the greatest common factor of 42 and 28.
  b Find the least common multiple of 42 and 28.

13 Calculate **a** $2^{-2} \times 2^6 \times 2^{-1}$ **b** $8^{\frac{1}{2}} \times 8^{\frac{1}{6}}$ **c** $\dfrac{5^4 \times 5^{-2}}{5^2}$

14 Simplify **a** $\dfrac{6}{\sqrt{3}}$ **b** $\dfrac{1}{\sqrt{2}-1}$ **c** $\dfrac{\sqrt{3}}{\sqrt{3}+\sqrt{2}}$

> **Reflect**
> Did you prefer the MAA or MAI style questions? What do you need more practice in.

1 Number

Modelling and investigation

DP ready   Approaches to learning

Critical thinking: Analysing and evaluating issues and ideas
Communication: Reading, writing and using language to gather and communicate information
Self-management: Managing time and tasks effectively

DP link
This activity is similar in style to the MAI course as it investigates a real-life context.

Building a model of the solar system

	Mercury	Venus	Earth	Mars	Jupiter	Saturn	Uranus	Neptune
Diameter (km)	4879	12 104	12 756	6792	142 984	120 536	51 118	49 528
Distance from the Sun (10^6 km)	57.9	108.2	149.6	227.9	778.6	1433.5	2872.5	4495.1

Elizaveta is going to create a model of the solar system using some balls to represent planets. She has four types of ball available. In order of size with their approximate diameters, these are the balls:

tennis ball: 7 cm   volleyball: 20 cm   football: 22 cm   basketball: 24 cm

She organizes the sizes of the planets into order and groups those that are a similar size.

- Mercury and Mars are the smallest; she represents each of these using a tennis ball.
- Venus and Earth are next in size; she represents each of these using a volleyball.
- Uranus and Neptune are bigger; she represents each of these using a football.
- The largest are Jupiter and Saturn; she represents each of these using a basketball.

To determine whether this arrangement forms an accurate scale model of the true planet sizes, Elizaveta divides the planet diameter (in km) by the diameter of the ball (in cm) used to represent it.

By considering these calculations, comment on whether Elizaveta be able to make a realistic model with these balls.

Elizaveta finds some Styrofoam balls with these diameters: 1, 1.5, 2, 2.5, 3, 3.5, 4, 4.5, 5, 6, 7, 8, 9, 10, 12, 13, 15, 17, 20, 25, 30, 40 (measurements in cm).

Since Mercury is the smallest planet, she chooses the 1 cm ball to represent it.

How many times larger is Venus than Mercury, to 1 dp? Which ball would represent Venus?

How many times larger is Earth than Mercury, to 1 dp? Which ball would represent Earth?

Choose the balls whose sizes would be closest in scale to the other planets.

The distances from the Sun are in units of 10^6 km. If Elizaveta used the same scale to represent these as she did to represent the diameters, Neptune would be 9 km from the Sun in her model! Instead, she uses a scale that is much smaller so that her model will fit in the room.

She begins by placing Mercury 10 cm from the Sun.

How many times further away than Mercury is Venus? Calculate your answer to the nearest cm. How far away from the Sun will Venus be in the model?

On this scale how far would you place Neptune from the Sun? Elizaveta's classroom is 10 m by 10 m. Does she have room for her model?

What would the distances from the Sun be for the 8 planets?

25

3 Units and ratio

Example 5
a What is the ratio of squares to triangles?
b What is the ratio of triangles to squares?
c What is the ratio of squares to shapes?

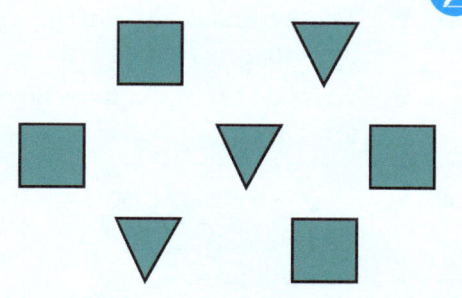

a	4 : 3	There are 4 squares and 3 triangles
b	3 : 4	
c	4 : 7	There are 4 + 3 = 7 shapes altogether.

Key point

The ratio of two numbers p and q is $p:q$. A ratio shows the relative sizes of two quantities.

Like fractions, you normally express ratios in their simplest terms.

If you multiply or divide both numbers in a ratio by the same constant, the value of the ratio does not change. For example, the ratio of 12 : 8 is equivalent to 3 : 2.

Internal link

You learned about fractions in section 1.8

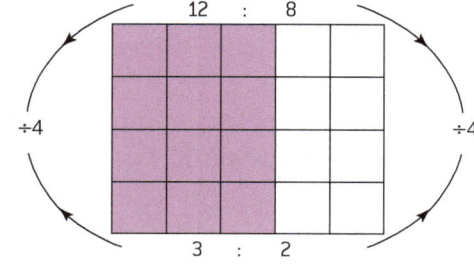

Note

Would a ratio remain the same if you added a constant to both sides, or if you subtract a constant from both sides?

You should simplify ratios in the same way as you simplify fractions. Normally ratios are written using integers and in their simplest terms. Ratios in which one of the figures is one are called **unitary ratios**. These can be written using figures that are not integers.
For example,

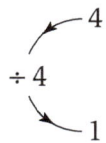 :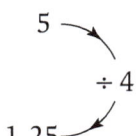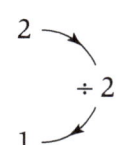

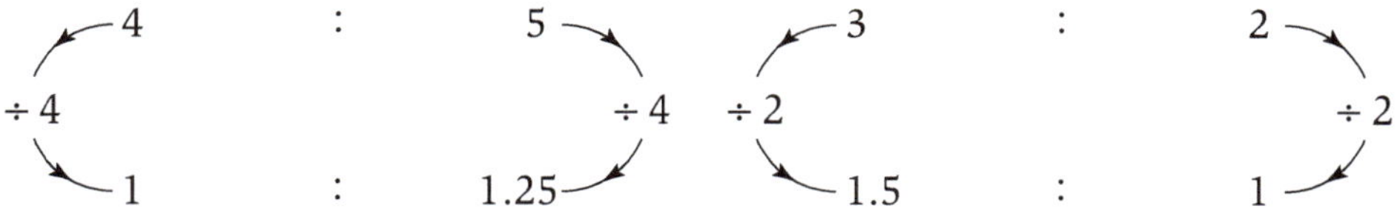

You write the ratio 4 : 5 as a unitary ratio of 1 : 1.25 or 0.8 : 1.
You write 3 : 2 as the unitary ratio 1.5 : 1 or 1 : 0.667.

Example 6
a To make a mortar you mix cement to sand in the ratio 1 : 3. (That is 1 part cement to 3 parts sand). If you use 5 buckets of cement:
  i calculate how much sand would you use
  ii determine how much mortar you will make.

Note

If you are given a ratio of two quantities in a real-life situation, the first quantity corresponds to the first number in the ratio, and the second quantity to the second number. Here, you mix sand to cement in the ratio 1 : 3. Sand corresponds to 1, and cement corresponds to 3.

57

NUMBER AND ALGEBRA

> **b i** Three fifths of the Physics class are boys. Find the ratio of boys to girls in the class.
>
> **ii** Write down the ratio of boys to girls as a unitary ratio in the form $1 : n$.

a i	$1 : 3$ is the same as $5 : 15$. You will need 15 buckets of sand.	
ii	The total amount of mortar is $5 + 15 = 20$ buckets.	The fractions add to make 1.
b i	If $\frac{3}{5}$ of the class are boys then $1 - \frac{3}{5} = \frac{2}{5}$ are girls. The ratio of boys to girls is $\frac{3}{5} : \frac{2}{5} = 3 : 2$	Multiply by 5.
ii	$3 : 2 = 1 : \frac{2}{3}$	Divide by 3.

> **Note**
>
> We wrote the unitary fraction in exact form $1 : \frac{2}{3}$. You could have written $1 : 0.666\ldots$, but this is less accurate because of the recurring decimal.

Suppose you wanted to make 20 buckets of mortar with cement to sand in the ratio $1 : 3$. Working backwards, you can find out how many of each to mix.

For a ratio of $1 : 3$, you will need to split the 20 buckets into groups of $1 + 3 = 4$ buckets

In each group, 1 bucket is cement and 3 buckets are sand.

So in 5 groups there are 5×1 buckets of cement and $5 \times 3 = 15$ buckets of sand.

For a different mix, the ratio of cement to sand is $1 : 4$. To make the same quantity, split 20 into groups of $1 + 4 = 5$ buckets.

In each group, 1 bucket is cement and 4 buckets are sand.

Now there are 4×1 buckets of cement and $4 \times 4 = 16$ of sand.

Exercise 3.3a

1 Express these ratios in the form $1 : n$.
   a $2 : 6$ b $4 : 6$ c $6 : 2$ d $8 : 5$

2 Express these ratios in the form $n : 1$.
   a $6 : 3$ b $9 : 5$ c $1 : 4$ d $4 : 10$

3 A box contains red and black balls. $\frac{5}{8}$ of the balls are red. What is the ratio of red balls to black balls? Write this as a unitary ratio in the form $1 : n$.

4 Write these ratios in their simplest terms.
   a $8 : 12$ b $15 : 10$ c $2 \text{ cm} : 5 \text{ mm}$ d $8 \text{ kg} : 500 \text{ g}$
   e $45 \text{ min} : 2 \text{ h}$ f $330 \text{ ml} : 1.2 \text{ l}$ g $1.5 \text{ m} : 450 \text{ cm}$ h $20 \text{ sec} : 0.5 \text{ min}$

5 Dean makes up a juice drink using concentrate to water in the ratio $2 : 7$. His sister makes her drink using 3 parts concentrate to 9 parts water. Whose drink is the strongest?

6 The ratio of female to male workers in the labour force was $16 : 18$ in France while in Chile the ratio was $20 : 28$. Which of the two countries has the greater proportion of female workers?

7 In a mortar mix, the ratio of sand to cement is $3 : 1$. If I have 4 tonnes of sand, how much cement do I need?

8 Brass is an alloy made from a mixture of copper and zinc in the ratio $13 : 7$. If I use 35 g of zinc, how much copper will I need? What weight of brass will this produce?

Dividing into a given ratio

You can also divide a quantity into a ratio.

Example 7

a Two brothers own a company and their shares are in the ratio $4 : 7$. Their annual profit is $132 000 and they want to split it in the ratio of their shares. Calculate how much of the profit each brother gets.

b A box of chocolates contains plain chocolates and milk chocolates in the ratio $3 : 5$. If there are 32 chocolates in the box, how many plain and how many milk chocolates are there?

c Students in a school can choose physics, chemistry or biology for their group 4 subject. They choose these in the ratio $3 : 2 : 5$. If there are 60 students in the IB Diploma class, how many choose each subject?

a $132\,000 \div (4 + 7) = 12\,000$ $12\,000 \times 4 = \$48\,000$ $12\,000 \times 7 = \$84\,000$	Split the shares into $4 + 7$ parts. One brother has 4 parts. The other has 7 parts.
b $32 \div (3 + 5) = 4$ $4 \times 3 = 12$ $4 \times 5 = 20$ There are 12 plain and 20 milk chocolates	Split the shares into $3 + 5$ parts. There are 3 parts plain and 5 parts milk.
c $60 \div (3 + 2 + 5) = 6$ $6 \times 3 = 18$ $6 \times 2 = 12$ $6 \times 5 = 30$ 18 take physics, 12 take chemistry and 30 take biology	Split the shares into $3 + 2 + 5$ parts. There are 3 parts physics, 2 parts chemistry and 5 parts biology.

NUMBER AND ALGEBRA

Ratios are used for **scales** such as map scales or the scales used in models. Often these are expressed as unitary ratios in the form $1 : n$. This means that 1 cm in the map or the model represents n cm in real life.

Example 8

A map has a scale of 1 : 50 000. Varun measures the distance he walks to school on the map. If the distance on the map is 2.5 cm, determine how far Varun walks to school (in km).

2.5 cm = 50 000 × 2.5 = 125 000 cm	Multiply the distance on the map by the map scale to get the real distance.
125 000 ÷ 100 000 = 1.25 km	To convert cm to km ÷ 100 and ÷ 1000

Example 9

Aurelia has a 1 : 72 scale model of a plane. If the wingspan of the real plane is 10.8 m, what is the wingspan, in cm, of the model plane.

10.8 × 100 = 1080 cm 1080 ÷ 72 = 15 cm	To convert m to cm × 100. Divide the real wingspan by the model to get the model wingspan.

Exercise 3.3b

1. $42 is divided in the ratio 2 : 5. What is the difference between the largest and smallest shares?
2. What is the ratio of 2 cm : 5 mm in its simplest terms? (You must make sure that both quantities are in the same units).
3. An area of 80 m² is divided between grass and paving in the ratio 11 : 5. What are the areas of grass and paving?
4. Jean, Michel and Boris divide some sweets in the ratio of their ages. Jean is 12 years old, Michel is 8 and Boris is 7. If they have 81 sweets, how many does each get?
5. 18 carat rose gold is an alloy that is made using gold, copper and silver in the ratio 300 : 89 : 11. If a ring weighs 6 g, how much of each metal is there in the ring?
6. Hans makes a model of the tallest building in London, the Shard, to a scale of 1 : 1024. If his model is 303 mm tall, how tall, in m, is the Shard?
7. The distance between Brooklyn and Manhattan is 15 km. How far is this, in cm, on a map which is to the scale 1 : 25000?

3.4 Percentages

Percentage of a quantity

> **Key point**
>
> A percentage can be expressed as a fraction or as a decimal.
>
> Divide by 100 to change from a percentage to a fraction or a decimal.

> **Key point**
>
> A **percentage** means *parts per hundred*.

For example, 25% is 25 parts per hundred.

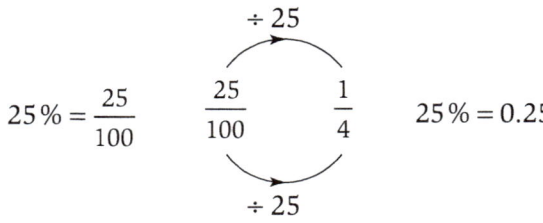

$25\% = \dfrac{25}{100}$ $\qquad 25\% = 0.25$

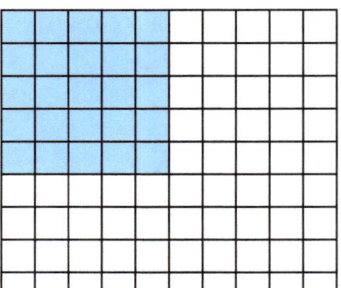

Fractions and decimals can be expressed as percentages.
Multiply by 100 to change to a percentage.

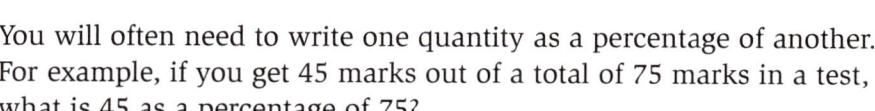

$0.35 = (0.35 \times 100)\% = 35\%$

You will often need to write one quantity as a percentage of another. For example, if you get 45 marks out of a total of 75 marks in a test, what is 45 as a percentage of 75?

To find the percentage, first write the result as a fraction and then convert to a percentage.

45 marks out of 75 is $\dfrac{45}{75}$.

As a percentage, this is $\dfrac{45}{75} \times 100 = \dfrac{15 \times 4}{1} = 60\%$.

> 3 Units and ratio
>
> **Internal link**
> You learned how to simplify fractions in section 1.8.

Example 10
a Write 35% as a fraction.
b 2400 out of a group of 6000 students said that they preferred MAI to MAA. Write this as a percentage.
c Write 5% as a decimal.

a $\dfrac{35}{100} = \dfrac{7}{20}$	Divide by 100.
b $\dfrac{2400}{6000} \times 100 = 40\%$	
c $5\% = \dfrac{5}{100} = 0.05$	First write 5% as a fraction, and then convert this fraction to a decimal.

You will also need to find percentages of a quantity. For example, you can find 20% of $150 as shown.

Write the percentage as a fraction or decimal and then multiply by the amount.

$20\% = 0.2$ then $150 \times 0.2 = \$30$

Example 11
Find 12% of €25.

$12\% = 0.12$ $0.12 \times 25 = €3$	First write the percentage as a decimal number. Then multiply the quantity by the decimal.

Example 12
Find 60 g as a percentage of 1.2 kg.

$1.2 \text{ kg} = 1200 \text{ g}$ $\dfrac{60}{1200} \times 100 = 5\%$	Ensure that the quantities are in the same units.

61

NUMBER AND ALGEBRA

Exercise 3.4a

1 Write these fractions as percentages.

   a $\dfrac{17}{20}$ b $\dfrac{2}{3}$ c $\dfrac{18}{35}$

2 Write these decimals as percentages.

   a 0.34   b 1.75   c 0.675

3 Write these percentages as:

   i fractions (in their lowest trems)   ii decimals.

   a 35%   b 12.5%   c 140%

4 a Leila scores 35 marks out of 56 in a Spanish test. What is her mark as a percentage?
   b Kwaku scores 75% in the same test. How many marks out of 56 did he get?

5 Out of the voters in Atown, 56% voted for the Rhombus Party. If there were 125 300 voters in Atown, how many voted for the Rhombus Party?

6 A gardener buys a packet containing 750 seeds. Of these seeds, 75% will successfully germinate. Of the seeds that germinate, 64% will grow to maturity. How many mature plants can the gardener expect to grow from his packet?

   Another packet states that out of 1000 seeds, 70% will germinate and 48% will grow to maturity. If both packets cost the same, which is the better buy?

DP style Applications and Interpretation HL

7 An isolated area of farming land has a simple food chain. Airborne insects are eaten by sparrows, and sparrows are eaten by a population of hawks.

   On average one sparrow will eat 90 insects in a day, and a hawk will eat three sparrows in a day.

   The area is 3 km² and the insect population favoured by the sparrows is stable (that is, the population size neither increases or decreases) if no more than 1% of their numbers are eaten each day. Initially there are 300 insects per m². The sparrow population remains stable if no more than 0.3% of their population is eaten each day by hawks.

   a Find the maximum number of sparrows the area can support without a decline in the insect population.
   b For this number of sparrows, find the maximum number of hawks the area can support.

   The farmers spray the land with insecticide that reduces the number of airborne insects to 60 per m².

   c Find the maximum population of sparrows which is now sustainable without the insect population decreasing.

   After a short time the sparrow population has reduced to the new levels but the hawk population still remains at its previous level.

   d Assuming there is no time for the sparrow population to reproduce, determine how many days from this point it will be before the population of sparrows becomes extinct.
   e Comment on the effect of this extinction on the populations of insects and hawks, assuming there is no further intervention by the farmers.

Percentage increase and decrease

Percentages can be used to increase or to decrease an amount.

Example 13

If global temperatures increase by 2%, find the new average temperature of a city with previous average temperature of 25 °C.

3 Units and ratio

We require 100% + 2% = 102% of 25 °C.	If something is increased by 2% then the new amount is 102% of the original.
$102\% = \dfrac{102}{100} = 1.02$	Change to a decimal.
$1.02 \times 25 = 25.5$ °C	To find 102% you need to multiply by 1.02.

In a similar way you can find percentage decreases.

Example 14
Find the sale price of an item that is advertised as 15% off when the original price was $32.

We require 100% − 15% = 85% of $32	After a decrease of 15%, you need to find 85% of the original amount.
$85\% = \dfrac{85}{100} = 0.85$	Change to a decimal.
$0.85 \times \$32 = \$27.20$	To find 85% you need to multiply by 0.85.

In percentage problems, always take care with units. If you are looking for one quantity as a percentage of another, they must both be in the same units.

Example 15
a Increase $250 by 10%.
b Decrease 60 marks by 15%.

a $1.1 \times 250 = \$275$	If 100% is increased by 10%, then it will become 110%. Multiply by 1.1.
b $60 \times 0.85 = 51$ marks	If 100% is decreased by 15% then there will be 85% left. Multiply by 0.85.

Example 16
Sven puts his money into a bank account that pays him interest so that his money increases by 5% each year. If he pays in € 240, then how much will he have after **i** 1 year **ii** 2 years?

i $240 \times 1.05 = €252$	If 100% is increased by 5%, then it will become 105%. Multiply by 1.05.
ii $252 \times 1.05 = €264.60$	To find the amount after 2 years, multiply by 1.05 again.

Higher Level

20% off
SALE PRICE
$160

A ticket on an item in a sale states that its price has been reduced to $160 after a 20% reduction. The shopkeeper decides to remove the item from the sale and restore it to its original price. He calculates 20% of $160 which is $32 and adds this

63

NUMBER AND ALGEBRA

to the sale price and puts a new ticket on selling the item at $192. Is this a correct calculation?

An assistant points out that the 20% reduction was on the *original* price, not on the sale price, so the calculation must be wrong. She argues that if the price had been reduced by 20% then the original amount, x, has been multiplied by 0.8. So to find x we need to solve $0.8x = 160$.

> **Internal link**
>
> To recap solving linear equations, see section 2.5a.

$$0.8x = 160$$
$$x = \frac{160}{0.8}$$
$$x = 200$$

Example 17

A box of biscuits has a label saying it includes 20% extra free. If it now weighs 144 g, find the original weight of the packet before 20% was added.

$1.2x = 144$ $x = \dfrac{144}{1.2}$ $x = 120$ g	After an increase of 20%, the packet would be 120% of the original weight.

Exercise 3.4b

1. A hotel chain increases its prices by 8%. If the price of a room was $120, what will it be after the increase?

2. The average annual inflation rate in the US for the last century has been 3.15% per year. If the price of new car is $36 000, how much would you expect this to rise to next year if it increases by 3.15%?

3. In a sale, all prices in a shop are decreased by 15%. If a coat was priced at $140, what will the sale price be?

4. Tina has a loyalty card that gives her 12.5% off the cost of meals in the Binomial Burger Bar. If the advertised cost of a meal is $9.60, what will Tina have to pay?

5. **a** In a clearance sale, a store reduces its prices by 30%. How much are they selling an item that previously cost $3.70?
   b In the same sale an item is being sold for $15.40. Calculate its original price.

6. During the year, a shop increases the price of soap powder by 10% in March and a further 10% in September. What is the overall increase during the year?

> **Hint**
>
> Let the original price be x. Multiply x by 1.10 for the first increase. Then multiply this number by 1.10 again for the second.

3 Units and ratio

3.5 Direct proportion

Suppose an apple costs 40p. Then two apples cost 80p, and three apples cost £1.20. The total price of the apples increases by the same amount each time as the number of apples increases.

We say that the number of apples is **directly proportional** to the total price of the apples.

> **Key point**
> If a quantity y is a constant multiple of another quantity x, then y is **directly proportional** to x.

Example 18

12 oranges cost €13.20. Assuming each orange costs the same amount:
a calculate the price of 36 oranges
b find how many oranges you could buy for €16.50.

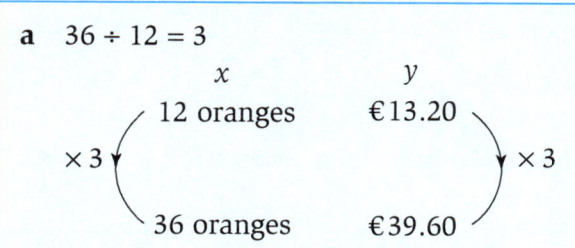

a $36 \div 12 = 3$

	x	y
	12 oranges	€13.20
$\times 3$		
	36 oranges	€39.60

The cost of 36 would be €39.60.

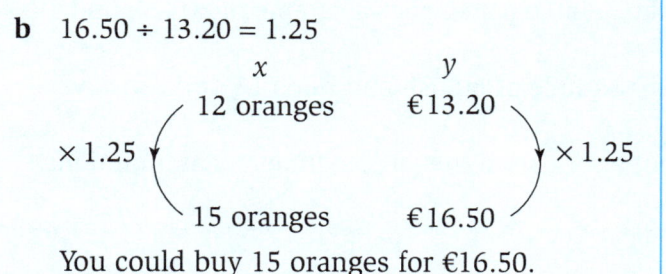

Find the number which you multiply 12 by to get 36.

If $12 \times 3 = 36$ then $13.20 \times 3 = 39.60$.

b $16.50 \div 13.20 = 1.25$

	x	y
	12 oranges	€13.20
$\times 1.25$		$\times 1.25$
	15 oranges	€16.50

You could buy 15 oranges for €16.50.

Find the number you multiply 13.20 by to get 16.50.

If $13.20 \times 1.25 = 16.50$ then $12 \times 1.25 = 15$.

Exercise 3.5

In this exercise you should assume that the quantities are in direct proportion.

1 20 l of petrol costs £24. What is the cost of 40 l?
2 If Maria can earn $75 for 6 hours work, how much would she earn for 18 hours work?
3 If I can walk 3 km in 45 minutes, how far could I walk in 1 hour?
4 What would be the cost of 200 g of flour if 1 kg costs $7.
5 24 pencils cost $4.56. What is the cost of 50?
6 A piece of apple pie in a restaurant costs €4.50. Instead of buying a piece I decide to make an apple pie at home.
   The main ingredients in the recipe I will use are as follows. The recipe will be large enough to make 6 pieces.
       160g sugar
       5 g ground cinnamon
       600 g cooking apples
       400 g plain flour
       200 g butter cut into cubes
       1 medium egg
   The costs of the ingredients at the supermarket are:
       Sugar 75¢ for 1 kg
       Cinnamon 80¢ for 40 g

NUMBER AND ALGEBRA

Cooking apples €1.85 per kilogram
Plain flour €1.80 for 1 kg
Butter €1.50 for 250 g
Eggs €1.80 for 12

a Find the cost of making the apple pie.
b Express the cost of making the pie as a percentage of the cost in the restaurant.

DP style   Analysis and Approaches HL

7 An alternative way to solve proportion problems is to write the unknown term as x and use the fact that the ratio of the two quantities is always equal.
For example if x and y are directly proportional and if $y = 12$ when $x = 5$ and we need to find the value of x when y is equal to 15, we can write the proportion, $\frac{x}{y}$, as $\frac{x}{15} = \frac{5}{12}$.

a Solve the equation given above to find the value of x.
b Find the value of y when x is equal to 9.

x and y are directly proportional. It is given that when $x = a$ $y = 6$ and when $x = 2$ $y = a + 1$.

c Find the value of a.

DP style   Applications and Interpretation HL

8 In order to work out the number of fish in a lake, a biologist catches a sample of 60 fish and tags them.
A week later he returns to the lake and catches a sample of 80 fish and finds 12 of these have been tagged.
Use proportions to find an estimate for the number of fish in the lake, stating any assumptions you are making.

> **Key point**
>
> The **exchange rate** between a pair of currencies is how much one currency will buy of another. Exchange rates change by the second.

3.6 Currency

'Currency trading' is the buying and selling of currencies in the foreign exchange market.

The table shows how much of each currency you would need to buy 1 USD. The rates will vary over time.

Currencies used by the top 20 economies in the world on 13 Feb 2019

Country	Currency	Symbol	Code	Exchange rate (1 USD)
Australia	Dollar	$	AUD	1.41
Brazil	Real	R$	BRL	3.72
Canada	Dollar	$	CAD	1.32
China	Renminbi (Yuan)	¥	CNY	6.76
Eurozone	Euro	€	EUR	0.88
India	Rupee	₹	INR	70.81
Indonesia	Rupiah	Rp	IDR	14 056
Japan	Yen	¥	JPY	110.71
Mexico	Peso	$	MXN	19.34
Russia	Rouble	₽	RUB	65.73
Saudi Arabia	Riyal	ريال	SAR	3.75
South Korea	Won	₩	KRW	1 123.40
Switzerland	Franc	CHF	CHF	1.01
Turkey	Lira	₺	TRY	5.25
United Kingdom	Pound	£	GBP	0.77
United States	Dollar	$	USD	1.00

3 Units and ratio

Most currencies can be subdivided into 100 parts (cents, etc.). When writing a currency amount you should give your answer as an exact amount or to 2 d.p.

Do not round amounts of money to 3 s.f. If your average monthly salary was $2 773.50 and your employer rounded this to 3 s.f. you would only receive $2 770, and might not be very happy!

Example 19

a Use the table to convert 50 USD to these currencies:
   i BRL   ii KRW
b Use the table above to convert the following amounts to US dollars (USD):
   i 27.40 GBP   ii 100 000 IDR

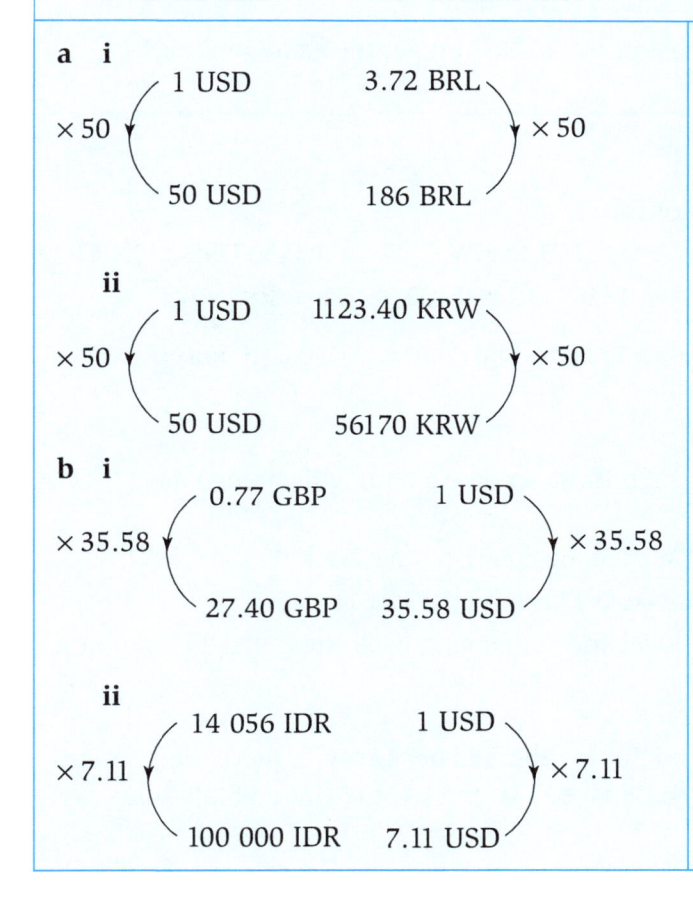

a i
   1 USD → 3.72 BRL
   × 50   × 50
   50 USD → 186 BRL

When looking at your answer, ask yourself whether you would have more dollars or more of the currency. This is a good way to check your answer.
$3.72 \times 50 = 186$ BRL

ii
   1 USD → 1123.40 KRW
   × 50   × 50
   50 USD → 56 170 KRW

$50 \times 1123.40 = 56170$ KRW

b i
   0.77 GBP → 1 USD
   × 35.58   × 35.58
   27.40 GBP → 35.58 USD

Find the multiplier
$27.40 \div 0.77 = 35.58$

ii
   14 056 IDR → 1 USD
   × 7.11   × 7.11
   100 000 IDR → 7.11 USD

Find the multiplier
$100\,000 \div 14\,056 = 7.11$

Investigation 3.1

In order to compare the cost of living in various countries, Michel collects information about the average cost of a 1.5 l bottle of water. Here are the results for six countries.

Country	Cost
China	4.34 CNY
Indonesia	5 058 IDR
Japan	155.80 JPY
Russia	57.84 RUB
Switzerland	1.20 CHF
United States	1.75 USD

How can you compare the cost in these countries?

NUMBER AND ALGEBRA

Assuming the cost of a bottle of water is representative of the cost of living in general, use the data to rank these countries in order of the cost of living.

To find whether the cost of water is representative of the cost of living, Michel looks at another factor: the cost of a pair of jeans in each country.

Country	Cost
China	212.32 CNY
Indonesia	439 795 IDR
Japan	6576.70 JPY
Russia	4504.70 RUB
Switzerland	110.98 CHF
United States	44.59 USD

Rank the countries in the same way according to cost of jeans. Do you get the same ranking? How would you account for any differences?

Exercise 3.6

1. Using the table at the beginning of section 3.4, convert:
   - a 100 SAR to USD
   - b 1000 MXN to USD
   - c 43 USD to JPY
   - d 0.30 USD to INR
   - e 72 EUR to USD
   - f 1.25 USD to TRY
   - g 1850 USD to CAD
   - h 6 BRL to USD.

2. Léonie is travelling from Switzerland to Turkey for a holiday. She changes 1250 CHF into Lira. The exchange rate is 1 CHF to 5.23 TRY.
   - a Calculate how much Léonie receives in TRY.

   While on holiday she spends 5000 Lira. When she returns, Léonie's bank will change any banknotes over 50 TRY back to CHF.
   - b Find the maximum amount of money, in TRY, that she could change back.

   The exchange rate that Léonie gets for changing the money back is 5.58 TRY to 1 CHF.
   - c Calculate how much money, in CHF, she receives for exchanging back the unused banknotes.

DP style Analysis and Approaches SL

3. Safa has just arrived in Germany from the United States. She fills her car with petrol and notices that 40 litres costs her €53.60. She remembers that just before she left the United States she filled her 13 gallon tank for $60.00.

   Supposing that fuel prices are the same in the USA as they are in Germany and that 1 gallon is approximately 3.79 litres, find the exchange rate at the time. Give your answer in the form $1 : € x$.

Chapter summary

- ☐ 1 m = 100 cm, 1 m² = 100² cm² = 10 000 cm², 1 m³ = 100³ cm³ = 1 000 000 cm³.
- ☐ 1 cm = $\frac{1}{100}$ m, 1 cm² = $\frac{1}{100^2}$ m² = $\frac{1}{10 000}$ m², 1 cm³ = $\frac{1}{100^3}$ m³ $\frac{1}{1 000 000}$ m³.
- ☐ 1 l = 10³ cm³, 1 cm³ = $\frac{1}{1000}$ litres = 1 ml.
- ☐ The ratio of two numbers p and q is $p : q$. A ratio is used to show the relative sizes of two quantities.
- ☐ A percentage can be expressed as a fraction or as a decimal. Divide by 100 to change from a percentage to a fraction or a decimal.
- ☐ If a quantity y is a constant multiple of another quantity x, then y is **directly proportional** to x.
- ☐ The **exchange rate** between a pair of currencies is how much one currency will buy of another.

Chapter 3 test

1 Convert:

   a 2.34 km to m   **b** 3 250 mm to m   **c** 250 nm to mm   **d** 125 g to kg.

2 1 tonne (t) is 1000 kg. A container is loaded with 48 000 cans of tomatoes which weigh 454 g. Calculate the weight of these cans in tonnes.

3 A sheet of metal has an area of 1.94 m². It is cut into 5000 identical pieces with no wastage.

   a Find the area of each piece of metal after they have been cut.
   b If the whole sheet of metal weighs 2.47 kg, determine the weight of each piece after cutting.

(Use the most appropriate units for your answers).

4 A strand of human DNA is 2.5 nanometers in diameter. A powerful electron microscope magnifies the strand 10 million times. Calculate the diameter of the strand after magnification.

5 Convert:

   a 1720 mm² to cm²   **b** 3.45 cm³ to mm³   **c** 0.0025 m² to cm²   **d** 23 600 mm² to m².

6 The largest thermonuclear bomb tested was a Russian bomb with a yield of 50 megatons. In 2017, North Korea tested a weapon with a yield of 250 kilotons. Determine how many times larger the Russian bomb was than the North Korean bomb.

7 Write the ratio 15 : 24:

   a in its simplest form   **b** in the form 1 : n.

DP style   Analysis and Approaches SL

8 A caterer supplies both plain and fancy cakes for a party.

   a Out of the cakes in the box $\frac{7}{10}$ are plain. Write the ratio of plain to fancy cakes in the form $n : 1$.
   b Give that the caterer supplies 44 more plain cakes than fancy cakes, write down and solve an equation for the total number of cakes supplied, x.

9 A model boat is made to a scale of 7 : 80.

Calculate the height (in cm) of the mast in the model if the full-sized boat has a mast that is 4 m high.

DP style   Applications and interpretation SL

10 Bruce exchanges Australian dollars (AUD) to Indonesian Rupiah (IDR) at the airport.

If he receives 1 850 000 IDR for 200 AUD, calculate the value of 1 AUD in IDR.

Later, in a currency exchange kiosk, Bruce sees that the exchange rate is 9877 IDR to 1 AUD. Calculate how many more Rupiahs Bruce would have received if he had waited to change his money at this kiosk.

Higher Level

11 A new toothpaste tube contains 75 ml. This is 6.25% less than the old tube. How much toothpaste was in the old tube?

NUMBER AND ALGEBRA

Modelling and investigation

> **DP ready Approaches to learning**
>
> **Critical thinking:** Analysing and evaluating issues and ideas
> **Communication:** Reading, writing and using language to gather and communicate information
> **Self-management:** Managing time and tasks effectively

Bicycle gears

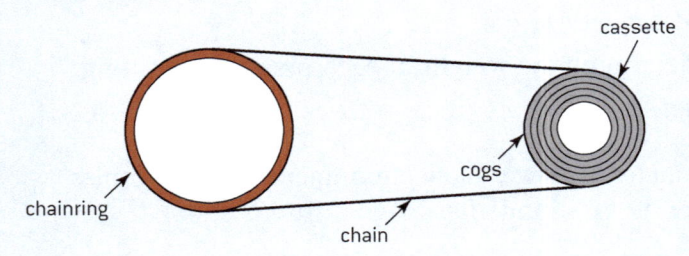

Bike riding is popular around the world.

Most bikes have both high gear ratios for cycling downhill fast and low gear ratios for cycling uphill slowly. Bikes have two sets of gearwheels:
- the larger front ones – the chainrings – are attached to the pedals
- the smaller rear ones – the cassette – are attached to the rear wheel of the bike.

The chain connects the two gearwheels.

On a standard set of gears, there are two chainrings and 11 cogs in the cassette. As you move from the larger to the smallest cog in the cassette, pedalling gets harder, but the speed at which you are cycling becomes faster. The smallest chainring is the easiest to pedal, but cycling speed is slower.

Each gearwheel is defined by its number of teeth.

Standard chainrings have 53 and 39 teeth.

The cogs in the cassette have 11, 12, 13, 14, 16, 18, 20, 22, 25, 28 and 32 teeth.

The gear ratio is defined as 'number of teeth in chainring : number of teeth in cassette'.

The hardest gear to cycle in is with the 53-tooth chainring at the front and the 11-tooth cog at the back. The gear ratio is 53 : 11 = 4.82 : 1. This means that one turn of the pedals will turn the rear wheel 4.82 times.

The easiest gear to cycle in is with the 39-tooth chainring at the front and the 32-tooth cog at the back. The gear ratio is 39 : 32 = 1.22 : 1. This gear is for cycling up steep hills.

Find the ratios for each of the 22 combinations of chainring and cog (to 3 s.f.).

'Cross-chaining' is using a combination of two big or two small gears, for example 53 and 32 or 39 and 11. Because there are many similar combinations, it is not necessary to cross-chain as it puts extra strain on the chain.

Put the ratios you found into order and find the combinations that will give you a full range of ratios and avoid cross-chaining by eliminating those that involve two big or two small gears.

A compact set of gears has chainrings with 48 teeth and 34 teeth combined with cogs that have 10, 11, 12, 13, 14, 16, 18, 20, 22, 25 and 28 teeth.

Calculate the ratios that are possible with this set of gears and compare them with the standard set.

FUNCTIONS

4 Graphing functions

Learning outcomes

In this chapter you will learn about:
- Graphing linear functions using technology
- Graphing quadratic functions using technology
- Mappings of the elements of one set to another. Illustration by means of sets of ordered pairs, tables, diagrams and graphs.
- Modelling with linear and quadratic functions

Key terms
- Graph
- Parabola
- Vertex
- Mapping
- Mapping diagram
- Domain
- Relation
- Image
- Range
- Function
- Vertical line test

4.1 Mappings

Suppose you have two sets, and every element of the first set is associated with an element of the other. This is called a **relation** between the two sets.

This table is an example of how the letters of the alphabet can be related onto the numbers 1 – 26.

A	B	C	D	E	F	G	H	I	J	K	L	M	N	O	P	Q	R	S	T	U	V	W	X	Y	Z
↓	↓	↓	↓	↓	↓	↓	↓	↓	↓	↓	↓	↓	↓	↓	↓	↓	↓	↓	↓	↓	↓	↓	↓	↓	↓
1	2	3	4	5	6	7	8	9	10	11	12	13	14	15	16	17	18	19	20	21	22	23	24	25	26

Using this code, you would write I LOVE MATHEMATICS as 9 / 12 15 22 5 / 13 1 20 8 5 13 1 20 9 3 19.

This type of relation is often associated with a **mapping diagram**.

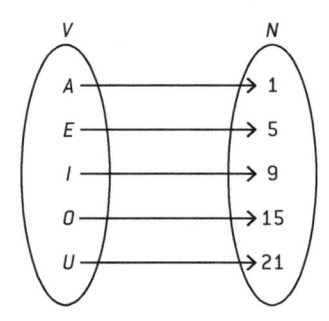

> **Internal link**
> In section 1.2, a **set** was defined as a collection of objects.

This diagram shows part of the relation above, but instead of the whole alphabet the relation only applies to the set of vowels, $V = \{A, E, I, O, U\}$.

The set $V = \{A, E, I, O, U\}$ is the called **domain** of the relation, and the set $N = \{1, 5, 9, 15, 21\}$ is called the **range**.

A relation gives you a set of pairs of objects: (A, 1), (E, 5), (I, 9), (O, 15), (U, 21) where the first coordinate in each pair is from the domain and the second coordinate is from the range.

FUNCTIONS

> **Note**
> Can you list the coordinate pairs that each of these relations gives?

> **Note**
> When you transform an element of a set, in this case using a relation, the result is called its **image**.

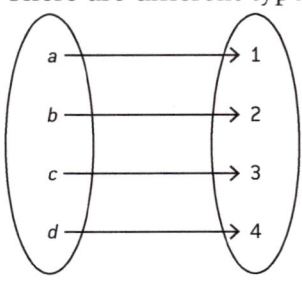

There are different types of relation:

This type of relation is **one-to-one**: every element in the domain is related to one and only one element in the range.

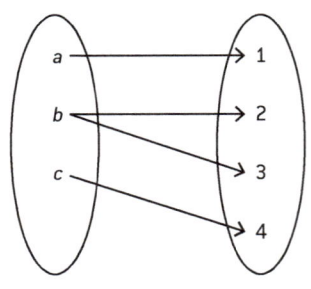

This is **one-to-many**: elements of the domain can have more than one image.

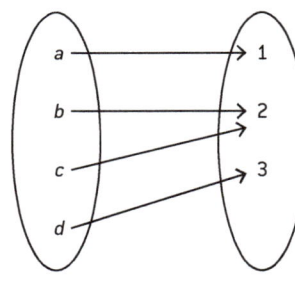

This is **many-to-one**: more than one element from the domain can have the same image.

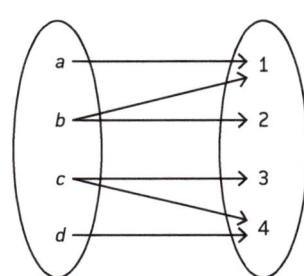

This is **many-to-many**: elements can have more than one image, and more than one element can have the same image.

A **mapping** is a special kind of relation. A relation is a mapping if every element of the domain maps to only one point in the range (a point in the range *can* have two or more points in the domain mapping to it, but every point in the domain *must* map to only one point in the range).

> **DP link**
> Although mappings can occur between any types of sets, the ones that you will be dealing with in the DP programme will mostly be mappings between sets of numbers.

> **Key point**
> Only one-to-one and many-to-one relations are mappings because each point in the domain maps to one point in the range.
> One-to-many and many-to-many relations are not mappings as one point in the domain can map to more than one point in the range.

Here is a mapping diagram:

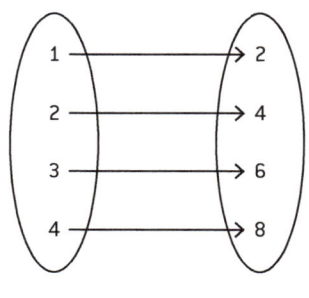

> **Key point**
> The term **function** is often used to describe a mapping. If x is an element in the domain and it maps to y in the range, then we write $f: x \to y$ or $f(x) = y$.

In this diagram, the domain is the set $\{1, 2, 3, 4\}$ and $f(1) = 2$, $f(2) = 4$, $f(3) = 6$, $f(4) = 8$. You can describe the mapping as $(1, 2), (2, 4), (3, 6), (4, 8)$.

To write the function you could write $f : x \to 2x$, $f(x) = 2x$ or $y = 2x$.

4 Graphing functions

Coordinate diagrams are generally used to show functions. You **plot** points in the domain on the *x*-axis and points in the range on the *y*-axis.

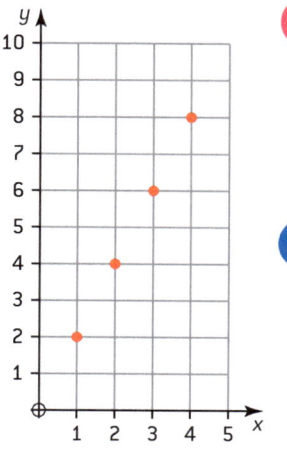

> **Command term**
>
> **Plot** means you should mark the position of points on a diagram.

→ **Note**
Because you can plot the graph of a function in this way, we sometimes write a function as $y = f(x)$ for some function involving x, such as $y = 2x + 1$ or $y = 4x^2$.

Here the function is a set of distinct points because the domain is a set of integers. If the domain was instead $\mathbb{R}$, then the graph of the function would be continuous.

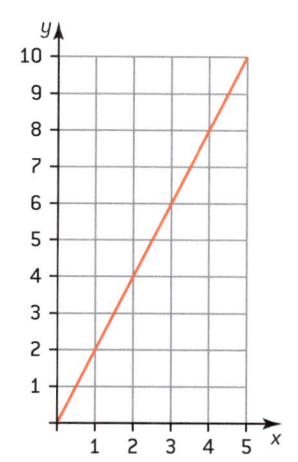

Example 1
Determine which type of relation each of these represents, and hence state whether the relation is a function.

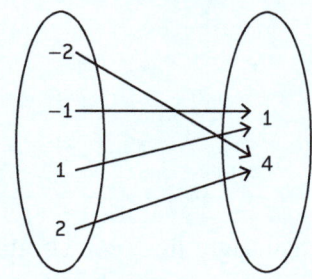

a

b

a function; many-to-one	Each element in the domain maps to only one point in the range.
b not a function; one-to-many and there is no image for −1.	1 maps to both −1 and 1, and 4 maps to both −2 and 2.

To draw the graph of a function you should calculate the coordinates of points related by the function, plot them and connect them with a smooth curve or a straight line.

Internal link

In sections 4.2 and 4.3 you will learn about the differences between functions whose graphs are straight lines and functions whose graphs are curves.

FUNCTIONS

Example 2
Draw a graph of the function $y = 5 - 2x$

x	y
−2	9
0	5
4	−3

$(-2, 9), (0, 5), (4, -3)$

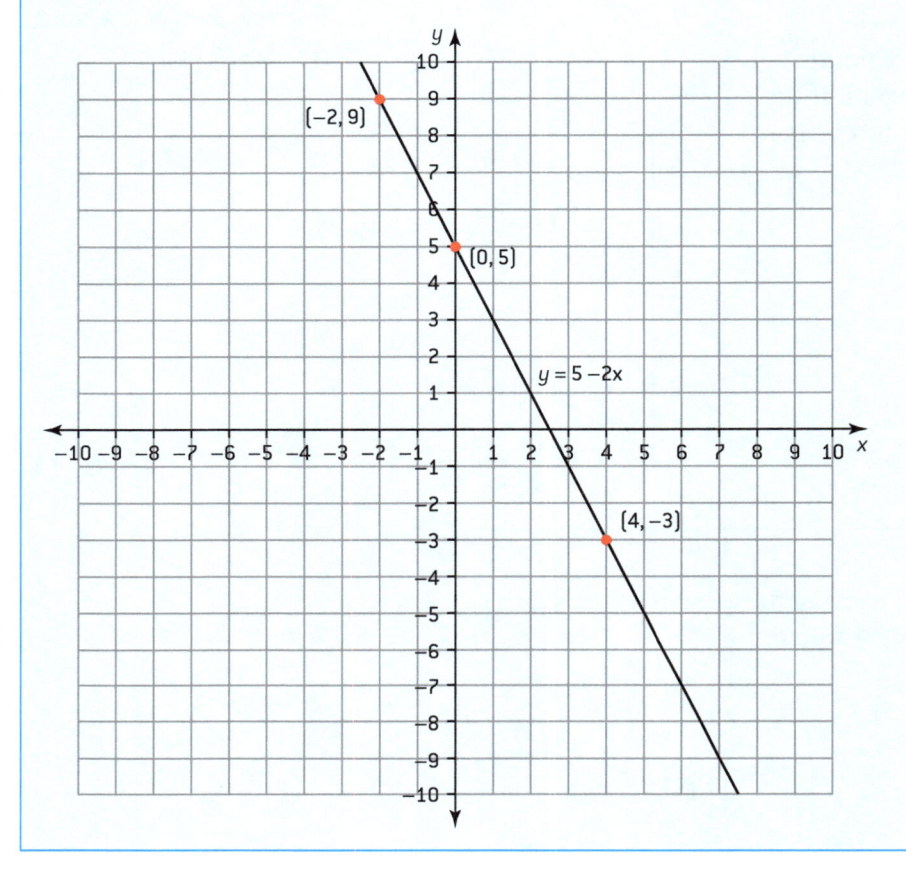

Choose a range of three values of x. Calculate y-coordinates and put them in a table of values.

$5 - 2(-2) = 9$

$5 - 2 \times 0 = 5$

$5 - 2 \times 4 = -3$

Plot the points on a graph.

Then draw a straight line through the points and label the line with its equation.

> **Command term**
>
> **Draw** means you should represent, by means of a labelled, accurate graph, using a pencil. A ruler (straight edge) should be used for straight lines. Graphs should have points correctly plotted (if appropriate) and joined in a straight line or smooth curve.

If the points given by a function do not lie in a straight line, you should make sure that you plot enough points to be able to draw a smooth curve through them. If possible, you should include any significant point, such as where the curve crosses the x- or y-axis.

Example 3
Draw a graph of the function $y = 2x^2 + 7x - 1$.

x	y
−4	3
−3	−4
−2	−7
−1	−6
0	−1
1	8
−1.75	−7.125

Choose a range of values of x. Calculate y-coordinates and put them in a table of values.

$2(-4)^2 + 7(-4) - 1 = 3$, etc.

74

(−4, 3), (−3, −4), (−2, −7), (−1, −6), (0, −1), (1, 8), (−1.75, −7.125)

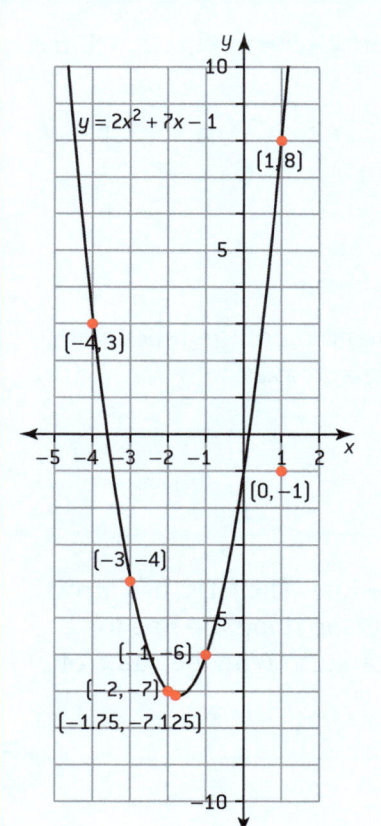

From the table, write the coordinates of the points.

Plot the points on a graph.

Then draw a smooth curve through the points and label it with its equation.

> **DP link**
>
> In the DP course, you will learn how to calculate the coordinates of the vertex (the bottom point) of a graph like this one.

> **DP ready** **International-mindedness**
>
> Coordinate geometry is often referred to as Cartesian geometry after one of its inventors. Descartes wrote his book, *la géométrie* in the early 17th century. In it he laid the foundations of modern analytic geometry. At around the same time Fermat wrote *ad locos planos et solidos isagoge* in which he independently produced many of the features of analytic geometry. Analytic geometry combined geometry and algebra as a single subject and provided the basis for later mathematical breakthroughs, like Newton and Leibniz developing the differential calculus (which you will learn about in both the MAA and MAI courses.)

Exercise 4.1

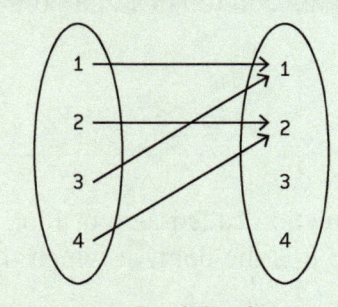

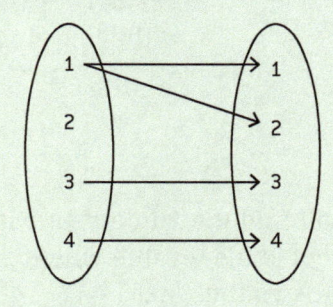

1. Determine which of these diagrams show a function

   a   b

2. Draw a graph of the function $y = 3x - 1$

3. Draw a graph of the function $y = x^2 - 3x - 4$

4.2 Graphing linear functions using technology

In section 4.1 you learned to draw the graph of a function by plotting points on paper. In this section you will look at functions whose graphs are straight lines.

Your GDC can plot the graph of a function for you. Your calculator is likely to either use the $y = \ldots$ notation, where you will enter the equations as Y1, Y2, etc, or the function notation where you enter equations as $f1(x)$, $f2(x)$, etc.

Some GDCs have an equation entry screen and others have drop-down area in a graph screen to enter the equations of functions.

> **Key point**
>
> A **linear function** is a function whose graph is a straight line. It can be written in the form $y = mx + c$ where m and c are numbers.

FUNCTIONS

Example 4

Graph the function $y = 2x + 1$ with your GDC.

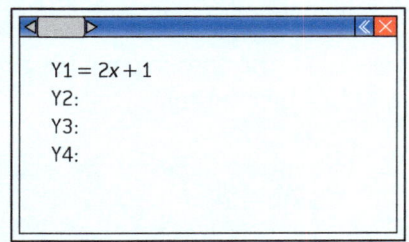

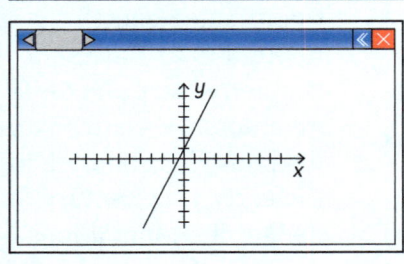

Y1 = 2x + 1 Y2: Y3: Y4:	Open the equation entry screen, type $2x + 1$ and press Enter (or EXE). To type x, you may have to press a key labelled something like X, T, θ.
[graph screen showing line]	Switch to the graph screen. The GDC displays the graph of the function $y = 2x + 1$ with the default axes.

Using the GDC you can trace points on the line. The GDC has arrow keys and you can use these to move the cursor along the line to display the coordinates of the point. You can also type the value of an x-coordinate.

Example 5

Find the coordinates of the point on $y = 2x + 1$ where $x = 1$.

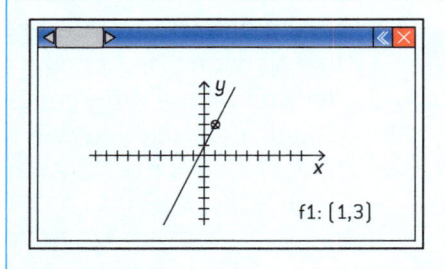

[graph with point, f1: (1,3)]	Using the trace function on your GDC, type the x-coordinate, 1. The GDC displays the coordinates of a point on the line (1, 2).

◉ Key point

The points where a line crosses the axes are the x- and y-intercepts.

GDCs will find the x-intercept with a function called zero or root. The x-intercept is the y-value when $x = 0$, so it is the point at which the graph crosses the y-axis.

Some GDCs also have a function that will find the y-intercept. If this function is missing then you will be able to trace a point where $x = 0$.

Example 6

Find the x- and y-intercepts of the function $y = 2x + 1$.

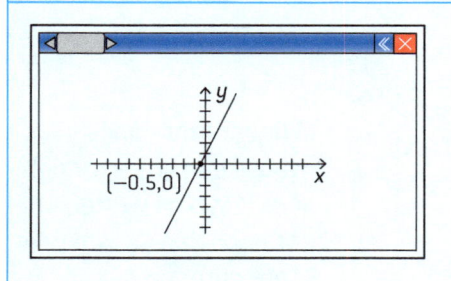

[graph showing point (−0.5, 0)]	Use the zero or root function to find the x-intercept. Follow any instructions on the screen. The GDC displays the coordinates of the point (−0.5, 0).

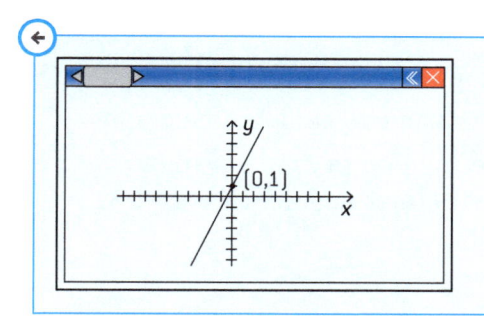

4 Graphing functions

Using the trace function on your GDC, type the *x*-coordinate, 0, or use the *y*-intercept function.
The GDC displays the coordinates of a point on the line (0,1).

In DP examinations, you will also have to **sketch** the graphs of functions.

Sketching is different from *drawing* an accurate plotted graph, but you should avoid making your sketches too unclear. You do not need to use graph paper for a sketch but it is advisable to use a pencil and a ruler. You should **label** axes, but you do not need to give a full scale. You should label key points (such as where the graph passes through the axes) with their coordinates.

> **Command term**
>
> **Sketch** a graph means you should represent by means of a graph (labelled as appropriate). The sketch should give a general idea of the required shape or relationship, and should include relevant features.
>
> **Draw** a graph means you must correctly plot coordinates and join them with a straight line or smooth curve. You did this in section 4.1
>
> **Label** means you should add labels to the diagram or graph. This might mean labels for the *x*- and *y*-axes, or the coordinates of points on the graph.

Example 7
Sketch the graph of the function $y = 2x + 1$.

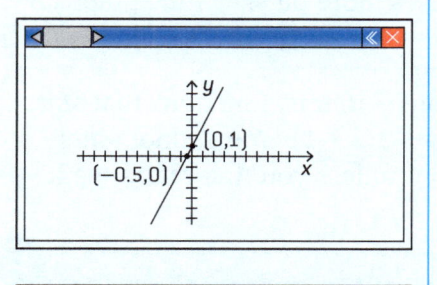

Use the GDC to graph the function $y = 2x + 1$ and find the *x*- and *y*-intercepts. These are the key points.

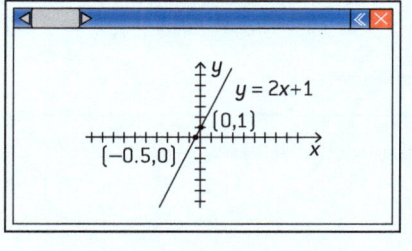

Draw and label the axes. A scale is not really necessary as the intercepts are labelled.
Label the intercepts with their coordinates.
Sketch the line using a ruler and passing through the labelled intercepts.
Label the equation of the function.

∞ **Internal link**

In section 2.5a you learned how to solve linear equations algebraically.

Example 8 will show how to solve a linear equation graphically, using your GDC.

Example 8
Solving the equation $2x + 3 = -6$ graphically, using your GDC.

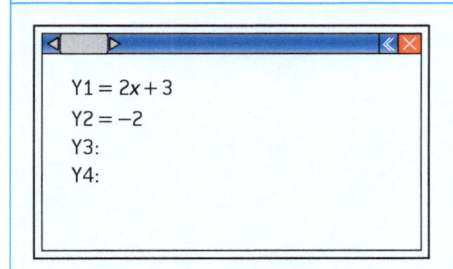

Y1 = 2x + 3
Y2 = -2
Y3:
Y4:

Solving the equation $2x + 3 = -6$ is equivalent to finding the point on the graph of $y = 2x + 3$ where $y = -6$.
Enter the functions $y = 2x + 3$ and $y = -6$.

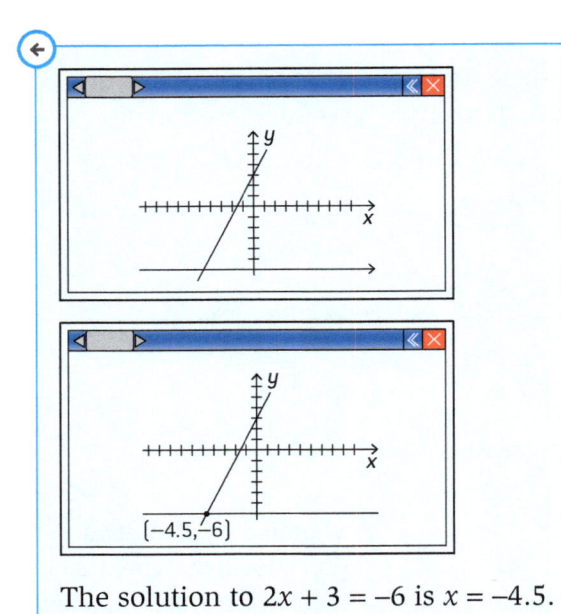

FUNCTIONS

Switch to the graph screen.

Your GDC will display two straight line graphs.

You can find the solution of $2x + 3 = -6$ by finding the point of intersection of $y = 2x + 3$ and $y = -6$.

Your GDC will tell you the coordinates of this point, which is $(-4.5, -6)$.

The solution to $2x + 3 = -6$ is $x = -4.5$.

DP ready: MAA & MAI

The MAA course focuses more on sketching graphs by analysing the equation of a function and finding key points by which to sketch a graph. The MAI course focuses more on sketching graphs by first plotting them on your GDC.

Internal link

See section 2.5c to recap rearranging an equation.

The GDC graphs linear *explicit* functions – that is, functions that start with '$y =$'. For example, $y = 3x - 4$ or $y = 2(x + 1)$. You cannot enter an *implicit* equation such as $2x + 3y = 6$ unless you first rearrange it to make y the subject.

Example 9

Graph these equations on your GDC:

a $y = 2(x + 1)$ **b** $2x + 3y = 6$

a

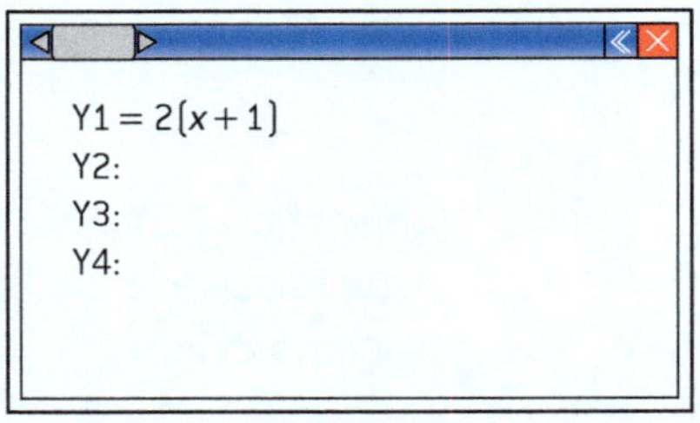

Enter the function $y = 2(x + 1)$

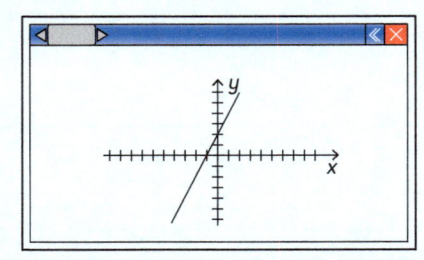

Switch to the graph screen.

Your GDC will display the graph of the function.

b

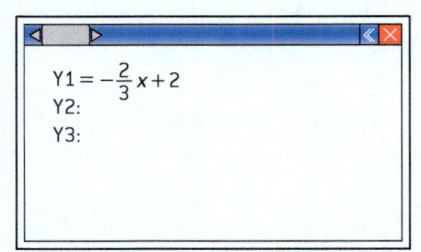

$2x + 3y = 6$
$3y = -2x + 6$
$y = -\dfrac{2}{3}x + 2$

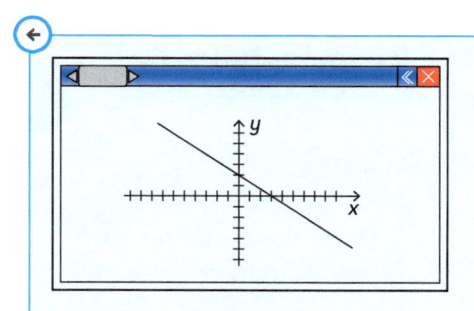

4 Graphing functions

Enter the function $y = -\frac{2}{3}x + 2$

Switch to the graph screen.

Your GDC will display the graph of the function.

Look at the pair of simultaneous equations $\begin{matrix} 5x + 3y = 29 \\ 2x + 3y = 17 \end{matrix}$.

Both equations are written as implicit functions. Writing these as explicit equations (where y is the subject) allows you to solve them using your GDC by finding the intersection of the two lines.

Internal link

In section 2.9, you learned to solve simultaneous equations.

Example 10

Solve the equations $\begin{matrix} 5x + 3y = 29 \\ 2x + 3y = 17 \end{matrix}$ graphically, using your GDC.

$Y1 = -\frac{5}{3}x + \frac{29}{3}$

$Y2 = -\frac{2}{3}x + \frac{17}{3}$

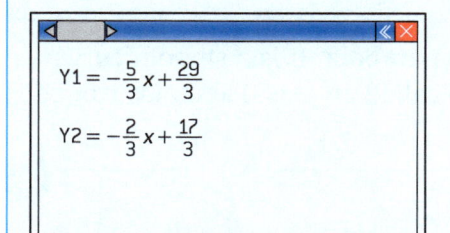

Rearrange the equations to make y the subject.

$y = -\frac{5}{3}x + \frac{29}{3}$

$y = -\frac{2}{3}x + \frac{17}{3}$

Enter the functions into your GDC

Switch to the graph screen.

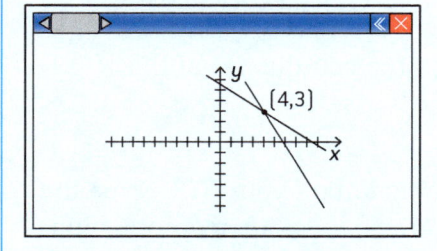

The GDC shows two straight lines.

Use the intersection function of your GDC to find the point where the lines cross.

$x = 4$ and $y = 3$

The intersection point is (4, 3) and so the solution is $x = 4$ and $y = 3$.

Exercise 4.2

1 Use your GDC to graph these functions, find the x- and y-intercepts and sketch their graphs.

   a $y = x - 4$ **b** $y = \frac{1}{2}x + 3$ **c** $y = 3 - 2x$

2 Use your GDC to plot $y = \frac{2}{3}x + \frac{4}{5}$ and find the point on $y = \frac{2}{3}x + \frac{4}{5}$ where $x = 1.75$.

3 Solve these equations graphically using your GDC:

   a $3x - 5 = 4$ **b** $4x - 3 = 2$ **c** $3(x - 4) = 2$

4 Solve the simultaneous equations $\begin{matrix} 3x + 2y = 3 \\ 4x + 4y = 12 \end{matrix}$ graphically, using your GDC.

FUNCTIONS

> **Key point**
>
> A **quadratic function** is in the form $y = ax^2 + bx + c$ or, in factorized form, $y = a(x-p)(x-q)$.

> **Internal link**
>
> You studied quadratic expressions in section 2.7. A quadratic expression is one where the highest power of x is 2, i.e. it contains a term in x^2.

4.3 Graphing quadratic functions using technology

Example 11

Graph the function $y = x^2 + 5x + 6$ with your GDC.

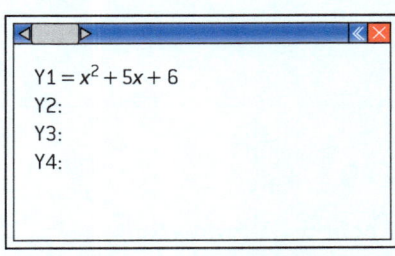

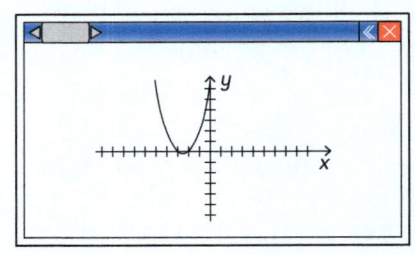

Y1 = $x^2 + 5x + 6$
Y2:
Y3:
Y4:

Open the equation entry screen, type $x^2 + 5x + 6$

Switch to the graph screen.

The GDC displays the graph of the function $y = x^2 + 5x + 6$ with the default axes.

The shape of the quadratic curve is a **parabola**. It is a smooth curve and symmetrical about a vertical line called an axis. Parabolas can be ∪-shaped or ∩-shaped.

Example 12

Find the x- and y-intercepts of the function $y = x^2 + 5x + 6$.

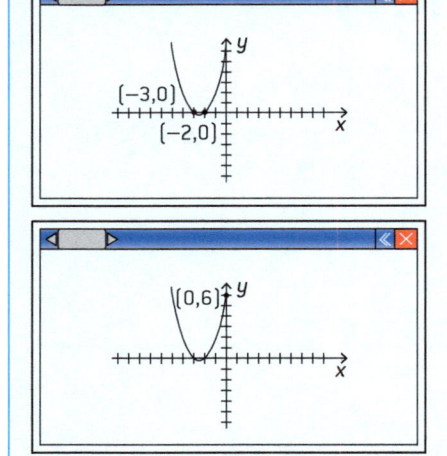

(−3,0)
(−2,0)

(0,6)

Use the zero or root function to find the x-intercepts. Follow any instructions on the screen.

The GDC displays the coordinates of the points $(-3, 0), (-2, 0)$.

Using the trace function on your GDC, type the x-coordinate, 0, or use the y-intercept function.

The GDC displays the coordinates of a point on the line $(0, 6)$.

> **Note**
>
> If you are asked to find the intercept, then the answer is a single number. In the example above, the y-intercept is 6. If you are asked for the coordinates of the y-intercept, you need to write (0,6). Generally, exam mark schemes will accept the coordinates if asked for the intercepts, but not vice versa.

There is another important point on the quadratic curve: the **vertex**, which is its lowest or highest point on the curve. To find this point you can use the minimum or maximum function on your GDC.

Example 13

Find the vertex of the function $y = x^2 + 5x + 6$.

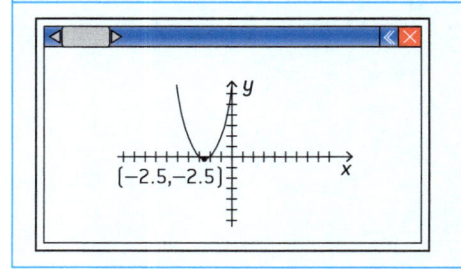

(−2.5, −2.5)

Use the minimum function of the GDC to find the vertex.

The GDC displays the coordinates of the point.

80

4 Graphing functions

When you sketch a quadratic function, you should show and label the key features: its intercepts and vertex.

Example 14

Sketch the graph of the function

a $y = 3x^2 + 4x - 4$
b $y = 2x^2 + 4x + 3$
c $y = 4x^2 - 12x + 9$

a

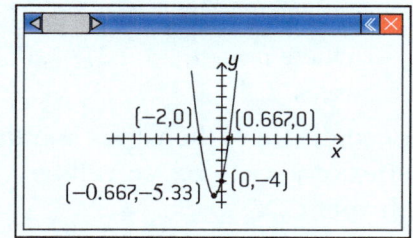

[GDC screen showing graph with points $(-2,0)$, $(0.667,0)$, $(0,-4)$, $(-0.667,-5.33)$]

[Sketch showing $y = 3x^2 + 4x - 4$ with points $(-2,0)$, $(0.667,0)$, $(0,-4)$, $(-0.667,-5.33)$]

Use the GDC to graph the function $y = 3x^2 + 4x - 4$.

Find the x- and y-intercepts and the vertex. These are the key points.

Draw and label the axes. A scale is not really necessary as points are labelled.

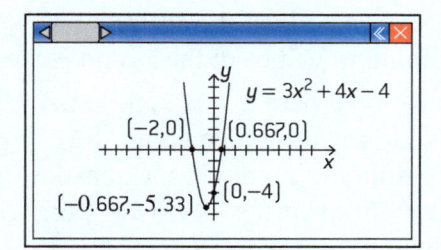

Sketch the curve and label the intercepts and the vertex with their coordinates.

Label the equation of the function.

b

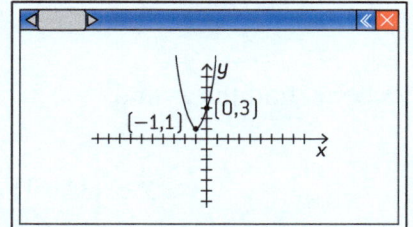

[GDC screen showing graph with points $(-1,1)$ and $(0,3)$]

[Sketch showing $y = 2x^2 + 4x + 3$ with points $(-1,1)$ and $(0,3)$]

Use the GDC to graph the function $y = 2x^2 + 4x + 3$.

Find the y-intercept and the vertex. There are no x-intercepts.

Draw and label the axes. A scale is not really necessary as points are labelled.

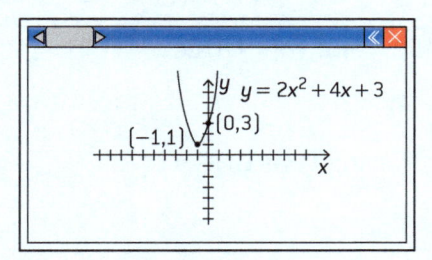

Sketch the curve and label the intercept and the vertex with their coordinates.

Label the equation of the function.

c

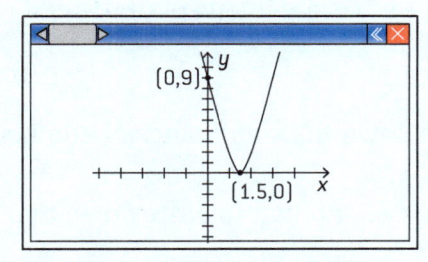

[GDC screen showing graph with points $(0,9)$ and $(1.5,0)$]

[Sketch showing $y = 4x^2 - 12x + 9$ with points $(0,9)$ and $(1.5,0)$]

Use the GDC to graph the function $y = 4x^2 - 12x + 9$.

Find the y-intercept and the vertex. The vertex is on the x-axis and so it is the x-intercept.

Draw and label the axes. A scale is not really necessary as points are labelled.

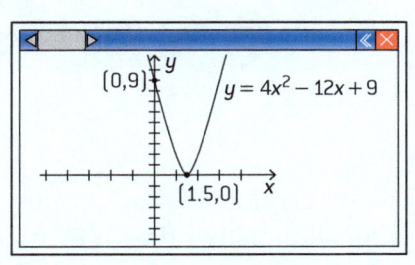

Sketch the curve and label the intercept and the vertex with their coordinates.

Label the equation of the function.

FUNCTIONS

DP ready: Analysis and approaches

This investigation is in the style of those from Analysis and approaches.

> **Command term**
>
> **Explain** means you should give a detailed account, including reasons or causes.

Investigation 4.1

1. Sketch the graphs of $y = x^2 - 3x + c$ where $c = -1, 0, 1, 2, 3, 4$. Label the y-intercept and the vertex of the curves.

   a **What** do you notice about the y-intercept and the value of c? **Explain** why this pattern exists.

   b **Describe** the pattern that you notice for the vertex of the curves and the value of c.

2. Sketch the graphs of $y = x^2 + bx + 1$ where $b = -4, -3, -2, -1, 0, 1, 2, 3, 4$. Label the vertices of these curves.

   What do you notice about the x-coordinate of the vertex and the value of b? Predict where the vertex of $y = x^2 + 6x + 6$ will be and confirm your prediction with your GDC.

3. For this part of the investigation, you may need to adjust the viewing window of your GDC. You can adjust the scales by changing the maximum and minimum values of the x- and y-axes.

   Sketch the graphs of $y = ax^2 + 6x + 6$ where $a = 1, 2, 3$. Label the vertices of these curves. What do you notice about the x-coordinate compared to the result you obtained for question 2? Predict what the x-coordinate of the vertex of $y = 5x^2 + 6x + 6$ will be and confirm your prediction with your GDC.

DP ready | Theory of knowledge

In an advanced mathematical textbook published in 1960, intended for students going on to study mathematics at university, there was a whole chapter devoted to techniques for manipulating quadratic functions and solving quadratic equations. The IB first approved the use of calculators in examinations in the 1980s, and in the 1990s they permitted some use of graphical display calculators. How do you think that this change has influenced what is in mathematics syllabuses over recent decades? Do you think that mathematicians need to be good at solving things by hand when there is technology that can perform the same functions at the press of a button?

Exercise 4.3

1. Use your GDC to graph these functions, find the x- and y-intercepts and draw a sketch.

   a $y = \frac{1}{2}x^2 - 2x - 3$ b $y = 9x^2 - 4$ c $y = \frac{3}{4}(x+1)^2$

2. Use your GDC to find the point on $y = x^2 + x + 1$ where $x = 1.5$

3. Solve these equations graphically using your GDC:

   a $\frac{1}{2}x^2 = 4.5$ b $x^2 + 2x = 3$ c $x^2 + 6x + 10 = 1$

4. Find the vertex of $y = x^2 - 5x + 4$ using your GDC.

DP style | Analysis and Approaches SL

5. A quadratic curve $y = ax^2 + bx + c$ has a y-intercept of 9 and a vertex at $(2, 1)$.

   a State the value of c.

   b Sketch the curve and write down the coordinates of another point on the curve.

   c Use the points the curve passes through to write down two linear equations in a and b.

   d Solve these two equations to find the equation of the curve.

4.4 Linear and quadratic models

You can model many situations in science, economics, etc. by linear functions. You can use a graph of the function, either drawn by hand or with a GDC, to calculate values of the function.

4 Graphing functions

Example 15

The final velocity, v, of an object, accelerating at a rate of a is given by the formula $v = u + at$ where u is the initial velocity and t is the time.

If $u = 33$ ms^{-1} and $a = -10$ ms^{-2}, use the function $v = 33 - 10t$ to model the motion of a cricket ball. You can enter this into your GDC as $y = 33 - 10x$, where y takes the place of v and x takes the place of t.

Use your GDC to graph the function $v = 33 - 10t$.

- **a** Find the value of v when $t = 2$ s.
- **b** Find the value of v when $t = 4$ s. Comment on your result.
- **c** Find the value of t when $v = 0$.
- **d** Find the value of t when $v = 10$ ms^{-1}.

a

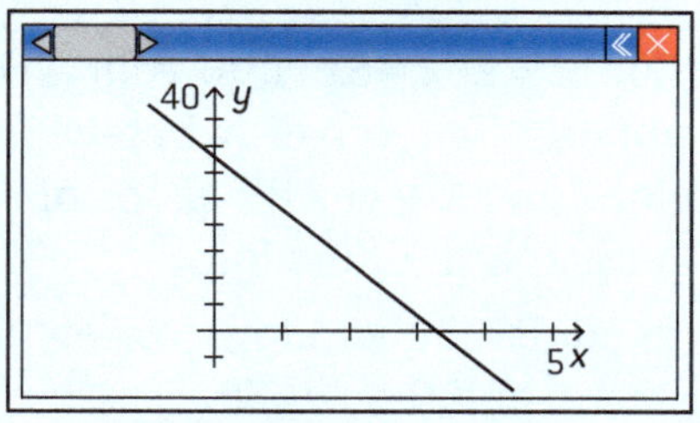

You will need to adjust the window to view the function to $-1 \leq x \leq 5$ and $-10 \leq y \leq 40$.

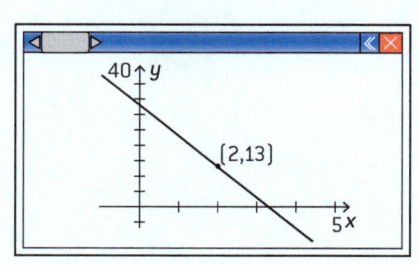

Use the trace function to find y when $x = 2$.

$v = 13$ ms^{-1}

b

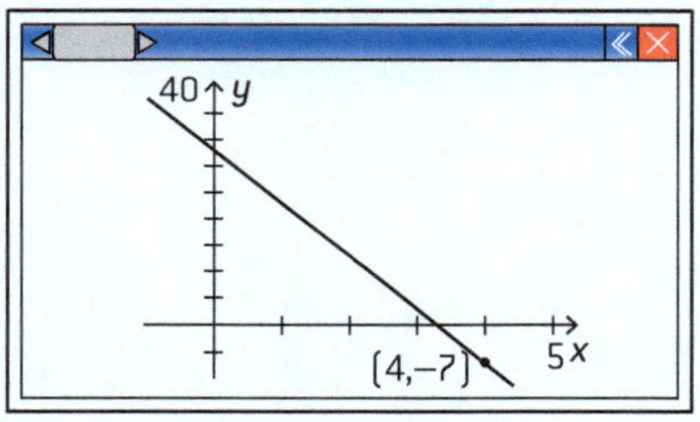

Use the trace function to find y when $x = 4$.

$v = -7$ ms^{-1}. The direction of the ball's motion is downward.

In the DP course you will learn that the sign of velocity tells you whether the object is moving in the positive or the negative direction.

c

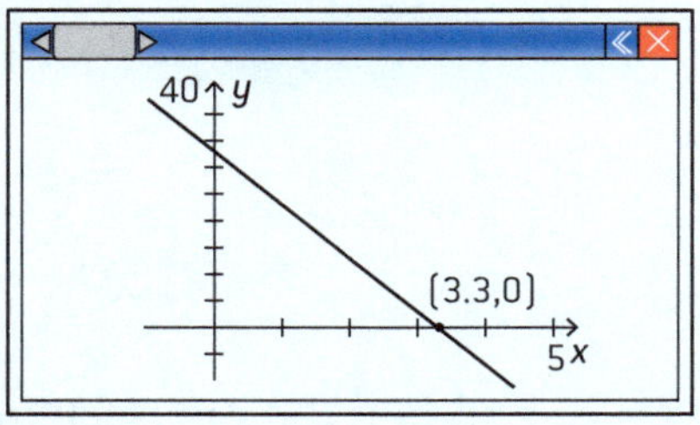

Use the zero (or root) function.

$t = 3.3$ s.

d

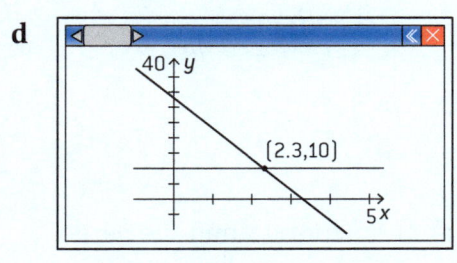

Draw the line $y = 10$ and find the intersection.

$t = 2.3$ s.

FUNCTIONS

You can also model situations in the same way with quadratic functions.

Example 16

The height, s, of an object, accelerating at a rate of a is given by the formula $s = ut + \dfrac{1}{2}at^2$ where u is the initial velocity and t is the time.

A football is kicked vertically upward with $u = 28$ ms^{-1} and $a = -10$ ms^{-2}.

a Find the value of s when $t = 2$ s.
b Find the value of t when $s = 0$.
c Find the value of t when $s = 25$ m.
d Find the maximum height of the football.

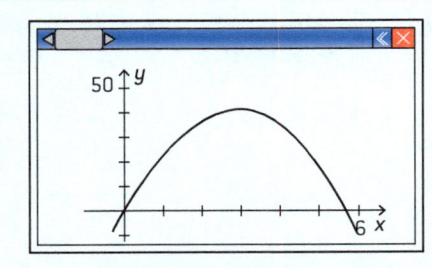

Enter the function $y = 28x - 5x^2$ into your GDC to model the motion of a football, where y takes the place of s and x takes the place of t. Use your GDC to graph the function.

You will need to adjust the window to view the function to $0 \leq x \leq 6$ and $0 \leq y \leq 50$.

a $s = 36$ m

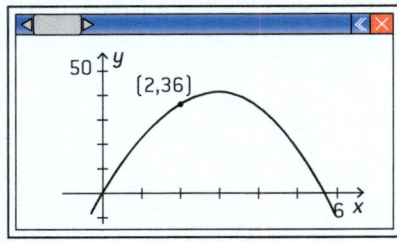

Use the trace function to find y when $x = 2$.

b $t = 0$ s and 5.6 s.

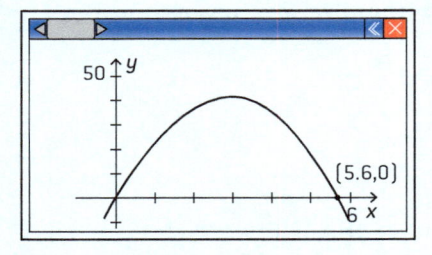

Use the zero (or root) function.

c $t = 1.11$ s or 4.49 s.

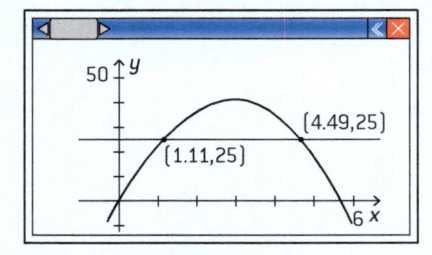

Draw the line $y = 25$ and find the intersection.

d Maximum $s = 39.2$ m when $t = 2.8$ s.

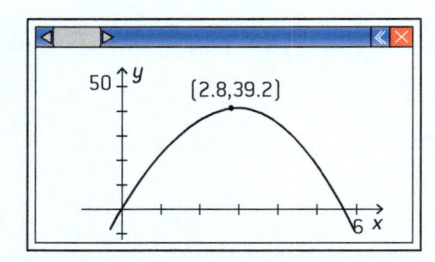

Use the maximum function to find the vertex of the curve.

4 Graphing functions

Investigation 4.2

Use your GDC to complete this table.

equation	$y=2x-4$	$y=2x-3$	$y=2x-2$	$y=2x-1$	$y=2x$	$y=2x+1$	$y=2x+2$	$y=2x+3$	$y=2x+4$
y-intercept									

Comment on the pattern that you see.

Confirm your results by examining the y-intercepts of some other linear functions.

The **gradient** of a line is a measure of how steep it is. To find the gradient with a GDC you will need to use a function referred to as dy/dx. (On some GDCs you will need to use the *derivative* function). When using this function, you choose a point on the line and the GDC will give the value of the gradient. The gradient of a straight line will be the same for every point on the line.

Use you GDC to complete this table.

equation	$y=-4x+1$	$y=-3x+1$	$y=-2x+1$	$y=-x+1$	$y=1$	$y=x+1$	$y=2x+1$	$y=3x+1$	$y=4x+1$
gradient									

Comment on the pattern that you see.

Confirm your results by examining the gradients of some other linear functions.

Use you GDC to complete this table.

equation	$y=x^2-3$	$y=2x^2-x-2$	$y=2x^2+2x-1$	$y=x^2+4x$	$y=3x^2-3x+1$	$y=x^2+3x+2$	$y=x^2+x+3$
y-intercept							

Comment on the pattern that you see.

Confirm your results by examining the y-intercepts of some other quadratic functions.

Higher Level

4.5 Finding the equation for a linear model

As seen in the investigation, in a linear model of the form $y = mx + c$, m represents the gradient or slope of the graph of the model. The gradient is a measure of the rate at which y changes with respect to x. It is the amount that y increases or decreases as x increases by one unit. Finding m will enable us to find the equation for a linear model. To find m you need to know two pairs of x and y values.

If two points on a straight line are (x_1, y_1) and (x_2, y_2), then the gradient of the line (or the rate of increase of y with respect to x) is given by $\dfrac{y_2 - y_1}{x_2 - x_1}$.

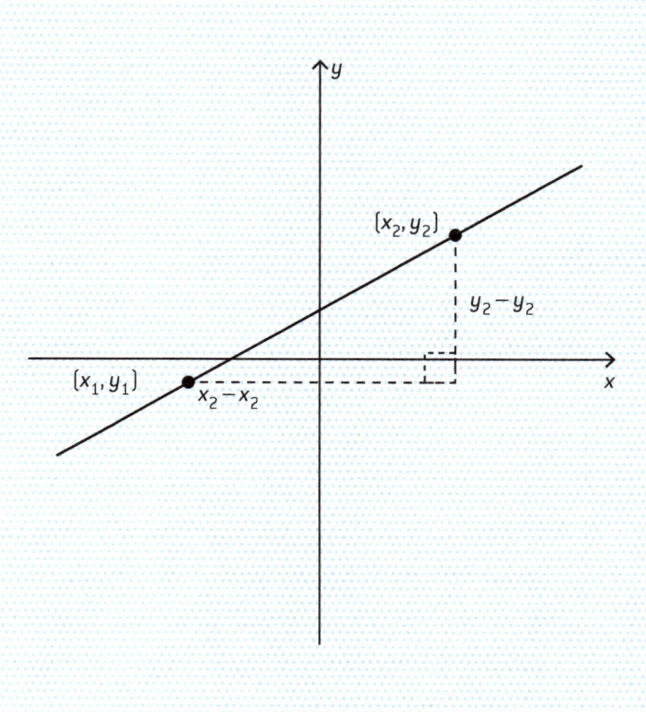

FUNCTIONS

Example 17

The temperature on a beach (T) between the times of 0700 and 1400 can be modelled by the function $T = mt + c$ where t is the time in hours after midnight. At 0700 the temperature is 12°C and at 1200 the temperature is 24°C.

a Find the rate of increase of the temperature in degrees per hour.
b Find the values of m and c for the model.
c Hence predict the temperature at 1400.

a $\dfrac{24-12}{5} = 2.4$ °C/hour	The rate of increase will be the total increase divided by the length of time between the two points.
b $m = 2.4$ $12 = 2.4 \times 7 + c$ $c = -4.8$	The value of m is simply the rate of increase of temperature. As the equation must be satisfied by both the sets of values given, either can be substituted to find c.
c $T = 2.4t - 4.8$ $T = 2.4 \times 14 - 4.8 = 28.8$	The second point can be used as a check $2.4 \times 12 - 4.8 = 24$

> **DP ready: Applications and interpretation**
>
> The following questions are more in the style of those you would find on the MAI paper.

Exercise 4.4

1. The quantity of items sold, q and their selling price, s are connected by the formula $q = -20s + 1200$.
   Use your GDC to graph the function for $0 \le s \le 25$ and $0 \le q \le 1300$.
   Find:

   a The quantity sold when the selling price is 20.
   b The selling price when 1000 items are sold.

2. The profit, $P(x)$ made when selling x television sets is modelled by the function $P(x) = -20x^2 + 1400x - 12000$.
   Use your GDC to graph the function for $0 \le x \le 100$ and $0 \le y \le 15000$.
   From the graph find:

   a The number of television sets that must be sold before the company break even.
   b The maximum profit and the number of television sets that must be sold to achieve this.

> **→ Note**
>
> Break even means to make zero profit.

Chapter summary

- ☐ A function is a mapping for which there is only one value of y for each value of x.
- ☐ A **linear function** is a function whose graph is a straight line. It is in the form $y = mx + c$.
- ☐ The points where a line crosses the axes are the x- and y-**intercepts**.
- ☐ A **quadratic function** is in the form $y = ax^2 + bx + c$ or, in factorized form, $y = a(x-p)(x-q)$. Its graph is a parabola.

Chapter 4 test

1. Use your GDC to graph the function $y = 2(2 - x)$ and find the coordinates of the x- and y-intercepts.

2. Use your GDC to graph the function $y = 2.05x - 3.65$ and find the coordinates of the point on the line where $x = 3.25$.

3. Use your GDC to draw the graph of $y = 5 - \frac{1}{2}x$ and **hence** solve the equation $5 - \frac{1}{2}x = 2$.

   > **Command term**
   >
   > **Hence** means you should use the preceding work to obtain the required result.

4. Sketch the graph of $y = \frac{1}{2}x^2 + 2x - 3$, showing the coordinates of the intercepts and vertex.

5. Use your GDC to draw the graph of $y = x^2 - 3x - 4$ and hence solve the equation $x^2 - 3x - 4 = 2$.

6. Use your GDC to draw the graph of $y = x^2 + 4x - 1$. Find the coordinates of the x- and y-intercepts and the vertex. Show that the vertical line through the vertex is equidistant from the intercepts.

7. Which of these graphs are functions?

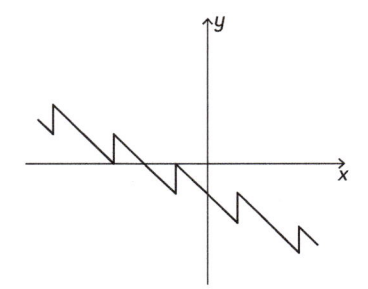

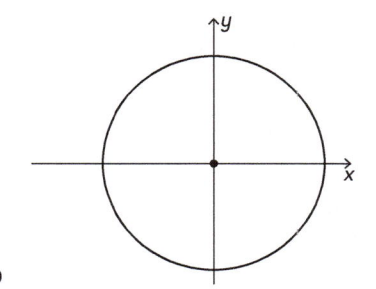

   a   b

DP style   Analysis and Approaches SL

8. Without using your GDC, draw the graph of the function $y = (x + 3)(2 - x)$ for $-4 \leq x \leq 4$, showing clearly the values of the x- and y-intercepts and the coordinates of the vertex.

DP style   Applications and Interpretation SL

9. A total of 25 m of fencing is being used to make a rectangular enclosure in a field to contain some sheep. One side of the enclosure is a straight wall and the other three sides are made using the fencing, as shown in the diagram.

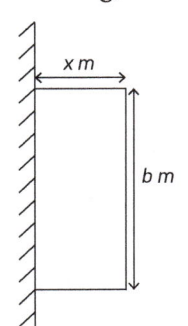

   If one side of the enclosure is x m long, write down the length, b cm of the other side in terms of x and hence find the area of the enclosure in terms of x.

   Graph the area function using your GDC and find the maximum area for the enclosure.

FUNCTIONS

Modelling and investigation

DP ready   Approaches to learning

Critical thinking: Analyzing and evaluating issues and ideas

Communication: Reading, writing and using language to gather and communicate information

During the second world war, a Russian economist Leonid Kantorovich developed linear programming as a method for achieving the best result in a situation where the constraints can be represented as linear functions. Linear inequalities are used to represent any restrictions.

An inequality can also have two variables, x and y, such as $x + 3y < 9$. Instead of the solution being a portion of the number line, the solution of this inequality is a region of the Cartesian plane.

First, you must look at the points where $x + 3y = 9$. This is a straight line. You can draw this by finding several points on the line that satisfy its equation.

On one side of this line $x + 3y < 9$ and on the other $x + 3y > 9$.

To decide which side is which, you can choose one point, for example the point $(0,0)$. At this point $x = 0$ and $y = 0$. Substituting this into the expression $x + 3y$, $0 + 3 \times 0 = 0$ and $0 < 9$, so $(0,0)$ is in the region $x + 3y < 9$. The required region is to the left of the line. This can be verified by trying other points.

Consider the following problem which will be solved by linear programming.

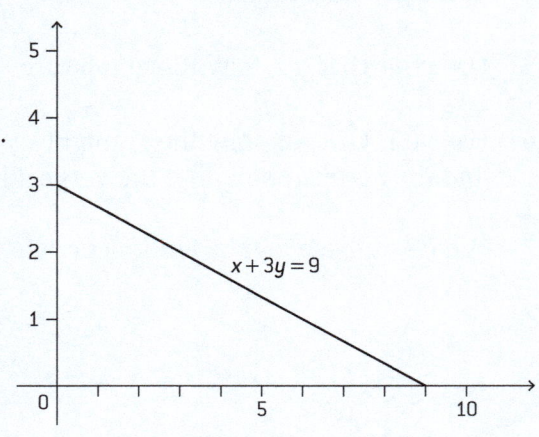

You are responsible for the transportation of supplies to a remote area that has been struck by an earthquake. Supplies can be transported by plane or truck and you have a budget for getting them to the area.

Let x be the number of trips by plane and y the number of trips by truck.

1. The cost of a plane is $1000 per trip and the cost of a truck is $500 per trip. Your budget is $62 500. Show that $2x + y \leq 125$.

2. There are 5 planes and 15 trucks available.

   Planes can make 2 trips per day

   Trucks will take 2 days per trip (1 day to reach the site and a second to return).

   Write inequalities in the form $x \geq a$, $x \leq b$, $y \geq c$ and $y \leq d$ for the number of trips by plane and truck that are possible in 6 days.

3. On graph paper, or using an online graphing package, draw the lines representing the equations $2x + y = 125$, $x = a$, $x = b$, $y = c$ and $y = d$

   Indicate on your graph the region containing the values of x and y which satisfy all the inequalities. This is known as the feasible region.

4. Planes can deliver 1 tonne of supplies per trip. Trucks can deliver 2 tonnes of supplies per trip.

   Let A be the amount of supplies that can be delivered to the area in 6 days. Write down an expression for A in terms of x and y.

   The fundamental theorem of linear programming states that the maximum or minimum value of any linear function will occur at one of the vertices of the feasible region.

   Use the theorem to find the maximum amount of supplies that can be delivered in the first six days and the number of planes and trucks that should be hired.

GEOMETRY AND TRIGONOMETRY

5 Geometry

Learning outcomes

In this chapter you will learn about:
- Geometric concepts: point, line, plane, angle
- Angle measurement in degrees.
- The triangle sum theorem
- Properties of triangles and quadrilaterals, including parallelograms, rhombuses, rectangles, squares, kites and trapezoids; compound shapes
- Three-figure bearings, compass directions
- Simple geometric transformations: translation, reflection, rotation, enlargement

Key terms

- Point
- Line
- Line segment
- Parallel
- Angle
- Perpendicular
- Supplementary
- Acute
- Obtuse
- Vertically opposite
- Corresponding
- Alternate
- Co-interior
- Complementary
- Bisect
- Reflection
- Rotation
- Translation
- Enlargement
- Vector
- Stretch

5.1 Points, lines, planes and angles

The idea of a **point** is fundamental in geometry. A point is a location in space. It is dimensionless, that is it has no length, width or depth. A point is shown by a dot, •.

A straight **line** connects points and has one dimension only, length. It has no depth or breadth. A line through two points continues infinitely. A line which has two endpoints is called a **line segment**.

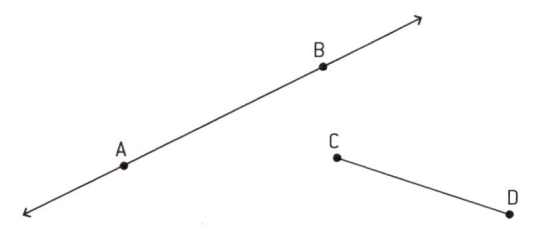

The line through A and B is (AB) and the line segment joining C and D is [CD].

If two lines do not meet, then they are **parallel**. Arrows are used to show that two lines are parallel.

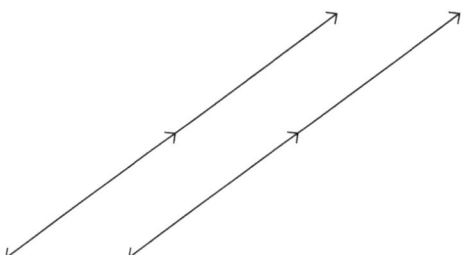

DP ready | Theory of knowledge

Mathematical ideas are based on axioms, or 'self-evident truths' and are developed logically from them. The first such system was the geometry of Euclid in ancient Greece. The axioms of plane geometry defined the point, line, plane and angle, which are not defined in terms of any other objects. Euclidean geometry has changed little in the last 2000 years.

Key point

A point is a dimensionless location in space.

A line is one-dimensional and extends infinitely in both directions.

A line segment is a line with two endpoints.

Two lines are parallel if they are the same distance apart and never touch.

GEOMETRY AND TRIGONOMETRY

The amount of turn between two line segments around the point where they meet is the **angle** between them.

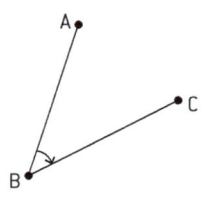

This angle can be described as AB̂C or, if the description is clear because there are no other angles at the point B which could cause confusion, as B̂.

Angles are measured in degrees. A full turn that rotates all the way round and back to the start is 360°.

> **DP link**
>
> DP students taking MAA SL and HL and MAI HL will learn about an alternative measure of angles known as radians. 1 radian measures out an arc length on a circle equal to its radius.

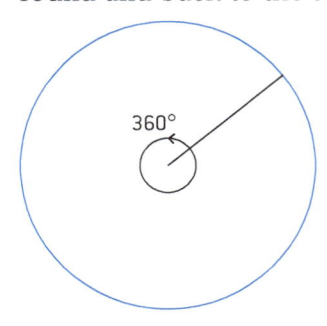

The angle on a straight line is known as a straight angle. The measure of a straight angle is 180°.

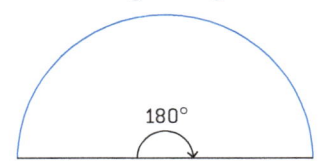

Half the angle in a straight line is a right-angle. You show that an angle is a right angle with a symbol like a box in the corner.

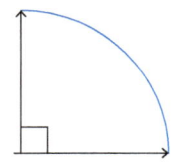

A right angle is 90°. Two lines at right-angles are called **perpendicular.**

A full turn is 360°, a straight angle (180°) is a half-turn and a right-angle (90°) is a quarter-turn.

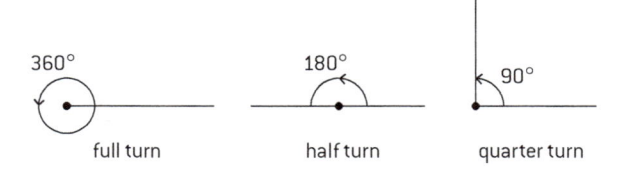

full turn   half turn   quarter turn

If you split a straight angle in two, then the angles formed by splitting it are called **supplementary**. Supplementary angles add up to 180°.

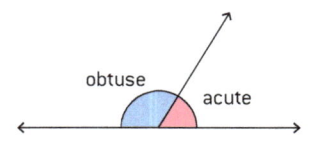

obtuse   acute

One of these angles is **obtuse** and the other is **acute**. An obtuse angle is between 90° and 180° and an acute angle is less than 90°.

90

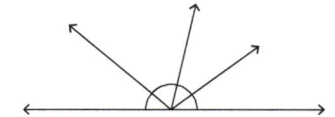

5 Geometry

Any group of angles on a straight line will add up to 180°.

Example 1

a Calculate the angle marked a.

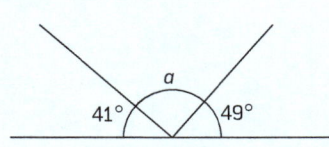

b Calculate the angle marked b.

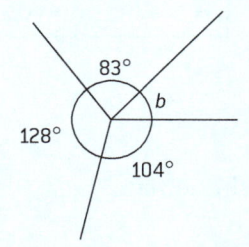

a $41 + a + 49 = 180$
$90 + a = 180$
$a = 90°$

A straight angle is 180°.

b $83 + 128 + 104 + b = 360$
$315 + b = 360$
$b = 45°$

The full turn is 360°.

Investigation 5.1

1 On a sheet of graph paper (or squared paper), draw two parallel lines.

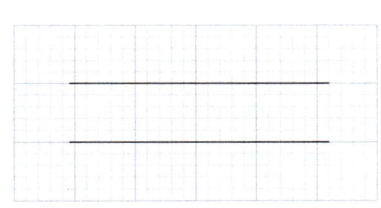

2 Draw another line that crosses the two parallel lines.

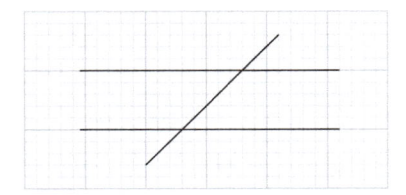

3 For reference, label the angles as shown.

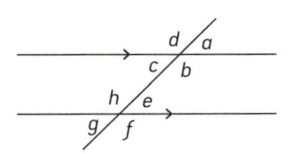

4 Using a protractor, measure all the angles.

5 What do you notice about the angles a and b?

What do you notice about the angles b and c?

What can you deduce about the angles a and c? Try to explain why this follows from the first two observations you made.

What do you notice about b and d? Give a reason.

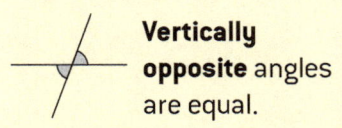

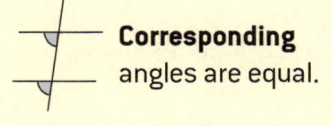

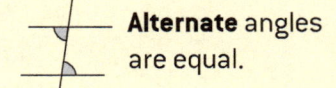

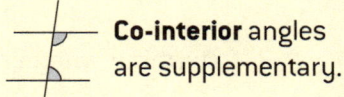

> **Key point**
>
> When two lines cross
>
> **Vertically opposite** angles are equal.
>
> When a line crosses two parallel lines:
>
> **Corresponding** angles are equal.
>
> **Alternate** angles are equal.
>
> **Co-interior** angles are supplementary.

91

GEOMETRY AND TRIGONOMETRY

> 6 Copy and complete the following, writing your answers in terms of angle a and giving reasons.
>
> angle b = ... (because ....)
>
> angle c = ... (because ....)
>
> angle d = ... (because ....)
>
> 7 What do you notice about angles a and e?
>
> 8 What do you notice about angles c and h?

Exercise 5.1

1 Find the angles marked with letters.

i 117°, a

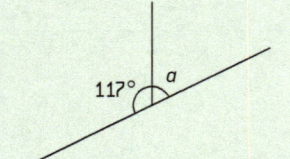

ii b, c, 26°

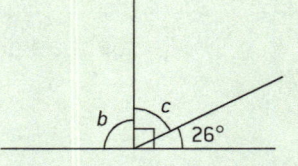

iii 62°, d, 51°, 24°

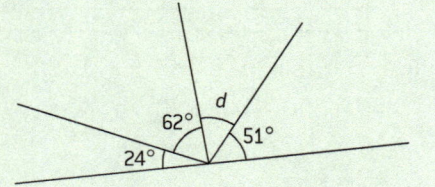

iv 127°, e, 80°

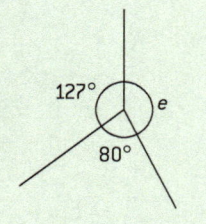

v $2f$, 59°, f, 55°

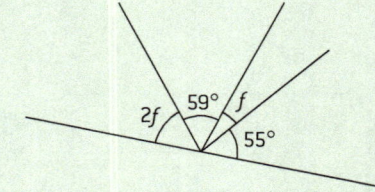

vi g, $3g$, $5g$

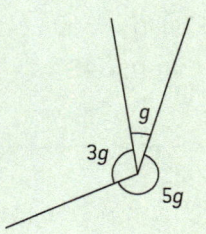

2 i 41°, a

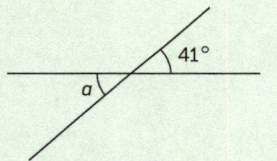

ii 143°, b

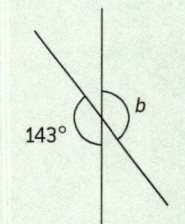

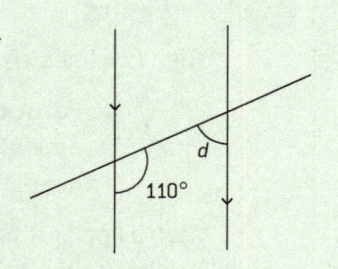

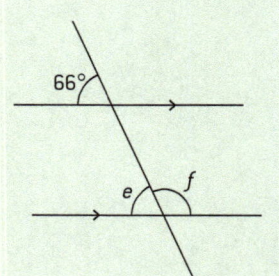

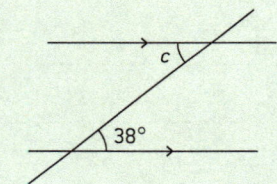

iii c, 38°

iv d, 110°

v 66°, e, f

vi 62°, g, h

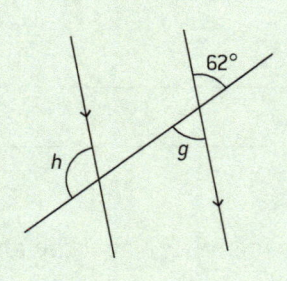

3 Find all angles marked with letters.

A, 30°, 47°, t, s, r, v, p, q, u, 103°, B

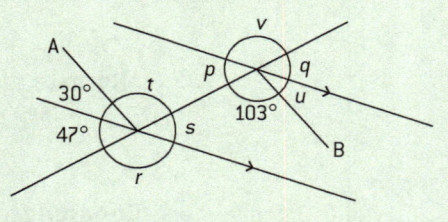

Determine whether the lines marked A and B are parallel. Justify your answer.

5.2 The triangle sum theorem

Investigation 5.2

a   Draw a triangle on a sheet of paper and carefully cut the triangle out with a pair of scissors.

Mark the angles of the triangle A, B and C. (Mark them on both sides). Put a dot in the corner.

Tear (or cut) the angles from the triangle.

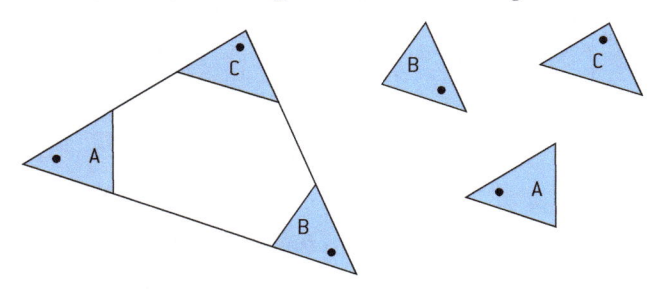

Carefully place the three angles (the points marked with dots) along the side of a ruler. What do you notice? What does this suggest about the three angles of the triangle?

Part **a** was a demonstration of an important result in geometry about the angle sum of a triangle. You have not, however, shown that the result is true for *any* triangle. In part **b**, you will **prove** the result for *all* triangles.

b   ABC is a triangle. The line through P and Q passes through A and is parallel to [BC].

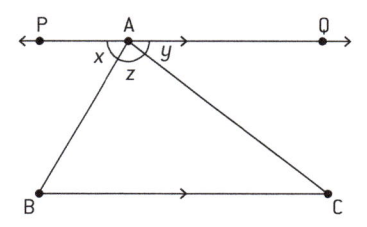

  i   Let angle PÂB = x. Label another angle that is the same size as x. Give a reason.
  ii Let angle QÂC = y. Label another angle that is the same size as y. Give a reason.
  iii What is the sum of x, y and z?
  iv What does your answer to part **iii** tell you about the angles of a triangle.

> **Command term**
> **Prove** means you should use a sequence of logical steps to obtain the required result in a formal way.

DP ready **Applications and Interpretation**

If you prefer the approach in part a then you may prefer MAI, but if you prefer the more formal proof in part b then you may prefer MAA.

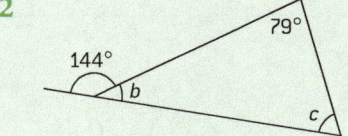

◉ **Key point**
The angle sum of a triangle is 180°.

Exercise 5.2
Find the lettered angles.

1   (triangle with angles 69°, 47°, a)

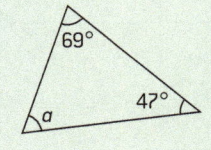

2   (triangle with angles 79°, 144° exterior, b, c)

GEOMETRY AND TRIGONOMETRY

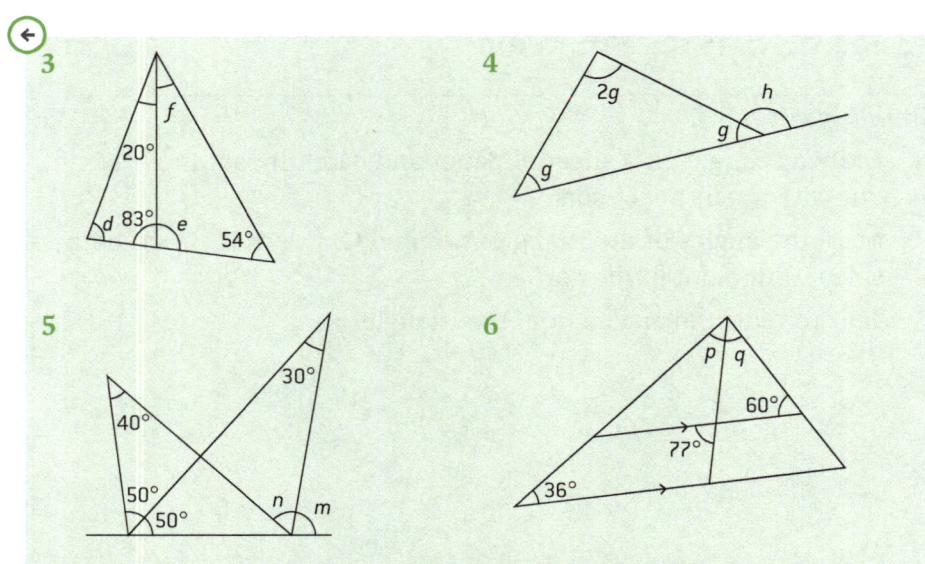

3 [triangle with angles 20°, f, 83°, d, e, 54°]

4 [triangle with 2g, g, g, h]

5 [figure with angles 40°, 30°, 50°, 50°, n, m]

6 [triangle with p, q, 60°, 77°, 36°]

7 ABC is a triangle. Extend the side [BC] to pass through point D.

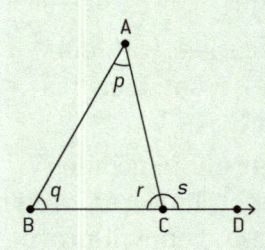

[diagram of triangle ABC with p at A, q at B, r and s at C, D on extension]

Let $B\hat{A}C = p$ and $A\hat{B}C = q$. Let $A\hat{C}B = r$. Write down a relation between p, q and r.

Let $A\hat{C}D = s$. Write down a relation between r and s.

Hence, find an expression for s in terms of p and q.

5.3 Properties of triangles and quadrilaterals

Types of triangle

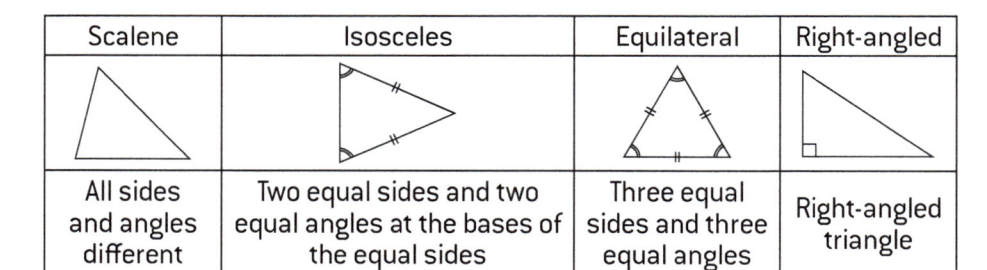

Scalene	Isosceles	Equilateral	Right-angled
All sides and angles different	Two equal sides and two equal angles at the bases of the equal sides	Three equal sides and three equal angles	Right-angled triangle

Equal length sides are shown by having the same number of dashes:

Equal size angles are shown by having the same number of arcs:

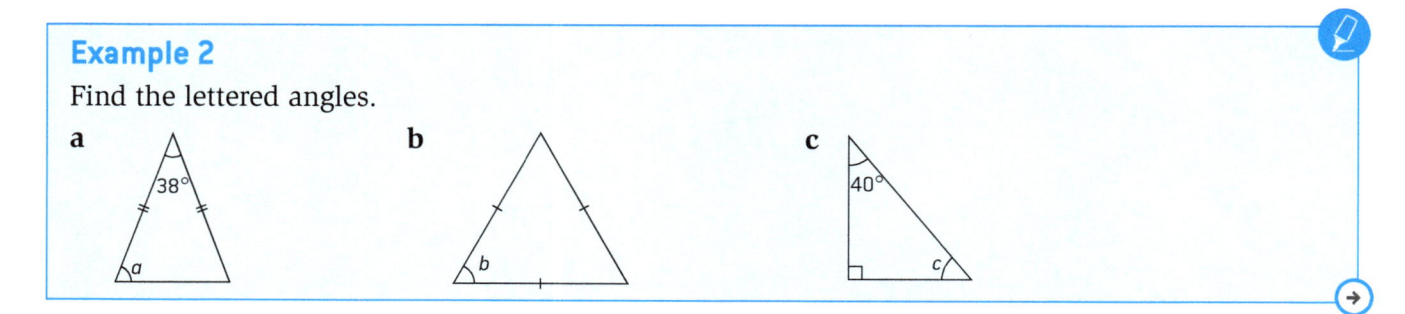

Example 2
Find the lettered angles.

a [isosceles triangle with 38° at top, a at base]

b [isosceles triangle with b at base]

c [right-angled triangle with 40° at top, c at base]

a $a + a + 38 = 180$
          $2a = 180 - 38$
          $2a = 142$
          $a = 71°$
	The base angles of the isosceles triangle are equal.

b $b + b + b = 180$
          $3b = 180$
          $b = 60°$
	The three angles of the equilateral triangle are equal.

c $c + 40 + 90 = 180$
          $c = 180 - 90 - 40$
          $c = 50°$
	Note that $40° + 50° = 90°$ Angles of a right-angled triangle are **complementary** (they add up to $90°$).

Exercise 5.3a

1 Find the lettered angles.

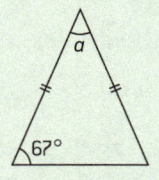

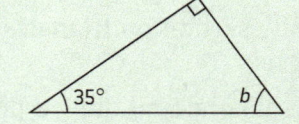

   i (triangle with base angle 67°, angle a at top)

   ii (right-angled triangle with 35° and angle b)

   iii (triangle with 106° and angle c)

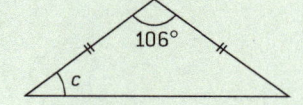

2 Find the lettered angles.

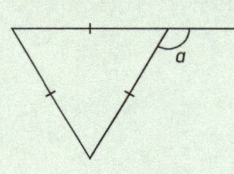

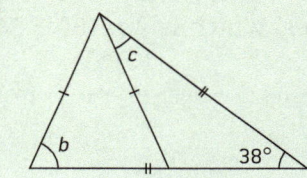

   i (isosceles triangle with exterior angle a)

   ii (triangle with angles b, c, and 38°)

   iii (triangle with angles d, e, and 30°)

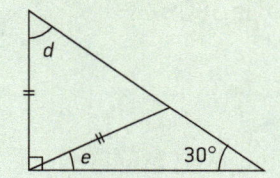

Types of quadrilateral

Parallelogram	Rhombus	Rectangle	Square	Kite	Trapezoid
Opposite sides are parallel and the same length opposite angles are equal	All sides are equal and opposite sides are parallel; opposite angles are equal	Opposite sides equal and all angles are 90°	All sides are equal and all angles are 90°	Two pairs of adjacent sides are equal; one pair of opposite angles is equal	Two parallel sides

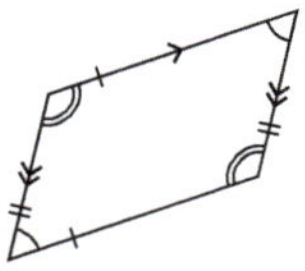

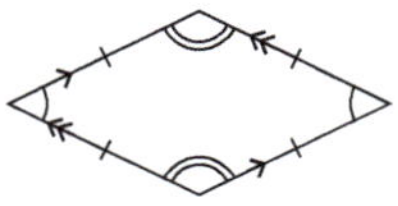

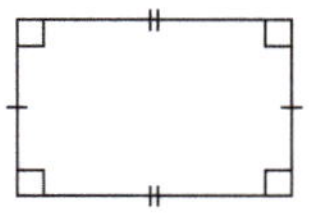

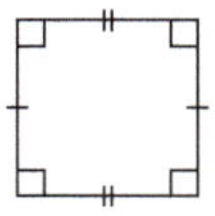

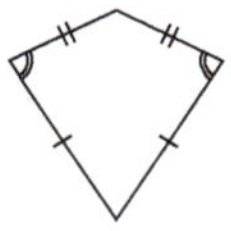

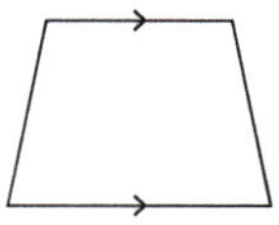

Investigation 5.3

Draw a parallelogram, a rhombus, a rectangle, a square, a kite and a trapezoid. Your drawings need to be accurate so that sides that should be equal in length are equal, sides that should be parallel are parallel and angles that should be right-angles are right-angles.

(Use an *isosceles* trapezoid, in which the two non-parallel sides are equal in length).

Draw the diagonals of each of the shapes.

Measure the angle between the diagonals.

Measure the lengths of the diagonals.

6 Right-angled triangles

Example 6

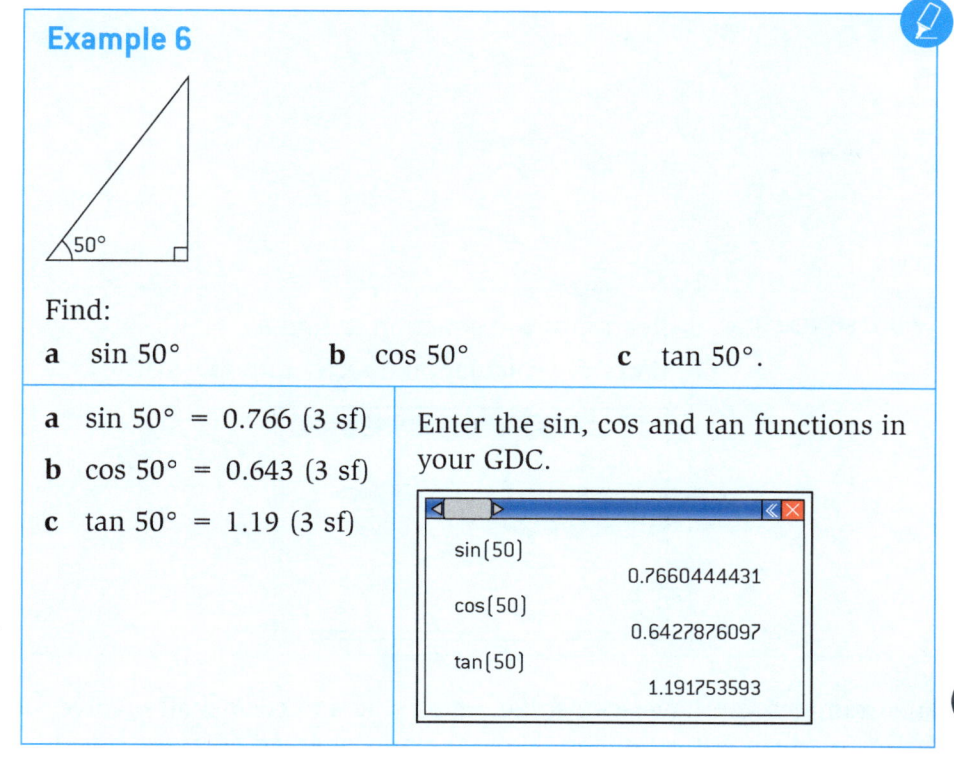

Find:
a sin 50°   b cos 50°   c tan 50°.

a sin 50° = 0.766 (3 sf) b cos 50° = 0.643 (3 sf) c tan 50° = 1.19 (3 sf)	Enter the sin, cos and tan functions in your GDC. sin(50) 0.7660444431 cos(50) 0.6427876097 tan(50) 1.191753593

Finding lengths of sides in right-angled triangles

Because the ratios are the same for any right-angled triangle with a given angle, you can use them to find the length of one side of the triangle when we know another. You can also use them to find the angle in a right-angled triangle when you know two of the sides. You will need to choose which of the three ratios to use, depending on the combination of sides that you are working with.

"SOHCAHTOA" is a helpful way to remember these definitions.

> **Key point**
>
> Use *Sine* when you have one of Opposite and Hypotenuse and want to know the other.
>
> Use *Cosine* when you have one of Adjacent and Hypotenuse and want to know the other.
>
> Use *Tangent* when you have one of Opposite and Adjacent and want to know the other.

Example 7

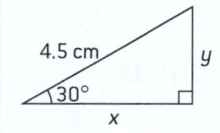

Find the missing lengths x and y.

x is adjacent to the angle so you should use cos $\dfrac{x}{4.5} = \cos 30°$ $x = 4.5 \cos 30°$ $x = 3.90$ cm (3 sf) y is opposite the angle so you should use sin $\dfrac{y}{4.5} = \sin 30°$ $y = 4.5 \sin 30°$ $y = 2.25$ cm (3 sf)	Rearrange to find x and to find y. Enter the calculation directly into the GDC. 4.5cos(30) 3.897114317 4.5sin(30) 2.25

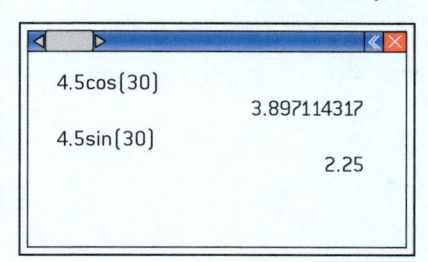

GEOMETRY AND TRIGONOMETRY

Example 8

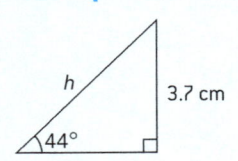

Find the length of the hypotenuse, h.

You have *opp* and want to find *hyp*, so use sine $$\frac{3.7}{h} = \sin 44°$$ $h \times \sin 44 = 3.7$ $$h = \frac{3.7}{\sin 44°}$$ $h = 5.33$ cm (3 sf)	Rearrange the equation to find h. Enter the calculation directly into the GDC. 3.7/sin(44) 5.326359197

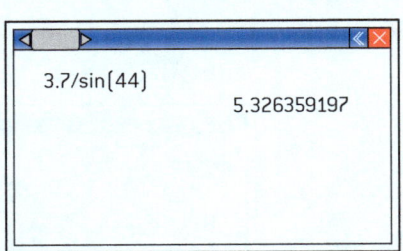

The examples you have seen so far, using sine and cosine, all involve the hypotenuse. When you are given the opposite and adjacent sides, you will use the tangent of the angle.

Example 9

a Find the length of the side marked a.

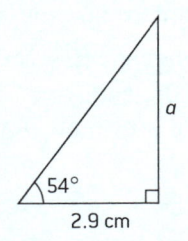

b Find the length of the side marked b.

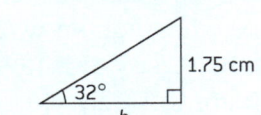

a Find the opposite side given the adjacent, using tan. $$\frac{a}{2.9} = \tan 54°$$ $a = 2.9 \tan 54°$ $a = 3.99$ cm (3 sf)	Rearrange the equation to find a. Enter the calculation directly into the GDC. 2.9tan(54) 3.991507569
b Find the adjacent side given the opposite, using tan. $$\frac{1.75}{b} = \tan 32°$$ $b \cdot \tan 32° = 1.75$ $$b = \frac{1.75}{\tan 32°}$$ $b = 2.80$ cm (3 sf)	Rearrange the equation to find b. This is similar to the rearrangement you used when finding the hypotenuse above. Enter the calculation directly into the GDC. 1.75/tan(32) 2.800585426

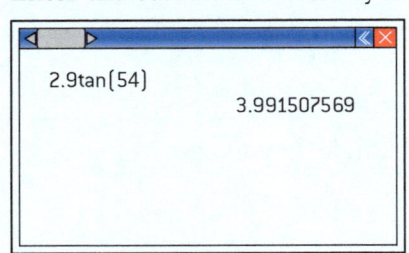

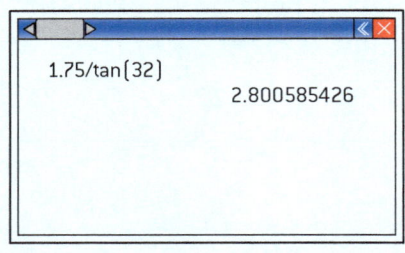

6 Right-angled triangles

Example 10

a A ladder should be at 75° to the horizontal to be safe. If my ladder is 3.7 m long, what height can I safely reach?

b A ship is sailing on a bearing of 156°. When it arrives at its destination it is 35 km south of its starting point. How far has it travelled?

a Let the height reached be y m.

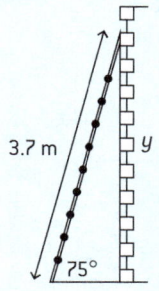

$$\frac{y}{3.7} = \sin 75°$$
$$y = 3.7 \sin 75°$$
$$y = 3.57 \text{ m (3 sf)}$$

3.7sin(75)   3.573925557

b Let the distance travelled be d km.

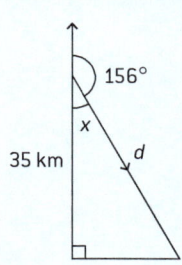

$$\frac{35}{d} = \cos 24°$$
$$d = \frac{35}{\cos 24°}$$
$$d = 38.3 \text{ km (3 sf)}$$

$\dfrac{35}{\cos(24)}$ 38.31226975

The angle x is $180 - 156 = 24°$.

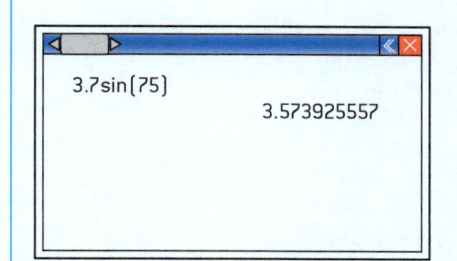

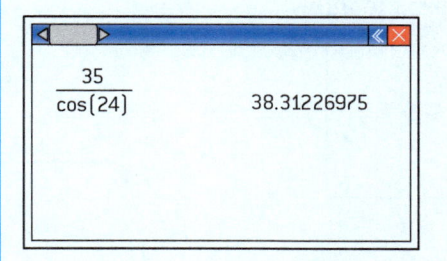

It is always useful to check that the hypotenuse is the longest side after your calculations. If not, then you have made a mistake.

These triangles will help you with rearranging the equations.

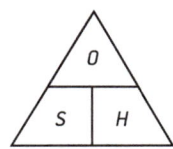

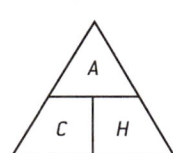

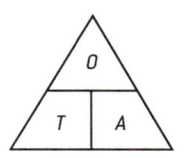

The diagrams show you graphically that

$$\sin = \frac{\text{opp}}{\text{hyp}} \qquad \cos = \frac{\text{adj}}{\text{hyp}} \qquad \tan = \frac{\text{opp}}{\text{adj}}$$

$\text{opp} = \sin \times \text{hyp} \quad \text{adj} = \cos \times \text{hyp} \quad \text{opp} = \tan \times \text{adj}$

$$\text{hyp} = \frac{\text{opp}}{\sin} \qquad \text{hyp} = \frac{\text{adj}}{\cos} \qquad \text{adj} = \frac{\text{opp}}{\tan}$$

> **Note**
>
> Remember you have already learned that "SOHCAHTOA" is a helpful way to remember these definitions.

GEOMETRY AND TRIGONOMETRY

Exercise 6.3a

1. Find:
   a sin 46°
   b cos 21°
   c tan 87°

2. Find the lettered lengths.

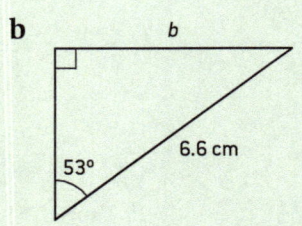

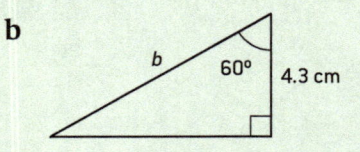

   a — 7.2 cm, 41°, side a
   b — 6.6 cm, 53°, side b
   c — 4.25 cm, 41°, side c
   d — 10.2 cm, 37°, side d
   e — 12.3 cm, 53°, side e
   f — 23.1 cm, 61°, side f

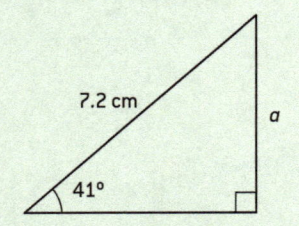

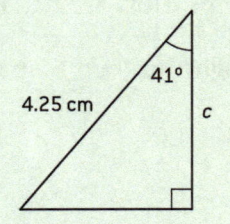

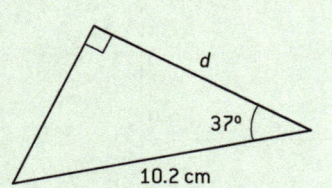

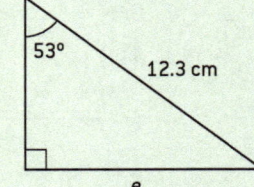

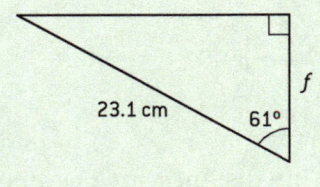

3. Find the lettered length.

   a — 3.5 cm, 36°, side a
   b — 4.3 cm, 60°, side b
   c — 3.9 cm, 38°, side c
   d — 34 cm, 49°, side d

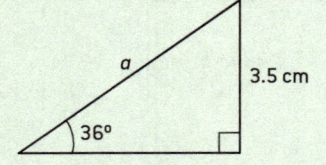

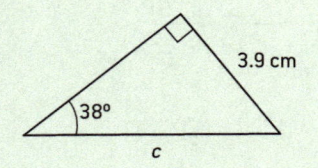

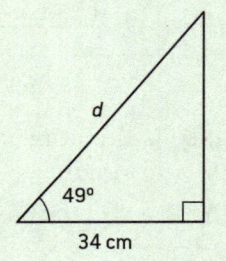

4. Find the lettered sides.

   a — 7.7 cm, 32°, side a
   b — 5.5 cm, 34°, side b
   c — 6.1 cm, 61°, side c
   d — 1.8 cm, 36°, side d
   e — 6 cm, 45°, side e
   f — 7.1 cm, 41°, side f

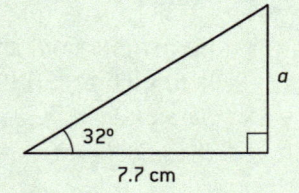

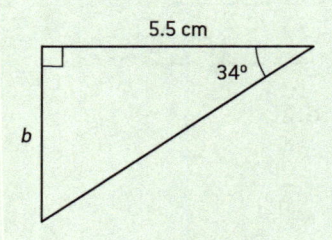

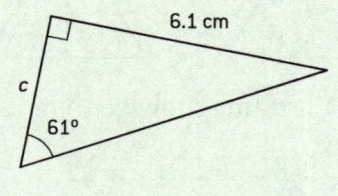

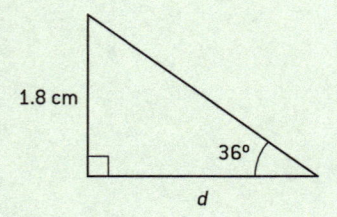

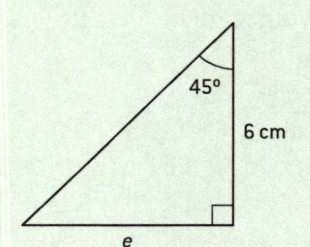

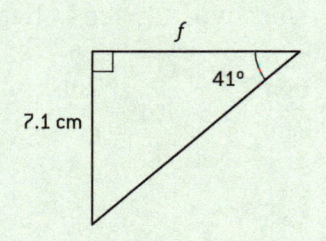

5. A plane is flying on a bearing of 073°. If plane has travelled a distance 183 km North, how far East has it travelled?

6. A kite is flying so that its string is taut. The string is 42 m long and makes an angle of 68° with the ground. How high is the kite?

6 Right-angled triangles

Finding angles in right-angled triangles

If you are given two sides of a right-angled triangle, then it is always possible to find the size of an angle. You find an angle from the trigonometric ratio with the inverse trigonometric functions. These functions are $\sin^{-1}$, $\cos^{-1}$ and $\tan^{-1}$.

Example 11

Find θ using your GDC.

a $\sin\theta = 0.234$
b $\cos\theta = 0.897$
c $\tan\theta = 1.51$

a $\sin\theta = 0.234$
  $\theta = \sin^{-1}(0.234)$
  $\theta = 13.5°$ (3 sf)

b $\cos\theta = 0.897$
  $\theta = \cos^{-1}(0.897)$
  $\theta = 26.2°$ (3 sf)

c $\tan\theta = 1.51$
  $\theta = \tan^{-1}(1.51)$
  $\theta = 56.5°$ (3 sf)

Enter the $\sin^{-1}$, $\cos^{-1}$ and $\tan^{-1}$ functions in your GDC.

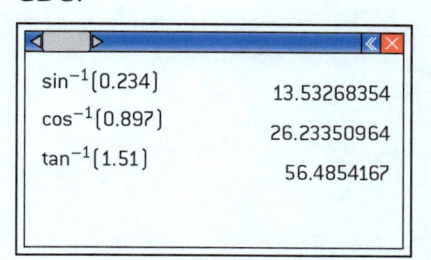

$\sin^{-1}(0.234)$	13.53268354
$\cos^{-1}(0.897)$	26.23350964
$\tan^{-1}(1.51)$	56.4854167

Example 12

Find θ using your GDC.

a triangle with hypotenuse 12.6 cm, side 8.23 cm, angle θ

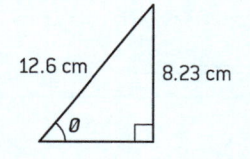

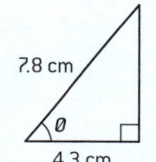

b triangle with side 7.8 cm, side 4.3 cm, angle θ

c triangle with side 5.95 cm, side 4.24 cm, angle θ

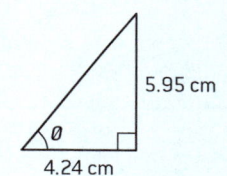

a $\sin\theta = \dfrac{8.23}{12.6}$
  $\theta = \sin^{-1}\left(\dfrac{8.23}{12.6}\right)$
  $\theta = 40.8°$ (3 sf)

You have opposite and hypotenuse, so use sine ratio.

Use $\sin^{-1}$ and enter the calculations directly into your GDC.

b $\cos\theta = \dfrac{4.3}{7.8}$
  $\theta = \cos^{-1}\left(\dfrac{4.3}{7.8}\right)$
  $\theta = 56.5°$ (3 sf)

You have the adjacent and hypotenuse, so use cos ratio.

c $\tan\theta = \dfrac{5.95}{4.24}$
  $\theta = \tan^{-1}\left(\dfrac{5.95}{4.24}\right)$
  $\theta = 54.5°$ (3 sf)

You have the opposite and adjacent, so use tan ratio.

133

GEOMETRY AND TRIGONOMETRY

Example 13

a Two radio beacons at A and B are used to guide planes to a landing strip. A is 25 km North of B and 35 km east. Calculate the bearing of A from B.

b A plank is leaning against a vertical wall. The plank is 2.1 m long and reaches 1.8 m up the wall. Calculate the angle between the plank and the horizontal ground.

a

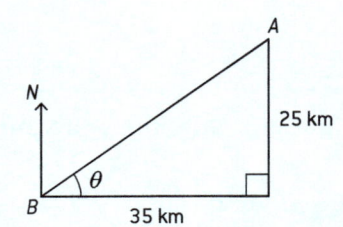

$\tan\theta = \dfrac{25}{35}$

$\theta = \tan^{-1}\left(\dfrac{25}{35}\right)$

$\theta = 35.5°$ (3 sf)

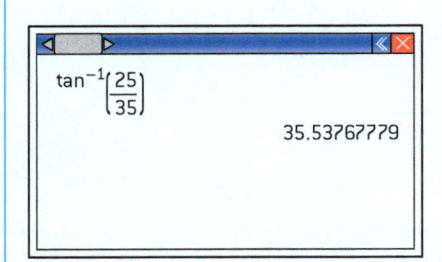

$90 - 35.5 = 54.5$

The bearing is 054.5°.

Calculate the angle θ.

$\tan^{-1}\left(\dfrac{25}{35}\right)$

35.53767779

Find the bearing.

b

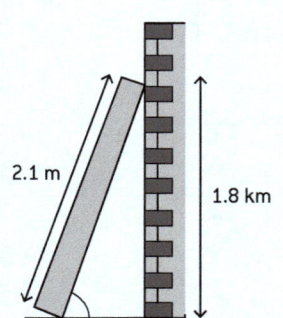

$\sin\theta = \dfrac{1.8}{2.1}$

$\theta = \sin^{-1}\left(\dfrac{1.8}{2.1}\right)$

$\theta = 59.0°$ (3 sf)

Calculate the angle θ.

$\sin^{-1}\left(\dfrac{1.8}{2.1}\right)$

58.99728087

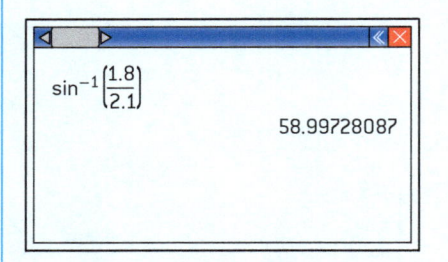

Exercise 6.3b

1 Calculate the angles.

  a $a = \sin^{-1} 0.793$ **b** $b = \cos^{-1} 0.184$ **c** $c = \tan^{-1} 0.891$

2 Find the lettered angles.

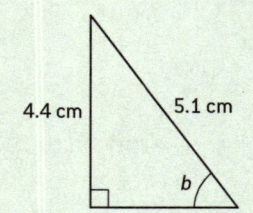

  a 4.3 cm, 2.5 cm, angle a

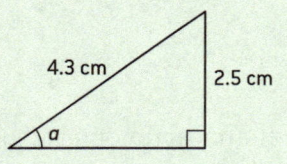

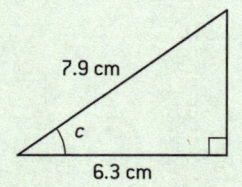

  b 4.4 cm, 5.1 cm, angle b

  c 7.9 cm, 6.3 cm, angle c

  d 4.9 cm, 6.5 cm, angle d

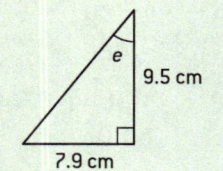

  e 9.5 cm, 7.9 cm, angle e

  f 2.3 cm, 3.2 cm, angle f

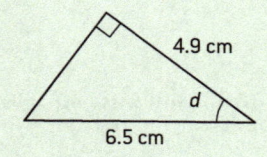

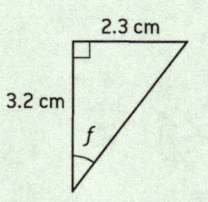

3 A ship sails to a harbour that is 54 km south and 44 km west of the starting point. Find the bearing of the harbour from the starting point.

4 A children's slide is 1.9 m long. If the height of the slide is 1.4 m, calculate the angle between the slide and the horizontal.

6 Right-angled triangles

Higher Level

6.4 Problem solving with right-angled triangles

Problems with right-angled triangles may involve the use of Pythagoras' theorem and/or trigonometry. In problems that need several steps to obtain a solution, avoid rounding results until you reach the final answer. Either keep the full value that your calculator stores or, at the very least, record intermediate results to one or two extra significant figures.

Example 14

A post 3.7 m long is placed at an angle against a vertical fence. The base of the post is 1.05 m from the fence on horizontal ground.

a Calculate the height of the point where the post meets the fence.
b Safety regulations say that the post must make an angle of at least 70° with the ground. Is the post safe?

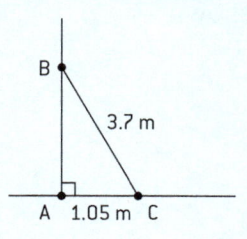

a $AB^2 + 1.05^2 = 3.7^2$
    $AB = \sqrt{3.7^2 - 1.05^2}$
    $AB = 3.55$ m (3 sf)

Draw a diagram of the fence, the post and the ground. A vertical fence means it is at right angles to the ground.

Use Pythagoras' theorem to find the length AB.

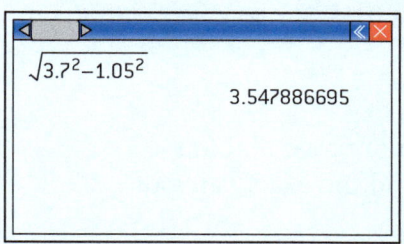

$\sqrt{3.7^2 - 1.05^2}$
3.547886695

b $\cos A\hat{C}B = \dfrac{1.05}{3.7}$
    $A\hat{C}B = \cos^{-1} \dfrac{1.05}{3.7}$
    $A\hat{C}B = 73.5°$ (3 sf)

   $73.5° > 70°$, so the post is safe.

Use cosine to find angle $A\hat{C}B$.

Use the lengths you were given rather than the one you have just calculated, in case of any errors.

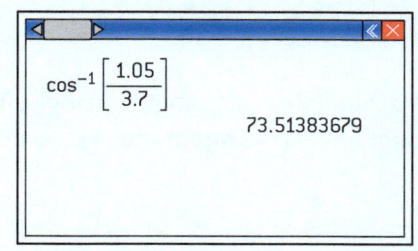

$\cos^{-1}\left[\dfrac{1.05}{3.7}\right]$
73.51383679

Exercise 6.3c

1 In the diagram, $C\hat{B}D$ and $C\hat{A}B$ are right-angles. AB and CD are parallel.

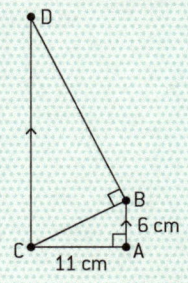

Calculate the size of the angle $C\hat{D}B$.

GEOMETRY AND TRIGONOMETRY

DP style — Analysis and Approaches HL

2. A surveyor is trying to find the height of a vertical tower on the other side of a river. Angle of elevation is the angle above the horizontal of a distant object. The surveyor measures the angle of elevation of the top of the tower, which is 30°. He then moves right to the edge of the river, which is 20 m closer to the tower, and measures the angle of elevation again. It is now 35°.

   Let h be the height of the tower and w the width of the river. Write down two equations in h and w and solve these to find the height of the tower.

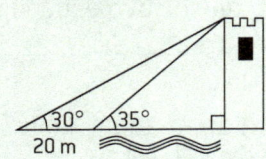

   Calculate the height of the tower.

DP style — Analysis and Approaches

3. Consider the right-angled triangle formed by dividing an equilateral triangle of side length 2 into two congruent triangles as shown.

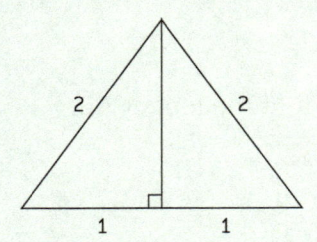

   a Use the diagram to prove that $\tan 60° = \sqrt{3}$ and find the exact value of $\tan 30°$.

   Consider the diagram shown:

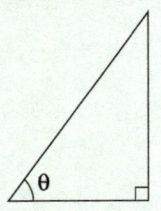

   Let $\tan \theta = t$

   b Find an expression for $\tan(90° - \theta)$ in terms of t.

   c Hence solve:

   i $\tan \theta + 3\tan(90° - \theta) = 2\sqrt{3}$

   ii $\tan \theta + \tan(90° - \theta) = \dfrac{4}{\sqrt{3}}$

Chapter summary

☐ Pythagoras' theorem says that in a right-angled triangle, if the two sides at right-angles are a and b, and if the side opposite the right angle (the **hypotenuse**) is c then $a^2 + b^2 = c^2$.

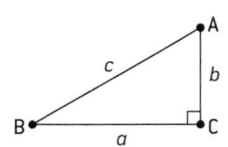

☐ The converse of Pythagoras' theorem states if $a^2 + b^2 = c^2$ then the triangle is right-angled.

☐ The midpoint of the line joining (x_1, y_1) and (x_2, y_2) is $\left(\tfrac{1}{2}(x_1 + x_2), \tfrac{1}{2}(y_1 + y_2)\right)$

☐ The distance between the points (x_1, y_1) and (x_2, y_2) is $\sqrt{(x_2 - x_1)^2 + (y_2 - y_1)^2}$

$$\sin\theta = \frac{\text{opp}}{\text{hyp}} \qquad \cos\theta = \frac{\text{adj}}{\text{hyp}} \qquad \tan\theta = \frac{\text{opp}}{\text{adj}}$$

☐ "SOHCAHTOA" is a helpful way to remember these definitions.

☐ These equations can be used to find:
   ☐ a side, if you know the angle and one other side
   ☐ an angle, if you know the lengths of two sides.

Chapter 6 test

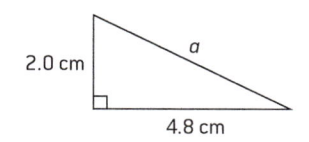

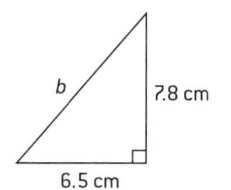

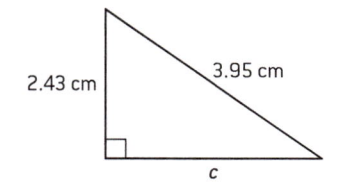

1 Find the lettered lengths.

a Triangle with legs 2.0 cm and 4.8 cm, hypotenuse a.

b Right triangle with sides 6.5 cm, 7.8 cm and hypotenuse b.

c Right triangle with legs 2.43 cm and c, hypotenuse 3.95 cm.

d Right triangle with sides 5.7 cm, 18.9 cm and hypotenuse d.

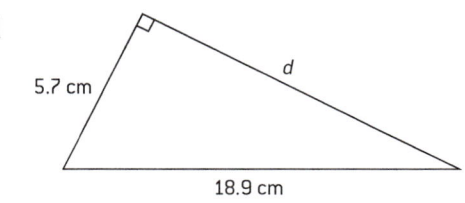

e P, Q, R collinear with PQ = 1.5 cm, QR = 2.3 cm; A below P (right angle at A); SA vertical; QS = e; RS = 4.6 cm.

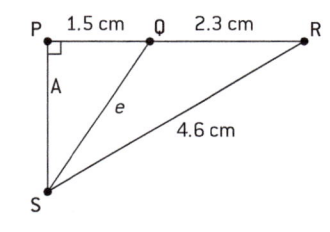

2 A ship sails to a port that is 26 km South and 44 km West of its starting point. How far does the ship travel?

3 Find the lengths of the sides marked p, q, r and s.

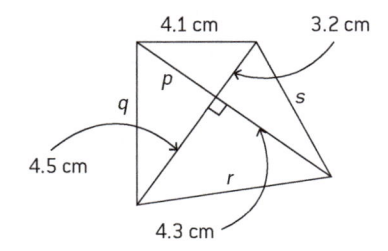

(Figure with 4.1 cm, 3.2 cm, 4.5 cm, 4.3 cm)

4 Find the midpoint of the line joining (5, 8) and (1, 2).

5 Find the distance between the points (−3, 6) and (4, −2).

6 Use your GDC to find the values of:

a sin 34° **b** cos 52° **c** tan 13°
d $\sin^{-1} 0.235$ **e** $\cos^{-1} 0.775$
f $\tan^{-1} 0.653$.

7 Find the lettered lengths.

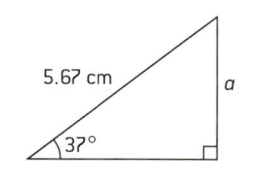

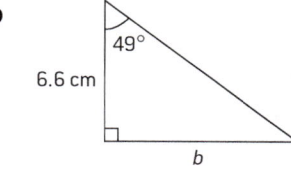

a Right triangle, 37° angle, adjacent 5.67 cm, opposite a.

b Right triangle, 49° angle, side 6.6 cm, side b.

c Right triangle, 53° angle, hypotenuse 7.67 cm, side c.

d Right triangle, 55° angle, side 1.95 cm, side d.

e Right triangle, 33° angle, hypotenuse 12.1 cm, side e.

f Right triangle, 48° angle, side 7.89 cm, side f.

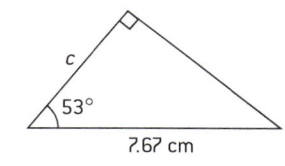

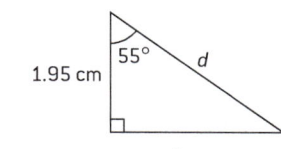

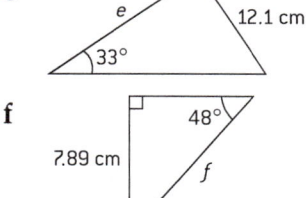

8 A 3.3 m ladder leans against a vertical wall. The angle between the ladder and the horizontal ground it stands on is 76°. How high up the wall does the ladder reach.

9 Find the lettered angles.

a Right triangle, angle a, opposite 4.36 cm, adjacent 5.57 cm.

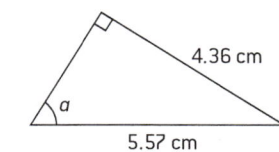

b Right triangle, angle b, hypotenuse 13.5 cm, adjacent 9.25 cm.

c Right triangle, angle c, opposite 2.39 cm, adjacent 4.75 cm.

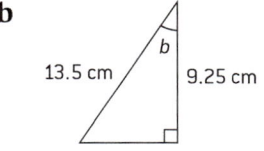

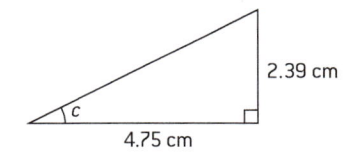

GEOMETRY AND TRIGONOMETRY

10 A plane travels to a point that is 245 km north and 367 km east. What is the bearing of the destination?

11 A plane flies 230 km on a bearing of 127°. Calculate:

   a the total distance travelled east
   b the total distance travelled south.

DP style — Applications and Interpretation SL

12 Some workers are constructing an aerial walkway between two trees on horizontal ground. They put up a ramp to the walkway that is 10 m from the base of a tree and at an angle of 20° to the horizontal.

It is decided that the ramp is too steep and it must be remade so that it is at an angle of 15°. Calculate how much further away from the foot of the tree the ramp must start.

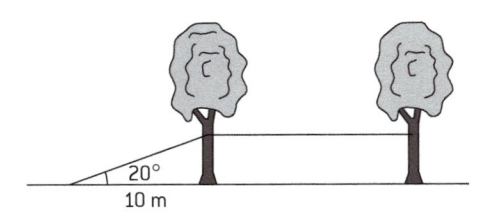

DP style — Analysis and Approaches SL

13 If the sides of a rhombus are 4.2 cm long and one of the diagonals is 5.7 cm, find the angles in the rhombus.

> **Internal link**
> Recall the properties of a rhombus, which you studied in chapter 5.

DP style — Applications and Interpretation HL

14 A right-angled triangle with angles 30°, 60° and 90° can be thought of as half an equilateral triangle, and hence the shorter side adjacent to the 60° angle will be half the hypotenuse.

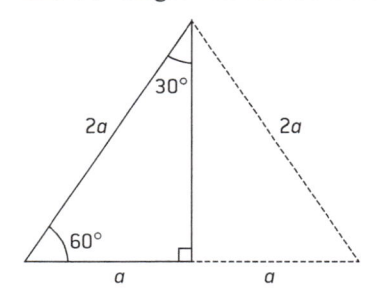

Consider the rectangle shown (Ailles rectangle). This will be used to calculate the exact values of the trigonometric ratios for 15° and 75°.

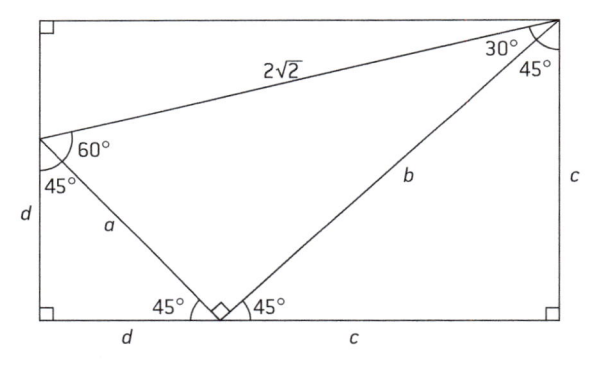

   a Write down the length a.
   b Use Pythagoras' theorem to find the length b.
   c Use Pythagoras' theorem to find the lengths:
      i c **ii** d.
   d Show the angles 15° and 75° on the diagram.
   e Hence find the exact values of:
      i $\cos 15°$ **ii** $\tan 75°$.

6 Right-angled triangles

DP style **Applications and Interpretation HL**

15 a The start of a yacht race is 2 km from a harbour. The bearing of the harbour from the start is 220°.

From the start of the race a yacht sails west until the harbour is on a bearing of 105°. By dividing the triangle shown into two right-angled triangles, find the distance travelled during this part of the race.

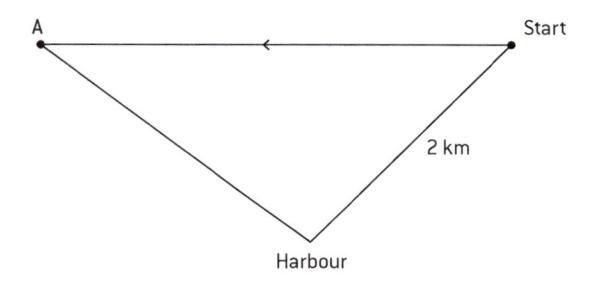

b In the second stage of the race the yacht sails 6.2 km from A to B and then turns through an angle of 135° before sailing 4.8 km to C.

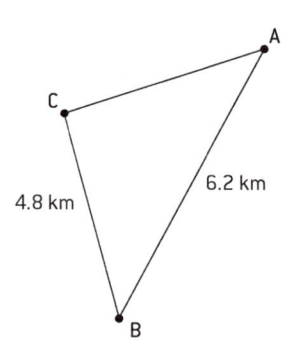

   i Write down the angle ABC.
   ii Find the distance from C back to A.

Modelling and investigation

DP ready **Approaches to learning**

Critical thinking: Analysing and evaluating issues and ideas
Organization skills: Managing time and tasks effectively

DP ready **International-mindedness**

In early trigonometry, calculations were done with the aid of tables of values of the trigonometric ratios. The earliest such table, equivalent to a table of values of sines, was made by Hipparchus in Greece around 140 BC. The term sine, cosine and tangent come from Latin words. The learning of ancient Greece passed through India and the Arab world, reappearing in Western Europe many centuries later.

The term for *sine* came from the Latin word for a bay and it was used to describe a chord of a circle, that is a line joining two points on its circumference. Originally the length of this chord was used, but later, just half the length of the chord was used to define the sine.

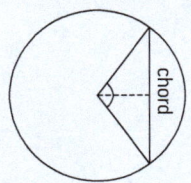

The term *tangent* was from the Latin for touch and the tangent to a circle is a line that touches the circle at a point. The tangent and the radius at the point of contact are at right-angles.

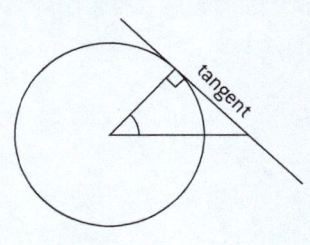

139

GEOMETRY AND TRIGONOMETRY

1. In the following diagram, show that the sides marked *s*, *c* and *t* are equal to the sine, cosine and tangent of the angle θ. The circle is a *unit circle*, that is its radius is 1.

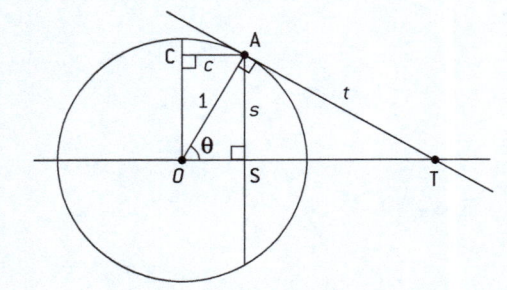

   The sine is, in fact, half the length of the chord. The origins of the term cosine have to do with its relation to the complementary angle.

   In the diagram, the angle alongside θ is $90° - \theta$, the complementary angle and the cosine is the sine of the complementary angle.

2. Using ruler, compasses and a pencil or, if you have access to an online geometry package, using Desmos or Geogebra, construct the diagram above. You can also use some GDCs to draw this construction.

   a Begin by drawing a circle and a horizontal line through the point O.

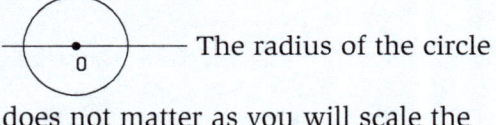

      The radius of the circle does not matter as you will scale the diagram later.

   b Draw a line segment from O to a point A on the circumference.

   c Construct a *chord* from A perpendicular to the horizontal line.

   d Construct a *tangent* to the circle at A.

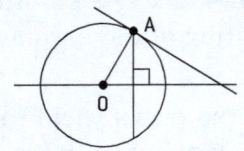

   e Construct a *radius* from O that is perpendicular to the horizontal line.

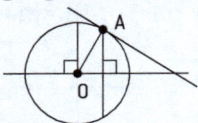

   f Construct a line segment from A perpendicular to the chord.

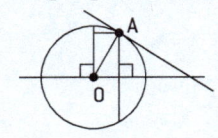

   g If you are working with a geometry package, check your diagram by moving the point A around the circle. (Do not go beyond the horizontal line or the radius you drew). If you have drawn the figure correctly the lines will move with the point.

   h Use the measurement tool to measure OA.

   i Use the measurement tool to measure the angle marked θ.

   j Use the measurement tool to measure the lengths marked *s*, *c* and *t*.

   k To scale your results to those you would get with a *unit circle*, divide your values of *s*, *c* and *t* by the length of OA.

   l Compare your results with the sin, cos and tan of the angle in your construction.

   m Move the point A. The measurements should all change. Divide the new values by OA and compare these results with the sin, cos and tan of the new angle.

GEOMETRY AND TRIGONOMETRY

7 Volumes and areas of 2- and 3-dimensional shapes

Learning outcomes

In this chapter you will learn about:
- The circle, its centre and radius, area and circumference. The terms diameter, arc, sector, chord, tangent and segment
- Perimeter and area of plane figures
- Familiarity with three-dimensional shapes (prisms, pyramids, spheres, cylinders and cones)
- Volumes and surface areas of cuboids, prisms, cylinders, and compound three-dimensional shapes

Key terms
- Centre
- Radius
- Circumference
- Diameter
- Arc
- Sector
- Chord
- Tangent
- Segment
- Irrational
- Perimeter
- Area
- Polyhedron
- Prism
- Cuboid
- Cylinder
- Pyramid
- Cone
- Sphere
- Vertex
- Edge
- Face

7.1 Perimeter and area of plane figures

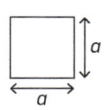

The sides of a square have length a. The perimeter of a square of side a is $4a$. The area is a^2.

Rectangles

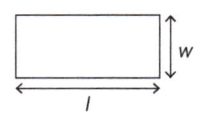

The length of a rectangle is l and its width is w.

You find its perimeter by adding the lengths of each of its sides: $l + w + l + w = 2l + 2w = 2(l + w)$.

Example 1
Find the perimeter and area of a rectangle measuring 3 cm by 5 cm.

| Perimeter = $2(l + w)$
$= 2(3 + 5)$
$= 2 \times 8$
$= 16$ cm
Area = $l \times w$
$= 3 \times 5$
$= 15$ cm² | It is usually best to draw a diagram to help you. |

Key point
The **perimeter** of a two-dimensional figure is the distance around its boundary. Perimeter is a measure of length so it is measured in cm, m, or km etc.

Key point
The **area** of a two-dimensional figure is a measurement of the amount of space inside its boundary. Area is measured in square units, such as cm².

Key point
The perimeter of a rectangle is $2(l + w)$.

Key point
The area of a rectangle is lw.

141

GEOMETRY AND TRIGONOMETRY

Parallelograms

The sides of a parallelogram are a and b.

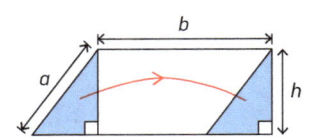

Take a right-angled triangle from one side and move it over to the other side. This makes a rectangle with the same area as the parallelogram. The perpendicular height of the triangle is h, and so the height of the rectangle is h.

The area of the rectangle is bh where h is the perpendicular height of the parallelogram.

> **Key point**
> The area of the parallelogram is bh

Triangles

The diagonal of a parallelogram splits it into two identical triangles.

The perimeter of the triangle is the sum of the lengths of its sides.

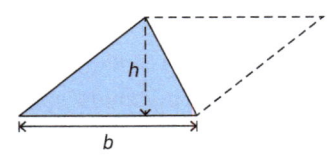

> **Key point**
> The area of the triangle is $\frac{1}{2}bh$.

Example 2a

Find the perimeters of these shapes.

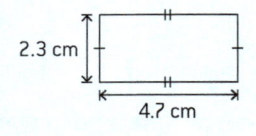

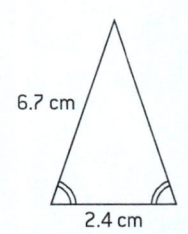

a 2.3 cm, 4.7 cm

b 6.7 cm, 2.4 cm

a $2.3 + 4.7 + 2.3 + 4.7 = 14$ cm

b $2.4 + 6.7 + 6.7 = 15.8$ cm

Missing side is 6.7 cm (isosceles triangle).

Example 2b

For this compound shape, find:
a the perimeter
b the area.

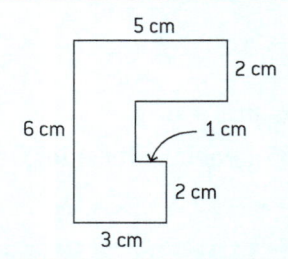

(5 cm, 2 cm, 6 cm, 1 cm, 2 cm, 3 cm)

a $3 + 6 + 5 + 2 + 3 + 2 + 1 + 2 = 24$ cm

Missing sides are 3 cm and 2 cm.

b $A = (5 \times 2) + (2 \times 2) + (3 \times 2)$
$= 10 + 4 + 6$
$= 20$ cm^2

Divide the composite shape up into shapes you know how to find the area of.

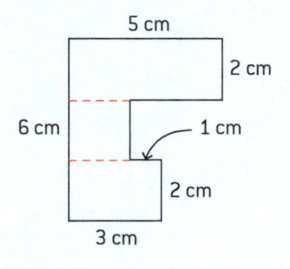

7 Volumes and areas of 2- and 3-dimensional shapes

Trapezoid

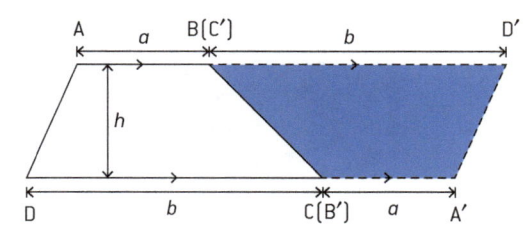

If you fit two trapezia together as shown, you get a parallelogram.
Area of two trapezia = $(a + b)h$ (using the formula for area of parallelogram).
Therefore area of one trapezoid is $A = \frac{1}{2}(a + b)h$

> **Key point**
> The area of a trapezoid is $\frac{1}{2}(a+b)h$.

Example 3
Find the areas of these shapes.

a 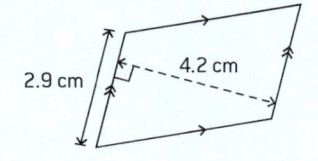
b 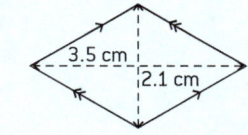
c 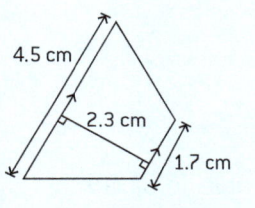
d

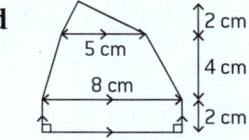

a Area = $b \times h$ $= 2.9 \times 4.2 = 12.2$ cm² (3 s.f.)	Two pairs of parallel sides mean this is a parallelogram.
b Area = $4\left(\frac{1}{2} \times 3.5 \times 2.1\right)$ $= 14.7$ cm²	The shape consists of 4 identical right-angled triangles with base 3.5 cm and height 2.1 cm.
c Area = $\frac{1}{2}(a+b)h$ $= \frac{1}{2}(4.5 + 1.7) \times 2.3$ $= 7.13$ cm²	One pair of parallel sides mean this is a parallelogram.
d Area = $(2 \times 8) + \left(\frac{1}{2}(5+8) \times 4\right) + \left(\frac{1}{2} \times 5 \times 2\right)$ $= 16 + 26 + 5$ $= 47$ cm²	This is a *compound* shape, made from a rectangle, a trapezoid and a triangle.

If you look at formulae for finding an area, for example $l \times w$, πr^2 or ½ × base × height, they all involve multiplying one length by another. The base units for area are m².

143

GEOMETRY AND TRIGONOMETRY

Exercise 7.1

1 Find the perimeters of these shapes.

a 3.2 cm, 0.9 cm (rectangle)

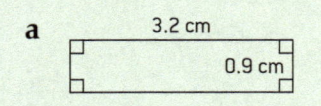

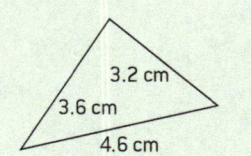

b 3.2 cm, 3.6 cm, 4.6 cm (triangle)

c 7 cm, 4 cm, 2 cm, 2 cm, 1 cm, 2 cm, 2 cm, 2 cm, 1 cm

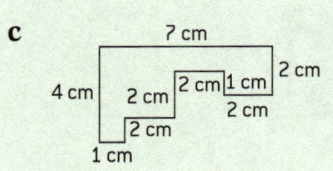

d 2.7 cm, 6.1 cm

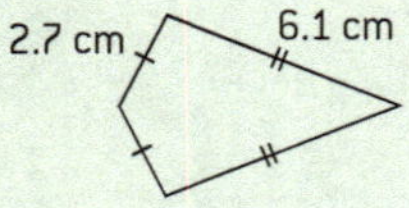

2 Find the areas of these shapes.

a 3.2 cm, 4.5 cm (rhombus/kite)

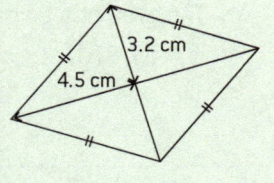

b 3.8 cm, 3.8 cm, 3.9 cm, 7.7 cm

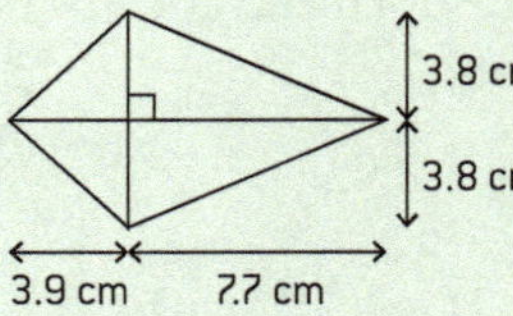

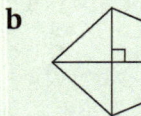

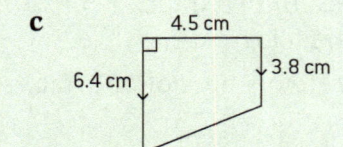

c 4.5 cm, 6.4 cm, 3.8 cm (trapezium)

d 2.9 cm, 6.2 cm (parallelogram)

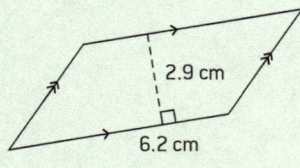

DP style   Analysis and Approaches HL

3 The diagram shows the lines $y = 2x - 1$, $y = 2x + 2$, $x = 1$ and $x = 3$. The points of intersection are shown as A, B, C and D.

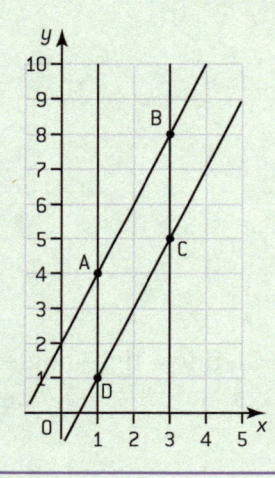

   a Using [AD] as the base find the area of the parallelogram ABCD.

   b Find the length of [AB].

   c Use your answers to **a** and **b** to find the shortest distance (the perpendicular distance) between the lines $y = 2x - 1$ and $y = 2x + 2$

7.2 The circle

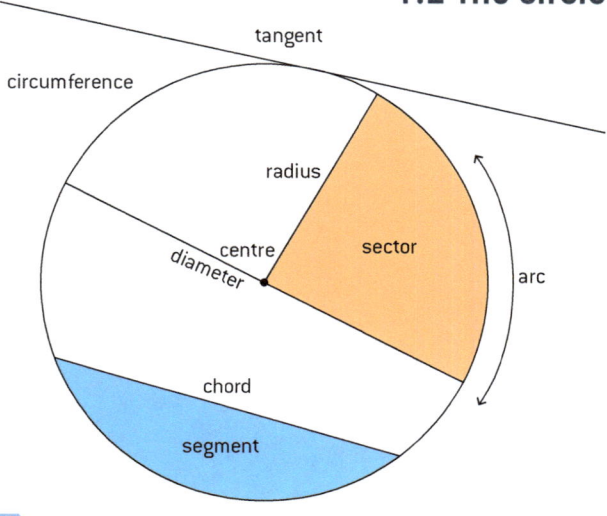

Labels on circle diagram: tangent, circumference, radius, centre, diameter, sector, arc, chord, segment

DP ready   Theory of knowledge

The ratio of the circumference of a circle to its diameter has been used in mathematics for centuries. The earliest recorded reference is in the Rhind Papyrus and is an example of Ancient Egyptian mathematics. Other civilisations have their own references. There is plenty of archaeological evidence of the building of circular structures in many cultures around the world.

7 Volumes and areas of 2- and 3-dimensional shapes

π is an **irrational** number. It cannot be written as an exact value. Mathematicians have calculated increasingly accurate approximations for π over the centuries. To 3 significant figures $\pi = 3.14$. For calculation you should always use the built-in value stored in your GDC which is 3.141592654… to provide sufficient accuracy.

Since the diameter (d) is twice the radius (r) $d = 2r$ and $C = 2\pi r$

You can also write the area of the circle in terms of the radius. $A = \pi r^2$

Example 4
Find the circumference and area of a circle with a radius of 5.6 cm. Give your answers to 3 s.f.

Circumference $= 2\pi r$
$= 2 \times \pi \times 5.6$
$= 35.2$ cm

Area $= \pi r^2$
$= \pi \times 5.6^2$
$= 98.5$ cm²

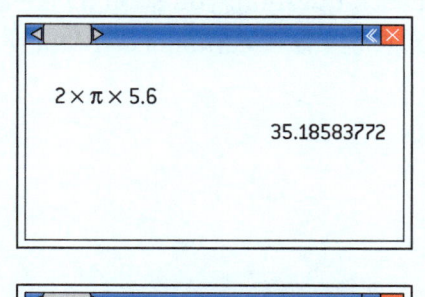

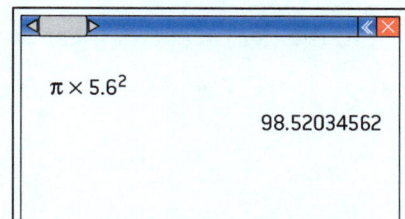

$2 \times \pi \times 5.6$ 35.18583772

$\pi \times 5.6^2$ 98.52034562

Example 5
Find the radii of circles with:
a   circumference = 44 cm   b   area = 60 cm²

a   Circumference $= 2\pi r$
$44 = 2\pi r$
$r = \dfrac{44}{2\pi}$
$r = 7.00$ cm (3 s.f.)

to solve the equation for r, divide by 2π

$\dfrac{44}{2\pi}$ 7.002817496

b   Area $= \pi r^2$
$60 = \pi r^2$
$r^2 = \dfrac{60}{\pi}$
$r = \sqrt{\dfrac{60}{\pi}}$
$r = 4.37$ cm (3 s.f.)

To solve the equation, divide by π then take square roots.

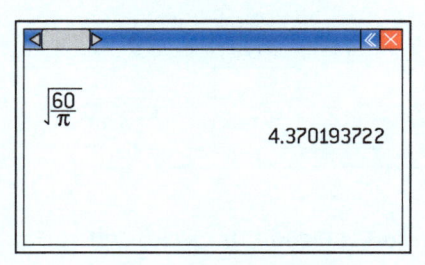

$\sqrt{\dfrac{60}{\pi}}$ 4.370193722

> **Key point**
>
> A **circle** is a two-dimensional shape made by drawing a curve that is always the same distance from a point called the **centre**.
>
> The distance around the edge of the circle is the **circumference**. This is the same as its perimeter.
>
> The part of the circumference between two points on the circle is an **arc**.
>
> A straight line joining two points on the circumference is a **chord**. If a chord passes through the centre, it is a **diameter**.
>
> The **radius** is the distance from the centre to the circumference of the circle.
>
> A chord cuts off an area called a **segment** and two radii cut off an area called a **sector**.
>
> A straight line that touches the circumference at a point is a **tangent**.
>
> The angle between a tangent and the radius at the point of contact is 90°.

> **Key point**
>
> The ratio of a circle's circumference (C) to its diameter (d) is π. $\dfrac{C}{d} = \pi$

> **Key point**
>
> Circumference of a circle $C = 2\pi r$
>
> Area of a circle $A = \pi r^2$

GEOMETRY AND TRIGONOMETRY

You can divide circles into major and minor segments, sectors and arcs. When these are equal, you have divided the circle into two semicircles.

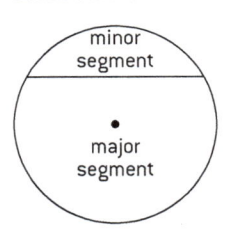

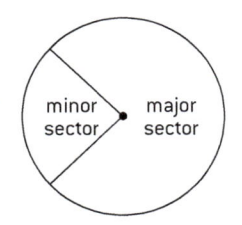

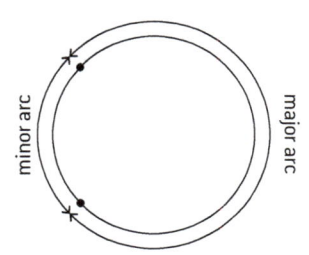

Exercise 7.2

In each question, you should give answers to 3 s.f. where appropriate.

1 Find the circumference of these circles.

a 7 cm

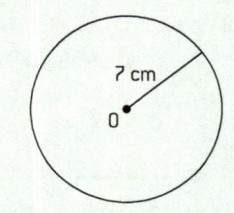

b 11.2 cm

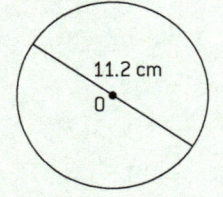

Hint
In part b, first find the radius of the circle.

2 Find the perimeters of these shapes.

a 3.5 cm

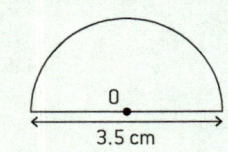

b 2.1 cm, 2.1 cm

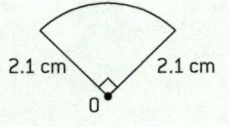

3 Find the area of these circles.

a 9.8 cm

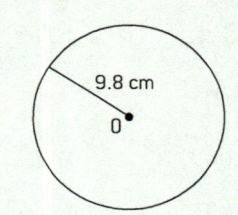

b 2.8 cm

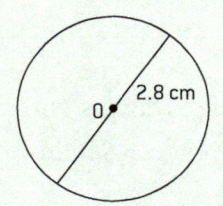

4 Find the areas of these shapes.

a 4 cm, 4 cm, 6 cm

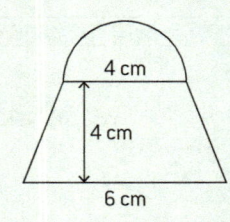

b 6.3 cm, 7.0 cm

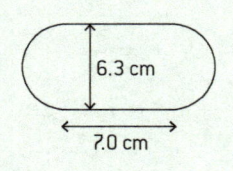

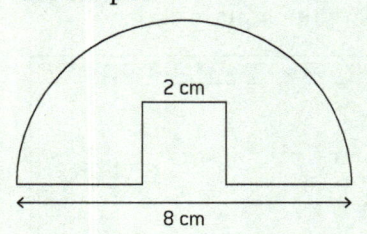

Hint
To find the perimeter, calculate all the individual lengths first. To find the area, subtract the area of the square from the area of the semicircle.

5 A compound shape is made from a semicircle with a square hole cut out. The shape is symmetrical. Find the area and perimeter of the shape.

2 cm, 8 cm

6 Find the radii of circles with:

a circumference = 32.5 cm

b area = 24.5 cm².

146

7 Calculate the length of the chord AB. (Hint: split the triangle AOB into two right-angled triangles).

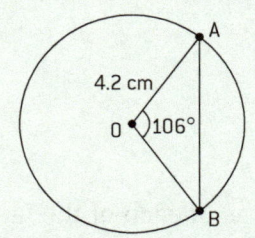

8 A tangent is drawn to a circle of radius 5 cm from a point A, 13 cm from its centre. Calculate the distance from A to the point where the tangent touches the circle.

Hint

The angle between a radius and a tangent is 90°.

7.3 Three-dimensional shapes

A 3-dimensional solid with straight sides is a **polyhedron**.

A prism is a 3-D solid with a constant cross-section (that is, if you cut into the solid at any point along its length, you will get the same shape as the one on the end face).

These solids are prisms:

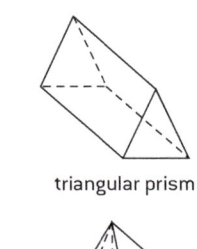

triangular prism 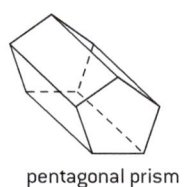   pentagonal prism 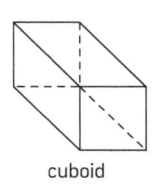   cuboid 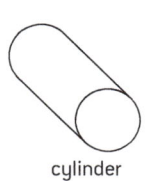   cylinder

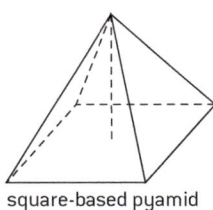

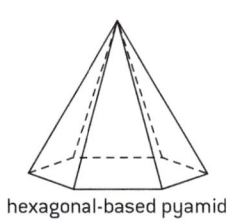

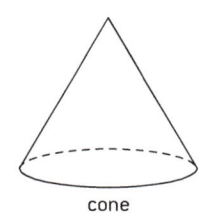

square-based pyramid   hexagonal-based pyramid   cone   sphare

A **pyramid** is a polyhedron that has a base which gives it its name and triangular sides that meet at the apex.

A cone has a circular base and a curved surface.

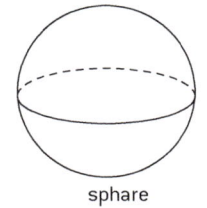

A **sphere** is a three-dimensional shape so that every point on its surface is the same distance from the centre.

DP ready   International-mindedness

For thousands of years, the largest structures in the world were pyramids. When you hear of pyramids, you tend to think of those in Egypt, but they are in many other parts of the world as far apart as China, India, Mexico, Peru, Nigeria and Indonesia. Early examples were often ziggurats, which are stepped pyramids, or even just mounds of earth and rock. Later, stone masons developed the art of cutting the stones on the outer surface to create a smooth pyramid. The existence of these ancient monuments has prompted people to speculate about the intervention of aliens in their building. However, the distribution of the weight of such buildings, with the majority of material nearer the ground and less weight pushing down from higher up allowed stable, very large structures to be built, often taking centuries to be completed as they were extended over the years.

Note

The pyramids and cone shown here are *right-pyramids* and *right-cones*, that is, the apex is directly above the centre of the base.

GEOMETRY AND TRIGONOMETRY

> **Key point**
>
> Volume is the amount of three-dimensional space something takes.

> **Key point**
>
> Surface area is the total area of the surface of a three-dimensional object.

> **Key point**
>
> Volume of a cuboid, $V = lwh$.

> **Key point**
>
> Surface area of a cuboid, $S = 2lw + 2wh + 2hl$.

Volumes and surface areas of three-dimensional shapes

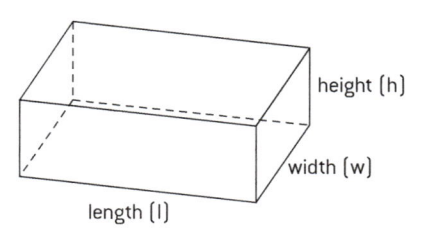

The surface area of a cuboid is the sum of the areas of each of the faces. Since a cube is a cuboid with equal length, width and height, say $l = w = h = a$

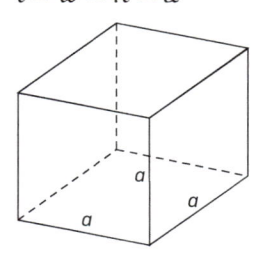

Then $V = a^3$ and $S = 6a^2$.

Examples of formulae for volume are $l \times w \times h$ and $\pi r^2 h$. These formulae involve multiplying three lengths together. The base units for volume are m³.

> **Internal link**
>
> Recall from chapter 3 that 1 cm³ = 1 ml.

Exercise 7.3a

1. A cuboid shaped box measures 1.2 m by 35 cm by 38 cm. Find its volume in m³ and its capacity in l.
2. Find the volume of a cuboid shaped box that measures 2.3 m by 0.45 m by 0.35 m in cm³. Find also the surface area of the box in cm².

DP style   **Applications and Interpretation SL**

3. Iresh sees an advertisement for a cuboid-shaped freezer with a capacity of 139 litres. Its dimensions are 84.2 × 69.7 × 55.7 cm. What is the difference between the volume of the freezer and its storage capacity?

> **Key point**
>
> The volume of a prism, $V = Ah$.

Volume of prisms

The volume of any prism is the cross-sectional area × height. A cuboid, a cube and a cylinder are special cases of this.

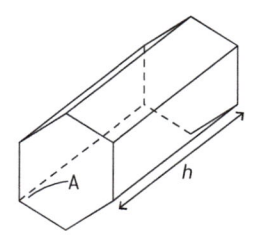

The surface area of a prism is 2 × cross-sectional area + perimeter of the cross-section × height.

In the same way the volume of a cylinder is the cross-sectional area × height.

> **Key point**
>
> The volume of a cylinder, $V = \pi r^2 h$.

148

Exercise 9.1

1. A bag contains 4 apples and 6 oranges. A piece of fruit is taken out of the bag at random. Find the probability that it is an apple.
2. In a prize draw, a box contains 50 tickets which either say "prize" or "lose". There are 5 tickets that say "prize". Find the probability of winning the draw.
3. Calculate the probably that a day of the week, chosen at random, contains the letter:
   a "T"
   b "Y"
4. 4 red balls, 3 blue balls and 5 yellow balls are in a bag. One ball is taken from the bag at random. Find the probability that the ball chosen is:
   a red
   b blue
   c red or blue.
5. Find the probability of rolling a 7 with a standard dice.
6. Find the probability of rolling a prime number with a standard dice.
7. The weather is classified as either hot, warm or cool. The probability the weather is hot is 0.6 and the probability it is warm is 0.32.
   a Find the probability the weather is:
      i cool   ii cool or warm   iii not hot.
   The probability it will rain on any day is 0.45.
   b Explain why you cannot work out the probability that the weather will be either warm or rainy.
8. On our street there are 15 houses on the left hand side, 7 of which have green curtains. There are also 12 houses on the right hand side and of these, 6 have green curtains. A house is chosen at random. Find the probability it is either on the right hand side or has green curtains (or both these things).

DP ready   Theory of knowledge

In the real world, probability is not about calculating how likely the outcomes of simple events like the outcomes of rolling a dice or tossing a coin are. An important area where probability is used is in decision making. For example, when a drug company introduces a new drug, two things need to be evaluated. First the effectiveness of the drug in curing the disease it is aimed at and second the likelihood of undesirable side effects. No drug is likely to be 100% effective and equally none is likely to be without unwanted side effects. Both considerations need to be evaluated along with ways of improving the drug's efficiency and reducing risk. When this has been done, mathematical, statistical techniques are used to evaluate the relative importance of each. In the same way, weather forecasts give the percentage probability of rain or sunshine.

9.2 Sorting data

If you toss two coins, then there could be 0, 1 or 2 heads. Notice that the event of tossing 1 head can happen in one of two ways, either HT or TH.

The sample space consists of four events:

HH   HT   TH   TT

It can be shown using a **sample space diagram** that shows each of the four possible outcomes.

If all the events in the sample space are equally likely then probabilities can be worked out using the formula $P(A) = \dfrac{n(A)}{n(U)}$

For example, the probability of getting exactly one head is $\dfrac{2}{4} = \dfrac{1}{2}$

	H	T
H	HH	HT
T	TH	TT

Rolling two dice results in many more events: 36 altogether. Writing out a list of all 36 events is quite difficult, but a sample space diagram

STATISTICS AND PROBABILITY

makes it easier. On the sample space diagram below, the sum of the values on the two dice are shown.

First dice

+	1	2	3	4	5	6
1	2	3	4	5	6	7
2	3	4	5	6	7	8
3	4	5	6	7	8	9
4	5	6	7	8	9	10
5	6	7	8	9	10	11
6	7	8	9	10	11	12

Second dice (row labels)

Sample space diagrams are a useful aid to finding probabilities.

Example 3

Two dice are rolled and their scores added. Find the probabilities of obtaining:

a   a "double" (two numbers the same)
b   a total of less than 6.

a

First dice

+	1	2	3	4	5	6
1	2	3	4	5	6	7
2	3	4	5	6	7	8
3	4	5	6	7	8	9
4	5	6	7	8	9	10
5	6	7	8	9	10	11
6	7	8	9	10	11	12

$P(\text{double}) = \dfrac{6}{36} = \dfrac{1}{6}$

Draw a sample space diagram. On the diagram indicate the events which are doubles.

b

First dice

+	1	2	3	4	5	6
1	2	3	4	5	6	7
2	3	4	5	6	7	8
3	4	5	6	7	8	9
4	5	6	7	8	9	10
5	6	7	8	9	10	11
6	7	8	9	10	11	12

$P(\text{less than } 6) = \dfrac{10}{36} = \dfrac{5}{18}$

Draw a sample space diagram. On the diagram indicate the events where the total is less than 6. (2, 3, 4 or 5).

Internal link

See section 1.2 for an introduction to Venn diagrams.

Venn diagrams for sorting data

A Venn diagram is commonly used to represent probabilities in an organised way.

The sample space is shown by the rectangle that represents the universal set, U. For example, if a dice is rolled then $U = \{1, 2, 3, 4, 5, 6\}$ and $n(U) = 6$.

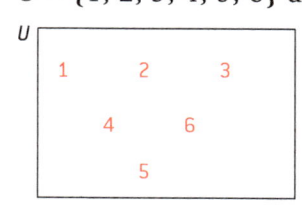

Now consider the event A "an even number", then $A = \{2, 4, 6\}$. These outcomes can be shown in a ring labelled A. The set $A' = \{1, 3, 5\}$.

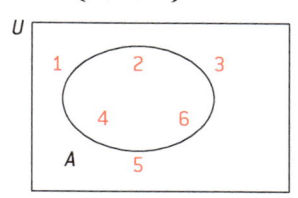

If B is the event "a multiple of 3", then $B = \{3, 6\}$. These outcomes can be shown in a ring labelled B. The set $B' = \{1, 2, 4, 5\}$.

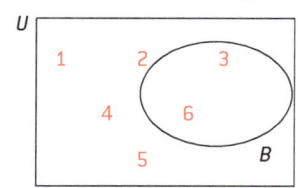

Showing both sets in the diagram with intersecting rings, you can see that $A \cap B = \{6\}$, $A \cup B = \{2, 3, 4, 6\}$, $A \cap B' = \{2, 4\}$, $A' \cap B = \{3\}$, $(A \cup B)' = \{1, 5\}$, etc.

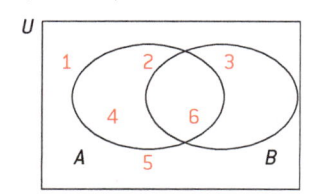

When using a Venn diagram to calculate probabilities, it is usually easier to show the number of outcomes in each ring, rather than its contents.

For example, there is one number in the intersection of A and B (that is, $n(A \cap B) = 1$) so we would put a 1 in this position in the Venn diagram. Similarly there are two numbers outside both circles so we would write a 2 here. The resulting Venn diagram is

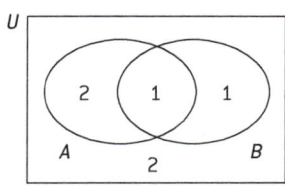

You can then use these figures to calculate probabilities. For example, the probability of a dice roll being even and a multiple of 3 is

$$P(A \cap B) = \frac{n(A \cap B)}{n(U)} = \frac{1}{6}.$$

Conditional probability

Sometimes you are given some extra information which will change the probability associated with an event. In the example above we could ask: given that the number rolled is even, what is the probability it is a multiple of 3?

Because we know it is even there are now just three possibilities and only one of these is a multiple of 3, so the answer is $\frac{1}{3}$.

> **Example 4**
>
> 20 students are asked about some of the subjects they are studying.
>
> 12 students study economics, 8 study design technology and 6 study Mandarin.
>
> 2 study economics and design technology, 3 study design technology and Mandarin, and 3 study Mandarin and economics. There is one student who studies all three subjects.
>
> Show this information in a Venn diagram and find the probability that a student chosen at random studies:
>
> a only one of the three subjects
>
> b exactly two out of the three subjects
>
> c at least 2 subjects, given they study Economics.

STATISTICS AND PROBABILITY

(Venn diagram: E, D, M with 1 in centre intersection)	Enter the student who studied all three subjects in the intersection.
(Venn diagram: E, D, M with 1 in centre, 2, 1, 2 in pairwise intersections)	Enter the number of students who studied two subjects in the intersections. (Do not include the student who studied all three.)
(Venn diagram: E, D, M with 8, 1, 4 in sole regions; 2, 1, 2 in pairwise; 1 in centre; 1 in complement)	Enter the number of students remaining in the three sets. Then, totalling the students entered so far, place any others in the complement.

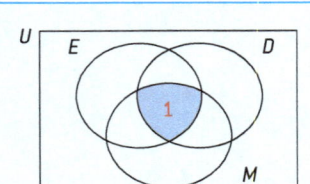

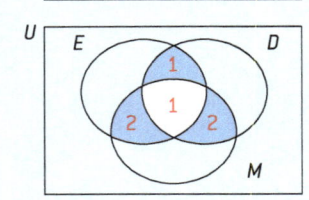

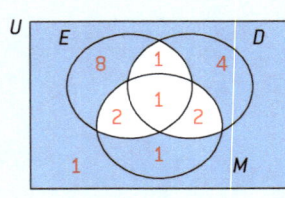

a P(studies only one) = $\dfrac{8+4+1}{20}$ = 0.65

b P(studies exactly two) = $\dfrac{1+2+2}{20}$ = 0.25

c P(studies at least 2 given they study economics) = $\dfrac{1+1+2}{12} = \dfrac{1}{3}$

Another similar diagram that helps to organise data and helps in the calculation of probabilities is a **contingency table** or **two-way table**. In the table, there are two variables. The use of the contingency table is shown in the following table.

Example 5

The voting preferences of 100 people in a survey are shown in this table:

Find the probability that a person chosen at random is:

a male
b a female voting orange
c an orange voter
d an orange voter given they are female
e female given they are an orange voter.

voting preference	blue	orange	Total
male	23	31	54
female	17	29	46
Total	40	60	100

a $\dfrac{23+31}{100} = 0.54$

b $\dfrac{29}{100} = 0.29$

c $\dfrac{31+29}{100} = 0.6$

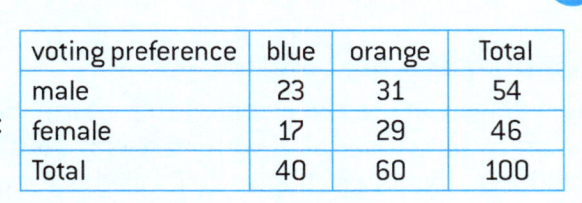

d $\dfrac{29}{46}$ This is now out of 46 as the total number of female voters was 46.

e $\dfrac{29}{60}$ This is out of 60 as the total number of orange voters was 60.

Exercise 9.2

1. Find the probability of getting 2 heads when two coins are tossed.

2. Roger rolls a dice and tosses a coin. Draw a sample space to show all possible outcomes. Find the probability that he rolls an even number and tosses a tail.

3. Find the probability of scoring a total of 7 when 2 dice are rolled.

4. Calculate the probability of getting a total of 10 or more when two dice are rolled.

5. A spinner with ten equal parts numbered from 1 to 10 is spun. A is the event "the spinner lands on an odd number". B is the event "the spinner lands on a number greater than 7".

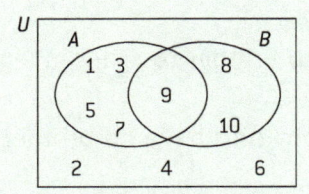

   [Venn diagram: U contains A and B. A has 1, 3, 5, 7; intersection has 9; B has 8, 10; outside: 2, 4, 6]

   The possible outcomes of the experiment and the events A and B are shown in the Venn diagram. Use the diagram to calculate the probabilities that the spinner lands on:
   a a number greater than 7
   b an odd number greater than 7
   c an even number less than or equal to 7.

6. The set U consists of the numbers {1, 2, 3, 4, 5, 6, 7, 8}.
   The numbers {1, 3, 4, 5, 7} are in set X and {2, 4, 6, 7} are in Y.
   Draw a Venn diagram showing where all the numbers from 1 to 8 belong.
   a List the outcomes that are not in Y and hence write down P(Y').
   b List the outcomes in X but not in Y and hence write down P($X \cap Y'$).
   c List the outcomes in X or Y or in both, and hence write down P($X \cup Y$).

7. There are 15 girls in grade 10. They can play touch rugby or football. 10 girls play touch rugby and 7 play football. 4 girls play both sports. Show these figures in a Venn diagram and hence calculate the probability that:
   a a girl chosen at random will play neither sport
   b a girl chosen at random plays only touch rugby.

DP style | **Applications and Interpretation SL**

8. In a class of 20 students, 10 study English, 9 study Spanish and 5 study French. None of the students study Spanish and French. 4 study English and Spanish and 2 study English and French. Show these figures on a Venn diagram and hence calculate the probability that:
   a a student chosen at random will study none of these languages
   b a student chosen at random studies only Spanish
   c a student chosen at random studies only English
   d a student studies Spanish, given that they study English
   e a student does not study Spanish, given that they study English.

9. There are two pre-IB classes, class 1 and class 2. The students in the two classes are asked whether they want to take MAA or MAI when they start the diploma programme.

Maths choice	MAA	MAI
class PIB1	6	12
class PIB2	13	9

   Find the probability that a student chosen at random will be:
   a a student in class 1
   b a student choosing MAA in class 2
   c a student choosing MAI
   d a student studying MAI given they are in class PIB1
   e a student in class PIB2 given they are studying MAA.

183

STATISTICS AND PROBABILITY

Investigation 9.2

When a red die and a blue die are rolled there are 36 possible outcomes which can be shown in a sample space.

+	1	2	3	4	5	6
1	2	3	4	5	6	7
2	3	4	5	6	7	8
3	4	5	6	7	8	9
4	5	6	7	8	9	10
5	6	7	8	9	10	11
6	7	8	9	10	11	12

Red dice (columns), Blue dice (rows)

1. Find the probability of rolling:
   a. a one on the red dice
   b. a six on the blue dice
   c. a one on the red dice and a six on the blue dice.

2. Find the probability of rolling:
   a. an odd number on the blue dice
   b. a number less than three on the red dice
   c. an odd number on the blue dice and a number less than three on the red dice.

3. Suggest a relationship, in terms of $P(A)$ and $P(B)$, between the probability of event A and B both occurring.

   The events in the question above are **independent** which means the outcome of one does not affect the outcome of the other.

   A version of the rule conjectured above will work with events that are not independent, but care needs to be taken to multiply the correct probabilities.

4. In a class of 30 students 16 are boys and 14 are girls. Ten of the girls have at least one brother or sister and so do 11 of the boys.
   a. Show this information in a contingency or two-way table.
   b. If a child is chosen at random from the class find the probability that:
      i. they are a girl
      ii. they have at least one brother or sister given they are a girl
      iii. they are a girl **and** have at least one brother or sister
   c. If a child is chosen at random from the class find the probability that:
      i. they are a boy
      ii. they have no brother or sister given they are a boy
      iii. they are a boy **and** have no brother or sister
   d. Use your answers to parts b and c to suggest what is the probability of both A and B occurring when A and B are dependent events.

> **Key point**
>
> For independent events, $P(A \text{ and } B) = P(A \cap B) = P(A) \times P(B)$ and for dependent events $P(A \text{ and } B) = P(A \cap B) = P(A) \times P(B \text{ given event } A)$

9.3 Tree diagrams

You saw how a sample space diagram can be used to illustrate the possible outcomes when you roll two dice. If you rolled three or more dice then such a diagram would no longer be useful. Another diagram that is used is called a **tree diagram**.

Each time a coin is tossed, the outcome will either be a head or a tail and the probability of each event will be $\frac{1}{2}$.

The event of a head (H) followed by another head is often written as HH.

As we want a head **and** then a second head, we use the fact that for independent events $P(HH) = P(H) \times P(H)$

The tree diagram below shows the four possible outcomes when tossing a coin twice and the associated probabilities.

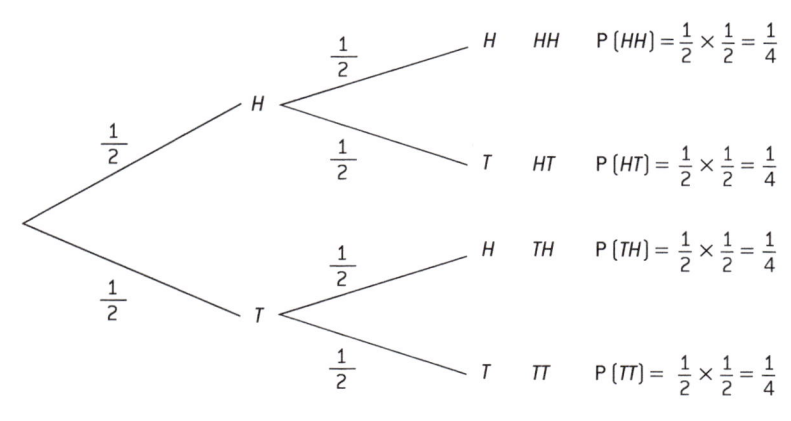

9 Probability

[Tree diagram for two coin tosses showing branches with probability 1/2 each, leading to outcomes HH, HT, TH, TT, each with probability 1/4]

$P(HH) = \frac{1}{2} \times \frac{1}{2} = \frac{1}{4}$

$P(HT) = \frac{1}{2} \times \frac{1}{2} = \frac{1}{4}$

$P(TH) = \frac{1}{2} \times \frac{1}{2} = \frac{1}{4}$

$P(TT) = \frac{1}{2} \times \frac{1}{2} = \frac{1}{4}$

> **Key point**
>
> A tree diagram shows a sequence of events. Each event has different outcomes shown by individual branches to which you assign probabilities.

An easy way to remember how to work out the probabilities of the combined events is that to find the probability of a particular outcome you multiply the probabilities on the branches leading to that outcome. For example, $P(HH) = \frac{1}{2} \times \frac{1}{2} = \frac{1}{4}$

To combine more than one outcome – for example *HT* **or** *TH* – you add the probabilities: $P(HT \text{ or } TH) = P(HT) + P(TH) = \frac{1}{4} + \frac{1}{4} = \frac{1}{2}$. Notice the events will always be mutually exclusive as you cannot go down two branches at the same time, so we can always add the probabilities. Notice how, at each stage, the sum of the probabilities is 1 $\left(\frac{1}{2} + \frac{1}{2} = 1 \text{ and } \frac{1}{4} + \frac{1}{4} + \frac{1}{4} + \frac{1}{4} = 1\right)$. This is because at each stage of the tree, the branches are **exhaustive**, that is the events include all possible outcomes.

Example 6

Three coins are tossed. What is the probability of getting 2 heads and 1 tail (in any order).

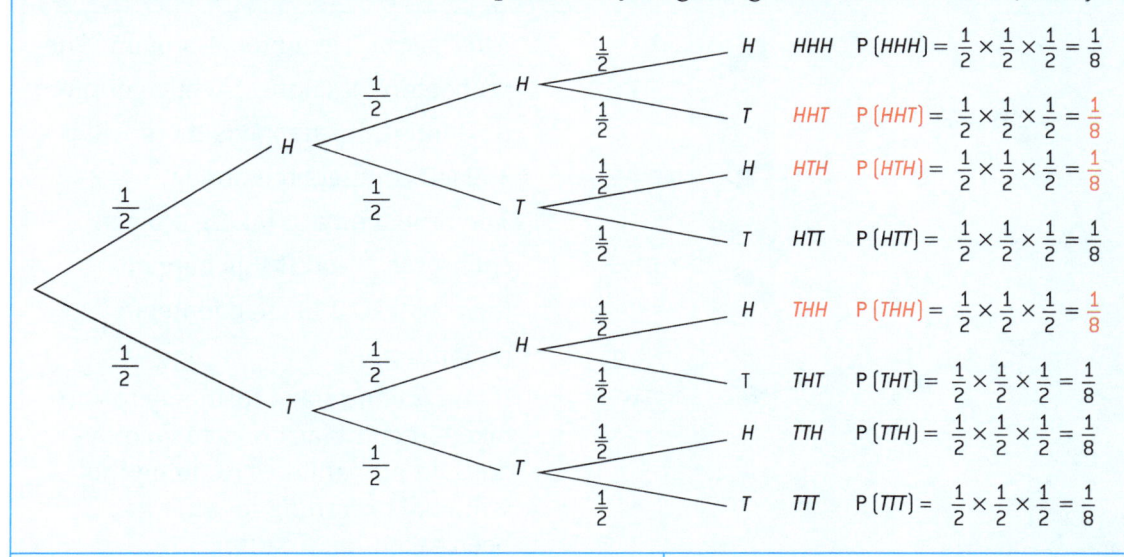

[Tree diagram for three coin tosses showing all 8 outcomes HHH, HHT, HTH, HTT, THH, THT, TTH, TTT each with probability 1/8]

$P(HHH) = \frac{1}{2} \times \frac{1}{2} \times \frac{1}{2} = \frac{1}{8}$
$P(HHT) = \frac{1}{2} \times \frac{1}{2} \times \frac{1}{2} = \frac{1}{8}$
$P(HTH) = \frac{1}{2} \times \frac{1}{2} \times \frac{1}{2} = \frac{1}{8}$
$P(HTT) = \frac{1}{2} \times \frac{1}{2} \times \frac{1}{2} = \frac{1}{8}$
$P(THH) = \frac{1}{2} \times \frac{1}{2} \times \frac{1}{2} = \frac{1}{8}$
$P(THT) = \frac{1}{2} \times \frac{1}{2} \times \frac{1}{2} = \frac{1}{8}$
$P(TTH) = \frac{1}{2} \times \frac{1}{2} \times \frac{1}{2} = \frac{1}{8}$
$P(TTT) = \frac{1}{2} \times \frac{1}{2} \times \frac{1}{2} = \frac{1}{8}$

Extend the tree diagram by adding another set of branches.

At each stage $P(H) = \frac{1}{2}$ and $P(T) = \frac{1}{2}$.

To get 2 heads and 1 tail, you could get *HHT*, *HTH* or *THH*

$P(HHT, HTH \text{ or } THH) = \frac{1}{8} + \frac{1}{8} + \frac{1}{8} = \frac{3}{8}$

185

STATISTICS AND PROBABILITY

Example 7

In a deck of 52 cards, 13 cards are labelled *H*. A card is drawn and replaced. A second card is drawn. What is the probability that one card is labelled *H* and the other is not?

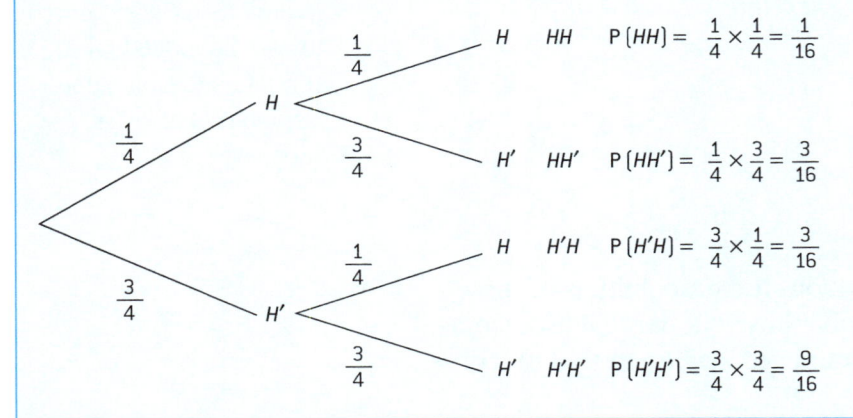

$$P(HH) = \tfrac{1}{4} \times \tfrac{1}{4} = \tfrac{1}{16}$$

$$P(HH') = \tfrac{1}{4} \times \tfrac{3}{4} = \tfrac{3}{16}$$

$$P(H'H) = \tfrac{3}{4} \times \tfrac{1}{4} = \tfrac{3}{16}$$

$$P(H'H') = \tfrac{3}{4} \times \tfrac{3}{4} = \tfrac{9}{16}$$

If one card is labelled *H* and the other is not this can be either (*H H'*) or (*H' H*).

$$P(1\ H) = \tfrac{3}{16} + \tfrac{3}{16} = \tfrac{3}{8}$$

13 out of 52 cards are labelled *H*, hence

$$P(H) = \tfrac{1}{4}$$

$$P(H') = 1 - \tfrac{1}{4} = \tfrac{3}{4}$$

When the second card is drawn, the probabilities remain the same

Example 8

There are 5 counters; 3 of them are black and 2 are white. After taking two counters, find the probabilities of 3, 2, or 1 black counter remaining. Check that the sum of these probabilities is 1.
What will happen after you take a third counter? Find the probabilities of 2, 1 or 0 black counters remaining.

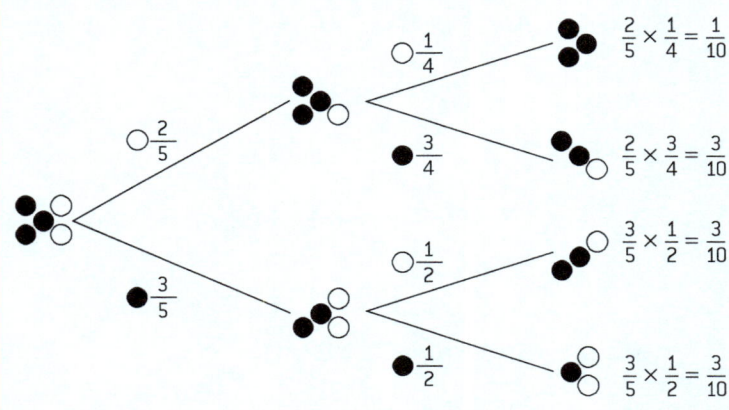

$$P(3\ \text{black}) = \tfrac{2}{5} \times \tfrac{1}{4} = \tfrac{1}{10}$$

$$P(2\ \text{black}) = \tfrac{2}{5} \times \tfrac{3}{4} + \tfrac{3}{5} \times \tfrac{1}{2} = \tfrac{3}{5}$$

$$P(1\ \text{black}) = \tfrac{3}{5} \times \tfrac{1}{2} = \tfrac{3}{10}$$

$$\tfrac{1}{10} + \tfrac{3}{5} + \tfrac{3}{10} = 1$$

After taking 1 counter, 4 remain. The probability of taking a white counter is $\tfrac{2}{5}$ and if this happens there will be 3 black counters remaining.

The probability of taking a black counter is $\tfrac{3}{5}$ and if this happens there will be 2 black counters remaining.

If you go one stage further, you can take either a black or white counter and the probabilities of doing this will vary according to what has been taken the first time.

Calculate the probabilities of each outcome by multiplying along the branches.

There are two ways of getting 2 black counters, so you must add these results together to get the combined probability.

$$P(2 \text{ black}) = \frac{1}{10} \times 1 + \frac{3}{10} \times \frac{1}{3} + \frac{3}{10} \times \frac{1}{3} = \frac{3}{10}$$

$$P(1 \text{ black}) = \frac{3}{10} \times \frac{2}{3} + \frac{3}{10} \times \frac{2}{3} + \frac{3}{10} \times \frac{2}{3} = \frac{3}{5}$$

$$P(0 \text{ black}) = \frac{3}{10} \times \frac{1}{3} = \frac{1}{10}$$

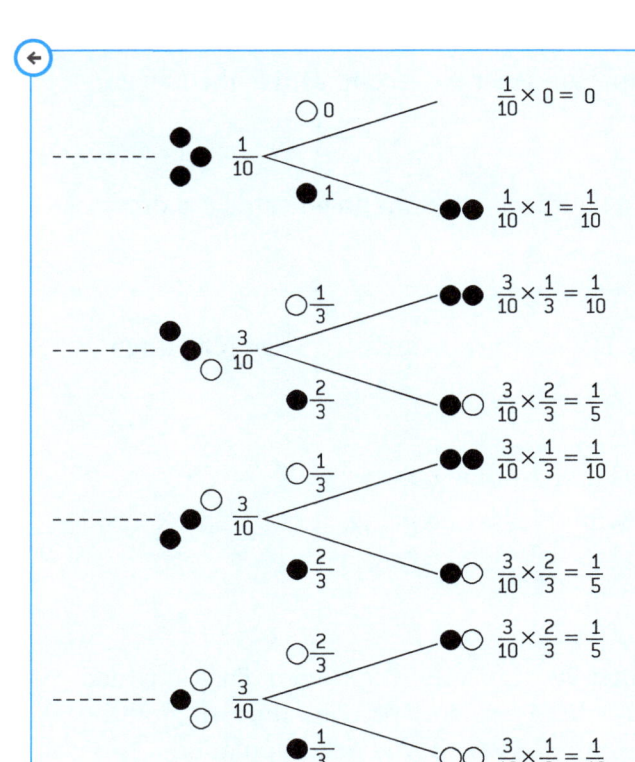

Continue the tree to the next stage and multiply the probabilities along the branches.

Add the probabilities together to get the 3 combined probabilities.

Exercise 9.3

1. The faces of an unbiased dice are painted so that 4 are green and 2 are blue. The dice is rolled twice. Draw a tree diagram to show the possible outcomes and their probabilities. Find the probability that:

   a both faces are green

   b both faces are the same colour

   c both faces are different colours.

2. A fair dice is rolled and a coin is tossed. Draw a tree diagram to show the possible outcomes and the probabilities of this experiment. Find the probability that:

   a a 5 is rolled and a tail is tossed

   b an even number is rolled and a head is tossed.

3. A coin is biased so that the probability of a head is 0.6 and the probability of a tail is 0.4. The coin is tossed 3 times. Draw a tree diagram to show the outcomes and their probabilities. Calculate the probability of obtaining:

   a 3 heads   **b** 3 tails   **c** 1 head   **d** at least 2 heads.

4. A spinner has 5 sectors: 3 red and 2 blue. A second spinner has 4 sectors: 3 red and 1 blue. On each spinner, each sector is equally likely. The two spinners are spun at the same time. Draw a tree diagram to show the outcomes and their probabilities. Find the probability of:

   a 2 red sectors   **b** 1 red and 1 blue sector   **c** 2 blue sectors.

STATISTICS AND PROBABILITY

5 A card is taken from a set of 52 cards. 12 of these cards are green. A second card is then taken, without the first being replaced.
   Use a tree diagram to find the probabilities that:
   a two green cards are drawn   b one green card is drawn   c no green cards are drawn.

DP style   Analysis and Approaches HL

6 Daya and Raquel are playing tennis. The probability Daya wins a game is $\frac{1}{3}$. They play three games.
   a Find the probability Daya loses all three.
   b Hence write down the probability that Daya wins at least one game.
   c Find the probability that both Daya and Raquel win at least one game.

DP style   Applications and Interpretation HL

7 An environmentalist wishes to test how many fish in a lake are suffering from a disease which is infecting the lake. One of the early indicators of the disease is grey patches appearing on the skin. It is also known that similar patches occur naturally in 10% of the fish population.
   The environmentalist catches 80 fish and finds that 30 have the grey patches.
   Let p be the probability a fish has the disease. Assume all fish with the disease have the grey patches and the sample caught is representative of the population of the fish in the lake.
   a Draw a tree diagram to show the possible ways that a caught fish has grey patches, and write down the corresponding probabilities on your diagram.
   b Hence find an estimate for the proportion of fish in the lake with the disease.

Chapter summary

- The probability of an event happening $= \dfrac{\text{number of ways it can happen}}{\text{total number of outcomes}}$

- Relative frequency of an event $= \dfrac{\text{number of times an event occurs}}{\text{total number of trials}}$

- A trial is an individual repetition of an experiment

- $P(A) = \dfrac{n(A)}{n(U)}$

- $P(A') = 1 - P(A)$

- A tree diagram shows a sequence of events. Each event has different outcomes shown by individual branches to which you assign probabilities.

- $P(A \text{ or } B) = P(A \cup B) = P(A) + P(B)$ whenever A and B are mutually exclusive

- For independent events $P(A \text{ and } B) = P(A \cap B) = P(A) \times P(B)$ and for dependent events $P(A \text{ and } B) = P(A \cap B) = P(A) \times P(B \text{ given event } A)$

Chapter 9 test

1. A box contains 3 red balls, 2 blue balls and 1 white ball.

   Find the probability that a ball taken at random is:

   a red **b** blue or white
   c yellow **d** not white.

2. A bag contains some coins. There are twice as many 10 ¢ coins as 20 ¢ coins. Find the probability that a coin taken at random from the bag is a 10 ¢ coin.

3. A standard dice is rolled. Find the probability that a number greater than 3 is rolled.

4. Two coins are tossed. Find the probability that the sides uppermost are:

   a the same **b** different.

5. Two standard dice are rolled. Find the probability that the product (i.e. the result when they are multiplied) of the two numbers is:

   a odd **b** even.

6. The faces of a regular six-sided dice are numbers 1, 1, 1, 3, 6, 6. The dice is rolled twice. Draw a sample space diagram and use it to find the probability of getting a total of:

   a 2 **b** 4 **c** 6
   d 7 **e** 9 **f** 12

7. A tetrahedral dice has 4 faces numbered 1, 2, 3, 4 and an octahedral dice has eight faces numbered 1, 2, 3, 4, 5, 6, 7, 8.

   The two dice are rolled together. Show the outcomes on a sample space diagram and use it to find the probability that the total is:

   a greater than 9
   b less than 4
   c 6 or 7 or 8 or 9.

8. A spinner has eight equal sectors numbered 1 to 8. *A* is the event "the spinner lands on an even number" and *B* is the event "the spinner lands on a number less than 5".

   Draw a Venn diagram showing the outcomes and the events *A* and *B*. Use the diagram to find the probability of getting:

   a an even number less than 5
   b an odd number greater than or equal to 5.

9. In class IB2, there are 16 students. 8 of the students wear glasses and 9 have black hair. There are 4 students who do not wear glasses and who do not have black hair.

   Show the figures in a Venn diagram and hence find the probability that a student chosen from the class at random

   a wears glasses and has black hair
   b has black hair but does not wear glasses
   c has black hair given that they wear glasses.

10. In a set of 52 cards, 4 cards are gold. One card is drawn from this set. The card is noted and replaced and another is drawn. Draw a tree diagram and use it to find the probability that both cards are gold cards.

11. The probability of rain on any one day is 0.35. Find the probability of there being no rain and show the different possible outcomes over two successive days on a tree diagram.

    Find the probability of:

    a rain on two days
    b rain on just one of the days
    c no rain on either day.

12. Look again at the set of cards used in question 10. A card is drawn from this set. The card is retained and another is drawn. Draw a tree diagram and use it to find the probability that both cards are gold cards. Compare this result to that you got to question 10.

STATISTICS AND PROBABILITY

DP style — Applications and Interpretation SL

13 Paulina and Leah are doing a survey on whether or not students are happy, overall, with the food in the cafeteria.

They record the responses to their survey in the table below:

	Happy	Not happy
Students surveyed by Paulina	20	32
Students surveyed by Leah	12	16

   a Use the data to find the approximate proportion of students who are happy with the food in the cafeteria.

   b Vince was surveyed and said he was happy with the food. Find the probability he was surveyed by Leah.

The principal decides to select two students at random and will ask them the same question.
If they are both unhappy with the food in the cafeteria he will organize a food committee.

   c Find the approximate probability that a food committee with be organised.

DP style — Analysis and Approaches SL

14 The Venn diagram below shows the number of elements in each region.

A: 4, A∩B: 2, B: 6, outside: 3

Find

   a $P(A)$ **c** $P(A \cup B)$

   b $P(B')$ **d** $P(A \cap B)'$

Higher Level

DP style — Analysis and Approaches HL

15 Students collected weather data for two weeks. They found on 8 days the sun shone and it rained on 10 days. On 3 days there was no rain and no sunshine.

One of the 14 days is selected at random. By drawing a Venn diagram, find the probability that on the day chosen it was sunny with no rain.

DP style — Applications and Interpretation HL

16 A match in a tennis tournament is played as 'the best of three sets'. The two players play each two sets and if either player wins both then the game is over. If they have each won one set then the third is played.

Cheryl is playing in this tournament. She knows that her chance of beating her opponent in any set is $\frac{1}{3}$.

   a Draw a tree diagram to show the possible outcomes of the match and hence calculate the probability Cheryl will win.

   b Cheryl wins the first set. Write down the probability she will go on to win the match.

9 Probability

Modelling and investigation

DP ready | Approaches to learning

Critical thinking: Analysing and evaluating issues and ideas
Communication: Reading, writing and using language to gather and communicate information
Organization skills: Managing time and tasks effectively

One of the oldest problems in probability was suggested by Chevalier de Méré, a French nobleman:

The first variation was to roll a dice four times and winning if you get a six.

The second variation involved rolling two dice twenty-four times and winning if you get a double six.

Méré argued that if the chance of getting a six in one roll of the dice was $\frac{1}{6}$ then in four rolls it would be $\frac{4}{6} = \frac{2}{3}$ which is greater than a half. With two dice he figured that if there were 36 possibilities and one of these was a double six then the chance of a double six was $\frac{1}{36}$. With twenty-four rolls, he had a $\frac{24}{36} = \frac{2}{3}$ chance of getting double six, the same as rolling one dice and again more than a half. So Méré deduced that he had more chance of winning than losing.

Can you see anything wrong with Méré's argument? Pascal and Fermat were able to prove him wrong. Here you are going to follow their argument and arrive at the probabilities of both events.

Méré was correct in his initial statement that the chance of getting a six in one roll of the dice is $\frac{1}{6}$.

1 **a** Draw a tree diagram showing the four throws of a dice where the outcomes for each throw are six (S) and not a six (S′).
   b Write the probabilities of S and S′. (You do not need to write these on every branch of the tree diagram.)

Calculating the probability of getting "at least one six in four throws" (this is equivalent to finding the complementary event of "not getting at least one six in four throws".)

   c Rewrite "not getting at least one six in four throws" in terms of S′.
   d Use your tree diagram to find this probability of "not getting at least one six in four throws".
   e Use the result P(S′) = 1 − P(S) to find the probability of getting "at least one six in four throws".
   f Write this probability as a decimal to find whether it is greater than or less than a half.

Looking at the two dice problem is obviously more complicated, but the method of calculating the probability is the same.

2 **a** Draw a sample space diagram to find the probability of scoring a double six in one throw. Show that this probability P(D) = $\frac{1}{36}$ and write down P(D′)

Drawing a tree diagram to show the results of rolling two dice 24 times in not practical. However, to solve the problem, you only need to use one branch of the tree and the pattern of this branch is the same regardless of its length.

   b Rewrite the complement of "getting at least one double six in twenty-four rolls" in terms of D′.
   c Without drawing the tree diagram, calculate the probability of "not getting at least one double six in twenty-four rolls" and hence of "getting at least one double six in twenty-four rolls".
   d Write this probability as a decimal to find whether it is greater than or less than a half.

3 From your results to 1 and 2, explain why Chevalier de Méré's arguments are wrong and why he was consistently losing the game.

CALCULUS

10 Speed, distance and time

Learning outcomes

In this chapter you will learn about:

→ speed = $\frac{\text{distance}}{\text{time}}$

→ Average rate of change of y with respect to x is $\frac{\text{change in } y}{\text{change in } x}$.

Key terms

→ Speed
→ Gradient
→ Distance-time graph
→ Rate of change

Key point

Speed is the rate of change of distance with time.

Key point

speed = $\frac{\text{distance}}{\text{time}}$

Note

When an object does not travel with a constant speed, the formula above tells you the average speed over the whole journey. Example 1 explains this further.

Internal link

In section 3.1 you learned that the SI unit for speed was m s^{-1}

10.1 Speed, distance and time

Speed is a measurement of how fast something is moving. When an object travels with a constant speed, then its speed, distance and time are connected by the formula: speed = $\frac{\text{distance}}{\text{time}}$

The units of speed are distance per unit of time, so they are metres (the unit of distance) per second (the unit of time), sometimes written m/s or more usually m s^{-1}.

1 m s^{-1} is the speed of something that travels 1 metre in 1 second.

When you are measuring the speed of a car travelling along a road or of a tennis ball being served, the unit that is commonly used is kilometres per hour. This may be written km/h, km h^{-1} or kph.

1 km h^{-1} is the speed of something that travels 1 kilometre in 1 hour.

Example 1

a A bullet travels 3000 m in 2.4 sec. Calculate its speed in ms^{-1}.

b A car travels 320 km in 4 hours. Find its average speed in km/h.

a speed = $\frac{\text{distance}}{\text{time}}$

= $\frac{3000}{2.4}$

= 1250 ms^{-1}

b average speed = $\frac{\text{distance}}{\text{time}}$

= $\frac{320}{4}$

= 80 km/h

The car's speed is not always the same over the journey. Here, we find average speed, which is the total distance travelled divided by the time taken.

10 Speed, distance and time

You can use a triangle to rearrange the formula speed = $\frac{\text{distance}}{\text{time}}$.

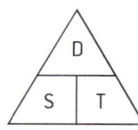

[Triangle with D on top, S and T on bottom]

The diagram shows you graphically that:

speed = $\frac{\text{distance}}{\text{time}}$ distance = speed × time   time = $\frac{\text{distance}}{\text{speed}}$

> **Internal link**
> In Section 6.3 you used a triangle like this [triangle with O on top, S and H on bottom] to rearrange the formula $\sin = \frac{\text{opp}}{\text{hyp}}$

Example 2

a A cricket ball travels at a speed of 41.1 m/s. The cricket pitch is 20 m long. Calculate how long the ball takes to travel the length of the pitch.

b A plane travels at a speed of 870 km/h. Determine how far it travels in 3½ hours.

a time = $\frac{\text{distance}}{\text{speed}}$
= $\frac{20}{41.1}$
= 0.487 sec (3 s.f.)

b distance = speed × time
= 870 × 3.5
= 3045 km

Questions may involve the conversion of units for speed.
For example, since there are 1000 m in 1 km and 3600 sec in 1 hr,
1 km h^{-1} = 1000 m h^{-1}
= $\frac{1000}{3600}$ m s^{-1}
= 0.278 m s^{-1}

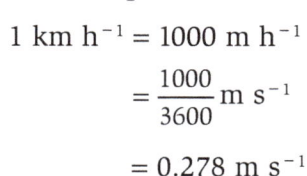

> **Internal link**
> In section 3.1 you learned to convert between different units of measure.

Example 3

A car travels 24 km in 30 min. If average speed is $\frac{\text{distance}}{\text{time}}$, find the car's average speed in:

a km h^{-1}
b m s^{-1}

a average speed is 24 ÷ 0.5 = 48 km h^{-1}
b 24 km = 24 000 m
30 min = 30 × 60 sec = 1800 sec
average speed is 24 000 ÷ 1800 = 13.3 m s^{-1} (3 s.f.)

First convert 30 minutes to 0.5 hours, then use the formula.

Example 4

Calculate the distance travelled by a bus travelling at 85 km h^{-1} for 1 hr 12 min. Give your answer in km.

12 min = $\frac{12}{60}$ = 0.2 hours
So total time is 1.2 hours.
distance = speed × time
= 85 × 1.2 = 102 km

First convert 1 hr 12 min to hours.

CALCULUS

> **Note**
> In Example 4, you could have alternatively converted the time into minutes first. You should try both methods and see what you prefer.

Example 5

a Calculate how many metres a car will travel in 10 seconds at a speed of 50 km h^{-1}.

b Calculate how many minutes the Maglev train takes to travel the distance of 30 km from the airport to Shanghai at an average speed of 257 km/h. Give your answer to the nearest minute.

a $50 \text{ km h}^{-1} = \dfrac{50 \times 1000}{60 \times 60} \text{ m s}^{-1}$ — Convert km h^{-1} to m s^{-1}

distanced travelled $= \dfrac{50 \times 1000}{60 \times 60} \times 10$ — Use distance = speed × time

$= 139$ m (3 s.f.)

b time $= \dfrac{30}{257}$ h — Use time = distance ÷ speed

$= \dfrac{30}{257} \times 60$ min — Convert hours to minutes

$= 7$ min

> **Internal link**
> You studied finding angles using trigonometry in section 6.3b.

Exercise 10.1a

1 It takes 3½ hours to drive from Sydney to Canberra, a distance of 330 km. Calculate the average speed of the journey.

2 The distance from Amsterdam to New York is 5840 km and the flight takes 8½ hours. Calculate the average speed of the plane on the journey.

3 Calculate the distance travelled by a car travelling at 92 km h^{-1} for 2 hr 20 min

4 Fernanda misses her bus home and walks a distance of 7 km. She can walk at a speed of 5 km/h. Find how long it takes her to walk home (giving your answer in hours and minutes).

5 A glacier has retreated by 750 m in 25 years. Calculate the average speed of retreat of the glacier in centimetres per day during this period.

6 Convert 50 km/h to m/s?

7 A cyclist on a time trial travels 3.5 km in 5 minutes 32 seconds. Calculate her speed in km/h.

DP style Applications and Interpretation

8 A river has a width of 40 m and is flowing with a steady current parallel to the banks at a speed of 0.3 m s^{-1}. Philipp wishes to row across the river and can row at a speed of 0.4 m s^{-1}. He begins to row, with his boat pointing perpendicular to the banks.

   a Find how long it will take him to reach the opposite bank.
   b Find how far the current will have taken him downstream during this time.
   c By considering how far he actually travels each second during his crossing, find his actual speed (distance travelled divided by time) relative to the banks.
   d Find the angle to the bank at which he is travelling.

   A second person leaves at the same time as Philipp from the side of the river directly opposite him, also rowing perpendicular to the banks. They meet when Philipp is 10 m from the bank he is rowing towards.

   e Find how far they are downstream from their starting point when they meet.
   f Find the speed at which the second person is rowing.

   After they have met, Philipp is directly in line with the point he is aiming for on the opposite bank. To ensure he no longer moves downstream he steers the boat at an angle such that if rowing in still water at 0.4 m s^{-1} he would be moving upstream at 0.3 m s^{-1}. This helps to cancel out the effect of the current.

   g Use trigonometry to find the angle to the banks at which he should steer so he is no longer moving downstream.
   h Find how long it will take him to complete his journey.

10 Speed, distance and time

Distance and time are often shown on a graph with distance on the vertical axis and time on the horizontal axis. This is known as a **distance–time graph**.

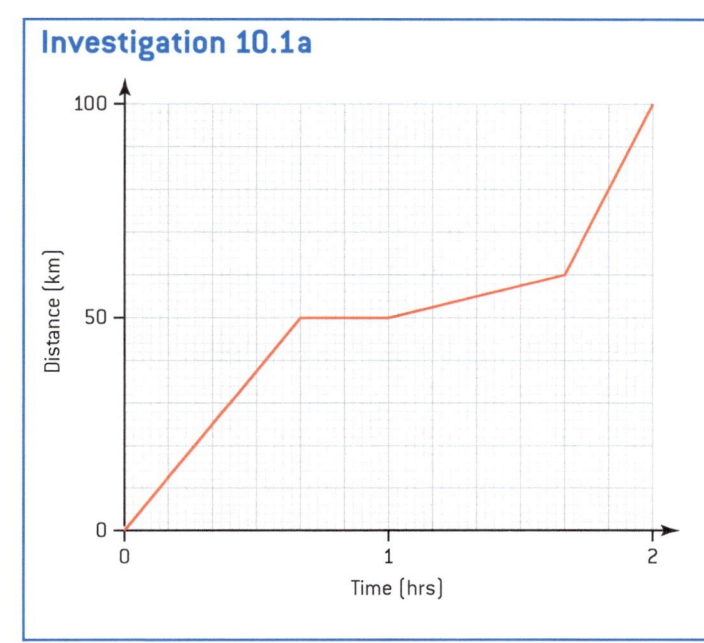

Investigation 10.1a

This graph shows a car that is travelling a distance of 100 km in 2 hours.

1. How far does the car travel in the first 40 minutes?
2. What is the speed of the car during the first 40 minutes?
3. Describe what is happening between 40 minutes and 1 hour.
4. In which part of the journey is the car moving fastest?
5. What is the speed of the car between $t = 1$ hr and $t = 1$ hr 40 min?
6. What is the speed between $t = 1$ hr 40 min and $t = 2$ hrs?

In a graph, the steeper a line is, the faster the rate of change. A horizontal line means that there is no change. The steepness of a graph is referred to as its gradient.

The horizontal change in a straight line is called the 'change in x' and the vertical change in a straight line is called the 'change in y'.

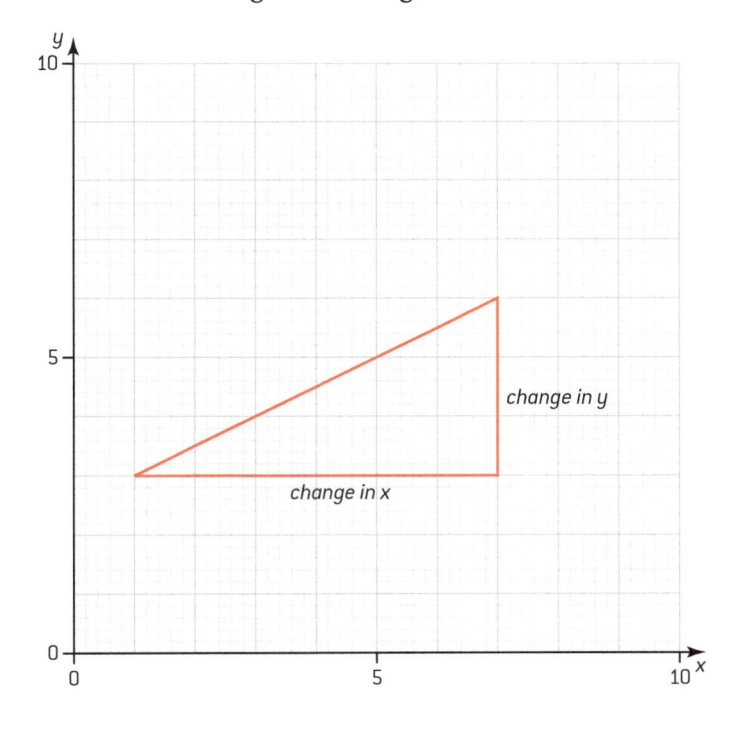

Internal link

Refer back to section 4.4.

DP link

The gradient function is sometimes written $\frac{dy}{dx}$. You can use this function to find the gradient of a curved line at a certain point on the line. This is part of the topic of calculus and will be studied in detail by all diploma students.

The **gradient** of a straight line is defined as $\frac{\text{change in } y}{\text{change in } x}$

This line has a gradient of $\frac{3}{6} = \frac{1}{2}$

A horizontal line has a gradient of zero and a vertical line's gradient is undefined.

Key point

Speed is the gradient of a distance–time graph

195

CALCULUS

In the distance-time graph, distance travelled is on the vertical axis and the time taken is on the horizontal axis. The change in y is distance travelled and the change in x is the time it takes.

So, the gradient of a distance-time graph is $\dfrac{\text{distance}}{\text{time}}$ which is speed.

As the gradient of a straight line is the same for every point on the line, it follows that the speed is the same for every point on a straight-line distance-time graph.

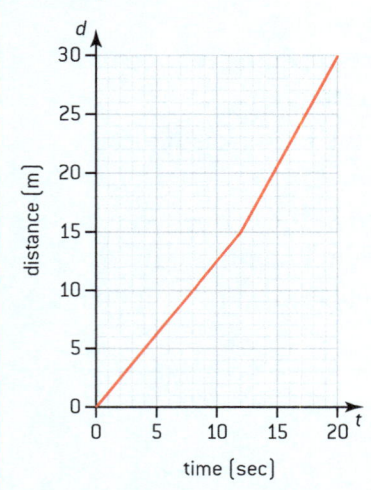

Example 6

The graph shows the motion of a particle.

a   Find the speed of the particle in the first 12 seconds.
b   Find the speed of the particle from $t = 12$ to $t = 20$.
c   Find the average speed of the particle during the 20 seconds it is in motion.

a   speed $= \dfrac{\text{distance}}{\text{time}}$
    $= \dfrac{15}{12}$
    $= 1.25$ ms^{-1}

The graph is a straight line over the first 12 seconds, which means constant speed.

b   speed $= \dfrac{\text{distance}}{\text{time}}$
    $= \dfrac{30 - 15}{20 - 12}$
    $= \dfrac{15}{8}$
    $= 1.875$ ms^{-1}

The graph is a different straight line from 12 to 20 seconds, so this represents a different constant speed.

c   average speed $= \dfrac{30}{20}$
    $= 1.5$ ms^{-1}

Because the speed is not constant over the whole 20 seconds the average speed formula is used.

When an object is travelling so that its distance from a given point is decreasing, it will have a graph with a negative slope. A negative slope is a downward slope and a positive slope is an upward slope.

10 Speed, distance and time

Example 7

A cyclist sets off from home. His distance from home is shown in this distance-time graph.

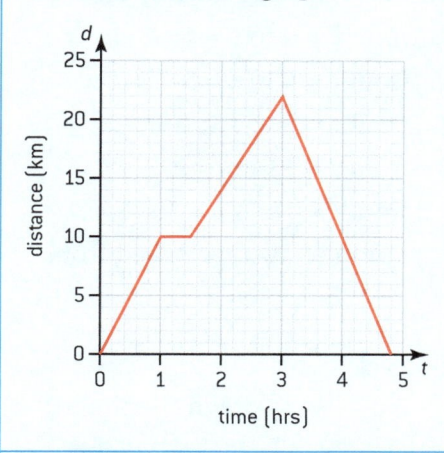

a State the time at which the cyclist is stationary.
b Write down the cyclist's furthest distance from home.
c Find the time when the cyclist starts to return home.
d Calculate the cyclist's speed:
   i   from $t = 0$ to $t = 1$ hr,
   ii $t = 1$ hr 30 min to $t = 3$ hrs,
   iii $t = 3$ hrs to $t = 4$ hrs 50 min.

a $t = 1$ hr to $t = 1$ hr 30 min	The graph is horizontal when the cyclist is stationary.
b 22 km	Furthest distance is when the graph changes direction.
c After 3 hrs	
d i $\dfrac{10}{1} = 10$ km h^{-1}	
ii $\dfrac{22-10}{1.5} = \dfrac{12}{1.5} = 8$ km h^{-1}	
iii $\dfrac{22}{1\frac{5}{6}} = 12$ km h^{-1}	1 hr 50 min is $1\frac{5}{6}$ hrs.

DP link

DP students will study *velocity* which is speed in a given direction. Velocity is a vector quantity and so has direction as well as magnitude. A negative velocity is in the opposite direction to a positive velocity.

Speed is the **magnitude** of the gradient, so the negative sign is ignored.

DP ready Theory of knowledge

Albert Einstein's theory of special relativity states that the maximum speed at which all matter can travel is the speed of light in a vacuum, 299 792 458 m s^{-1}. Particles in the Large Hadron Collider have reached speeds of over 99% of the speed of light. In the fictional series *Star Trek* and *Star Wars*, space ships are able to travel faster than the speed of light, going into *hyperdrive*.

Exercise 10.1b

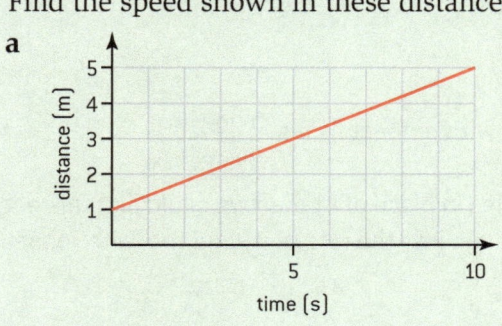

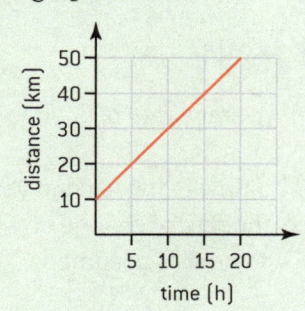

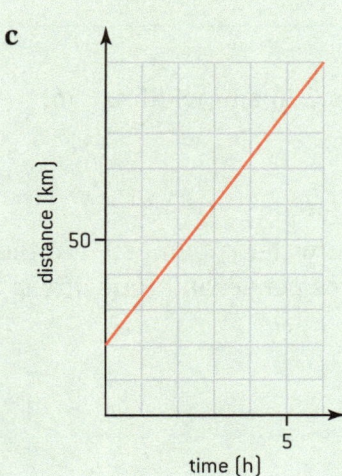

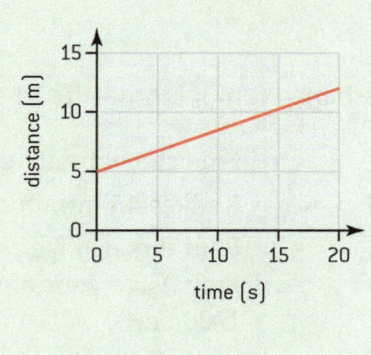

1 Find the speed shown in these distance-time graphs.

   a
   b
   c
   d

197

LESSON 6
INDIFFERENCE TO THE SEARCH FOR MEANING

Objective: This lesson will look at how people sometimes avoid and can be indifferent to the search for meaning.

OPENING ACTIVITY

Carry out a survey in your class, asking the following question: 'Do you ever find yourself reflecting on deep, meaningful topics in your life? Yes or no?' What percentage of the class said 'yes' and what percentage said 'no'? Write the findings on the board.

As a result of these findings, can you conclude that your class group are indifferent to, or actively engaged in, the search for meaning?

AN INCREASINGLY INDIFFERENT SOCIETY

Indifference is the state where one is unconcerned about acting to improve a situation. People are indifferent to many things; for example, people can be aware of injustice in the world but do not feel moved to do anything about it. In the same way, people can be indifferent to the search for meaning in life. In previous lessons we studied how for many centuries society has actively concerned itself with a search for meaning: the search for answers to the big questions of life such as 'Where did I come from?', 'Where did all that exists come from?' 'Where will I go after death?', 'Why is there evil?', 'Why does God allow bad things to happen?' and the list goes on. Today, while the search for answers to these questions goes on, many people believe that these and other questions can be answered by science, whereas in the past people were more likely to look to their religious context to find answers. For some people the belief that happiness can be purchased in the latest fashion item, or car, or IT appliance leads to indifference about the need to find happiness in God. We live in a world that strongly suggests that happiness can be bought and therefore people do not stop to reflect on some of the bigger questions of life. However, sometimes a change in the circumstances of a person's life can make the search for meaning unavoidable.

COLIN FARRELL ON THE MEANING OF LIFE

Each episode of the RTÉ TV series, *The Meaning of Life*, starts off in the same way with Gay Byrne asking the following questions:

- What's it all about?
- Why are we here?
- Is there a God?
- What happens when we die?

Byrne interviews public figures about these questions, and acknowledges that, like him, none claim to be religious experts, but all have had cause to think about the meaning of life. One episode of the programme is an interview with the actor, Colin Farrell. This interview reveals Farrell to be the perfect example of someone who, during a certain phase in his life, avoided the search for meaning. As an up-and-coming actor in LA, Farrell filled his days with materialistic things and it took a life-changing moment for him to eventually begin to search for meaning.

During the interview Farrell admits that as a teenager he craved fame. He believed that celebrity would give his life meaning and it was this idea of fame that initially brought him to acting. Having moved to LA, Farrell soon became one of the most sought-after actors in Hollywood and worked with people like Steven Spielberg, Samuel L. Jackson, Kevin Spacey, Angelina Jolie and Tom Cruise.

During his time in LA, Farrell also began to use drugs and misuse alcohol. The Irish actor was to realise, however, that fame and fortune would not give him the meaning to life he was yearning for.

In the interview, Farrell talks about the negative aspect of fame in LA and the crucial moment that triggered his search for meaning:

> The negative aspect to all this good fortune was ... loneliness. I never figured it in; missing my family, all of my friends – never figured it in!

Farrell admits that at one point in his life he was completely drowning in his addictions. When talking about his faith after leaving rehab, Farrell reveals:

> When I came out I tried hard to be an atheist. But I didn't have the faith! And I really tried hard!

OVER TO YOU

- Some people ignore or avoid searching for meaning in their lives. Why do you think that Colin Farrell avoided the search for meaning for some time?
- What event caused him to begin to ask deep questions?
- Do you think Colin Farrell still continues to avoid the search for meaning today? Why/why not?

Causes of indifference

Some believe that in recent history society has become increasingly indifferent. The following factors are some of the causes of this indifference:

MATERIALISM

Materialism is the theory that physical matter is the only fundamental reality; material goods are considered to be more important than spiritual experience. In a world dominated by fashion, appearance and celebrity, one may easily forget to set aside time to explore the key questions in life.

LOSS OF HOPE

For various reasons, some people do not see the point in exploring the key questions of life. When people feel that their efforts will not yield a desired result, they can become indifferent. In such a case the person can believe that taking a particular course of action will not change anything. They may be disillusioned, heartbroken or demotivated for one reason or another.

CYNICISM

When one faces an experience which causes a sense of disillusionment and betrayal, it can result in a sense of hopelessness in the world. The world can become a place where to be 'cool' is to be cynical and indifferent.

TECHNOLOGICAL ADVANCEMENT

Technology has offered ready-made answers to a wide variety of questions. A person may query the necessity to 'search' for meaning when technology seems to provide answers. However, there are some questions that Google can't answer. These questions are often the ones that we must work out for ourselves, such as 'What gives my life meaning?'

LEARNED HELPLESSNESS

When one continuously fails to accomplish something, or after investing a considerable effort does not see evidence of a result, some people develop what is termed 'learned helplessness'. This is where the person believes that regardless of the effort they invest in a particular thing, it will still not yield the desired result.

LESSON 6 – INDIFFERENCE TO THE SEARCH FOR MEANING

THE DANGER OF INDIFFERENCE

During his speech at the White House Millennium Lecture series, Holocaust survivor and Nobel Peace Prize laureate Elie Wiesel said the following:

> What is indifference? Etymologically, the word means 'no difference'. A strange and unnatural state in which the lines blur between light and darkness, dusk and dawn, crime and punishment, cruelty and compassion, good and evil.
>
> What are its course and inescapable consequences? Is it a philosophy? Is a philosophy of indifference conceivable? Can one possibly view indifference as a virtue? Is it necessary at times to practice it simply to keep one's sanity, live normally, enjoy a fine meal and a glass of wine, as the world around us experiences harrowing upheavals?
>
> Of course, indifference can be tempting — more than that, seductive. It is so much easier to look away from victims. It is so much easier to avoid such rude interruptions to our work, our dreams and our hopes. It is, after all, awkward, troublesome, to be involved in another person's pain and despair. Yet, for the person who is indifferent, his or her neighbours are of no consequence. And, therefore, their lives are meaningless. Their hidden or even visible anguish is of no interest. Indifference reduces the other to an abstraction ...
>
> In a way, to be indifferent to that suffering is what makes the human being inhuman. Indifference, after all, is more dangerous than anger and hatred. Anger can at times be creative. One writes a great poem, a great symphony, one does something special for the sake of humanity because one is angry at the injustice that one witnesses. But indifference is never creative. Even hatred at times may elicit a response. You fight it. You denounce it. You disarm it. Indifference elicits no response. Indifference is not a response. Indifference is not a beginning, it is an end.

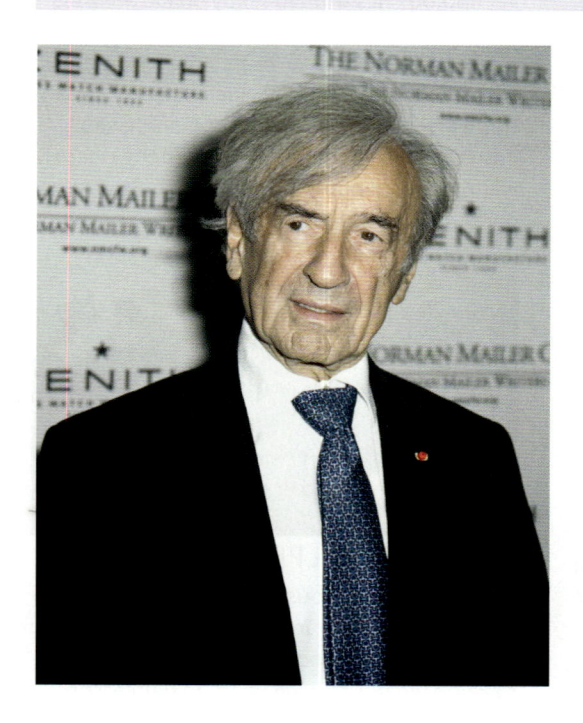

Elie Wiesel

Faith can help people overcome indifference. From the perspective of our faith, we believe that the dignity of human beings rests on the fact that we are created by God out of love, and we are called to grow in relationship with God. God has put the desire for happiness in the human heart and that desire will only be fulfilled by becoming the people that God intends us to become, human beings fully alive, in God's image and likeness. We will look more closely at how faith can give meaning to life in the next lesson.

> ❛ *Indifference is not a beginning, it is an end.*
>
> Elie Wiesel

THINK IT THROUGH

- The factors listed in this lesson are only some of the reasons that cause humans to avoid the search for meaning. Can you think of any other reasons why people may be indifferent?
- According to Elie Wiesel, why can indifference be tempting?
- 'Indifference … is more dangerous than hatred or anger.' Do you agree with this statement? Explain your answer.

JOURNAL

Reflect on times when you have been indifferent to the search for meaning. Can you identify what caused this indifference?

SUMMARY

- Some people can be indifferent to the search for meaning.
- Some factors which may cause indifference include: materialism, loss of hope, cynicism, technological advancement and learned hopelessness.
- At certain times of our lives, circumstantial factors can force us to reflect.

LESSON 7
FAITH GIVES MEANING TO LIFE

Objective: This lesson will explore what faith means and how it can give meaning to life, and will outline the key beliefs of Christianity.

OPENING ACTIVITY
Match the captions with the photos.

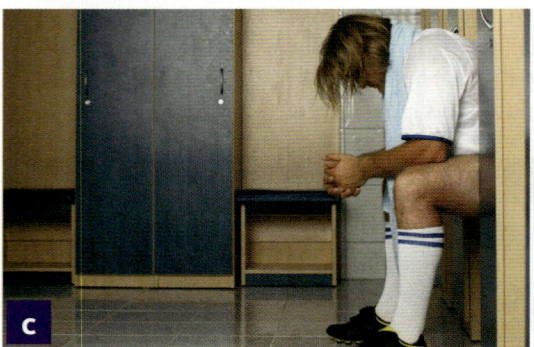

'My faith in my religion means that I want to be married in a church.'
A ☐ B ☐ C ☐ D ☐

'Please God, we have faith that you will keep us safe.'
A ☐ B ☐ C ☐ D ☐

'We carry out this ritual because we have faith that our dead relatives and friends will pass onto the afterlife.'
A ☐ B ☐ C ☐ D ☐

'God, we have faith that you will help us win the game.'
A ☐ B ☐ C ☐ D ☐

Faith and religion

Religious faith is a belief in a transcendent (otherworldly) being and gives meaning to hundreds of millions of people across the world. For Muslims, praying five times a day reminds them of the importance of Allah in their lives. Hindus address the concept of death through a beautifully symbolic ritual on the River Ganges. Jews remember God's intervention in their lives each Saturday with a Sabbath meal, while Buddhists use meditation to reflect on the concept of God. Christians often wear a cross to remind them of the suffering, death and Resurrection of Jesus. Some sports stars bless themselves when they run onto the pitch; many couples choose to get married in a church; and when a loved one dies most families choose to bury them with religious rites.

SECTION A: SEEK AND FIND

WHAT IS FAITH?

In a religious context, faith is a gift from God. To have faith means to have a trusting belief in a supreme power which we may not fully understand. Belief in this supreme power gives purpose and meaning to our lives. If there is no God, then how are we here? If there is no afterlife, then what happens to our soul when we die? What is a soul? Belief in God and an afterlife gives us great hope that when a loved one dies, death is not the end – we will see them again. Faith makes us realise that there is something else out there and that sometimes this 'something else' may not be the most logical path to follow, but we are drawn to it nonetheless. It reminds us that we should not live our lives with only ourselves in mind. Faith gives us a vision to live by. It helps to inform our conscience to do what is right. Ultimately, faith offers us support during the trials and tribulations of life.

Girl on pilgrimage on the Santiago de Compostela trail

OVER TO YOU
- Write your own response to the question, 'What is faith?'
- How can faith help people find meaning in life?

Just as the search for meaning has taken place for centuries now, so too have people expressed their religious faith. Indeed, the two are inextricably linked. Searching for meaning can cause us to reflect upon and express our faith.

CHRISTIAN FAITH

Christians believe in and follow the teachings of Jesus Christ. In the Old Testament we hear the story of how God entered into a covenant with humankind, that he would be their God and they would be his people. Again and again human beings turned away from God and broke their side of the covenant, but God always continued to seek them out and rescue them. He sent the prophets to teach them how to change their ways and to re-embrace their side of the covenant. Finally God sent his Son, Jesus, the second person of the Blessed Trinity, into the world to become one of us and to show us God's love in action in the everyday events of life. In his life he revealed to us who God wanted us to be. Through his death and Resurrection he showed us the depth of the love that God has for us and he won for us the grace to reach our full potential, as people made in the image of God. He also restored our relationship with God, which had been broken by sin. He opened up the possibility of realising our search for happiness and fulfilment by deepening our relationship with God and by helping us become the people God intends us to be.

LESSON 7 – FAITH GIVES MEANING TO LIFE

The word 'creed' comes from the Latin *credo* and means 'belief'. The Nicene Creed is a profession of faith used in Christian celebrations. It was written in the city of Nicaea in modern-day Turkey in the third century by the early Christian community, and was adopted at the First Council of Nicaea in 325 CE. Its purpose was to distinguish the early Christian believers from their Jewish counterparts. It summarises the faith of the Christian Church:

> I believe in one God,
> the Father almighty,
> maker of heaven and earth,
> of all things visible and invisible.
>
> I believe in one Lord Jesus Christ,
> the Only Begotten Son of God,
> born of the Father before all ages.
> God from God, Light from Light,
> true God from true God,
> begotten, not made, consubstantial with the Father;
> through him all things were made.
> For us men and for our salvation
> he came down from heaven,
> and by the Holy Spirit was incarnate of the Virgin Mary,
> and became man.
>
> For our sake he was crucified under Pontius Pilate,
> he suffered death and was buried,
> and rose again on the third day
> in accordance with the Scriptures.
>
> He ascended into heaven
> and is seated at the right hand of the Father.
>
> He will come again in glory
> to judge the living and the dead
> and his kingdom will have no end.
>
> I believe in the Holy Spirit, the Lord, the giver of life,
> who proceeds from the Father and the Son,
> who with the Father and the Son is adored and glorified,
> who has spoken through the prophets.
>
> I believe in one, holy, catholic and apostolic Church.
> I confess one Baptism for the forgiveness of sins
> and I look forward to the resurrection of the dead
> and the life of the world to come. Amen.

Christians believe that Jesus is the Son of God, that God is the creator of the universe, and that in God there are three persons: the Father, Son and Holy Spirit. Christians believe in heaven, life after death, the resurrection of the body and the forgiveness of sins. Christians believe in a loving God who is close to us and who cares for us. God's greatest act of care was to send his Son Jesus into the world. It is our faith in God and in God's Son, Jesus, through whose life, death and Resurrection we come to know the extent of God's love for us, that will lead us to true happiness.

THINK IT THROUGH
- Read the Nicene Creed again and identify what it tells us about God the Father, Son and Holy Spirit.
- What other beliefs are expressed in the Creed?
- How do you think the Christian faith gives meaning to people's lives?

GROUP WORK
Using large sheets of paper, work in groups and try to list as many positive 'I believe ...' statements as you can think of. Try to focus particularly on faith statements. Then write up a 'Class Creed' on a separate sheet of paper.

SUMMARY
- Faith provides answers to the search for meaning.
- Religious faith offers meaning to hundreds of millions of people around the world.
- Religious faith means to have trust in a supreme power.
- Christians have faith in and follow the teachings of Jesus Christ.
- The Nicene Creed records the key beliefs of Christianity.

LESSON 8
THE QUESTION OF SUFFERING AND EVIL

Objective: This lesson will investigate the meaning of suffering and evil as understood from a religious perspective.

OPENING CONVERSATION
Has any recent news event made you question the role of God in the world today? Explain your answer.

The struggle

There are certain moments in life when people find themselves struggling, for example because of bullying, a broken family, poverty, or the death of a loved one. For some, such suffering can bring desolation, despair and hopelessness. It causes them to question: Why does God allow all of this? What type of God allows earthquakes and floods to occur? Another question that ought to be asked during times of suffering would be: Why do humans allow evil to exist?

For some people, suffering offers the opportunity to look at their lives anew and perhaps gain added meaning in their lives. For example, it sometimes takes the occurrence of a major disaster in one part of the world for the rest of us to realise how lucky we really are. Disasters also make us rally round to help each other; we can transform bad situations by our good choices and actions.

Suffering can sometimes encourage thanksgiving: in some parts of Ireland today, the death of a loved one is marked by a ritual called a 'wake'. Along with being a time of deep grief, the 'wake' celebrates the life of the loved one through story, song and prayer. For millions of Christians worldwide, the cross is a powerful symbol as it reminds them of the suffering of Jesus and that God is their 'companion' in suffering. Two millennia on, the cross has become a moving symbol inspiring devotion and prayer.

For millions of people worldwide whose daily lives have become a struggle for one reason or another, their suffering renews their faith in a God.

The entrance to Auschwitz Concentration Camp in Poland. The sign reads, 'Labour makes you free'

NIGHT BY ELIE WIESEL

Elie Wiesel's famous work *Night* recounts his experiences with his father, Shlomo, in the Nazi German concentration camps of Auschwitz-Birkenau and Buchenwald in 1944–45. The events of the book take place at the height of the Holocaust and towards the end of World War II. Wiesel writes about his own questioning of God and his increasing disgust with humanity.

Eliezer 'Elie' Wiesel was a studious and deeply pious Orthodox Jewish teenager who, along with his parents and his sisters, was crammed into a closed cattle wagon with eighty others and transported to Auschwitz-Birkenau, with no light, little to eat or drink and barely able to breathe. On their arrival at Auschwitz-Birkenau, men and women were separated. Eliezer and his father were sent to the left; his mother, Hilda, and his sisters, Beatrice and Tzipora, to the right. He learned years later that his mother and Tzipora were taken straight to the gas chamber. He was sixteen years old when Buchenwald, the camp he was later transferred to, was finally liberated by the US army in April 1945. It was too late for his father, who had died after a beating while Wiesel lay silently on the bunk below for fear of being beaten too.

In *Night*, Elie recalls how during the hanging of a child, which the camp is forced to watch, he hears someone ask: Where is God? Where is he?

> Behind me, I heard the same man asking: Where is God now? And I heard a voice within me answer him: Here He is – He is hanging here on this gallows …

This, the central event in *Night*, is the moment where Wiesel gains insight; insight into death, insight into the essence of the Divine. It was this one horrendously cruel event which, incredibly, offered the opportunity for the author to reflect on what the concept of God meant to him and enabled him to recognise God's presence even in the disgusting events that were taking place around him.

The following reflection describes the impact reading *Night* had on one fifth year student:

> My name is Aisling and I'm seventeen years old. Our class read *Night* by Elie Wiesel. I loved it, but it made me angry to know how these people were murdered, tortured and mutilated. I found myself wanting to jump into the world of the book and end these atrocities.
>
> I felt that the moment where the child is hanged definitely caused Elie to question God, and whether God was dying with the child – who was not only murdered but suffered tremendously, taking a half hour to finally die. Those of us reading this extract should ask ourselves these important questions: How has the Jewish religion survived after such a terrible event like the Holocaust? Why do we believe in God and what is the reasoning behind our beliefs?
>
> Elie has difficulty accepting that his God would allow this brutal hanging to happen, but I realise that if there is a God, he put us here to live, to take care of ourselves, each other and the earth. I think what we actually do is not under his control. He can only help us to help ourselves in the situation of a Holocaust or any other disaster.

OVER TO YOU

► Write a similar reflection about a book or film that gave you some insight into finding meaning in suffering.

WHY DOES GOD LET US SUFFER?

Father Richard Leonard, an Australian Jesuit, addressed the many myths that people believe about the role of God in human suffering in his book *Where the Hell is God?* Father Leonard details six steps which contradict what some people believe about God's role in human suffering:

» God does not directly send pain, suffering and disease. God does not punish us.
» God does not send us accidents to teach us things, though we can learn from them.
» God does not will earthquakes, floods or other natural disasters to happen.
» God did not create Jesus purely for death. Jesus did not just come to die – God used his death to announce the end of death.
» Our world is one in which suffering, disease and pain are realities; otherwise, it would be heaven.
» God does not kill us off.

Father Leonard wrote his book to remind us of the power of a loving God. He wanted to reach out to people who are in pain and who are struggling to understand how they can reconcile their faith with the terrible things that have happened to them or their family. Father Leonard hopes to get people to look at their language and how they are presenting God to the world. He says:

Language creates reality. I think we have to be careful with what we say. It is easy to have throw-away lines like: God is punishing us, God only sends the biggest crosses to those who can bear them, or it's all God's will so just offer it up. They get you off the hook but what sort of an image of God sits behind them? It is a punishing and tyrannical God who doesn't seem to care.

JOURNAL

Think of a time in your life when you suffered in some way. What helped you to cope with this struggle? How do you think faith might give you hope when faced with future struggles?

GROUP WORK

Look up newspapers or news items on radio and/or television for reports that show good news stories and events happening in the world at this time. Try to find stories of people reaching out to help others. Create a collage with images and captions to show hope in the midst of suffering in our world.

SUMMARY

- Suffering can cause people to question: Why does God allow all of this?
- Another question that ought to be asked during times of suffering would be: Why do humans allow evil to exist?
- God does not directly cause or will pain and suffering.
- God is a companion in suffering, not someone external to it.

Devastation caused by the earthquake in Haiti in 2010

LESSON 8 – THE QUESTION OF SUFFERING AND EVIL

LESSON 9
THE BIG QUESTIONS OF LIFE AND DEATH

Objective: This lesson will investigate some perspectives on one's approach to life and will discuss finding meaning in life and death.

OPENING ACTIVITY
Write a bucket list – a list of things you would like to do before you die.

How am I going to live?

Coming to terms with suffering and death has concerned the greatest thinkers from the beginning of time. Life is not controllable and not completely safe. Acceptance of the inevitability of death leads one to the meaningful question: How am I going to live so that when my dying comes, I can look back with a sense of contentment, with few regrets and with many thanks? The journey towards death is one we can only make ourselves; it is a solitary undertaking.

THE CHRISTIAN PERSPECTIVE

Just as faith can give meaning to life it can also give meaning to death. Faith in the Resurrection of Christ is the foundation of the Christian perspective on death. Christian faith offers a consoling and influential way of facing and even celebrating the death of our body. This is because of the belief in the resurrection of the body and in eternal life. Eternal life is living for ever with God in the happiness of heaven. Just as Christ is risen and lives for ever, so all of us will live in a new way after our death and will rise on the last day.

Father Ronald Rolheiser is a member of the Missionary Oblates of Mary Immaculate. He is also a Catholic theologian, speaker and spiritual writer who has given much thought to the subject of life after death and how it should affect our lives in the here and now:

> It makes a huge difference, unconsciously, as to how restless or peaceful we are. When we no longer believe in a life hereafter, we will, one way or the other, put unfair, restless pressure on this life. Belief in life after death is important, not because it can affect our present lives with fears of hellfire or with the promise of a heaven that can be a soothing narcotic when life can't deliver what we want, but because only the infinite can provide the proper horizon against which to view the finite … Belief in life after death is meant to give us proper vision so that we can, precisely, enjoy the real joys of this life without perpetually crucifying ourselves because they, and we, aren't perfect.
>
> (From www.ronrolheiser.com)

THINK IT THROUGH
- Do you believe in life after death?
- How does this affect your life now?
- What is your understanding of the Christian teaching on eternal life?

FIGHTING FOR LIFE

Shortly before he died, sixteen-year-old Dónal Walsh came to national prominence when he wrote a letter that made a plea for an end to suicide, especially among young people. This is his letter:

A few months left, he said. There it was; I was given a timeline on the rest of my life. No choice, no say, no matter. It was given to me as easy as dinner.

I couldn't believe it, that all I had was sixteen years here, and soon I began to pay attention to every detail that was going on in this town.

I realised that I was fighting for my life for the third time in four years and this time I have no hope. Yet still I hear of young people committing suicide, and I'm sorry but it makes me feel nothing but anger.

I feel angry that these people choose to take their own lives, to ruin their families' lives and to leave behind a mess that no one can clean up.

Yet I am here with no choice, trying as best I can to prepare my family and friends for what's about to come and leave as little a mess as possible.

I know that many of these people could be going through financial despair and have other problems in life, but I am at the depths of despair and, believe me, there is a long way to go before you get to where I am.

For these people, no matter how bad life gets, there are no reasons bad enough to make them do this; if they slept on it or looked for help they could find a solution, and they need to think of the consequences of what they are about to do.

So please, as a sixteen-year-old who has no say in his death sentence, who has no choice in the pain he is about to cause and who would take any chance at even a few more months on this planet, appreciate what you have, know that there are always other options and help is always there.

OVER TO YOU
- What is your reaction to this letter?
- Do you appreciate what you have?
- How can you begin to be more grateful for what you have?
- If you believed that someone was feeling suicidal, what could you do to help?

DÓNAL'S FAITH GAVE MEANING TO HIS LIFE AND DEATH

Dónal's letter had a huge impact on the country and he gave moving interviews speaking about his battle with cancer and his faith in God. In an interview with Dónal on *The Saturday Night Show*, Brendan O'Connor said: 'You seem to have a very clear perspective on what is important in life … I know what has helped you a lot through this is your faith, isn't it?' Dónal replied, 'It is a huge part of it. I wouldn't be here at all without it. I see [it as if] God has given me this challenge. I may be used as a symbol for other people to appreciate life more … then I'll be happy to die.'

REFLECT AND DISCUSS

Read the following extracts from an interview with Dónal Walsh and discuss the questions that follow:

Some days I would wake up and I could easily appreciate the beauty of the world that I was leaving behind, although it does make me upset that I will never get to experience the feeling of living that I had on the bike or in the gym, or that I will never get to see my sister walk up the aisle next to the love of her life, or that I will never get to travel the world and see places like New Zealand, Asia or America, or that I won't get the chance to see my four best friends do as good in life as I know they will. But I have to remember that God is using me; whether he is using me as a symbol for people to appreciate life more or whether his first two mountains weren't high enough for me, all I know is that I am walking with him even though it is along his path.

I live in a part of the world that is surrounded by mountains. I can't turn my head without finding a bloody hill or mountain, and I suppose those were God's plans for me – to have me grow up around mountains and grow climbing a few too. And that's exactly what I've done: I may have grown up in body around them but I've fully grown and matured in mind climbing his mountains.

He's had me fight cancer three times, face countless deaths and losses in my life, he's had my childhood dreams taken off me but at the end of the day, he's made me a man.

I am always called brave, heroic, kind, genuine, honourable and so many other kind compliments, but I have to try and explain to everyone why I seem to reject them. I have never fought for anyone but myself, therefore I cannot be brave or heroic, I've only been kind because my religion has taught me so.

What impact could I ever make on the world if I was fake or how could I ever be honourable if I was not honoured to be here.

I am me. There is no other way of putting it – Dónal Walsh from Tralee, one body, one mind with a few other tales thrown in.

I've climbed God's mountains, faced many struggles for my life and dealt with so much loss. And as much as I'd love to go around to every fool on this planet and open their eyes to the mountains that surround them in life, I can't. But maybe if I shout from mine they'll pay attention.

▶ How did Dónal's faith help him approach his life and death?
▶ What is the main message that Dónal wanted to give people?
▶ A person's outlook on life is evident when death is imminent – when and how does one develop an outlook on life?
▶ What is your outlook on life?

Dónal Walsh

Comparative Religious Studies

All the great religions of the world define themselves, ultimately, by how they view death. Research the beliefs about death and an afterlife in one world religion.

YOU WILL FIND ADDITIONAL INFORMATION ON WWW.SEEKANDFIND.IE

JOURNAL

How am I going to live so that when my dying comes, I can look back with a sense of contentment, with few regrets and with many thanks?

Write your response to the question by reflecting on your life now and your hopes and dreams for the future.

SUMMARY

- Faith in the Resurrection of Christ is the foundation of the Christian perspective on death.
- Christians believe in the resurrection of the body and in eternal life.
- Eternal life is living for ever with God in the happiness of heaven, entered after death by the souls of those who die in the grace and friendship of God.
- Dónal Walsh showed how faith can give meaning to life and death.

LESSON 10
THE ORIGINS OF PHILOSOPHY

Objective: This lesson will introduce the origins of philosophy and the key people involved in developing philosophical thought.

OPENING CONVERSATION
What are the first thoughts that come to mind when you think of the word 'philosophy'?

Examining life and searching for meaning

Philosophy begins with human beings and our attempt to examine and understand the world around us. In the first lesson we studied how archaeological sites such as Newgrange and the Royal Tombs of Ur have revealed evidence of the search for meaning undertaken by ancient civilisations. However, this was merely the dawn of humanity's quest for meaning. Philosophy was brought to a higher level in Classical Greece. As recorded in Plato's *Apology*, the Greek philosopher Socrates said that 'the unexamined life is not worth living'. He believed life to be pointless unless we spend time contemplating and studying it. So how exactly does one examine life, what does the term 'philosophy' actually mean and where did philosophy begin?

WHAT IS PHILOSOPHY?

The word 'philosophy' comes from the Greek *philosophia*, and literally translates as 'love of wisdom'. It refers to thinking about thinking, setting aside time in our lives to contemplate life at a deeper level. 'Theology' also comes from the Greek, and means the study of the gods. When you, as a Senior Cycle student, ponder concepts such as what it is you want to do with your life and what the point is of doing your Leaving Certificate exams, you too become a philosopher. Through the act of questioning, you join billions of human beings before you who have also participated in philosophy.

Socrates, Academy of Athens, Greece

PHILOSOPHY CONTAINS THE FOLLOWING MAIN AREAS OF STUDY:

Metaphysics: The study of what reality is, for example the study of the relationship between the mind and the body.

Epistemology: Concerned with whether knowledge is possible and, if so, what the nature and scope of knowledge is.

Ethics: Also known as 'moral philosophy', concerns the issue of what is the best way to live and whether this question can be answered.

Political Philosophy: Concerns the government and the relationship of the individual to communities, including the state. Includes questions about justice, law, property and the rights and obligations of the citizen.

Aesthetics: Looks at beauty, art, enjoyment and how beauty is created.

Logic: The study of valid arguments and how they are formed.

THE ORIGINS OF PHILOSOPHY

Several cultures have contemplated philosophical questions and built traditions based on such questions. Philosophy is said to have had its origins in Greece in the sixth century BCE. Whereas earlier societies used myth to help people to understand reality, Greek philosophy used reason. In fact, the Western way of thinking, political and legal structures and education are very much derived from the Greek invention of philosophy and politics.

The cities of Greece of the sixth century BCE were thriving commercial centres. Greek society flourished artistically, politically and creatively. The Greeks were in the process of developing the basic structure of democracy (i.e. a society should not be ruled by a dictator but rather by politicians elected by the people).

They were also an adventurous, sea-faring civilisation who explored extensively. Hence, the Greeks were quite a progressive people. During their explorations they had learned geometry from the Egyptians and knowledge of the calendar from the people of Asia Minor.

Prior to this, people had a mythical understanding of the world. They used myths to understand what they could not explain. Philosophers, however, were dissatisfied with these mythical explanations and began to challenge them. As Athens was the cultural centre of Greece at the time, philosophy started from here and soon began to move society in a new post-mythical direction.

LESSON 10 – THE ORIGINS OF PHILOSOPHY

Timeline of early Greek philosophy

THE NATURAL PHILOSOPHERS
- The earliest known philosophers.
- Concerned with our true nature as human beings, how the universe began and our place within it.
- Believed that the universe was created from one of the natural elements of fire, air, water or earth.
- Were also known as pre-Socratic philosophers because they came before Socrates.
- One of the Natural philosophers by the name of Thales believed everything originated from water.

THALES
- A Natural philosopher.
- The first man to whom the name of 'wise' was given.
- A politician, geometer, astronomer and thinker.
- Credited with correctly predicting the solar eclipse of 585 BCE.
- Disregarded the mythical legends of his ancestors.
- Focused instead on knowledge of the world and the stars.
- Laid the philosophical foundations for subsequent thinkers of the time such as the Sophists.
- Made it acceptable to question age-old traditions.

THE SOPHISTS
- Educated men.
- Travelled from place to place offering tuition on grammar and rhetoric (the art of debating, argument and applying logic).
- Also taught statesmanship and generalship.
- Charged for their services and were employed by the wealthy to provide their children with professional training.

PROTAGORAS
- Concerned with the person and their place in the world.
- Believed that it was impossible to know absolute truth, as truth was a matter for each individual.
- Believed that the difference between good and evil cannot be fully known.
- Later philosophers including Socrates disagreed with Protagoras.

SOCRATES
- Concerned with the question of ethics (knowing the difference between right and wrong).
- Believed that it was not possible for any human to fully know truth.
- Wanted to establish a universal definition of justice.
- Worked to find laws and limits which society could abide by.
- Socrates' philosophy involved taking the role of an ignorant questioner – asking probing questions to show the experts how little they actually knew.
- Socratic wisdom is knowing that we do not know everything.
- Encouraged others to question their beliefs and knowledge also.
- Was critical of the Athenian government and because of this was executed in 399 BCE.

OVER TO YOU
- What were the earliest philosophers known as?
- From what did the Natural philosophers believe the universe was created?
- The Natural philosophers were also known as Pre-Socratic. Why was this?
- Thales was a Natural philosopher and the first man to whom what name was given?
- What qualifications did Thales have?
- Thales is credited with correctly predicting what event?
- Thales made what acceptable for following philosophers?
- Describe the function of the Sophists in early Greek culture.
- Why was Protagoras important to the philosophical world?
- Socrates was concerned with which crucial philosophical concept?
- How did Socrates play a crucial part in the development of our modern judicial system?
- How and why did Socrates die?

THINK IT THROUGH
- From what you have learned, what are some of the influences philosophers have had on society?

SUMMARY
- Philosophy originated in sixth-century BCE Greece. Greek culture was politically and creatively advanced for the time. This progressive environment helped to nourish philosophical development.
- The earliest philosophers were the Natural philosophers who were concerned with the creation of the universe.
- One example of a Natural philosopher was Thales, who disregarded the myths of his ancestors and made it acceptable to question age-old traditions.
- The Sophists were educated men who travelled around offering tuition on rhetoric, statesmanship and generalship.
- Protagoras believed that it was impossible to know absolute truth as truth was a matter for each person.
- Socrates wanted to establish a universal definition of justice.

LESSON 11
INTRODUCING PLATO

Objective: This lesson will introduce the philosopher Plato and examine his influence on learning.

OPENING ACTIVITY

Divide into groups of four for this exercise. Each group needs a large sheet of paper. Write the word 'Education' in the centre of the sheet. Discuss the following:

- What does education mean to me?
- Does education have a positive or negative influence on society?
- What would the world be like without education?
- From where has the idea of school and formal education come?

Significant points which arise are to be written around the word 'Education'. You are invited to discuss your ideas with the rest of the class.

Who was Plato?

Ancient Greek philosopher, student of Socrates, teacher of Aristotle and founder of the Academy (a famous school in Athens), Plato is considered to be one of the most important philosophers of all time. The son of a wealthy and noble family, Plato (427–347 BCE) was a student of Socrates and this experience seems to have dissuaded him from a political life. Since Socrates did not write anything, what is known of his activity of engaging his fellow citizens in conversation derives primarily from the writings of Plato.

THE INFLUENCE OF SOCRATES ON PLATO

Plato was profoundly affected by both the life and death of his influential mentor Socrates (469–399 BCE), and his encounters with the older man changed the course of his life. Plato had been preparing for a career in politics. The activity of the older man, however, provided the starting point of Plato's philosophising. Socrates appears to have been a critic of democracy and irritated some with his discussions on justice and the pursuit of goodness. His attempts to improve the Athenians' sense of justice clashed with their politics and societal thinking of the time and this, it is thought, may have been the reason for his execution. Resentment against Socrates grew, and in 399 BCE he was charged with impiety and corrupting the youth. The ensuing trial and eventual execution had a traumatic effect on the young Plato and it was this event that led his attempt to create the perfect society.

You may not realise it, but Plato is partly responsible for the third level university system that exists today. Following the death of Socrates, Plato travelled to Italy, Sicily, Egypt and Cyrene in search of knowledge. Returning to Athens at the age of forty, he turned to philosophy, opening an academy on the outskirts of Athens dedicated to the Socratic search for wisdom.

The School of Athens by Raphael (1509–10), a fresco at the Apostolic Palace, Vatican City. This fresco features nearly every great Greek philosopher, but determining which are depicted is difficult.

PLATO'S ACADEMY

Founded in the 380s, Plato's Academy was the forerunner of the modern university (hence the English term 'academic'). Plato's Academy was the earliest known organised school in Western civilisation and functioned for 150 years. It became an influential centre of research and learning and produced many students of outstanding ability. One of these students was Aristotle who for twenty years was also a member of the Academy. He started his own school, the Lyceum, after Plato's death.

PLATO'S WRITINGS

Plato wrote several documents about various topics, including politics and art, religion and science, justice and medicine, virtue and vice, crime and punishment, pleasure and pain, love and wisdom, and most of his writings have survived to the present day. He wrote in the form of dialogue, where a number of characters argue a topic by asking questions of each other. This form of writing suited a philosopher like Plato as his use of dramatic elements like humour draws the reader in. Using dialogues allowed Plato to raise various points of view in order to interrogate the subject, thus allowing the reader to decide which perspective is valid.

THE DIALOGUES OF PLATO

The dialogues contain huge numbers of characters, in addition to Socrates and other authority figures, some of whom are meant to symbolise certain classes of reader (e.g. Glaucon, the interlocutor in Plato's Allegory of the Cave, may be representative of talented and politically ambitious youth). These characters not only carry forward the plot but inspire the reader to join in the discussion in their imagination. Inspiring the reader to philosophical activity is the main purpose of the dialogues. Because Plato himself never appears in any of these works, and because many end with the issue unresolved, some scholars believe that Plato was not recommending any particular point of view.

STUDYING PLATO'S DIALOGUES

Let us study a contemporary example of Plato's dialogue process:

Q: How is a tree created?
A: A tree is created from a seed.
Q: But how does the seed get there?
A: The seed can be germinated as a result of many factors, e.g. animal, wind etc.
Q: But where does the seed come from?
A: The seed comes from the tree.

In a similar manner Plato would have encouraged his students to find meaning through playing the role of an ignorant questioner.

THINK IT THROUGH

▶ In pairs, debate one of the following topics using the Plato model of debate, whereby the questioner continues to pose a question after each answer:

- Who is the most famous person in the world?
- Where do chickens come from?
- How does life begin?
- Why do bad things happen in the world if God is ultimately good?

Plato's Central Ideas

THEORY OF FORMS (OR IDEAS)

The central idea of Plato's philosophy was his Theory of Forms (or Ideas). This theory is based on the premise that people believe that they know things that, in truth, they do not know. The term that Plato used to refer to Forms, or ideas, comes from the verb *eidō*, 'to look'. Therefore, when Plato refers to ideas he refers to how a thing looks or appears. Plato's term 'Forms' refers to the real or true world, a world of perfect forms which is eternal or changeless. According to Plato, the sensory or material world – that is, everything we can see, hear, taste, touch and smell – is false, a passing shadow, and is merely an image or copy of the real world. Plato taught that by rational inquiry through discussion and reflection we are able to free ourselves from a false notion of the world and realise the true form of things. Plato used his Allegory of the Cave to explain his Theory of Forms. We will explore this in the next lesson.

We perceive the outside world thanks to our five senses. This, however, is not evidence that we are dealing with the material likeness of what we perceive in the outside world. For example, we cannot say 'there is a textbook here', just because we see one. That is because the eyes that see the textbook are merely an agent. There are receptor cells at the rear of the retina in the eye. These cells turn the photons that land on them into an electrical current and nerves then carry that current to the visual centre in the brain. The visual centre in the brain interprets the signal and then forms an image. In other words, when we say 'I see' something, we actually see the effect created in our brains by the alteration of the light waves reaching the eye through electrical signals. All of these facts regarding the sense of sight also apply to hearing, touch, taste and smell. What we call 'real' is actually an interpretation of electrical signals transmitted to the brain. Plato believed it naïve to say that the world we live in is real simply because we perceive it as the world, because what we perceive is merely a reflection of it in our brains.

THEORY OF THE SOUL

Plato's Theory of the Soul argues that the soul is composed of three parts: the appetitive, the rational and the spirited. These three parts also correspond to the three classes of a fair society.

Appetitive

The appetitive part of the soul is that which is responsible for the basic desires or 'appetite' within humanity. It is responsible for the simple cravings needed to stay alive, such as thirst and hunger, sexual excess or over-consumption. These desires for essential things should be controlled by the other parts of the soul.

Plato indicates that the appetitive soul corresponds to the working class of merchants and labourers.

Rational

The rational soul yearns for truth. It is responsible for all philosophical desires. It is the part of the soul that rationally instructs and restricts the other two.

The rational soul corresponds to the guardian class in Plato's theory. This social class consists of the philosopher kings to whom all of society should listen and follow unquestioningly.

Spirited

The spirited soul is the source of emotions such as love, honour and victory. In the soul which seeks justice, the spirit becomes the enforcer of the rational soul, guaranteeing that the commands of reason are followed. Emotions such as anger and indignation are the result of the frustration of the spirit.

The spirited soul parallels the ancillary class of soldiers and enforcers who make certain that the orders of reason from the philosopher kings are obeyed by all of society.

OVER TO YOU

▶ Write a paragraph explaining which of Plato's theories discussed above, the Theory of Forms or the Theory of the Soul, is more important today, and give reasons why. Once completed, read your paragraph to the student sitting beside you. Share your ideas with the class.

SUMMARY

- Plato is considered to be one of the most important philosophers of all time.
- Socrates inspired Plato to move towards philosophy and away from politics.
- Plato opened a school on the outskirts of Athens called the Academy.
- Aristotle was a member of Plato's Academy for nearly twenty years.

LESSON 11 — INTRODUCING PLATO

SECTION B — CHRISTIANITY

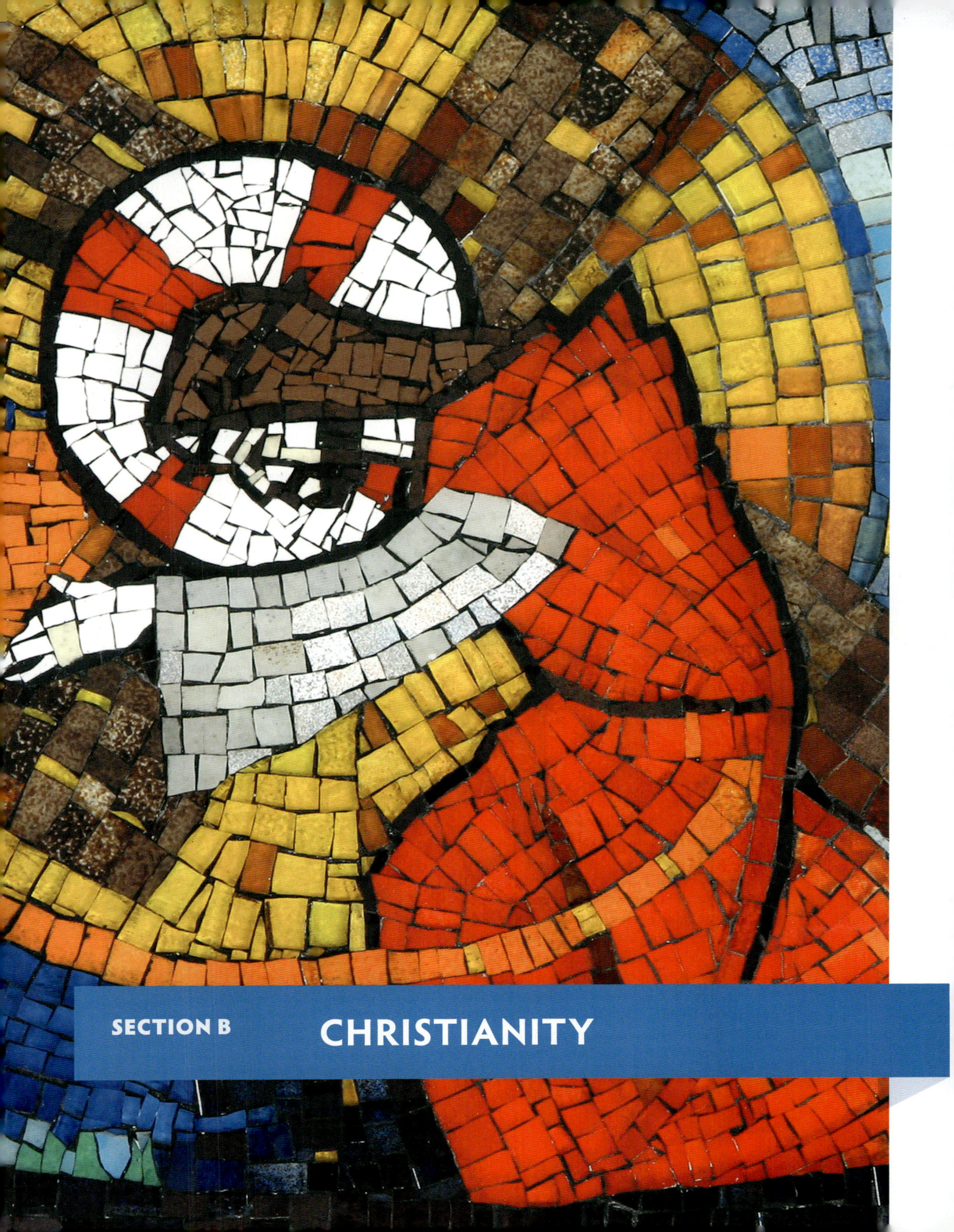

LESSON 15
SETTING THE SCENE

Objective: This lesson will explore the cultural and political context of Roman rule in Palestine during the time of Jesus.

OPENING CONVERSATION
The place, time and circumstances of a person's birth can have a major influence on how their life takes shape. What aspects of your early life do you think might have influenced the person you are today?

Setting the scene for the life of Jesus

Throughout history there have been several key figures who have had a profound effect on the world. No one single individual, however, has exerted more influence than Jesus, who lived in the first century in Palestine. But how do we know for certain that Jesus actually existed? Perhaps he is just a mythical character created simply to act as a moral compass for humanity?

A man by the name of Jesus did indeed live in Palestine in the first century. We know this to be the case, as objective (i.e. neutral) historical documents record the fact. The Jewish historian Josephus and the Roman historian Tacitus, both writing in the first century, mention Jesus. Josephus refers to Jesus as a 'wise man', a 'doer of wonderful works' and 'a teacher' who was condemned to death on a cross. Tacitus mentions 'Christus' as a person convicted by Pontius Pilate during the reign of Tiberius. Both sources confirm the fact that Jesus did indeed exist.

In order to appreciate the situation that Jesus found himself in during his life, it is essential to have studied the political, social and religious context of Palestine in the first century. Only then can we study Christology, the part of theology concerning Jesus Christ, in any meaningful depth. Let us try to imagine the world he inhabited two thousand years ago.

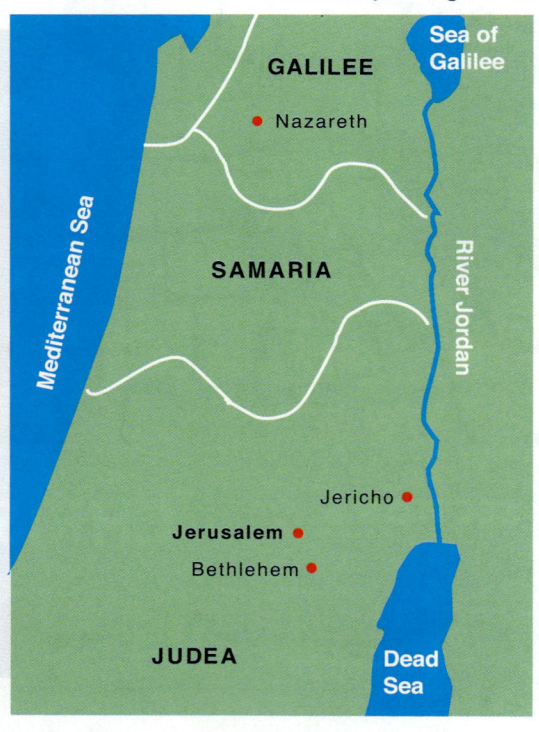

PALESTINE AT THE TIME OF JESUS

Palestine was split into three major provinces: Galilee in the north, Samaria in the centre and Judea in the south. Galilee was a relatively poor province where overcrowding and disease were rampant. Judea was quite the opposite: it was an affluent and vibrant province where the capital city of Jerusalem thrived. Jesus, as written about in the Bible, although born in Bethlehem in the province of Judea, was actually raised in the province of Galilee, in the small town of Nazareth, which was inhabited mainly by Jews. You may also recall how Jesus travelled on pilgrimage during the Jewish festival of the Passover from Galilee to the city of Jerusalem. Jews were required to travel to Jerusalem and offer sacrifices at the Temple three times a year.

SECTION B: CHRISTIANITY

REFLECT AND DISCUSS

Look closely at the map of Palestine from the time of Jesus. Find the locations mentioned so far. Can you identify any other locations associated with Jesus? With a partner, try to recall which events in the life of Jesus occurred at each location.

> *For thousands of years, the Jewish people were subject to foreign rule.*

THE CULTURAL CONTEXT

Jerusalem, a cosmopolitan and ethnically diverse city, was the main city of Palestine in the first century. Greek was the most common language spoken across the Roman Empire; however Jews of the time also used Hebrew, Aramaic and Latin. Aramaic was Jesus' natural spoken language. The shops and marketplace were the focal point of village life, while the synagogue acted as the central meeting place as well as being the seat of the local Jewish government.

Strict moral, social and religious rules formed the basis of Jewish family life. The husband was the spiritual and legal head of the household, responsible for sheltering and protecting the family. In first-century Palestine, women were considered second-class citizens, akin to slaves.

The economy of first-century Palestine was supported primarily by three areas: agriculture, trade and government building projects. There was a large disparity between the rich and poor. The upper class comprised of the temple priests, the middle class contained traders, merchants and craftsmen. The Pharisees, scribes and teachers would also have been included in the middle class. The lower class was made up of labourers, slaves and the unemployable (lepers, the blind, the crippled). The level of taxation imposed by the Roman government formed a heavy burden on the people. The tax collectors were local men who became outcasts and traitors amongst their society.

THE POLITICAL CONTEXT

For thousands of years, the Jewish people had been subject to foreign rule (Egyptian, Syrian, Babylonian, Persian, Greek) with only short periods of autonomy. During Jesus' lifetime the country found itself under foreign rule once again when the Romans arrived in 63 BCE. As a Palestinian Jew, Jesus would have been well aware of the many waves of foreign invasion that sought to conquer the Jewish people through the ages.

The Old City of Jerusalem

LESSON 15 — SETTING THE SCENE

HEROD THE GREAT

By the time of Jesus' birth sixty years after their arrival, Rome had already established a two-tiered system of government consisting of Roman overseers and Jewish leaders who exercised control in the name of Rome. It was their policy to appoint native rulers where possible in their colonies. Consequently, in order to keep the Jews satisfied, a native, Herod the Great, was made king of the Jews. After word reached him of the prophecy that a baby born in Bethlehem was to become 'king of the Jews', he ordered the execution of all baby boys aged two years and under living in Bethlehem and its surrounding area.

PONTIUS PILATE

Whilst Rome appointed native Jewish leaders, they simultaneously assigned Roman officials in Palestine to ensure that the occupied country was adhering to Roman ideology in a peaceful fashion. Appearing in all four Gospels, Pilate was the fifth prefect (i.e. magistrate) of the Roman province of Judea from 26–36 CE. The primary function of a prefect was a military one, but as a representative of the empire, Pilate would have been responsible for the collection of imperial taxes as well as having limited judicial functions. In the Gospel according to Matthew, Pilate washes his hands of Jesus and reluctantly sends him to his death.

The Roman historian Tacitus

ROMAN RULE IN PALESTINE

In general, Roman rule was quite enlightened and conquered peoples were allowed a large measure of self-governance and a freedom to practice their own customs and religion. The Jews were allowed to observe their ancient worship of God in the temple and synagogue and to observe their feasts and festivals.

Nevertheless, the potential for war existed at all times. It might take only one small incident from either an officer or a member of the public to incite violent conflict. Both the Jewish leaders and Roman leaders were acutely aware of this and used the forces at their command to ensure no such small spark ignited. According to historians, constant fear of unrest was a critical factor in Rome's response to Jesus' call for a restoration of the kingdom. The 'kingdom' Jesus referred to, however, was not a political one. Ironically, Jesus had no interest in politics. This tense situation was to persist for forty years after the death of Jesus and resulted in the Great Jewish Revolt of 66–70 CE.

OVER TO YOU

- Two historians have written about Jesus. Name them.
- There were three major provinces in Palestine at the time of Jesus. What were they?
- At the time of Jesus, which country was in control of Palestine?

RESEARCH PROJECT

Research the political and religious situation in Israel today. Present your findings in the next class.

YOU WILL FIND ADDITIONAL INFORMATION ON WWW.SEEKANDFIND.IE

SUMMARY

- In addition to the Gospels, two historical documents record the fact that a man by the name of Jesus existed in first-century Palestine: one was written by a Jewish historian, Josephus, the other by a Roman historian, Tacitus.
- Palestine during the time of Jesus was a place in great turmoil. During the first century it found itself under foreign rule once again, on this occasion by the Romans.
- Herod the Great and Pontius Pilate were two political leaders who affected the life of Jesus.
- The tense situation that existed in Palestine was to continue for forty years after the death of Jesus and resulted in the Great Jewish Revolt of 66 CE.

LESSON 15 — SETTING THE SCENE

LESSON 16
RELIGIOUS GROUPS IN FIRST-CENTURY PALESTINE

Objective: This lesson will describe the religious authority and groups in Palestine at the time of Jesus.

OPENING ACTIVITY
With a partner, try to recall the main religious groups in first-century Palestine that you covered in your Junior Cycle. Try to list three points of information about each group.

The religious context
It is important to remember whilst reading through this lesson that Jesus did not live or die a Christian. Jesus was a Jew. The Jews, also known as the Jewish people, are a nation and an ethnic group that originated in the Ancient Near East. Hebrew is considered to be the language of the Jewish people. Not alone did the Roman occupation have political ramifications for the Jews, it had religious consequences also.

In order to understand the situation Jesus faced during Holy Week in Jerusalem, we must first look at the key religious groups and the religious authority of the time. Some of them played a crucial part in the events leading up to Jesus' crucifixion.

THE SANHEDRIN
Although the Jews were under no illusion that they were under Roman rule, they were permitted a certain degree of self-governance. Despite the fact that the Romans ruled Palestine at the time of Jesus, the Jews believed that it was God and not Caesar, the Roman emperor of the time, who ruled their people. Realising the importance religion played in the lives of the Jewish people, the Romans commanded and obtained the loyal support of the Jewish Sanhedrin in governing Palestine. The Hebrew word 'Sanhedrin' means 'to sit together'. The Sanhedrin was a religious council composed of high priests. It served as both the ruling council of the Jewish religion and its highest court of law. In 57 BCE, five regional Sanhedrin were set up by the Romans to regulate the internal affairs of the Jews. They convened on an ad hoc basis and their powers varied depending on Roman policy. The Sanhedrin's members divided into two rival groups: the Sadducees and the Pharisees, and each claimed to uphold the valid morals of the Jewish religion. Both groups collectively formed a council of seventy elders from whom a high priest was elected to direct the Sanhedrin's activities. The Sanhedrin operated as a court of law for Jews, punished Jews who failed to obey the Jewish religious laws and had its own Temple guards to maintain order. It was before the Jerusalem Sanhedrin that Jesus was tried after he had been arrested in the Garden of Gethsemane.

SECTION B: CHRISTIANITY

THE HIGH PRIEST

The High Priest chaired the Sanhedrin and acted as a supreme judicial body. The High Priesthood was a hereditary office. Hence, the Temple, until it was destroyed, remained in the control of one family for most of the first century. The Temple was the place where offerings described in the course of the Hebrew Scriptures were carried out, including daily morning and afternoon offerings with special offerings on Sabbath and Jewish holidays.

The Romans considered the High Priesthood to be a political office. The primary function of the High Priest was to collect taxes and convince the Romans not to interfere with the Temple by maintaining stability and ensuring that the Jews did not rebel. The Jews, on the other hand, considered the role of the High Priest to be a religious office. According to the Hebrew Scriptures, the High Priest supervised the Temple and Temple sacrifices. Caiaphas was the High Priest in power at the time of Jesus' trial. As the High Priest did not have power to condemn anyone to death, Caiaphas referred Jesus on to Pontius Pilate, as only a Roman overseer could sanction an execution.

THE SADDUCEES

The Sadducees were the great pragmatists of the day. As wealthy lay-nobles, priests and aristocrats, they sought to conserve their wealth and power through an attempt at a compromise with Rome. Most of the members of the Sanhedrin were from the Sadducee group. As the most powerful Jews, rather than spend their time speculating on the life-to-come, they were much more concerned with present-day affairs. In the Gospels, it is evidently the Sadducees who are the main opponents of Jesus at the time of his trial and death. They believed that Jesus' radical brand of religion threatened their power and status.

THE PHARISEES

The Pharisees were in many ways the idealists of Jewish society. Most of the Scribes (the 'theologians' of the day) were Pharisees. The Pharisees sought to live a life of spiritual purity by a meticulous following of the Torah (the Jewish law consisting of the first five books of the Hebrew Scriptures: the books of Genesis, Exodus, Leviticus, Numbers and Deuteronomy). They did not believe in compromise with the Romans (like the Sadducees did) nor in revolutionary activity (like the Zealots did). Many Pharisees were highly committed and deeply spiritual people. They believed that the only way to ensure the survival of the chosen people of God was through the strict observance of the Law of Moses.

Because of this they were easily recognisable: for example, keeping holy the Sabbath was a very important fundamental law rigorously upheld by the Pharisees. Primarily scholars and educators, the Pharisees were politically astute and well studied, and taught and worshipped in their own way. Although popular and well respected, the Pharisees had no power. They debated new ways in which Jews could view the law of the Torah. Unlike the Sadducees, the Pharisees believed in the concept of the resurrection of the dead in a future messianic age.

THE ESSENES

The Essenes were a Jewish religious group that thrived from the second century BCE to the first century CE. They were fewer in number than the Pharisees and the Sadducees and were characterised by their withdrawal from the world. They lived in monastic-type communities because they believed that the only way to be faithful to God was to withdraw from the world with all its imperfections and devote their lives to prayer and contemplation. They also practiced poverty and abstinence. The Essenes have gained prominence in recent times as a result of the discovery of extensive religious documents known as the Dead Sea Scrolls, commonly believed to have been their library. The Dead Sea Scrolls are a collection of 972 texts from the Hebrew Bible and other biblical documents found between 1947 and 1956 at Qumran, which is located on the northwest shore of the Dead Sea. These texts are considered to be incredibly important as they are the oldest known surviving copies of biblical documents. They are written on parchment and papyrus in Hebrew, Aramaic and Greek.

THE ZEALOTS

The Zealots were a group founded in the year 6 CE. They were a radical, militant group who believed it was their duty to oppose the presence of the Romans and expel them by force of arms. The Zealots anticipated a political king who would banish the Romans through force and restore Israel to the chosen people. The movement arose out of the inherent situation of societal and political injustice, with the Zealots appealing in particular to those who suffered most under Roman rule, especially in relation to the payment of taxes. Most notably, the Zealots led the unsuccessful Great Jewish Revolt of 66–70 CE.

Jesus and the Pharisees, fresco from San Marco Church, Milan

Ruins in Masada with the Dead Sea in the background, Israel

OVER TO YOU

- What does the Hebrew word 'Sanhedrin' mean?
- What was the name of the High Priest who was in power during the trial of Jesus?
- Which religious group was said to have been the 'idealists of Jewish society' in first-century Palestine?
- Why were the Pharisees easily recognisable?
- The Essenes have become more widely known in recent years as a result of the discovery of what religious documents?
- What was the aim of the Zealots?

GROUP WORK

Dividing into four groups, imagine each group represents a different religious group in first-century Palestine: Sadducees, Pharisees, Essenes or Zealots. Write a short speech justifying your beliefs and giving your opinion on Roman occupation. Share your speech with the other groups and try to convince them to join your religious group.

SUMMARY

- The Sanhedrin was effectively a religious council that existed during the life of Jesus.
- The High Priest chaired the Sanhedrin.
- The Sadducees were wealthy nobles, priests and aristocrats who sought a compromise with Rome.
- The Pharisees sought to live a life of spiritual purity by following the laws of the Torah.
- The Essenes were monastic communities said to have lived throughout Judea.
- The Zealots sought people in Judea to rebel against the Roman Empire and expel it from the Holy Land.

LESSON 16 — RELIGIOUS GROUPS IN FIRST-CENTURY PALESTINE

LESSON 17
JESUS THE MESSIAH

Objective: This lesson will explain different expectations of the Messiah at the time of Jesus and will explore other names and titles for Jesus.

OPENING CONVERSATION
Recall a time in your life where you waited anxiously for something that you wanted, something that you imagined would make your life better or make you happier. What was it like waiting and anticipating? What was it like when it finally arrived or happened? Was it what you expected?

Messianic expectation

To fully comprehend the essence of Jesus' teachings and the effect they would have had on the people he preached to, we must first understand the key beliefs held by Jewish people in the first century. Throughout the Old Testament the ancient people of Israel knew that some things were not as they ought to be with the human condition: wars and violence, injustice and discrimination, hatred and resentment, lying and stealing, adultery and dishonesty – the list goes on. What could be their hope against this backdrop? The foundation of the hope of God's people was their belief in God's faithfulness to his twofold promise of forgiveness for their sins and of setting them free from the consequences of their sins. This was the foundation of their expectation of a Messiah, or 'Anointed One', whom we now know is Jesus the Christ. Within this context we understand the identity and mission of Jesus.

By the time of Jesus' birth, Jewish history had for centuries taught that a Messiah would herald a new era of global peace. The Jews believed that the Messiah would come to save them from whichever political power was occupying their land at the time. As we have studied in a previous lesson, Rome was the political force in control of the Holy Land at the time of Jesus. Various religious and social groups within Judaism at the time of Jesus understood the coming of the Messiah differently. There were primarily three different expectations of the Messiah at the time: Davidic, Prophetic and Priestly.

DAVIDIC MESSIAH
There was a general expectation among Jewish people at the time that the Messiah would be a new King David, who would deliver Israel from foreign rule and restore the former glories of the time of King David's rule. He would be a leader who would guide them into battle against foreign forces occupying Palestine. One example of this expectation can be seen in the Bible when, subsequent to Jesus' birth, three wise men arrive in Bethlehem with gifts to welcome the Messiah into the world. They believed that Jesus

was the political leader they had been waiting for to rule over the kingdom of Israel.

PROPHETIC MESSIAH

The Zealots looked forward to a Messiah whom God would send to expel the Romans from Palestine and restore the Kingdom of God (i.e. the Holy Land) to the chosen people (i.e. the Israelites). Some of the Apostles (e.g. Simon) were Zealots and initially followed Jesus in the belief that he would lead them in a violent revolution and liberate them from oppression just as Moses had freed the Israelites from slavery in Egypt.

PRIESTLY MESSIAH

The Essenes, the monastic community associated with the Dead Sea Scrolls, also looked forward to the coming of the Messiah. Their yearning was directed not towards an earthly Messiah but towards a heavenly one, who would bring a heavenly kingdom. The Essenes hoped the Messiah would find people who were prepared to re-establish the true priesthood and kingship of David and to battle the forces of spiritual darkness. Their mission was to prepare the way for the Messiah and to bring spiritual light to the world.

MESSIANIC REFERENCES IN THE BIBLE

The concept of the Messiah is frequently referred to in both the Old and New Testaments of the Bible. The Hebrew word for 'anointed one' is *Messiah*, which is translated *Christos* in Greek and Christ in English. The ancient Israelites held an anointing ritual to instal those who had been chosen for a special work of service or mission. They would pour sacred oil over these 'chosen ones', or anoint them, to signify that they had been chosen, filled with the spirit of God and set aside for this special work. Among those anointed were priests and kings and sometimes prophets. Within this context, God promised to send 'the Anointed One', the Christ. Hence the title 'Christ' names and identifies Jesus to be the Anointed One whom God sent to fulfil his promises. Luke proclaims, 'God anointed Jesus of Nazareth with the Holy Spirit and with power' (Acts 10:38). Jesus' mandate and mission came directly from God: he was sent to restore the holiness and justice that was central to the original divine plan of Creation.

In the Gospel of Mark, Peter proclaims Jesus outright as the Messiah. Similarly, in John 1:41 we are informed that after meeting Jesus, Andrew found his brother Simon and said to him, 'We have found the Messiah'. We must keep in mind that Jesus was fully aware of the messianic expectations that his followers anticipated of him. He knew that some expected him to lead them into battle and to set up and rule over an independent Jewish kingdom of Israel once again. However, Jesus on several occasions pointed to the fact that he was not interested in violence of any kind. He encouraged his followers to turn the other cheek, to love their neighbours as they loved themselves and to forgive their enemies.

THINK IT THROUGH
▶ Can you think of any examples from the life of Jesus where he showed that he was not interested in violence or leading people into battle?

'Jesus was fully divine and fully human, true God and true man.

What's in a name?

In the Bible and biblical times, the name of a person often captured the essence of that person's role in the saving plan of God. The connection between a person's name and who they were was inseparable. With that in mind, let us review some other key names or titles for Jesus.

LORD

The people of ancient Israel considered the divine name YHWH that God revealed to Moses to be so sacred it was unspeakable, not to be uttered by any person. In its place they used the name 'Lord'. Within this context we can see the significance of the early Church addressing and naming Jesus 'Lord', and Jesus using the divine name to identify himself (cf. Matthew 7:21; 22:41-46). The *Catechism of the Catholic Church* sums up the apostolic faith of the Church:

> By attributing to Jesus the divine title 'Lord', the … Church … affirm[s] from the beginning that the power, honour and glory due to God the Father are due also to Jesus. (CCC, 449)

SON OF MAN

Jesus used the title 'Son of Man' to identify himself and his mission in the four accounts of the Gospel (thirty times in St Matthew, fourteen times in St Mark, twenty-five times in St Luke and twelve times in St John). Rooted in the Scriptures of ancient Israel, most especially the books of Ezekiel and Daniel, the term 'Son of Man' refers to the 'ideal human', the one most faithful to YHWH.

SON OF GOD

The term 'Son of God' was used in a variety of ways by the sacred writers of the Scriptures, sometimes to describe a person known and revered as holy, who obeyed God's will and God's law. In short, a 'son of God' was a person steadfastly loyal and faithful in his love for God and all that God required. Such a 'son of God' prefigured the 'Son of God', who would come and live among us. Jesus revealed himself to be uniquely the Son of God: 'he is the only Son of the Father (cf. Jn 1:14, 18; 3:16, 18); he is God himself (cf. Jn 1:1)' (CCC, 454), and he and the Father are one (cf. Jn 14:11; 17:11). So Jesus could say to his disciples, 'No one knows the Father except the Son and anyone to whom the Son chooses to reveal him' (Mt 11:27).

Jesus was fully divine and fully human, true God and true man. Jesus was not a human person with God dwelling inside of him; he was a divine person in whom the divine nature and a human nature were united. We will look at this in more detail in the next lesson.

OVER TO YOU
▶ Which of the above titles of Jesus do you prefer, and why?

SUMMARY

- For centuries, Jewish history had taught that a Messiah, anointed by God, would come to bring a new era of peace to the Jewish people.
- There were three different expectations of the Messiah at the time of Jesus: Davidic, Prophetic and Priestly.
- Jesus was fully aware of the messianic expectations the Jewish people had of him at the time.
- There are a number of titles for Jesus that each reveal something about his identity, for example Christ/Messiah, Lord, Son of Man and Son of God.

LESSON 18
FULLY HUMAN, FULLY DIVINE

Objective: This lesson will explore the mystery of the Incarnation — that God took on human nature without giving up his divinity.

OPENING CONVERSATION

Can you think of any people that have 'secret identities' — from novels and movies, from folktales, comics or real life? How and when was their identity revealed?

God became one of us

There is often more to things than meets the eye. This was true of Jesus — a wandering Jewish preacher and teacher and a doer of amazing deeds, whom many misunderstood. The Gospels tell us that even Jesus' closest disciples only came to know him and the true nature of his identity and mission over time and gradually. To some of his enemies, Jesus was a false prophet; to others he was a blasphemer and a threat to Judaism. Jesus was not a superhero, nor did he have 'magical' powers. Jesus' power is the very power of God. This is why he could heal; teach with 'authority'; cast out fear and oppression; and overcome hatred and chaos. By his own dying and rising, he even had the power to overcome death. As his story unfolded his true identity emerged.

God has revealed that God the Son became one of us. This Mystery of Faith, the Incarnation, is the most unique event in human history and summarises the very heart of Christian faith — God became man in Jesus without giving up his divinity. Almighty God became a carpenter, learned and spoke a language, had a family history and practiced the customs of his religion and culture. He was like us, like you, in all things but sin.

Through the mystery of the Incarnation, God bridged the gap between humanity and divinity, between humankind and God. The Son of God took on flesh (a human nature) without losing his divinity (the divine nature). This does not mean that Jesus Christ is part God and part man. The Son of God, the Second Person of the Trinity, became truly man while remaining truly God. Jesus possesses two natures, one divine nature and one human nature, united in one divine Person, the Son of God. The Church names the mystery of the union of the divine nature and human nature in the one divine Person, Jesus, the 'hypostatic union'.

THE SEVEN 'I AM' STATEMENTS OF JESUS

John's Gospel uses the seven 'I am' statements to teach that Jesus is divine, truly God. These two words, 'I am', have their roots in the Book of Exodus when God reveals his identity, his name, to Moses. When Moses asks the voice in the burning bush, 'If I come to the Israelites and say to them, "The God of your ancestors has sent me to you," and they ask me, "What is his name?" what shall I say to them?', God replies, 'I am who I am … Thus you shall say to the Israelites, "I am has sent me to you"' (Ex 3:13-14). These words had a very clear meaning for the audience for whom John's Gospel was written, namely, Jews who came to believe in Jesus. How significant it is, then, that Jesus so often echoes this divine name and applies it to himself.

The seven 'I am' statements of Jesus are included in and are part of longer sermons, or discourses, of Jesus. They are: 'I am the bread of life' (Jn 6:35); 'I am the light of the world' (Jn 8:12); 'I am the gate' (Jn 10:9); 'I am the good shepherd' (Jn 10:11); 'I am the resurrection and the life' (Jn 11:25); 'I am the way, and the truth, and the life' (Jn 14:6); and 'I am the vine' (Jn 15:5).

JOURNAL

Look up the 'I am' statements in the Bible. Select the one that appeals to you the most. Write it out and decorate it.

Why did God take on human nature?

The question 'Why did God become man?' has been asked since the earliest days of the Church. Our human understanding of the Incarnation necessarily continues to grow, since we are dealing with *ultimate mystery* – something we could never have known on our own unless God revealed it to us. The *Catechism of the Catholic Church* sums up in the following manner the reasons why the Son of God took on 'flesh' in the Incarnation:

1. '*For us men and for our salvation* he came down from heaven' (Nicene Creed; CCC, 456)
2. 'The Word became flesh for us *in order to save us by reconciling us with God*' (CCC, 457)
3. 'The Word became flesh *so that thus we might know God's love*' (CCC, 458)
4. 'The Word became flesh *to be our model of holiness*' (CCC, 459)
5. 'The Word became flesh *to make us "partakers of the divine nature"*' (CCC, 460, quoting 2 Pt 1:4).

1. Jesus is the Saviour, the One who makes us 'safe' (from the Latin *salvare*, meaning 'to make safe or healthy') from all powers of evil. God the Father sent the Son to be one of us because humanity needed to be saved. Jesus said of himself, 'I am the light of the world. Whoever follows me will never walk in darkness but will have the light of life' (Jn 8:12); and 'I came that they may have life, and have it abundantly' (Jn 10:10). The 'they' that Jesus refers to here is not only the people who preceded him, and his contemporaries, it also includes us, right here, right now, and all people of all times.

2. Throughout history, humanity continued, many times and over and over again, to turn away from God's love and to sin. God's response to his people's sin is the constant story of God faithfully offering his forgiveness and reconciliation. The Son of God, our Redeemer, became man 'to set us free from sin, and make us sharers in God's mercy and reconcile us with God'.

3. You have more than likely seen 'John 3:16', the classic statement of Jesus as the expression of God's love, displayed on banners and billboards everywhere. John 3:16 reads: 'For God so loved the world that he gave his only Son, so that everyone who believes in him may not perish but may have eternal life.' Through the Incarnation and in the public life of Jesus we 'see in flesh and blood' and catch a glimpse of the depth and breadth of God's love at work in the world.

4. The call to holiness is the call to live as God first created us to live and, in so doing, to become the best people we can be. We are to be holy because God is holy. Jesus modelled how we are to live according to that call. Jesus is the 'way' of holiness. He said, 'I am the way, and the truth, and the life' (Jn 14:6). Jesus, the Holy One of God, succinctly summarised that 'way', commanding his disciples to 'love one another as I have loved you' (Jn 15:12).

5. Saint Athanasius, the great theologian of the Council of Nicaea and renowned Doctor of the Church, summarised the purpose of the Incarnation this way: 'The only-begotten Son of God, wanting to make us sharers in his divinity, assumed our nature, so that he, made man, might make men gods.' This is an amazing statement of faith; yet if we remember the first accounts of Creation, it should not surprise us. God created us in the divine image. When we do our best to live the 'way' of Jesus, we are closest to what is divine. We demonstrate to ourselves and to others who we are and who we are called to be – images of the living God.

REFLECT AND DISCUSS
The following story can help us to reflect upon why God became man in Jesus.

PARABLE OF THE BIRDS

There was a man who looked upon Christmas as a lot of humbug. He wasn't a Scrooge. He was a kind and decent person, generous to his family, upright in all his dealings with other people. But he didn't believe all that stuff about Incarnation. And he was too honest to pretend that he did. 'I am truly sorry to distress you,' he told his wife, who was a faithful churchgoer, 'but I simply cannot understand this claim that God becomes human. It doesn't make any sense to me.'

On Christmas Eve his wife and children went to church for the midnight service. He declined to accompany them. 'I'd feel like a hypocrite,' he explained, 'I'd rather stay at home. But I'll wait up for you.'

Shortly after his family drove away in the car, snow began to fall. He went to the window and watched the flurries getting heavier and heavier. 'If we must have Christmas,' he thought, 'it's nice to have a white one.' He went back to his chair by the fireside and began to read his newspaper.

A few minutes later he was startled by a thudding sound. It was quickly followed by another, then another.

He thought that someone must be throwing snowballs at his living room window. When he went to the front door to investigate, he found a flock of birds huddled miserably in the snow. They had been caught in the storm and in a desperate search for shelter had tried to fly through his window. 'I can't let these poor creatures lie there and freeze,' he thought. 'But how can I help them?' Then he remembered the barn where the children's pony was stabled. It would provide a warm shelter.

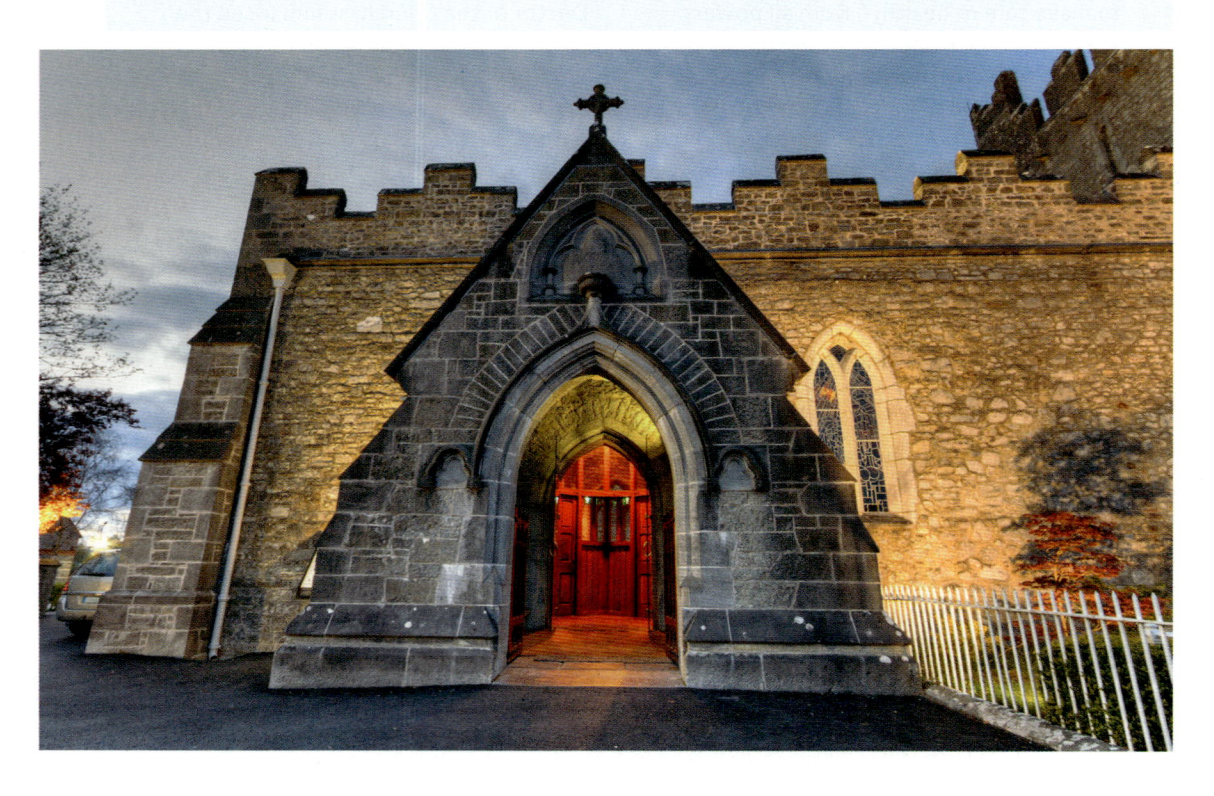

He put on his coat and tramped through the deepening snow to the barn. He opened the door wide and turned on a light. But the birds didn't come in. 'Food will lure them in,' he thought. So he hurried back to the house for bread crumbs, which he sprinkled on the snow to make a trail into the barn. To his dismay, the birds ignored the bread crumbs and continued to flop around helplessly in the snow. He tried shooing them into the barn by walking around and waving his arms. They scattered in every direction – except into the warm, lighted barn.

'They find me a strange and terrifying creature,' he said to himself, 'and I can't seem to think of any way to let them know they can trust me. If only I could be a bird myself for a few minutes, perhaps I could lead them to safety. …' Just at that moment the church bells began to ring. He stood silent for a while, listening to the bells pealing the glad tidings of Christmas. Then he sank to his knees in the snow. 'Now I understand,' he whispered. 'Now I see why You had to do it.'

- What do you think the man meant when he said, 'Now I see why You had to do it'?
- What does this story add to your understanding of the Christmas story?
- Why do you think God became human?

SUMMARY

- The Incarnation means that without losing his divine nature, God assumed human nature.
- Jesus, the only Son of God and the only Son of the Virgin Mary, was fully divine and fully human, true God and true man.
- This mystery is called the 'hypostatic union'.
- John's Gospel uses the seven 'I am' statements to teach that Jesus is divine, truly God.
- The *Catechism of the Catholic Church* sums up in the following manner the reasons why the Son of God took on 'flesh' in the Incarnation:

  » '*For us men and for our salvation* he came down from heaven' (Nicene Creed; CCC, 456)
  » 'The Word became flesh for us *in order to save us by reconciling us with God*' (CCC, 457)
  » 'The Word became flesh *so that thus we might know God's love*' (CCC, 458)
  » 'The Word became flesh *to be our model of holiness*' (CCC, 459)
  » 'The Word became flesh *to make us "partakers of the divine nature"*' (CCC, 460, quoting 2 Pt 1:4).

LESSON 18 – FULLY HUMAN, FULLY DIVINE

LESSON 19
THE ANNUNCIATION

Objective: This lesson will define the Annunciation and look at the roles of Mary and Joseph in the life of Jesus.

OPENING ACTIVITY

How much do you know about the Blessed Virgin Mary? With a partner, see how many answers you can come up with:

- How many prayers to Mary can you name?
- How many titles for Mary can you name?
- How many feast days associated with Mary can you name?
- How many places of pilgrimage associated with Mary can you name?

The Annunciation

The story of Jesus' life on earth began nine months before his birth, at his conception in Mary's womb. There would be no Christmas without Mary, a young Jewish woman who said 'Yes' to what must be the strangest and most challenging request in human history. The Latin word *annuntiare*, giving us 'Annunciation', means 'announcement'. Luke 1:26-38 is the account of the Annunciation – the announcement to Mary that God had chosen her to be mother of the Son of God, whom she was to name Jesus. You have read and listened to the telling of this story many times; and yet its meaning is inexhaustible and our coming to grasp that meaning is a lifelong task.

Read Luke's account of the Annunciation again now, slowly, dwelling on every word, imagining the scene:

> In the sixth month the angel Gabriel was sent by God to a town in Galilee called Nazareth, to a virgin engaged to a man whose name was Joseph, of the house of David. The virgin's name was Mary. And he came to her and said, 'Greetings, favoured one! The Lord is with you.' But she was much perplexed by his words and pondered what sort of greeting this might be. The angel said to her, 'Do not be afraid, Mary, for you have found favour with God. And now, you will conceive in your womb and bear a son, and you will name him Jesus. He will be great, and will be called the Son of the Most High, and the Lord God will give to him the throne of his ancestor David. He will reign over the house of Jacob forever, and of his kingdom there will be no end.' Mary said to the angel, 'How can this be, since I am a virgin?' The angel said to her, 'The Holy Spirit will come upon you, and the power of the Most High will overshadow you; therefore the child to be born will be holy; he will be called Son of God. And now, your relative Elizabeth in her old age has also conceived a son; and this is the sixth month for her who was said to be barren. For nothing will be impossible with God.' Then Mary said, 'Here am I, the servant of the Lord; let it be with me according to your word.' Then the angel departed from her. (Lk 1:26-38)

OVER TO YOU

▶ Share any words or phrases that stood out for you. Why did they, and what do they mean?
▶ What do you imagine was going on in Mary's head and heart as she listened to the angel?
▶ How do you think you would have responded if you were Mary?

REFLECT AND DISCUSS

Look at this painting of the Annunciation by Henry Ossawa Tanner (1859–1937). What do you think the artist conveys about Mary.

The Annunciation by Henry Ossawa Tanner (1859)

MARY'S 'YES'

Mary's first reaction to the angel was to be 'much perplexed'. Her confusion as to why God had chosen her is very understandable. She was a virgin and betrothed (engaged) but not yet married to Joseph. We can only imagine the questions swirling around in Mary's head as the angel told her why God had chosen her. While her hope, and 'the hope of Israel' (Acts 28:20), for the Messiah was being fulfilled, Mary's faith must surely have been tested. Could God really have the power to create life within her?

Mary's words of response were a sign of her deep trust in God: 'Here am I, the servant of the Lord; let it be with me according to your word' (Lk 1:38). These were the words of a brave, strong and faith-filled woman, who knew the implications of being pregnant before she was married. Some of her family, friends and others would question her fidelity to God's Law and hold her in disgrace. Yet Mary said 'Yes'.

LESSON 19 — THE ANNUNCIATION

JOSEPH'S SIDE OF THE STORY

Now we will consider the events of the Annunciation as experienced by Joseph. While Luke's account of the Annunciation focuses on Mary, Matthew's account tells Joseph's side of the story. Read it slowly and carefully:

> Now the birth of Jesus the Messiah took place in this way. When his mother Mary had been engaged to Joseph, but before they lived together, she was found to be with child from the Holy Spirit. Her husband Joseph, being a righteous man and unwilling to expose her to public disgrace, planned to dismiss her quietly. But just when he had resolved to do this, an angel of the Lord appeared to him in a dream and said, 'Joseph, son of David, do not be afraid to take Mary as your wife, for the child conceived in her is from the Holy Spirit. She will bear a son, and you are to name him Jesus, for he will save his people from their sins.' (Mt 1:18-21)

Joseph could simply have dismissed this as 'only a dream'. But clearly, he, like Mary, was a person of great faith. And he 'did as the angel of the Lord commanded him; he took her as his wife' (Mt 1:24).

THINK IT THROUGH

- Share any words or phrases that stood out for you. Why did they stand out and what do they mean?
- What do you imagine was going on in Joseph's head and heart as he listened to the angel?
- From reading Matthew's account of the Annunciation, what kind of person do you think Joseph was? Explain your answer.
- How do you think you would have responded if you were Joseph?

RESEARCH PROJECT

Saint Joseph has been an inspiration to many and is perhaps one of the most beloved saints among Catholics today. But how much do we really know about Joseph? His appearance in the Bible is relatively brief and rather obscure. Create a profile of St Joseph, including what we learn about him in the Bible, what the Catholic Church says about him, his feast day and popular prayers and devotion to St Joseph today.

YOU WILL FIND ADDITIONAL INFORMATION ON WWW.SEEKANDFIND.IE

JOURNAL

The Hail Mary is the most popular of all the prayers in honour of Mary. Write the following lines into your journal and explain what they mean to you in light of today's lesson:

> Hail Mary,
> full of grace,
> the Lord is with you.
> Blessed are you among women
> and blessed is the fruit of your womb,
> Jesus.

SUMMARY

- The Latin word *annuntiare*, giving us 'Annunciation', means 'announcement'.
- Mary's words of response were a sign of her deep trust in God: 'Here am I, the servant of the Lord; let it be with me according to your word.'
- While Luke's account of the Annunciation focuses on Mary, Matthew's account tells Joseph's side of the story.

LESSON 20
ONE SOLITARY LIFE

Objective: This lesson will outline some of the main events in the life of Jesus.

OPENING ACTIVITY

You already know the storyline of Jesus' life very well, but it is worth recalling some of the high points of his life. Draw a timeline and on it mark in as many key events in Jesus' life as you can think of, beginning with his birth in Bethlehem and ending with his Resurrection.

When you have completed your timeline, read the following summary points about Jesus' life and see if you remembered all the events that are mentioned.

Early life

- After many years of waiting on the part of the people of ancient Israel, Jesus was born of the Virgin Mary by the power of the Holy Spirit; his birthplace – a stable in Bethlehem – already signified his solidarity with the poor and the marginalised.
- This was soon followed by the Epiphany – meaning 'manifestation' – when three wise men, also known as the Magi, came from the East bearing gifts, signifying that Jesus had come for the whole world.
- Jesus' circumcision and presentation in the Temple reminds us that Jesus was born, raised, lived and died as a good and faithful Jew.
- Herod feared that the 'newborn king of the Jews' would threaten his power, so he ordered the massacre of all children two years of age and under living in Bethlehem and its surrounding area. Mary and Joseph, warned of this pending massacre in a dream, fled into Egypt, and returned after the death of Herod to raise their child in the town of Nazareth.
- For the next thirty years, Jesus 'shared the condition of the vast majority of human beings: a daily life spent without evident greatness, a life of manual labour' (CCC, 531). We know nothing of his childhood except for the incident in Jerusalem at the age of twelve when 'After three days [Mary and Joseph] found him in the temple, sitting among the teachers, listening to them and asking them questions' (Lk 2:46).
- Luke ends the account of Mary and Joseph finding Jesus in the Temple with the statement, 'Then he went down with them and came to Nazareth, and was obedient to them. ... And Jesus increased in wisdom and in years, and in divine and human favour' (Lk 2:51-52).

THINK IT THROUGH

▶ Read Luke 2:41-52, the Boy Jesus in the Temple. What questions do you imagine Jesus as a twelve-year-old might have been asking the teachers?

Jesus' public ministry

» Jesus' public ministry began around the age of thirty when he left the family home and went to where John, the son of Elizabeth and Zechariah, was baptising people in the River Jordan. Though John was reluctant to baptise him, Jesus insisted and John agreed. Matthew concludes his account of the baptism of Jesus, '… just as [Jesus] came up from the water, suddenly the heavens were opened to him and he saw the Spirit of God descending like a dove and alighting on him. And a voice from heaven said, "This is my Son, the Beloved, with whom I am well pleased"' (Mt 3:16-17). This affirmation of the identity of Jesus by God the Father was echoed again at Jesus' Transfiguration in the presence of the disciples Peter, James and John. Luke tells us that they heard a voice from heaven say, 'This is my Son, my Chosen; listen to him' (Lk 9:35).

» According to John's account of the Gospel, Jesus was prompted by his mother Mary to perform his first miracle at the wedding feast at Cana (cf. John 2:1-12).

» According to Mark, Jesus' first great public proclamation was about the Kingdom of God. 'The time is fulfilled, and the kingdom of God has come near; repent, and believe in the good news' (Mk 1:15). The Kingdom, or Reign, of God was a key theme of Jesus' preaching. The purpose of his life on earth was that God's kingdom of fullness of life and salvation for all would triumph and that God's will would be done 'on earth as it is in heaven'.

» While 'everyone is called to enter the kingdom', Jesus had a special outreach to the poor and marginalised. Feeding the hungry and witnessing to God's love for them was clearly a central aspect of Jesus' public ministry. The miracle of Jesus multiplying loaves and fishes to feed the hungry is told in all four accounts of the Gospel and twice in Mark and Matthew – only the Resurrection is recounted more often.

» Throughout his public ministry, Jesus devoted much of his time to teaching people, mainly by parables, how to live for God's kingdom, or reign. He admonished and warned his disciples and others that simply stating one's faith or sweet-talking God would not be enough. To enter the Kingdom of God – here and hereafter – a person must live the faith they profess. He said, 'Not everyone who says to me, "Lord, Lord," will enter the kingdom of heaven, but only the one who does the will of my Father in heaven' (Mt 7:21).

» Jesus worked many miracles as wonderful signs of God's loving and saving presence at work in the world. Jesus' miracles were not for show but to bring people to faith in his Father and in him. 'So miracles strengthen faith in the One who does his Father's works; they bear witness that he is the Son of God' (CCC, 548).

» Jesus gathered a community of disciples around him, first the Twelve and then others, both women and men, who would commit to follow his 'way' and bring his Good News to others. He chose the Twelve to be the leaders of his disciples, the Church. He warned them not to 'lord it over' others but to be servants, as he had shown himself to be during his life and especially when he washed his disciples' feet at the Last Supper.

OVER TO YOU

- Choose one event from Jesus' public ministry and imagine 'being there' as the event unfolds. Write an account of what happened as if you were a journalist reporting for TV or radio at the time. Think of some good headlines to draw in your audience.

> ' *The Kingdom of God has come near; repent, and believe in the good news.*
>
> Mk 1:15

The final week

» Throughout his public ministry, Jesus was ever journeying toward Jerusalem – and his final destiny. Jesus himself said, 'It is impossible for a prophet to be killed outside of Jerusalem' (Lk 13:33). He entered the holy city riding on a donkey as the people spread palms before him and hailed him like a king. Palm Sunday of the Lord's Passion marks the beginning of Holy Week.

» The night before he died, Jesus assembled with his disciples for the Passover meal. There, anticipating his death the next day, Jesus instituted the Eucharist. In this sacrament he gave and gives us his own body and blood, to be constantly celebrated and received as 'a living sacrifice of praise' to God (Eucharistic Prayer IV).

» Jesus was crucified on the hill of Calvary, just outside the city of Jerusalem. The Fourth Gospel tells us that his mother and the disciple whom he loved and other faithful women disciples stood at the foot of the cross witnessing his death. We are also told that on either side of Jesus were two thieves and that some of the chief priests and scribes mocked him, saying, 'He saved others; he cannot save himself' (Mk 15:31).

» The crucifixion and burial might have been the end, but for the Resurrection when Jesus 'rose again on the third day in accordance with the Scriptures' (Nicene Creed).

LESSON 20 – ONE SOLITARY LIFE

REFLECT AND DISCUSS

Here is how one man, Dr James Allen Francis, described the life of Jesus. He wrote this poem in 1926.

'ONE SOLITARY LIFE'

He was born in an obscure village,
the child of a peasant woman.
He grew up in another obscure village
where he worked in a carpenter shop
until he was thirty.

He never wrote a book.
He never held an office.
He never went to college.
He never visited a big city.
He never travelled more than two hundred miles
from the place where he was born.
He did none of the things
usually associated with greatness.
He had no credentials but himself.

He was only thirty-three.
His friends ran away.
One of them denied him.
He was turned over to his enemies
and went through the mockery of a trial.
He was nailed to a cross between two
    thieves.
While dying, his executioners gambled for
    his clothing,
the only property he had on earth.

When he was dead
he was laid in a borrowed grave
through the pity of a friend.

Nineteen centuries have come and gone
and today Jesus is the central figure of the
    human race
and the leader of mankind's progress.
All the armies that have ever marched,
all the navies that have ever sailed,
all the parliaments that have ever sat,
all the kings that ever reigned put together
have not affected the life of mankind on earth
as powerfully as that one solitary life.

- What do you think the author wanted to convey most of all about Jesus?
- Why do you think Jesus had such an impact, given that he did not have any of the trappings of wealth and status that we might expect an influential person to have?
- What is the most important thing that this poem says about Jesus?

SUMMARY

- We know very little about the early life of Jesus.
- Jesus' public ministry began when he was about thirty years old.
- Jesus devoted much of his time to teaching people, mainly by parables.
- Jesus worked many miracles as signs of God's loving and saving presence at work in the world.
- Jesus was crucified on the hill of Calvary but this was not the end.
- On the third day Jesus rose again in accordance with the Scriptures.

LESSON 21
THY KINGDOM COME

Objective: This lesson will take a closer look at what Jesus taught us about the Kingdom of God.

OPENING ACTIVITY
Recall what you can from the Junior Cycle course and what you have heard about the Kingdom of God before. Close your eyes and try to picture the Kingdom of God. What are five words or phrases that describe the Kingdom of God for you?

Kingdom of God

The phrase 'the Kingdom of God' occurs in the Gospel more than one hundred times. The Gospel or 'Good News' of the Kingdom of God was the heart and core of Jesus Christ's message. However, the theological concept of the Kingdom of God is a complex one. What did Jesus mean when he preached about the Kingdom of God? Jesus never offered an exact definition of the Kingdom of God but he made it clear that the kingdom he referred to was not a physical or political kingdom. According to Jesus, the Kingdom of God is within people. It is a kingdom that will be inherited by the righteous. It is a way of being in the world with others which will ultimately lead us to life forever with God in heaven. There are two elements to Jesus' theology of the Kingdom of God: the Kingdom of God on earth and the Kingdom of God in heaven.

Through his parables, Jesus taught his followers that the Kingdom of God was not a place but rather a renewed way of living. In his prayer the Our Father, Jesus looks forward to the coming of the kingdom: 'Thy Kingdom come, Thy will be done on earth as it is in heaven ...' In Mark's Gospel, Jesus begins his public ministry by announcing, 'The time is fulfilled, and the kingdom of God has come near; repent, and believe in the good news' (Mk 1:15). The words 'Kingdom of God' would have been taken to mean that the saving work of God had begun in Jesus. Jesus told his followers to listen to him and to reform their lives so that they would be received into the kingdom. He also taught them how to live in the kingdom. Jesus assured his followers that God's love would be with them at all times and that God's help would be available. Before he left them he promised to send the Holy Spirit to guide them. This same Holy Spirit is with us in the Church today. Because of God's saving work through the life, death and Resurrection of Jesus, it is possible for us with the grace of the spirit of Christ to 'repent' – to change our lives by turning away from sin and back toward God – and to live the Gospel as his disciples.

REFLECT AND DISCUSS
- Look up the following references in the Bible: Luke 11:20, Luke 17:21
- What do you learn about the Kingdom of God from these passages?
- What do these Bible accounts tell us about how Jesus wants us to live?

THE KINGDOM OF GOD IN THE PARABLES OF JESUS

Jesus used parables to teach his listeners about the Kingdom of God. Through these kingdom parables, by using everyday images and ordinary, everyday experiences, Jesus helped people to understand the true meaning of the Kingdom of God. He taught them about their need to accept God's invitation to change their lives and live for the kingdom. He explored with them who truly belonged to and would be welcomed into the kingdom.

One parable, the parable of the Great Dinner, used the image of a banquet or feast (cf. Luke 14:7-24). In this parable, which he addressed to the Pharisees, Jesus contrasts the Pharisees (those who thought they were invited to the feast and worthy of the kingdom promised by God) with those whom the Pharisees judged to be unworthy and 'not invited'. Imagine the Pharisees' reaction when Jesus concludes by having the master say, 'For I tell you, none of those who were invited will taste my dinner' (Lk 14:24). In short, all are invited to share in the Kingdom of God but not all will take up that invitation.

GROUP WORK
Working in small groups, write a modern-day parable based around a meal or party. Decide what message you want to give. Discuss who would be invited, who would turn up and what would be expected of the guests.

Look up the following passages and identify the parables in the Gospel of Matthew that involve feasts or banquets to get some ideas: Matthew 14:13-21; 15:32-39; 22:1-14; and 25:1-13.

Share your parable with the rest of the class.

THE GROWTH OF THE KINGDOM OF GOD

Jesus frequently discussed the theme of growth in his parables, especially of seeds and plants. Jesus' listeners would have comprised many farming folk, who knew all about seeds and harvests, bad weather and crop failure. They knew that progress comes slowly and that growth depended on carefully tending to the crop and waiting patiently until it is fully grown and ripe for harvesting. Similarly with the kingdom, it may seem to be progressing slowly, almost imperceptibly, but it is growing.

The Church has come to see this teaching as pointing, in part, to the activity of the Church on earth, preparing for the coming of the Kingdom of God in this world.

OVER TO YOU
- Create a poster to illustrate the growth of the Kingdom of God.
- Look up and read the following passages and identify the parables in the Gospel of Luke that involve growth and harvest to get some ideas: Luke 6:43-45, 8:4-15 and 13:6-9, 18-19.

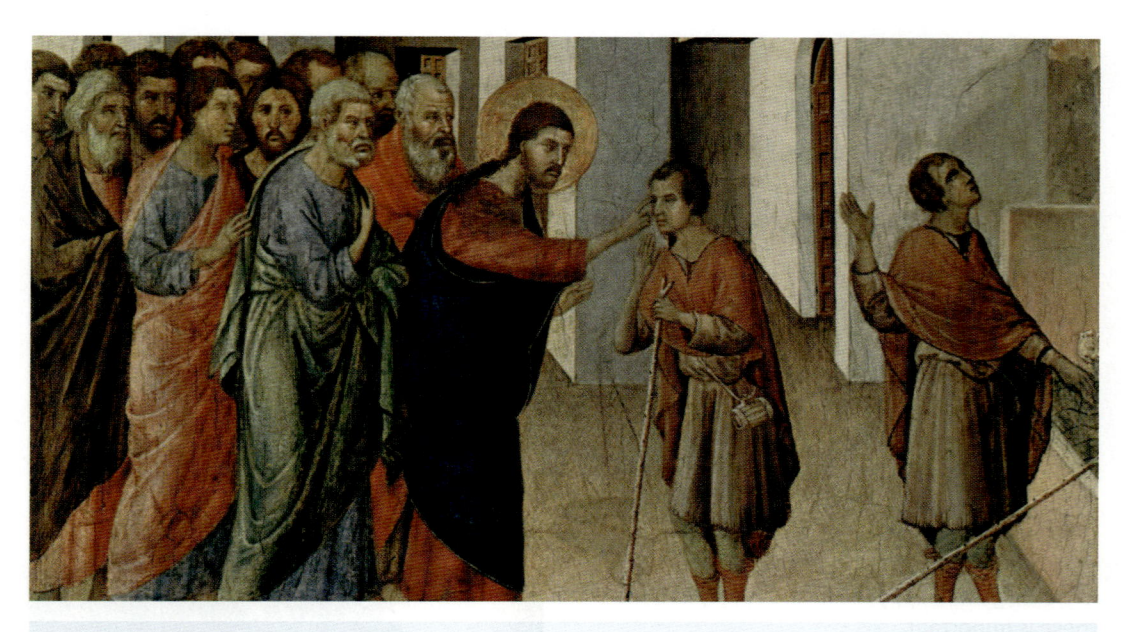

The Healing of a Blind Man by Duccio di Buoninsegna (1308–11)

THE KINGDOM OF GOD IN THE MIRACLES OF JESUS

One of the most powerful ways Jesus revealed the kingdom was through his miracles. In biblical times, illness was taken as a sign of God's displeasure and was sometimes understood as a punishment for sinfulness, not necessarily on the part of the person suffering but perhaps on the part of the ill person's parents. Thus, when Jesus enabled the blind man to see (cf. Matthew 9:27-30), helped a woman bent low to stand straight (cf. Luke 13:11-13), or cured a leper of his illness (cf. Matthew 8:1-3), he was revealing to people that God cares for those who suffer and that suffering is not a sign of God's displeasure or a punishment for sin. He was revealing to people the caring love of God at work in the world and calling them to believe in and trust in that love. These miracles of Jesus were signs pointing to the presence of the kingdom announced by the prophets and inaugurated in Jesus: the blind will be able to see, the sick will be cured, the poor are truly blessed, and those isolated at the edge of society will be included.

THINK IT THROUGH

▶ Read the following miracle stories:

- Matthew 14:13-21
- Luke 8:22-25
- John 11:1-46

▶ Choose one of the stories. What do you think it reveals about Jesus' vision of the Kingdom of God? Match it with one of the points below:

- There is no need to be afraid
- Death has no power over God
- In the Kingdom of God there is plenty for all

JOURNAL

Reflect on the words or phrases you used to describe the Kingdom of God in the opening activity. Are there any words or phrases you would change or add to this list now? Write out your top five words or phrases.

SUMMARY

- Jesus used the metaphor of the Kingdom of God as a teaching tool to explain what God's love offers to us and how God wanted people to live.
- Jesus used parables to teach people about the Kingdom of God.
- One of the most powerful ways Jesus revealed the kingdom was through his miracles.
- He was revealing to people that God cares for those who suffer and that suffering is not a sign of God's displeasure or a punishment for sin.

LESSON 21 – THY KINGDOM COME

LESSON 22
THE BEATITUDES

Objective: This lesson will explore the teaching at the heart of Jesus' message – the Beatitudes – and examine how the values of the Beatitudes are the values of the kingdom as articulated by Jesus.

OPENING ACTIVITY

Imagine you are going on a shopping spree with a credit card that has no financial limit but can be used only five times. Working in groups of three or four, try to agree on five things you would buy. Discuss why you want to purchase each item and how each item will contribute to your happiness. When you have done this, make a list of things that money can't buy. With your group, agree on your top five from this list that would help you live a long and happy life. Discuss why each of these is important.

If you were told you could have everything on this list or everything from your imaginary shopping spree, which would you choose, and why?

Jesus' guide to happiness

Jesus taught a very specific set of attitudes or values that people should live by in order to find happiness. The Gospels of Matthew and Luke summarise these in a collection of statements known as the Beatitudes. They are not meant to simply shape the way we think about things, they are indicators of how we ought to be in the world. They are, indeed, *be-attitudes*. They should shape the kind of people that we are and how we live our lives in the world with others. Jesus said that God promises a special blessing to anyone who lives by these attitudes and the values that go with them. Here is Matthew's version of what Jesus said:

> Blessed are the poor in spirit, for theirs is the kingdom of heaven.
> Blessed are those who mourn, for they shall be comforted.
> Blessed are the meek, for they shall inherit the earth.
> Blessed are those who hunger and thirst for righteousness, for they will be filled.
> Blessed are the merciful, for they will receive mercy.
> Blessed are the pure in heart, for they will see God.
> Blessed are the peacemakers, for they will be called children of God.
> Blessed are those who are persecuted for righteousness' sake, for theirs is the kingdom of heaven.
> Blessed are you when people revile you and persecute you and utter all kinds of evil against you falsely on my account. Rejoice and be glad, for your reward is great in heaven, for in the same way they persecuted the prophets who were before you. (Mt 5:3-12)

THINK IT THROUGH

The Beatitudes were originally written in Greek, and the first word in each one was *makarios*, which can be translated as 'blessed' or 'happy'.

▶ Read the list of the Beatitudes again, this time starting each one with the word 'happy'.
▶ Do any of the statements surprise you now?
▶ How do you respond to the description of these people as 'happy'?

THE BEATITUDES FOR US TODAY

To adopt the attitudes that Jesus outlined for us in the Beatitudes is not always easy. However, the best chance we have of doing so is by understanding what they mean for our lives today. The table below offers a summary and explanation of the Beatitudes to help us apply them to our lives.

GOD BLESSES …	IN OTHER WORDS, GOD BLESSES …	THIS SUGGESTS THAT GOD VALUES …
People who depend on God	People who know they don't have all the answers; people who are aware of God in their lives	Human beings in all our frailty and invites us to relationship with him
People who grieve	People who are mourning the loss of someone they love	Friendships and relationships and will restore them in heaven
People who are gentle	People who treat others with kindness; people who treat the earth with respect	Gentleness Being kind-hearted Compassion
People who hunger and thirst for what is right	People who strive to make life fair; people who won't settle for inequality or injustice	Justice Equality
People who are merciful	People who don't take revenge; who forgive and give others a fair chance to change	Mercy Forgiveness
People whose hearts are pure	People who are honourable; people who don't take advantage of others	Right living and relating Thinking properly about others
People who make peace	People who work to end war, conflict and division; people who aim to unite others	Unity Reconciliation Peacemaking
People who are treated badly for doing right	People for whom others make trouble because they stand up for what is right	Truth Honesty Fair play
People who are abused for following Jesus	People who live like Jesus, and who trust God's promises	What Jesus taught Our love for Jesus, self, others Our respect for Jesus, self, others

LESSON 22 – THE BEATITUDES

GROUP WORK
In groups, prepare a presentation on one of the Beatitudes as it applies to life in the world today. Each group might focus on a different beatitude. Present your finished work to the class.

JOURNAL
What changes would you suggest in our society to bring about the fullness of the values of the Beatitudes? What can you do right now to begin living out this way of life?

SUMMARY
- Jesus taught a very specific set of attitudes or values that people should live in order to find happiness.
- The Beatitudes were originally written in Greek, and the first word in each one was *makarios*, which can be translated as 'blessed' or 'happy'.
- The Beatitudes are not meant to simply shape the way we think about things, they are indicators of how we ought to be in the world.

LESSON 23
THE PASSION OF JESUS

Objective: This lesson will look at the Passion (the suffering and death) of Jesus.

OPENING CONVERSATION
Have you ever been deliberately and falsely accused of doing something, or do you know someone who has? How did that feel?
How do you think Jesus felt at being wrongly condemned to death?

Jesus freely accepted suffering – The Crucifixion

Jesus' faithfulness to his Father and the mission he was sent to accomplish resulted in his execution by crucifixion. This was a reality that Jesus faced with great anguish and wished might be otherwise (cf. Matthew 26:36-46), but that he freely accepted as the consequence of the fulfilment of his mission as the Saviour of the world. In explaining the parable of the Good Shepherd, Jesus said, 'No one takes [my life] from me, but I lay it down of my own accord' (Jn 10:18). Throughout his public ministry, Jesus experienced growing animosity and plotting against him. Jesus predicted that he would suffer and die because of his works and teachings. During all of this, Jesus faced his impending suffering and death with extraordinary resolve.

The cruel practice of punishing capital crimes by crucifixion was legendary in the ancient world of Jesus' time. So, when Jesus was falsely and unjustly executed in this fashion, the members of the early Church had no need for graphic descriptions to convey the horrific nature of his death – they would have been well aware of the brutality of Jesus' crucifixion. That Jesus would willingly accept death by crucifixion to accomplish the divine plan of Salvation was beyond the comprehension of his disciples. Given the miracles that Jesus' disciples witnessed him performing throughout his life, they would certainly have believed that he, the Son of God, could have avoided this cruel and excruciating suffering.

In the eyes of many onlookers, Jesus' death by crucifixion was the highest form of public shame. There was nothing glorious or splendid about what happened to Jesus on Calvary. For many of Jesus' disciples, the trauma was so dreadful and beyond their comprehension that they abandoned him as he hung on the cross. And, after his death, they struggled to come to grips with the fact that their great teacher, their Lord and Messiah, had died in this way. They did not understand fully what was taking place. That understanding would come later after Jesus had risen from the dead.

THINK IT THROUGH

- What do you think it felt like for Jesus to be aware of the suffering and death he would inevitably face?
- Have you ever wondered why Jesus would freely accept death by crucifixion?

GROUP WORK

Work in groups of four. Each member of the group reads one of the four Gospel accounts of the Passion:

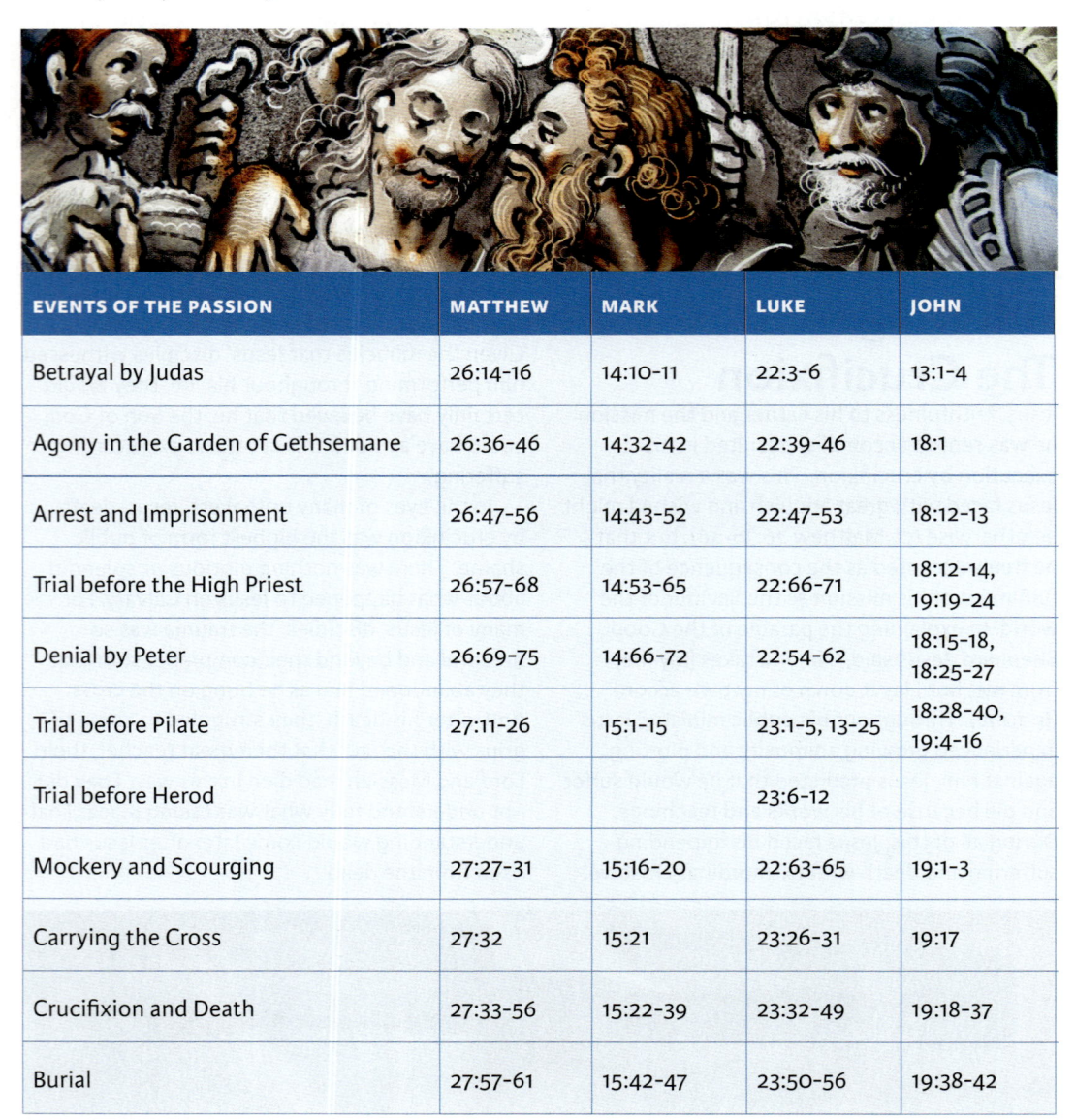

EVENTS OF THE PASSION	MATTHEW	MARK	LUKE	JOHN
Betrayal by Judas	26:14-16	14:10-11	22:3-6	13:1-4
Agony in the Garden of Gethsemane	26:36-46	14:32-42	22:39-46	18:1
Arrest and Imprisonment	26:47-56	14:43-52	22:47-53	18:12-13
Trial before the High Priest	26:57-68	14:53-65	22:66-71	18:12-14, 19:19-24
Denial by Peter	26:69-75	14:66-72	22:54-62	18:15-18, 18:25-27
Trial before Pilate	27:11-26	15:1-15	23:1-5, 13-25	18:28-40, 19:4-16
Trial before Herod			23:6-12	
Mockery and Scourging	27:27-31	15:16-20	22:63-65	19:1-3
Carrying the Cross	27:32	15:21	23:26-31	19:17
Crucifixion and Death	27:33-56	15:22-39	23:32-49	19:18-37
Burial	27:57-61	15:42-47	23:50-56	19:38-42

Discuss your findings, using these questions:

- Why do you think Judas betrayed Jesus?
- What does Jesus' prayer to his Father in the Garden of Gethsemane tell us about how he felt at that time?
- Are you surprised by Jesus' reaction to his arrest? Why/why not?
- What were the precise charges laid against Jesus by the High Priest in the Council and by the leaders before Pilate?
- Why do you think Pilate acted as he did?
- What were the last words that Jesus said?
- Where was Jesus buried?

OVER TO YOU

- Write the story of the Passion in one narrative, combining all the elements found in the four accounts of the Gospels.

A DEATH FOR LOVE

The greatest act of a person, the greatest virtue, is love. There are many stories of people dying for love of another; some of these stories are true (for example, the love that motivated St Maximilian Kolbe), others are fictional (such as the love of Romeo and Juliet). The sacrificial death of Jesus was the consequence of the love that he had preached, in both deeds and words, throughout his life. Jesus died to bring about the Kingdom of God's love. During his life he had denounced sin, evil, hypocrisy and deceit. His life lived to show the Kingdom of God alive in the world led to his persecution and death. Saint Paul used the Greek word *kenosis*, which means 'an emptying', to help us understand the depth of God's love for us revealed in the Incarnation and in the suffering, death and Resurrection of Jesus. The word *kenosis* reveals Jesus' love to be total and unconditional. John the Evangelist also helps us understand this mystery of divine love. He wrote: 'God so loved the world that he gave his only Son, so that everyone who believes in him may not perish but may have eternal life' (Jn 3:16). God the Father sent Jesus out of love for humankind, and Jesus lived and died and rose again because of his love for his Father and his love for us. Jesus' love for his Father and for humanity is the ultimate love story.

JOURNAL

'For God so loved the world that he gave his only Son, so that everyone who believes in him may not perish but may have eternal life' (Jn 3:16). Write this Scripture passage into your journal and reflect on what it means to you.

SUMMARY

- Jesus predicted that he would suffer and die.
- Although he was afraid, he accepted this.
- The Passion narrative describes the suffering and death of Jesus.
- The disciples struggled to come to grips with the fact that Jesus was crucified and died like a common criminal.
- Jesus lived and died (and rose again) because of his love for us.

LESSON 24
CHRIST IS RISEN!

Objective: This lesson will explore the Resurrection of Jesus Christ.

OPENING CONVERSATION
Think of examples of films, literature, poetry, music or art that tell the story of good triumphing over evil. Share your favourite examples.

The Resurrection – our hope

The ultimate triumph of good over evil is an age-old storyline that artists and musicians, poets, novelists and playwrights have interpreted down through the ages in theatre, cinema, art and literature: 'good' battles 'evil', and when all hope seems lost, good (usually) rises to triumph over evil once and for all. Such stories point to humanity's belief in the existence and ultimate power of good and its dominance over evil. This belief, which is embedded in the human heart, helps us find meaning in the hardships of life, and shows us how to see possibilities even in the most difficult situations.

Without the Resurrection, Jesus' life would simply be an epic story of a good man overcome by evil; a tragic figure meeting a violent and unjust death on a cross after a heroic life of loving and serving people. But Jesus was not simply a good and heroic man. He was Goodness and Love itself at work among us, whose love for and service of people was not defeated by his unjust execution. Jesus rose triumphantly and defeated death itself. The *Catechism of the Catholic Church* states: 'The Resurrection of the crucified one shows that he was truly "I Am", the Son of God and God himself' (CCC, 653). Christ's Resurrection assures us of our own resurrection to new life after death.

THE EMPTY TOMB
After the death and burial of Jesus, Mary Magdalene went back to the tomb in which Joseph of Arimathea and Nicodemus had buried Jesus. On finding the stone that was supposed to be blocking the entrance to the tomb rolled back and the tomb empty, Mary ran to Peter and John to share her astonishing discovery. Equally astonished, perhaps even bewildered, Peter and John rushed to the tomb to see for themselves. Peter, John and the other disciples grappled with the reality of the empty tomb – and were unsure what to make of it. The Fourth Gospel tells us that while they 'believed … they did not understand the scripture, that he must rise from the dead' (Jn 20:8-9). Jesus did foretell his Resurrection, but could it really be possible? Or did someone rob the grave and steal his body? The Risen Christ appeared to the disciples so they would not be in any doubt!

WITNESSES TO THE RESURRECTION

After the Resurrection, the Risen Lord Jesus appeared many times to his disciples. As they continued to struggle with faith and doubt, they responded to their encounters with the Risen Christ in different ways: some fell down in worship (cf. Matthew 28:9), some thought he might be a ghost (cf. Luke 24:37), some did not recognise him right away (cf. Luke 24:13-35; John 20:15-16), and some were outright resistant until they could touch him to make sure he was real (cf. John 20:25). All these encounters with the Risen Lord gradually helped the disciples to cement their belief in the Resurrection. Slowly they embraced and began to share the joyful news of Christ risen from the dead. It was in this sharing of faith that the early Church was rooted. Among those disciples who encountered the Risen Christ, Mary Magdalene and Thomas the Apostle stand out as two compelling examples. Let's look at how John the Evangelist describes their encounters.

MARY MAGDALENE

Mary Magdalene is the first disciple to whom the Risen Lord appears. In John 20:11-18 we read that Mary Magdalene stands weeping by the empty tomb because she thinks the body of Jesus has been stolen. The Risen Lord comes to her, but she thinks he is the gardener and does not at first recognise him. Then he calls her by name, and hearing his voice, Mary Magdalene recognises the Risen Christ and immediately embraces her beloved Jesus. He tells Mary Magdalene not to hold on to him. Instead, she must let go of him again in order to go and share the Good News of the Resurrection with others.

Mary Magdalene by Follower of Andrea Solari, circa 1524

LESSON 24 – CHRIST IS RISEN!

THOMAS THE APOSTLE

On that same Easter Sunday evening, 'the first day of the week', the Risen Christ's first appearance to the disciples as a group takes place. However, Thomas the Apostle is absent. When the other disciples tell him the extraordinary good news, Thomas refuses to believe until he can touch and confirm the reality of the Risen Lord's body for himself. That same evening the Risen Lord returns to the disciples again and offers his body to Thomas to touch. Thomas exclaims in faith: 'My Lord and my God!' (Jn 20:28). The Risen Lord gently admonishes him, saying, 'Have you believed because you have seen me? Blessed are those who have not seen and yet have come to believe' (Jn 20:29). In other words, our faith, the faith of all those who believe without seeing the Risen Christ face to face, is all the more 'blessed'.

Mary Magdalene and Thomas offer us two different perspectives and insights into the gift of faith: one focuses on the power of our emotions or feelings, and the other on our intellect or reason. Perhaps Mary was initially so overwhelmed by her emotions that she at first failed to recognise Jesus; Thomas, on the other hand, may have so rigidly adhered to the power of his intellect, looking for empirical evidence, that he too at first could not accept the fact that Jesus had risen from the dead. By sharing these two stories back to back, John the Evangelist teaches that there are many paths to faith. Faith is an invitation, calling forth a free response to relationship with the Lord that demands our whole being, mind and heart. Both in grappling with doubt and in responding to God's call in faith, we bring our whole being, mind and heart, into our relationship with God.

OVER TO YOU

- With a partner, read and compare the encounters of the Risen Lord with Mary Magdalene (cf. John 20:11-18) and Thomas (cf. John 20:24-29).
- Share your thoughts on how each of these disciples of Jesus responded to him.
- Compare Christ's message to each of them.

REFLECT AND DISCUSS

Consider this image entitled *The Risen Lord,* created by the Chinese Christian artist He Qi. The figure of the Risen Lord in the centre embodies the shape of a cross. He is surrounded on four sides by smaller figures: the women and the Apostles who went to the tomb are depicted at the bottom of the image, and the other disciples, some proclaiming faith in the Resurrection and some struggling with uncertainty and doubt, are shown at the top. In the foreground are bread on a paten and wine in a chalice, symbols of the Eucharist.

- How does this depiction compare with your own image of the Risen Lord?

'I am the resurrection and the life'

Jesus not only predicted his coming death and Resurrection but he also revealed the deeper meaning of those events. He declared, 'I am the resurrection and the life' (Jn 11:25). The Paschal Mystery of Jesus' death, Resurrection and Ascension is the heart and centre of the fulfilment of God's saving promise of salvation and flourishing new life. The Resurrection reveals the divine purpose of the Incarnation and Paschal Mystery of the Son of God: all humanity is empowered to live in justice and holiness, in right relationship with God, and with all creation. Christ defeated death and sin, and he opened the way for all of humankind to live in peace and eternal life with God. The deepest desire of the human heart can truly be fulfilled.

Jesus' Resurrection does not mean that we will escape from the challenges and problems of life. What it does mean, however, is that we now have the God-given power, the grace, not to be defeated by them. On our behalf, Christ defeated death and all of death's power, which is present in many events and experiences of life on earth, such as despair, dead ends, the loss of creativity, the loss of opportunity, the loss of imagination, the consequences of sin, and feelings of alienation from self, others and God.

JOURNAL

How could belief in the Resurrection make a difference in your life? How could it affect how you see the world?

The Ascension

The Ascension marks the end of the forty days the Risen Christ spent among his disciples. After those forty days, Christ was taken up into heaven to sit at the right hand of God the Father. The Acts of the Apostles describes the scene in more detail:

> So when they had come together, they asked him, 'Lord, is this the time when you will restore the kingdom to Israel?' He replied, 'It is not for you to know the times or periods that the Father has set by his own authority. But you will receive power when the Holy Spirit has come upon you; and you will be my witnesses in Jerusalem, in all Judea and Samaria, and to the ends of the earth.' When he had said this, as they were watching, he was lifted up, and a cloud took him out of their sight. While he was going and they were gazing up toward heaven, suddenly two men in white robes stood by them. They said, 'Men of Galilee, why do you stand looking up toward heaven? This Jesus, who has been taken up from you into heaven, will come in the same way as you saw him go into heaven.' (Acts 1:6-11)

THINK IT THROUGH

▶ Imagine yourself standing among Jesus' disciples, gazing upward as he disappears. What might be going through your mind?

SUMMARY

- Christ's Resurrection assures us of our own resurrection to new life after death.
- Among those disciples who encountered the Risen Christ, Mary Magdalene and Thomas the Apostle stand out as two compelling examples.
- The Paschal Mystery, Jesus' death, Resurrection and Ascension, is the heart and centre of the fulfilment of God's saving promise of salvation.

LESSON 24 – CHRIST IS RISEN!

LESSON 25
THE EARLY CHRISTIAN MOVEMENT

Objective: This lesson will introduce the origins of Christianity after the life of Jesus and will outline the key events in the development of the early Christian movement.

OPENING CONVERSATION
Think about a time in your life when you received really 'good news'. What was that news? Why was it so good? What did you do after you received this news?

Timeline of early Christianity

Christianity was established and spread because the early followers wanted to share the 'Good News' about Jesus Christ with the world.

THE EARLY CHURCH IN THE APOSTOLIC AGE

The Apostolic Age is the time after the Ascension of Jesus, when some of the Twelve Apostles are believed to have still been alive.

- 30 CE – Pentecost: The followers of Jesus experience God's gift of the Holy Spirit, as promised by Jesus.
- 36–69 CE – Oral transmission of the message and story of Jesus. Christianity is centred in Jerusalem.
- 46 CE – Paul begins his missionary journeys.
- 64 CE – The Roman historian Tacitus reports that Emperor Nero blames the fire that destroys much of Rome on the Christians. The persecution of thousands of Christians follows and, according to Church tradition, Peter and Paul are executed during this persecution and martyred in Rome. Despite this and other periods of persecution, the Christian faith survives and expands.
- 68–70 CE – The Dead Sea Scrolls are hidden in caves.
- 70–100 CE – Writing of the Gospels.
- 70 CE – The Jewish revolt against Rome fails. When the Roman army besieges and conquers the city of Jerusalem, some Christians are driven out of the city and thus Christianity spreads outside of Israel throughout the Roman Empire. Early Christian communities are set up in Ephesus, Corinth, Rome, Cathage and Alexandria. By the end of the second century, the faith had spread to Egypt, North Africa and Gaul.
- 81 CE – Domitian becomes emperor and styles himself as 'Master and God'. Christians are persecuted. The Church's early structure is established in terms of bishops, priests and deacons.
- 83 CE – Jewish authorities sever ties with Christians at the council in Jamnia, where it is decided that the Hebrew canon of scriptures is closed and that no Christian writing will be accepted as sacred texts.
- 98–117 CE – Trajan becomes emperor and reinforces persecutory policies toward Christians that stay in effect until the time of Aurelius.
- 150 CE – There are Christian communities throughout the Roman Empire and in places as far away as Arabia, Persia and India.
- By the beginning of the second century, congregations are documented in almost every city that Paul visits on his three missionary journeys.

The Roman emperor Nero

SECTION B: CHRISTIANITY

FIRST CHRISTIAN COMMUNITIES

Early Christian communities congregated in private homes and huts to sing hymns, listen to reading of the Scriptures, conduct all-night prayer sessions and celebrate events like the Last Supper.

In the early years of Christianity, the basic tenets of the religion were often unclear. Alexandria is where many of the doctrines of Christianity were clarified. Schools for priests were established in the city in the second century. In 313 CE, Alexandria became the centre of Christian theological studies and it was there that the doctrines of Christianity were shaped and unified.

Although most Christians identified Jesus as divine from a very early period, the first Christians saw Jesus as a unique agent of God. With the Council of Nicaea in 325, Jesus was identified as literally 'of the same substance, essence or being' as God. Within fifteen to twenty years of Jesus' death, St Paul refers to Jesus as the resurrected 'Son of God'. The phrase 'Son of Man' is more frequently used in the Gospel of Mark. The Gospel of John identifies Jesus as the human incarnation of the divine Word. The Book of Revelation refers to Jesus as the 'Alpha and Omega, the first and the last'.

The building of churches was largely forbidden until Constantine christianised the Roman Empire. The first churches were rather plain and their main objective was seen to be a space large enough for worship.

The Roman authorities observed the immediate and widespread growth of Christianity throughout the Roman Empire with suspicion. Although they were polytheists, the Romans had excused the Jews from observing the polytheistic beliefs of the empire. In gratitude for Herod the Great once helping Julius Caesar, the Jews were exempt from worshipping the emperor. The Romans considered the Christians to be a new, separate religion who were not eligible for the exemption granted to the Jews, and therefore considered them disloyal. Tacitus mentions how rumours began to circulate that Christians were cannibals, and this, along with their refusal to attend the popular vicious Roman games, led them to be hated.

OVER TO YOU
▶ Draw a timeline outlining the key events in the early Church in the Apostolic Period.

SAINT PAUL

The Apostles and other disciples worked night and day spreading the Good News of Jesus. They worked so effectively that their fellow Jews became more and more angry. A Pharisee named Saul from Tarsus was one of those angry Jews. He was so angry that, having received permission from the elders, he set out for Damascus with one purpose in mind: to seek out, arrest and bring back to Jerusalem for trial and punishment the enemies of Judaism. It was during this journey that Saul was knocked to the ground and blinded, which can be read as a physical manifestation of his blindness toward Jesus as Messiah. He experienced the Risen Lord, who asked, 'Saul, Saul, why do you persecute me?' (Acts 9:4). Saul accepted the Lord's call to become his disciple; he changed his name to Paul and spent the rest of his life spreading the Good News. He set out on a series of missionary journeys, first to his fellow Jews and then to Gentiles. Luke describes three of Paul's missionary journeys in Acts 13 and 14; 15:36–18:22; and 18:23–21:15.

LESSON 25 – THE EARLY CHRISTIAN MOVEMENT

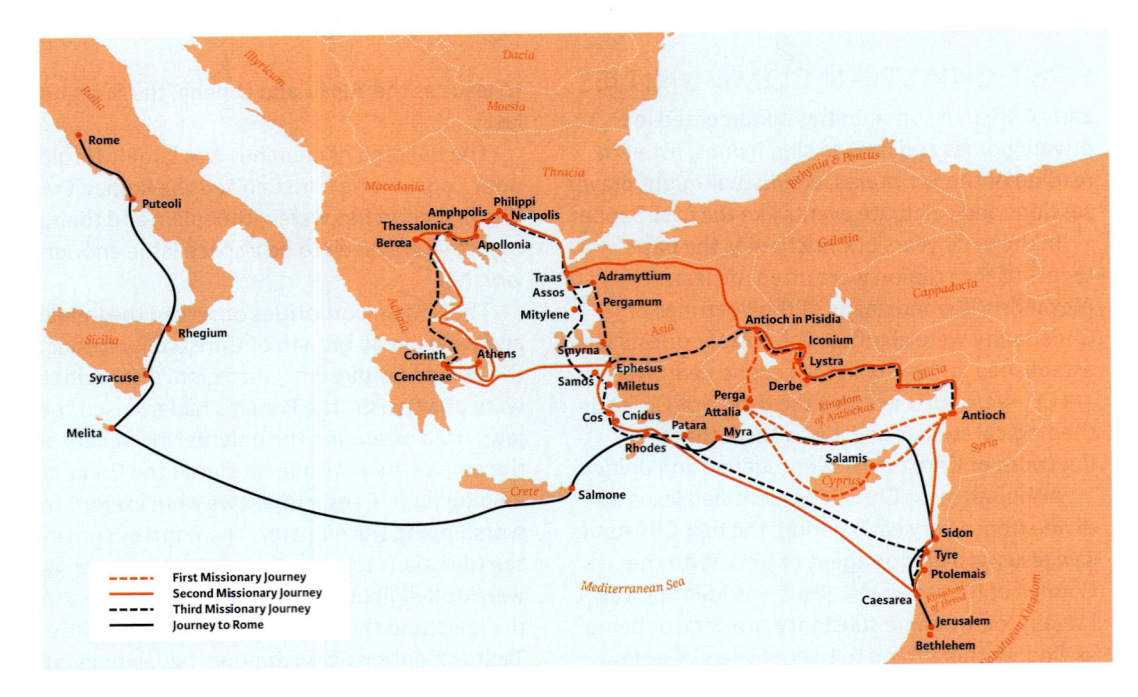

The Journeys of St Paul

A BRIEF SUMMARY OF SAINT PAUL'S THREE MISSIONARY JOURNEYS

First Missionary Journey (Acts 13 and 14): On his first missionary journey St Paul was accompanied by two companions, Barnabas and John Mark. This journey, which lasted about two years, took Paul and his companions to Cyprus and on to central Asia Minor and modern-day Turkey, proclaiming the Good News primarily to fellow Jews.

Second Missionary Journey (Acts 15:36–18:22): On his second missionary journey St Paul revisited some of the local churches he founded during his first missionary journey. He also travelled into Macedonia, in the northern part of what is Greece today. Paul spent most of his time in the port city of Corinth.

Third Missionary Journey (Acts 18:23–21:15): Saint Paul's third missionary journey was centred in Ephesus in Asia Minor. In addition to strengthening the churches he had founded, it was during this journey that Paul focused on his letter-writing campaign to proclaim the Good News and to clarify his teachings. The New Testament contains fourteen letters either written by Paul or attributed to him.

Paul's journey to Rome is considered his fourth and final evangelistic journey, and it was here that he continued to preach the Gospel until his death.

RESEARCH PROJECT
Research the accounts of the missionary journeys of St Paul. Include in your report:

- names of the disciples who accompanied Paul
- places Paul visited
- challenges and sufferings Paul endured
- an outline of Paul's teachings.

Share your report with the class.

YOU WILL FIND ADDITIONAL INFORMATION ON WWW.SEEKANDFIND.IE

JOURNAL
Reflect on the conversion of St Paul. Have you ever experienced a life-changing moment? Write about the experience.

SUMMARY

- The Apostles spread the Good News of the life, death and Resurrection of Jesus Christ and Christianity began to grow.
- The Roman authorities observed the immediate and widespread growth of Christianity throughout the Roman Empire with suspicion, and early Christians were persecuted.
- As a result of his three missionary journeys beginning in 46 CE, Paul played a crucial role in the initial expansion of Christianity.

LESSON 26
CHRISTIANITY: EXPANSION AND DIVISION

Objective: This lesson will look at the spread of Christianity and the major events that have occurred in its development.

OPENING ACTIVITY
In sixty seconds, name as many Christian denominations as you can.

Expansion and division in the Christian Church

This timeline highlights some of the main events in the history of Christianity:

- 196 CE – Controversy occurs between the Eastern Church (Greek-speaking) and the Western Church (Latin-speaking) regarding the day on which to celebrate Easter.
- 312 CE – The Conversion of Constantine: he had a vision in a dream that he was to conquer by the power of Christ; he led his army into battle and won.
- 313 CE – The Edict of Milan states that Christianity is officially accepted and recognised as a religion by the Roman government. Christianity now has political influence.
- 320 CE – Constantine moves the capital of the Roman Empire east to Constantinople (now Istanbul). This leads to the development of an Eastern (Greek-speaking) tradition based in Constantinople and a Western (Latin-speaking) tradition based in Rome.
- 325 CE – The Council of Nicaea: the first key council (gathering) of the Christian Church. Constantine called the council with a view to achieving unity within all Christian countries. It started in 318 and lasted for several years. It was this council that established 'The Nicene Creed'.
- 337 CE – Emperor Constantine is baptised shortly before his death.
- 380 CE – The Roman Emperor Theodosius I makes Christianity the official state religion.
- 432 CE/456 CE (there is disagreement as to the actual date, though 432 is traditionally given) – Patrick travels to Ireland as a missionary.
- 962–1806 CE – The era of the Holy Roman Empire in Central Europe. Its territory centres on the kingdom of Germany, including the neighbouring kingdom of Italy and Burgandy.

Stained-glass window of St Patrick

- 1054 CE – The Great Schism: refers to the split that takes place between the Christian Church of the East and West; the key areas of conflict were leadership of the Church, language differences and political differences between Latin and Greek speakers. Christianity was thereafter divided into the Catholic Church in the West and the Orthodox Church in the East.
- 1095–1291 CE – The Crusades: a series of religiously sanctioned military campaigns with the primary goal of restoring Christian control of the Holy Land. The crusaders came from all over Western Europe and were fought mainly by Roman Catholics and Orthodox Christians. The Crusades originally had the goal of recapturing Jerusalem and the Holy Land from Muslim rule in response to a call from the leaders of the Byzantine Empire for assistance against the expansion.
- 1200 CE – The Bible is available in twenty-two different languages.
- 1382 CE – The Bible is translated from Latin into English by John Wycliffe.
- 1462 CE – Johannes Gutenberg begins printing the Bible with his printing process.

- 1517 CE – Martin Luther nails his Ninety-Five Theses (i.e. topics for discussion) on the Wittenberg Church and the Protestant Reformation begins, resulting in the eventual establishment of the Anglican, Lutheran, Baptist, Methodist, Quaker and Presbyterian Churches.
- 1545–1563 CE – The Council of Trent is held and is seen as the beginning of the Counter Reformation.
- 1600–1800 CE – Christianity continues to expand throughout the world during the Age of Exploration, becoming one of the world's largest religions.

THINK IT THROUGH
▶ What do you think was the most significant event in the spread of Christianity?

Iconostasis in Russian Orthodox Church

THE FIRST GREAT SCHISM: THE DIVISION OF THE CHURCH INTO EAST AND WEST

Over the centuries the Roman Empire divided into East and West, with its centres of government in Constantinople and Rome respectively. Both capitals became equal centres of Catholic faith. Political and religious tensions emerged between the two parts of the Empire. The tensions eventually led to a division, or schism, between the Church in the East and the Church in the West.

The reasons for the schism are many and cannot be captured in this brief overview. Essentially, Eastern and Western Christianity was initially united in a profession of the apostolic faith, sharing the same creeds and sacraments. However, there was competition between the Pope of Rome and the Patriarch of Constantinople as to who should have universal jurisdiction in matters of Church governance. This tension was heightened by other disputes, for example about the kind of bread to be used for the Eucharist (leavened or unleavened), and whether priests and bishops must have beards.

The final breach of union within the Church is usually dated from 1054. In that year, legates sent by Pope Leo IX had an intense dispute with the Patriarch Peter Cerularius, and they mutually excommunicated each other. Thereafter, the Church split into the Roman Catholic Church and the Eastern Orthodox Church. This breach continues today. However, while separated from one another in many ways, the Roman Catholic Church and the Orthodox Church share in a rich history, which they express in a diversity of traditions. This reality has been expressed over and over again in recent years at the meetings between the various popes of the Roman Church and the patriarchs of the Orthodox Church.

RESEARCH ACTIVITY
Find out more about Eastern Orthodox Churches found in Ireland today. Present your findings to the class.

YOU WILL FIND ADDITIONAL INFORMATION ON WWW.SEEKANDFIND.IE

Statue of Martin Luther, Wittenberg, Germany

THE PROTESTANT REFORMATION

About five hundred years after the Great Schism, the Protestant Reformation resulted in many reformers and their followers separating themselves from the Roman Catholic Church. The major denominations of Christianity that emerged from the Reformation include Anglican (Church of Ireland), Presbyterian and Methodist.

History books mark the beginning of the Protestant Reformation as 31 October 1517, when Martin Luther, an Augustinian monk, nailed his Ninety-Five Theses to the door of the Castle Church in Wittenberg, Germany. In his theses Luther called for a variety of reforms within both the teachings and practices of the Roman Catholic Church.

Luther wanted to give priority to Scripture in the life of the Church. This eventually lead to his teaching of *sola scriptura* (scripture alone); in other words, the Bible alone is the measure of the faith. This, in turn, led to the denial of Tradition as a true source of faith and the Magisterium as the teacher of the faith.

Luther also called for reform to correct erroneous pastoral practices of the clergy. This led to Luther's teachings of *sola gratia* (grace alone) and *sola fide* (faith alone); in other words, a person is saved by grace and faith alone and not by any human effort. Luther could not resolve his disagreements with the Church and Pope Leo X excommunicated him on 3 January 1521.

The call for reformation grew wider and other reformers soon followed Luther's lead. Ulrich Zwingli (1484–1531) in Switzerland, John Calvin (1509–64) in France, and John Knox (1514–72) in Scotland were among these Protestant reformers. In England King Henry VIII challenged the pope's authority over his right to divorce and remarry. After protracted debate, the king by a decree of parliament declared himself to be the head of the Church in England.

The Catholic Church responded with her own efforts at reforming the Church. These efforts are known as the Catholic Reformation. The Council of Trent (1545–63) became the centre of the Catholic Reformation.

OVER TO YOU

- Identify the main beliefs that all Christians share.
- What are the main differences between Orthodox Christians and Catholic Christians?
- What are the main differences between Protestant Christians and Catholic Christians?

SUMMARY

- Christianity has experienced two major schisms during its history: the Great Schism and the Protestant Reformation.
- The Great Schism took place in 1054 between the Catholic Church in the West and the Orthodox Church in the East.
- The Protestant Reformation began in Central Europe during the sixteenth century and resulted in the eventual establishment of the Anglican, Lutheran, Baptist, Methodist, Quaker and Presbyterian Churches.

LESSON 27
IMAGES OF JESUS

Objective: This lesson will examine various images of Jesus.

OPENING ACTIVITY

As we know, Jesus was a real man who lived and died in Palestine in the first century. Close your eyes and picture Jesus. How would you describe your image of Jesus? Be as specific as possible – include physical attributes and personality traits that spring to mind.

Artistic depictions of Jesus

The Catholic Church has a long tradition of encouraging artists to express the faith of the Church through art. Indeed, the Church was the first great patron of the arts in the Western world. Works of art reach our imagination and 'speak' to us in ways that words alone cannot. Throughout the history of the Church, artists such as Michelangelo and Rembrandt have shaped our understanding of the Christian faith through their artistic expressions of their faith in God. Artistic presentations of Jesus by artists from cultures throughout the world continue to contribute to our image of Jesus.

JESUS OF THE PEOPLE

In 1999 the *National Catholic Reporter* newspaper sponsored a competition to see how artists imagined Jesus as the third millennium approached. The competition attracted 1,678 entries from nineteen countries. Sister Wendy Beckett, the well-known art expert, chose the winning painting, *Jesus of the People*. It is the work of Janet McKenzie, an American artist. Here is what the editor of the *National Catholic Reporter*, Michael Farrell, had to say about it:

> It was, to say the least, controversial. The first thing most people noticed was that Jesus 2000 was black. Then the artist told the world she had used a young woman as a model. The painting is basically what people call realistic or representational. I had frequently been asked what kind of image we were looking for. The point was not what we were looking for but what artists imagined.

REFLECT AND DISCUSS

Examine *Jesus of the People* closely. Spend some time in silence identifying and reflecting on all the details the artist has included: the colours, the background, the clothes, the facial expression and any other details you notice. Then, in small groups, share your impressions of the painting. Here are some suggestions to guide your discussion:

▶ Describe the picture in as much detail as possible.
▶ Comment on the clothing.
▶ Comment on the use of colour.
▶ Comment on the facial expression of Jesus.
▶ Does the artist's use of a female model affect your response? If yes, in what way?
▶ What is your response to the artist's presentation of Jesus as a black person?
▶ What is your response to this picture?
▶ If you were to create your image of Jesus, what qualities would you like to depict?

Jesus of the People by Janet McKenzie

❛ *Works of art 'speak' to us in ways that words alone cannot.*

LESSON 27 – IMAGES OF JESUS

JESUS IN *THE PASSION OF THE CHRIST*

Mel Gibson's film *The Passion of the Christ* is renowned for its brutality and proved controversial at the time of its release. The Passion of Christ – both the historical event and Mel Gibson's film – begins with the Agony in the Garden. In the film, the devil is watching Christ as he prays. Jesus agonises over the incredible suffering he is about to undergo in order to redeem humanity.

What is curious about this image of Jesus is the fact that, in contrast to the quietly assured Jesus commonly portrayed, Gibson's image of Jesus is much more mortal as he endures intense suffering. Jesus appears to be full of doubt and uncertainty, just as all humans are.

The image of the devil is also striking. It appears as an androgynous character. The devil confronts Jesus by asking:

> Do you really believe that one man can bear the full burden of sin? ... No one man can carry this burden I tell you. It is far too heavy. Saving their souls is too costly. No one. Ever. No. Never.

From beneath the devil's foot emerges a snake that slithers over to Christ, who is shedding tears and sweating blood. He seems not to notice the serpent until it is directly beneath him; he then stands and crushes the serpent's head under his foot. What do you believe this act symbolises?

The crushing of the serpent's head is but one way Christ conquers evil. The snake is an appropriate symbol for temptation; it is sneaky and deadly, lurking in the shadows until it is time to strike. So how does Christ deal with this tempter? He crushes it underfoot. This is a powerful moment in the opening scene of the film. It reminds us of the power of good over evil; the power of Jesus over evil.

Still from the film The Passion of the Christ

OVER TO YOU
- Does the image of Jesus in *The Passion of the Christ* appeal to you? Why or why not?
- Recall any other images of Jesus you are familiar with from art or film. What do they have in common? How do they differ?

SUMMARY
- The image of Jesus has been portrayed on numerous occasions down through the ages.
- *Jesus of the People* is the work of Janet McKenzie, an American artist.
- Mel Gibson's *The Passion of the Christ* offers the image of a mortal Jesus who endures intense suffering.

LESSON 28
THE CROSS AS SYMBOL

Objective: This lesson will look at the cross as symbol and will analyse various types of crosses.

OPENING CONVERSATION
Do you or any members of your family own or wear a cross? Can you think of any celebrity who wears a cross? Is this for decoration or does it symbolise their faith? Can you think of any athletes or footballers who make the sign of the cross as part of their preparation or celebration rituals?

The cross as symbol
Whether worn as an item of jewellery or positioned on top of a church building, the cross is the best-known religious symbol of Christianity. It is primarily seen as a representation of the instrument of the crucifixion of Jesus Christ. The cross reminds Christians of God's act of love in offering his son for sacrifice at Calvary. The cross also reminds Christians of Jesus' victory over sin and death. The earliest Christians did not use the cross as a symbol. For many the cross was a stark reminder of the humiliation suffered by Jesus. The use of the cross as a symbol for Christianity began towards the end of the fourth century. It became a powerful symbol for Christians who were being persecuted. The cross reminded them that Christ understood their suffering, and of Christ's victory over death.

Crosses are a prominent feature of Irish graveyards, either carved onto headstones or sculpted into individual pieces. Small crosses are sometimes even used to mark the site of fatal accidents. Followers of Catholicism, Orthodoxy and some branches of the Protestant Churches make the sign of the cross upon themselves as a mark of respect. In Ireland it is commonplace for followers to make the sign of the cross when passing a church, graveyard, grotto or other religious site.

Crucifix on the Old Bridge, Písek, Czech Republic

A Plain Cross

Greek Cross

Types of crosses

CRUCIFIX

The crucifix is the most widely recognised of all the crosses. A crucifix is a cross with the stripped and bloody body of Jesus hanging on it. Jesus is shown wearing a crown of thorns and the inscription 'INRI' is inscribed at the top of the cross. The letters 'INRI' are taken from the initial letters of *Iesus Nazarenus Rex Iudaeorum*, Latin for 'Jesus of Nazareth, King of the Jews'. This was the statement Pontius Pilate ordered to be ironically inscribed on Jesus' cross.

This form of the cross symbolises that Jesus suffered and died on the cross for the sins of humanity. It emphasises that it is Jesus' suffering, death and Resurrection that is important rather than the cross in isolation.

On one particular variation of the Christian crucifix, Jesus is portrayed on the cross, fully clothed, alive and in triumph. He is dressed in the rich clothes of a king and wearing a crown. The function of this cross is to serve as a reminder that Jesus does not remain on the cross. He had to die, yet he is risen. The theology of Jesus' Resurrection is the primary focus of this form of cross.

A PLAIN CROSS

This version of the cross is void of any image or figure of Jesus upon it. This version is to remind us that Jesus is no longer on the cross but is resurrected from the dead.

GREEK CROSS

This cross usually symbolises the Christian Church rather than being a symbol of Christ's suffering. The cross is seen on gravestones in the Roman catacombs. In the twelfth century, crusaders from England adopted the design for their own use, and took it back to England as the Cross of St George, which became the symbol used on the English flag. Another famous variation of the Greek cross is the emblem used by the International Red Cross, a humanitarian organisation founded more than one hundred years ago.

RUSSIAN ORTHODOX CROSS

The Russian Orthodox cross is quite different to the Western cross. The top bar symbolises the plaque that was hung over Christ's head. The main middle bar is the cross beam on which Christ's arms were stretched and nailed. The slanted bottom bar is the footrest.

CELTIC CROSS

The Celtic cross is one which is primarily associated with the Celtic regions of Ireland, Scotland and Wales. Our pre-Christian Celtic ancestors worshipped the sun. With the spread of Christianity throughout Western Europe, the Celtic clans had to find a way to merge their deep-rooted pagan beliefs with their newfound Christian ones. Hence, the Celtic cross was created merging the Christian cross with the circular sphere representing the pagan sun. It is essentially a Latin cross, with a circle enclosing the intersection of the upright and crossbar, as in the standing high crosses.

High crosses of Ireland

High crosses or Celtic crosses are to be found throughout Ireland on old monastic sites. These high crosses are considered to be Ireland's biggest contribution to Western European art of the Middle Ages. Some were probably used as meeting places for religious ceremonies. Others were used to mark boundaries.

As seen in the Monasterboice Cross, the ring initially served to strengthen the head and the arms of the high cross, but it soon became a decorative feature as well. The high crosses were status symbols, either for a monastery or for a sponsor or patron.

These high crosses are also known as the preaching crosses because people would use the images on them to help explain Christianity when teaching and preaching the faith. The early eighth-century crosses had only geometric motifs, but from the ninth and tenth century biblical scenes were carved onto the crosses. There were no crosses made after the twelfth century, until the Celtic Revival when similar crosses began to be erected in various contexts. The Celtic Revival, begun by Douglas Hyde, consisted of a variety of initiatives during the nineteenth and twentieth centuries which focused on renewing the traditions of Celtic literature and Celtic art.

Russian Orthodox Cross

Celtic Cross

Monasterboice Cross

LESSON 28 – THE CROSS AS SYMBOL

CLONMACNOISE – THE CROSS OF THE SCRIPTURES

Clonmacnoise is an ancient ecclesiastical site situated just south of Athlone in the centre of the country. It has one of Ireland's finest surviving high crosses. Pictured is the west face of the Cross of the Scriptures. Shown from the centre of the ring down is as follows:

- The Crucifixion is depicted in the crosshead.
- Flagellation is depicted in the top panel of the shaft.
- The arrest of Christ is depicted in the middle panel of the shaft.
- The soldiers guarding the tomb of Christ is depicted in the final panel of the shaft.

This cross is decorated with figures on all four sides.

OVER TO YOU

- Of all the crosses described in this lesson, which is your favourite? Explain your answer.
- Draw your own version of a cross and explain how your cross is a symbol for Christianity.

GROUP WORK

In small groups, create a collage called 'The Cross as a Symbol'.

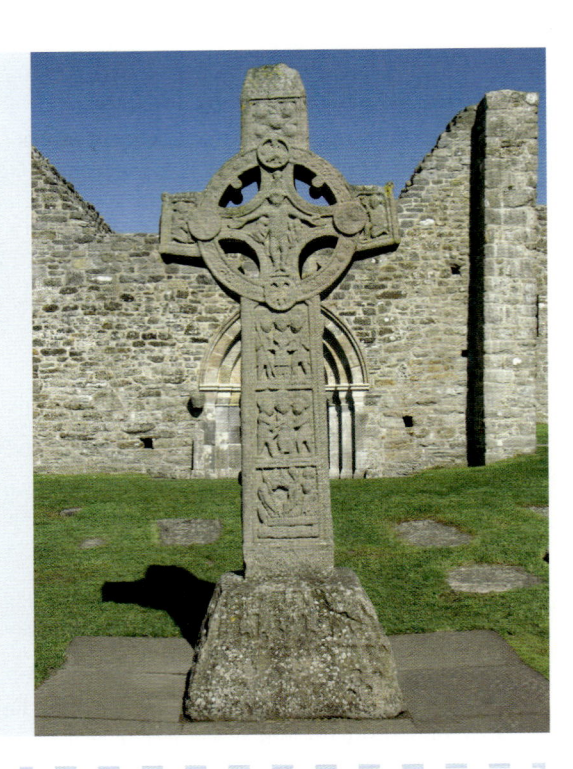

Comparative Religious Studies

Research the symbol of another world religion.

YOU WILL FIND ADDITIONAL INFORMATION ON WWW.SEEKANDFIND.IE

SUMMARY

- The cross is the main symbol of Christianity.
- There are a number of different types of crosses including the crucifix, plain cross and Celtic cross.
- The cross at Clonmacnoise is an example of an Irish high cross.

SECTION C
FAITH IN IRELAND

LESSON 29
ANALYSING RELIGIOUS FAITH IN IRELAND

Objective: This lesson will examine the census results from 1881 and 2011 in order to interpret the religious trends that have taken place in Ireland.

OPENING ACTIVITY

This is a 'vote with your feet' activity. At opposite ends of the room post two signs: AGREE and DISAGREE. Gather between the two signs, facing the teacher who will read a series of statements. If you strongly agree, walk and stand close to the AGREE sign; if you strongly disagree, walk and stand close to the DISAGREE sign; and if you are somewhere in the middle, find a place between the two signs that represents the strength of your opinion. You may be asked to explain your choice of position on the floor.

STATEMENTS

- Most people in Ireland don't know much about religions other than their own.
- Some religions are 'right' and some are 'wrong'.
- People of different religions can be friends.
- In Ireland, some religions are favoured over others.
- People who do not belong to a mainstream religion are looked down upon in our society.
- Contemporary Ireland is a pluralist society that accepts all religions as being equally valid.
- People are often in conflict as a result of religion.
- Religion makes a positive contribution to society.
- It is important to bring a faith perspective to questions about the future of society.

REFLECT AND DISCUSS

- What was it like to choose where you would stand?
- What issues or questions did this exercise make you think about?

Religious trends in Ireland

Historically Irish people have always been spiritual, and according to recent census records faith continues to play a crucial part in Irish people's lives.

A census is a process of attaining and recording information about members of a given population. The census in the Republic of Ireland is carried out by the Central Statistics Office (CSO) every five years. (It is important to note that the figures collated by the CSO are not for the island of Ireland, but for the twenty-six counties of the Republic.)

We will be analysing the figures relating to religion from the earliest census records in 1881 to those of 2011 but we will focus in particular on the last twenty years. The Irish population has increased in number from just over 3,870,020 in 1881 to 4,588,252 in 2011. It is important to keep in mind this population increase when analysing the statistics.

CATHOLICISM

Catholicism remained the predominant faith of Ireland according to the 2011 census, as it has done, according to census records, since at least 1881. Catholics represented just under 90% of the population in each of the censuses held from 1881 to 1911. It subsequently rose to a peak in 1961. Ever since then, its proportion of the total population has declined, falling marginally in the 1960s and 1970s, then accelerating to a more pronounced drop in the 1980s.

» While the proportion of Catholics continued to decline in 2011, to reach its lowest point at 84%, its congregation, at 3.86 million, was the highest since records began.
» The twenty years between 1991 and 2011 have seen significant increases in the non-Catholic population, driven not only by growing numbers with no religion but also by large increases in the religions of immigrants from Eastern Europe, Africa and Asia.
» Despite the recent arrival of large numbers of Polish Catholics, Catholicism has seen the slowest annual average growth of the religions presented.
» People who described themselves as lapsed Catholics in 2011 numbered 1,279.

OTHER CHRISTIAN DENOMINATIONS

» The fastest growing religion in percentage terms has been Orthodox.
» There were 45,223 Orthodox Christians in Ireland in April 2011 – more than double the number five years earlier (20,798), and over four times the number recorded in 2002 (10,437).
» While the majority (98.5%) simply ticked the category 'Orthodox' on the census form, a small proportion further defined their religion. Three classifications were returned, namely Greek Orthodox (0.17%), Russian Orthodox (0.39%) and Coptic Orthodox (0.02%).
» In 2011, four out of five of Ireland's Orthodox Christians were non-Irish. European nationalities accounted for 70% of Ireland's Orthodox Christians, with Romanian (26%) and Latvian (12.5%) nationalities being the largest.
» There were 129,039 members of the Church of Ireland in April 2011, an increase of 6.4% on 2006.
» The number of Presbyterians in Ireland in April 2011 stood at 24,600, up marginally on 2006 and continuing a pattern of increasing numbers since 2002 following long periods of decline up to 1991.
» There were 6,842 Methodists recorded in 2011, a drop from 12,160 in 2006 (though some of this difference may be due to a change in the questionnaire between 2006 and 2011).

OTHER RELIGIONS

JUDAISM
» There were 1,984 Jews living in Ireland in 2011.
» This increased from 394 in the 1881 census.
» The Jewish population was at its highest in 1946 when it peaked at 3,907.

ISLAM
» There were 49,204 Muslims in Ireland in April 2011, a rise on the number five years previously.
» Ireland's Muslim community has grown from just 3,875 persons in 1991, to 19,147 in 2002 to 32,539 in 2006.

HINDUISM
» There were 953 Hindus in Ireland in 1991 and Census 2011 showed a tenfold increase over the last twenty years to 10,688.

BUDDHISM
» According to the 2011 census, there were 8,703 Buddhists in Ireland.
» The first time Buddhists were recorded in the census was in 1991 and at that time there were just 953.

NO RELIGION, ATHEISTS AND AGNOSTICS
» The sum total of those with no religion, atheists and agnostics increased more than fourfold between 1991 and 2011 to stand at 277,237.
» The largest proportionate increase was in atheism, which has grown from 320 to 3,905 over the twenty years.

THINK IT THROUGH
▶ Do any of the figures surprise you? Explain your answer.
▶ What do you think has been the most significant change in religious faith in Ireland since 1881?
▶ Why do you think this change has happened?
▶ How do you think the figures will read in ten years' time?

GROUP WORK
You have been asked to present a news feature about the religious trends in Ireland from 1881 to 2011. Analyse the information given from the various censuses. Working in groups of three:

— One person focuses on the trends in Catholicism
— One person focuses on the trends in other Christian denominations
— One person focuses on the trends in other religions and no religion, atheists and agnostics.

Bring the information together and read your news report to the rest of the class.

SUMMARY
⊙ Historically Irish people have always been spiritual, and according to recent census records, faith continues to play a crucial part in Irish people's lives.
⊙ The CSO website contains the religious trends of Irish people from 1881 up to 2011.
⊙ Analysis of past Irish census records reveals that Ireland has become a much more religiously diverse country in recent times.

LESSON 30
FAITH ALIVE

Objective: This lesson will describe some of the ways in which faith is alive in Ireland today.

OPENING CONVERSATION
Have you ever heard your parents or grandparents talk about what religious faith and practice was like when they were young? What insights have they shared with you? How has religious practice changed?

Where is the faith?
Some people talk about faith dying out or say that religion is becoming irrelevant in a more secular world. However, as the most recent census showed, Ireland is filled with people who practice a variety of religious beliefs. Furthermore, the number of Roman Catholics in this country is at its highest level ever. So how are these people keeping their faith alive today?

SPIRIT RADIO BRINGS GOOD NEWS TO THE AIRWAVES
Spirit Radio, Ireland's first national Christian radio station, was launched in 2011. Spirit Radio plays contemporary Christian music alongside a mix of mainstream, positive chart music. Spirit's news and talk items feature Christian voices speaking about the issues of the day, while all Spirit's shows have the common denominator of highlighting how 'faith in God' makes a real difference.

Speaking about the launch, Rob Clarke, CEO of Spirit Radio, said:

> Today, across the nation, men and women are facing real and sometimes overwhelming challenges. Spirit Radio will reach into homes, cars and offices bringing a message of hope and direction. It will help people take steps to begin or renew their relationship with God. Spirit will help people discover fresh meaning and purpose.

THINK IT THROUGH
- How can listening to positive stories and songs make a difference to your day?
- What was the last 'good news story' or uplifting song you heard? Share your answer with a partner.

Closing Mass of the 50th International Eucharistic Congress, Croke Park

THE 50TH INTERNATIONAL EUCHARISTIC CONGRESS

One occasion that renewed the faith of many Catholics in this country was the 50th International Eucharistic Congress. A Eucharistic Congress is an international gathering of people that aims to:

- Promote an awareness of the central place of the Eucharist in the life and mission of the Catholic Church
- Help improve our understanding and celebration of the liturgy
- Draw attention to the social dimension of the Eucharist.

The Congress normally takes place every four years. It was held in Ireland in 1932, and then again in June 2012. In 2012, 25,000 participants on average attended each day of the week-long event. The closing ceremony was a sold-out event held in Croke Park, with 80,000 people attending and many more watching on TV. Ger Brennan was one of the thousands of people that volunteered at the Congress. Having played in Croke Park on many occasions with the Dublin football team, he found his involvement in the closing ceremony at GAA headquarters very special:

> Before I got involved I wouldn't have known what the Eucharistic Congress was. However, I began to realise what a big event it was and it gave me an opportunity to look at the aspects of my faith, what I believed in, and challenged me to reflect more deeply on what it means to be a Catholic.

This Congress stood out from previous ones in a number of ways. It was the first time that one of the daily themes was dedicated to ecumenism, with an extensive programme of events focusing on the importance of Christian unity. The 2012 Congress also had a greater emphasis on social media. One of the highlights of the Congress was the youth space where young people could tweet their questions and comments for the speakers.

Ecclesial movements

There are more than fifty ecclesial movements in the Catholic Church. Each one was founded by someone whose vision inspires the spirituality and action of the movement. For example, Jean Vanier is founder of l'Arche, and Frank Duff is founder of one of the oldest movements, the Legion of Mary, which he established in Dublin in 1921. On the feast of Pentecost in 1998, 300,000 members of these movements gathered in St Peter's Square in Rome at the invitation of Pope John Paul II.

The members of these movements find in them new possibilities for expressing and living their faith: for those in the L'Arche movement, in valuing life in all its forms; for those in the Legion of Mary, in giving a service to the Church on a voluntary basis to evangelise and seek conversions to the Church. Most people who belong to an ecclesial movement will say that the greatest benefit is the support they get from the other members.

THE FOCOLARE MOVEMENT

The Focolare movement is an international organisation that wishes to bring about the unity of people, groups and communities. The movement's name comes from the Italian word for 'hearth' or 'family fireside' and it sees the world as one family, in a communion of diversities. The Focolare movement believes a united world is not an impossible dream, but rather should be the goal of history and of every man and woman regardless of their religion or beliefs. The Focolare movement proposes the Gospel law 'Love one another' as the basis for relationships among people.

It was founded in 1943 during World War II in Trent, Italy, by Chiara Lubich. Chiara Lubich and her companions started off working with people in the poorest neighbourhoods of the city. After a few months of living their ideal of unity, they had a following of some five hundred people around them in Trent. It wasn't long before the message spread further afield. Today their movement is present in 182 countries and has approximately two million adherents. While the majority are Roman Catholic, there is a growing number of non-Catholics from 350 churches and ecclesial communities. The movement also includes many from other world faiths, for example Jews, Muslims, Buddhists, Hindus and Sikhs. There are also those in the movement who do not adhere to any particular religious faith.

The Focolare movement arrived in Ireland in 1971 and people from all around the country share in Focolare's spirituality for bringing the Gospel into everyday life.

Chiara Lubich

RESEARCH PROJECT

In 2010, Chiara Badano, a member of the Focolare movement, was beatified. Chiara Badano was a modern teenager: she liked to sing, dance, play tennis and skate, until cancer took her life at age eighteen, only two decades ago. Find out more about her life and beatification.

OR

World Youth Day is another large international Catholic gathering that takes place in different countries every few years. Most recently it has been held in Sydney, Madrid and Rio de Janeiro. Find out more about this event, including why it began, where the next one is being held and what people who have attended have to say about their experience.

OR

Find out about the 1932 Eucharistic Congress. How did it compare to the 2012 Congress? Why was this religious event of such historical significance?

YOU WILL FIND ADDITIONAL INFORMATION ON WWW.SEEKANDFIND.IE

SUMMARY

- Ireland's first national Christian radio station, Spirit Radio, launched in 2011.
- The 50th International Eucharistic Congress was held in Dublin in 2012 and was a time of renewal for many Irish Catholics.
- There are more than fifty ecclesial movements in the Catholic Church, including the Focolare movement.

LESSON 31
ADOLESCENT FAITH

Objective: This lesson will identify stages of faith development and describe one youth movement that is spreading the Catholic faith among young people.

OPENING ACTIVITY

On a blank piece of paper, draw a faith map to show the route you have followed in your journey of faith from childhood to the present time. Note any important moments along the way such as receiving the sacraments or the death of a loved one that made you reflect on your faith in a deeper way. Note if these events had a positive or negative impact on your faith. Identify people who have influenced your faith journey as well.

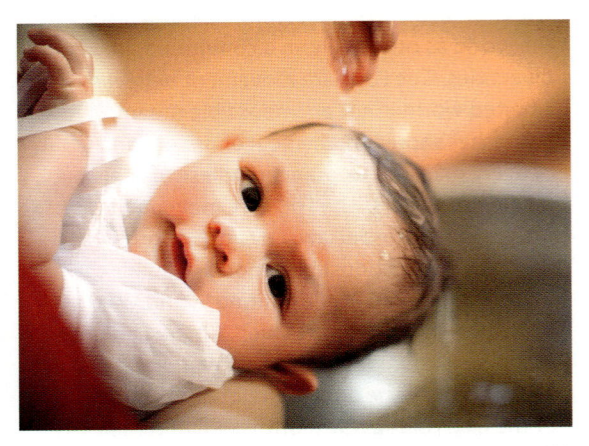

Stages of faith

Adolescence is a time of questioning in one's life: What am I going to do after school? Will I be able to pass the Leaving Cert? Will I get enough points? However, adolescence should also be a time for examining the deeper questions about life: Is there a God? Will I continue to attend my place of worship after I leave home and school? How important is my faith to me? What factors influence my belief systems and how will my faith develop?

Psychologist James Fowler developed a theory suggesting six stages of faith development. While it has been criticised by some who say that it is too intellectual and that the way in which growth in faith actually occurs is more complex and does not necessarily fit into clear stages, Fowler's theory has been very influential.

According to Fowler, in the first three stages, individuals in one way or another rely on some authority outside of themselves for their spiritual belief. In the second three stages,

SECTION C: FAITH IN IRELAND

Blessed Teresa of Calcutta

individuals gradually take on board a particular way of understanding themselves, their world and their relationships with others and with God. Their position is informed by their education, by the influences of those around them and by the teachings of their community of faith. Their faith becomes part of their self-definition rather than something imposed from outside.

1. Young children during the first stage of faith (intuitive–projective) follow the belief of their parents. They tend to imagine angels or other religious figures in stories as characters in fairytales.
2. In the second stage of faith (mythical–literal), children tend to respond to religious stories and rituals literally, rather than symbolically. As individuals move through adolescence to young adulthood, their beliefs continue to be based on authority focused outside themselves.
3. In the third stage of faith (synthetic–conventional), individuals tend to have a conformist acceptance of a belief with little self-reflection or examination of these beliefs. Most people remain at this level.
4. Those who move on to the fourth stage of faith (individuative–reflective) begin a radical move from dependence on others' spiritual beliefs to development of their own. Individuals are no longer defined by the groups to which they belong. Instead they choose beliefs, values and relationships which are important to their self-fulfilment.
5. In the fifth stage of faith (conjunctive), people still rely on their own views but move from being preoccupied with one's self to accepting other people's points of view. They tend to be more tolerant and begin to consider serving others.
6. Those who move to the sixth and final stage of faith (universalising) are rare. As older adults, they begin to search for worldwide values such as unconditional love and justice. Mother Teresa and Mahatma Gandhi are examples of people who reached this stage of spiritual development.

THINK IT THROUGH
- What stage of faith are most adolescents at?
- What stage of faith do you think you are at?
- Can you think of any other people who reached the sixth and final stage of faith?

YOUTH 2000

Youth 2000 was started by a young Englishman called Ernest Williams after World Youth Day in Santiago de Compostela in Spain in 1989, when Pope John Paul II called for young people to spread the Good News of Jesus among their peers. He said: 'It is to you young people that the task first falls of bearing witness to the faith and of bringing into the third millennium the Gospel of Christ, who is the Way, the Truth and the Life.'

In response to this, Ernest began to gather young people together in prayer, and soon this initiative, known as Youth 2000, spread to more than twenty-five countries all over the world. In Ireland there are around forty weekly prayer groups around the country, sixteen to eighteen weekend retreats throughout the year, a summer festival, an annual ball and various other social events – all organised by young people, for young people. Their motto is 'Youth leading youth to the heart of the Church'. Retreats and festivals are open to all young people between the ages of sixteen and thirty-five.

Here is what one person has to say about her experience with Youth 2000:

My name is Maura and I am from County Clare. I attended my first Youth 2000 retreat when I was sixteen after my school chaplain invited me along, and I can honestly say it was one of the best decisions of my life; in fact it was life-changing. I remember initially being nervous at the prospect of not knowing anyone there, and the idea of attending a retreat for a whole weekend was very daunting to say the least. I was brought up as a practicing Catholic but my idea of God was very impersonal. There was something stirring within me though and I really felt I should go. By the end of the retreat I did not want to leave! Looking back I really did not know what to expect and could never have imagined that attending that retreat would bring such peace and joy into my life, take it in a new direction and initiate a beautiful friendship with God.

One of my first impressions from the weekend was of how joyful everyone there was. Not only was their faith so important to them but God was a central part of their lives, someone relevant to them as young people. The happiness and joy I had tried to find in every place outside of the Church was now found. That weekend I became excited at the beautiful plans God has for my life and at the depth and limitlessness of his love for me. His love never fails and never gives up on us, no matter how far we might wander. It is an invaluable and precious experience to spend a whole weekend with fellow young Catholics, to spend time before Jesus in the Blessed Sacrament, to have an opportunity to offload all of your burdens and sins in confession and to return home a changed person. The happiness and joy I had in my heart leaving that weekend was overwhelming and a memory that will stay with me forever. From my experience in Youth 2000 I have begun to discover the direction the Lord wants my life to take and the desires he has put in my heart. When you open your heart to God, amazing things happen!

– Maura Garrihy

OVER TO YOU
- Find out more about Youth 2000 or another youth group in your area that provide opportunities for young people to engage in faith gatherings, prayer meetings or social action.
- Describe how these groups provide opportunities for young people to deepen their faith and put their faith into action in their lives.

' It is to you young people that the task first falls of bearing the faith ...

John Paul II

JOURNAL
Have you ever gone on a retreat? What was the experience like? Would you consider going on retreat in the future? Why or why not?

SUMMARY
- Adolescence is a time of questioning that can include asking meaningful questions about faith.
- Psychologist James Fowler developed a theory suggesting six stages of faith development.
- Everyone's journey of faith is different.
- Youth 2000 is a group for young people with the motto 'Youth leading youth to the heart of the Church'.

LESSON 32
RELIGIOUS DIVERSITY

Objective: This lesson will look at how Irish society respects and accepts difference, and will discuss ecumenism and interfaith dialogue.

OPENING CONVERSATION
Has there ever been a time in your life when you felt that you did not belong? How did it feel to be excluded? Have you ever excluded anyone? Are there any groups in our society that we exclude?

Difference and dialogue

Ireland has, for centuries now, been a predominantly Christian country. In the recent past, however, our country has rapidly developed into a more multicultural society. Until a few years ago, there were four main Christian Churches in Ireland: Roman Catholic, Church of Ireland, the Presbyterian Church and the Methodist Church. Since 1996, however, up to 200,000 immigrants have arrived in the Republic of Ireland – 5 per cent of the current population of four million. Many Black Majority Churches have been established and are developing at a fast rate all over the country. The 2011 census gave the number of Muslims in the Republic of Ireland as 49,204, as compared with 3,875 in 1991. The Buddhist community figure has risen from 986 to 8,703 during the same time period, while membership of the Hindu community has increased from 953 to 10,688. Living in such a diverse society presents a wonderful opportunity to explore various traditions. Living in such a diverse society also presents us with some challenges.

When we encounter people whose beliefs about things that we consider fundamental to how we see ourselves, our world, our relationships with one another and with God are different from our own, it can be difficult to know how to handle that difference. We live in a society that strives to respect difference and uphold freedom. Much as we might like for everyone to believe in something as fervently as we might believe, it is unrealistic to expect that this will happen. So rather than resisting difference, we need to see it as an opportunity to broaden our minds to new traditions and new cultures.

This requires an honest effort to learn about the beliefs and practices of those who are different from us so that we will understand where they are coming from. Ecumenism and interfaith dialogue are two methods of discourse.

When we enter into conversation and partnership with other faith traditions we must bring our true and honest selves into that dialogue. Our own faith beliefs and practices are part of our identity. As in our everyday friendships with others, good relationships with other believers come from an honest sharing of who we are and what we believe. Before we can engage in a faith dialogue with others we must be able to express our own beliefs. We must also listen with openness and respect to the beliefs of others.

INTERFAITH DIALOGUE

Interfaith dialogue happens when people from different faiths work together through dialogue to understand each other's faith background. The history of interfaith dialogue dates as far back as religion itself. History records many examples of interfaith initiatives throughout the ages. However, it was in the 1960s with the Second Vatican Council, and specifically the document *Nostra Aetate* (1965), that interfaith dialogue really gathered pace.

Since Vatican II, the Catholic Church has continued to state that it has the right and duty to proclaim the Gospel. It also recognises the value of what God is doing in the lives of other believers and thus engages in dialogue with them. The ultimate aim of this dialogue is the 'conversion of all towards God' (*Dialogue and Proclamation*, 41), and it can take many forms:

» The dialogue of life, in which people strive to live in an open and neighbourly spirit, sharing their human problems and preoccupations.
» The dialogue of action, in which Christians and others collaborate for the integral development and liberation of people.
» The dialogue of theological exchange, where specialists seek to deepen their understanding of their respective religious heritage, and to appreciate each other's spiritual values.
» The dialogue of religious experience, where persons rooted in their own religious tradition share their spiritual riches, faith and ways of searching for God or for the Absolute. (DP, 42)

Ecumenism

The movement to restore unity among Catholic, Protestant and Orthodox Christians is known as ecumenism. Catholicism, Protestantism and Orthodoxy are siblings within one family of God, the Body of Christ. While each one has distinct traditions, teachings and practices, all Christians are baptised and so are united in Jesus Christ as their leader. All Catholics must be committed to work for the unity of all the baptised. At the hour of his Passion, Christ himself prayed for unity among his followers: 'That they may all be one. As you, Father, are in me and I am in you, may they also be one in us …' (Jn 17:21).

IRISH COUNCIL OF CHURCHES

The Irish Council of Churches (ICC) was founded in 1922 and is an ecumenical Christian body.

The members of the Irish Council of Churches are:
- The Antiochian Orthodox Church
- The Church of Ireland
- The Greek Orthodox Church in Britain and Ireland
- The LifeLink Network of Churches
- The Lutheran Church in Ireland
- The Methodist Church in Ireland
- The Moravian Church (Irish District)
- The Non-Subscribing Presbyterian Church of Ireland
- The Presbyterian Church in Ireland
- The Religious Society of Friends
- The Rock of Ages Cherubim and Seraphim Church (Eternal Sacred Order of Cherubim and Seraphim)
- The Romanian Orthodox Church in Ireland
- The Russian Orthodox Church in Ireland
- The Salvation Army (Ireland Division).

The Irish Inter-Church Meeting (IICM) was established in 1973 as a forum between ICC's member churches and the Catholic Church. The Christian denominations who attend the IICM have all agreed to recognise the Common Certificate of Baptism. The essential elements of Baptism, according to the Catholic tradition, consist of immersing the candidate in water or pouring water while pronouncing the invocation of the Blessed Trinity. Water is poured 'in the name of the Father and of the Son and of the Holy Spirit'. Baptism is unrepeatable. 'Given once for all Baptism cannot be repeated' (CCC, 1272). The Common Certification of Baptism recognises this fact.

Of the members of the Irish Council of Churches, the Church of Ireland has the largest congregation, at 134,365 members according to the 2011 census. This census also shows that the second largest Christian denomination, other than Catholic, is the Orthodox Church (45,223 members). There are two branches of Orthodox Christianity: the Eastern Orthodox Church and the Oriental Orthodox Church. All of the Orthodox Churches in the Irish Council of Churches belong to the Eastern Orthodox Church.

The Catholic Church and the Orthodox Church share several characteristics, including the practice of seven sacraments and belief in the real presence of Christ in the Eucharist. Both Churches also honour Mary as the greatest of all the saints. Pope John Paul II recognised this as a significant element of the communion between the Catholic and Orthodox Churches when, in 1997, he proclaimed, 'It gives great joy and comfort to this sacred Synod that among the separated brethren too there are those who give due honour to the Mother of our Lord and Saviour ...' While there remain disagreements regarding the dogmas of the Immaculate Conception and of the Assumption, Catholics and Orthodox Christians share a common belief in Mary's divine motherhood and perpetual virginity. These beliefs, among others, unite the Church in a particular way.

There are many encouraging ecumenical initiatives in Ireland. One of these is the Week of Prayer for Christian Unity, which is held each year in January. During this week people are urged to pray for Christian unity and to engage in other activities to promote Christian unity. Each year a particular theme is chosen for the week. Christmas carol services and other annual events are also sometimes held jointly.

THINK IT THROUGH

▶ How can you contribute to building unity? Decide on an initiative that you can become involved in with a view to promoting ecumenism or interfaith dialogue. For example you might:

- Organise an interfaith or ecumenical prayer service
- Talk to your teacher about inviting a leader from another Christian Church to address your class
- Interview people from other traditions about their beliefs and faith practices.

GROUP WORK

Working in small groups, write the heading 'Diversity in Ireland' in the centre of a large sheet of paper. Using old newspapers or magazines, create a large display by cutting out relevant headlines and images. Glue these onto the sheet. Consider drawing images that symbolise the various religious traditions in Ireland working together. Display your work.

SUMMARY

- In recent times Ireland has changed from being a traditionally Christian country to being an increasingly multicultural society.
- Religious diversity presents Irish society with an opportunity to discover other traditions, and challenges us to come to a deeper understanding of the Christian and Catholic traditions.
- Ecumenism involves different branches within Christianity working together.
- Interfaith dialogue involves people from different faiths working together.

LESSON 32 – RELIGIOUS DIVERSITY

LESSON 33
ORIGINS OF JUDAISM

Objective: This lesson will explain the cultural context in which Judaism, one of the major world religions, originated.

OPENING ACTIVITY

To begin, under the heading 'Judaism Brainstorm', draw the below table in your RE journal. How much information can you remember about the Jewish religion from your Junior Certificate course?

When you have completed this task, in pairs, share your information. Discuss the facts with the whole class and write the common points on the board. Are there any points of information on the board that you did not remember?

FOUNDER	PLACE OF ORIGIN	SACRED TEXT	PLACE OF WORSHIP	PLACE OF PILGRIMAGE	MONOTHEISTIC/ POLYTHEISTIC

Context

Since the beginning of time, in every corner of the world, humanity has shared a common quest for meaning. Despite the thousands of miles that separated the ancient civilisations, they each established traditions and rituals that offered meaning in their quest. Judaism was the first great world religion to state explicitly a belief in only one God, which was in utter contrast to the polytheistic beliefs of the time. God revealed himself to the Jewish people, through his chosen leaders, as the God who created the world and all that is, the God of all creation and not just of a particular nation. The Jewish people believe that God not only created the universe but that every Jew can have an individual and personal relationship with God. They believe that God has chosen to have a special relationship with the Jewish people and that he will lead them, protect them from harm of any kind and vindicate them in the face of their enemies. Judaism is also the parent of two other monotheistic religions: Christianity and Islam.

With fourteen million followers worldwide, Judaism is one of the largest world religions. Let's take a closer look at what makes this one of the most beautifully spiritual religions in the world.

ORIGINS, FOUNDER AND LOCATION

According to Jewish law, a Jew is anyone born of a Jewish mother or who is a convert to Judaism in accordance with Jewish law. Judaism is a religious tradition that has its origins dating back nearly four thousand years in the land we now refer to as Israel. Abraham, his son Isaac and grandson Jacob are known as the Patriarchs of Israel. Their faith is founded on the covenant which God established with them: that he would be their God and they would be his people. The term 'Hebrew' refers to the descendants of the Patriarchs of Israel.

According to Jewish tradition, Jews trace their origins as a distinct people to the time when Abraham, the first patriarch, lived. Abraham was born Abram in Ur in Babylonia in the year 1800 BCE. At the time the Jewish people were nomadic, i.e. they spent their lives travelling around looking for water and rich pastures for their animals. Abraham was one such nomad living in Ur (modern-day Iraq) who believed in the one true God. When Abraham was aged seventy-five, God asked him to leave his father's house in Ur with his caravan (extended family) and go to the land of Canaan (modern-day Israel). In return, God would ensure that he and his elderly barren wife Sarah would be blessed with many descendants, who would become known as the Hebrews. They were to become God's chosen people. For God's part, he would be their God and would deliver them from evils of all kinds. This is the covenant that God established with his people. In addition to this, God also promised Abraham that Canaan would be set aside for the Hebrew race, and it became known as the Promised Land.

Map of Iraq showing Ur

TIMELINE	
THE OLD TESTAMENT	The history of Judaism is inseparable from the history of Jews themselves. The early part of the story is told in the Hebrew Bible (Old Testament). It describes how God chose the Jews to be an example to the world, and how God and his chosen people worked out their relationship.
THE BRONZE AGE	Jewish history begins during the Bronze Age in the Middle East. The birth of the Jewish people and the start of Judaism is told in the first five books of the Bible. God chose Abraham to be the father of a people who would be special to God, and who would be an example of good behaviour and holiness to the rest of the world. God guided the Jewish people through many troubles, and at the time of Moses he gave them a set of rules by which they should live, including the Ten Commandments.
THE BIRTH OF JUDAISM	The Jews, under God's guidance, became a powerful people with kings such as Saul, David and Solomon, who built the first great temple. From then on Jewish worship was focused on the Temple, as it contained the Ark of the Covenant and was the only place where certain rites could be carried out.
THE KINGDOM DECLINES	Around 920 BCE, the kingdom fell apart, and the Jewish people split into groups. This was the time of the prophets. Around 600 BCE the Temple was destroyed and the Jewish leadership was killed. Many Jews were sent into exile in Babylon. Although the Jews were soon allowed to return home, many stayed in exile, beginning the Jewish tradition of the diaspora – living away from Israel.
REBUILDING A JEWISH KINGDOM	The Jews grew in strength throughout the next three hundred years, despite their lands being ruled by foreign powers. At the same time they became able to practice their faith freely, led by scribes and teachers who explained and interpreted the Bible. In 175 BCE, the King of Syria desecrated the Temple and implemented a series of laws aimed at wiping out Judaism in favour of Zeus worship. There was a revolt by the Jews (164 BCE) and the Temple was restored. The rededication of the Temple is celebrated in the Jewish festival of Hannukah (Feast of Dedication).

(From bbc.co.uk)

OTHER ASPECTS OF THE JEWISH TRADITION

The name of God is so sacred to Jews that they avoid uttering it. Only the High Priest could pronounce the name of God – and only once a year in the prayer of the day of atonement. Once the Temple was destroyed in 70 CE, no Jew uttered the name again. From that time, devout Jews when reading the word YHWH in the Bible read *Adonai* (the Lord). Many Orthodox Jews go a step further and substitute *HaShem* ('the name') for God.

In the Jewish tradition, moral laws are understood as part of a covenant or sacred agreement with God, as part of a special relationship with God, not just as a set of random rules. Apart from the commonly known Ten Commandments, Jewish theologians have identified 613 commandments (*mitzvoth*) derived from the Torah that apply more specifically to Jews. They relate to the following areas: relationship with God, respect for the Torah, signs and symbols, prayers and blessings, love and brotherhood, treatment of the poor, treatment of Gentiles (non-Jews), marriage and family, holy times, dietary rules, business practices, property rights, law and punishment, prophecy, rituals and sacrifices. All these are important, especially to strict or Orthodox Jews today.

Isabella Lenga, a sixteen-year-old Jewish girl from England, speaks of such laws and especially of having to keep thirty-nine strict rules on the Sabbath, including not being able to turn on a light or the television:

> I believe those are the words of G-d ... I'm Jewish and I'm proud ... The importance of Jewish faith to me – it's my identity ... I have things with me all the time that remind me of my Judaism ... Obeying the laws really do bring me closer to G-d ... I find that it's really spiritual and I enjoy keeping the Sabbath.
> (From Channel 4, 4thought.tv)

OVER TO YOU
- Summarise the origins of Judaism in your own words.
- How do Jews show respect for the name of God?
- Apart from the Ten Commandments, how many other commandments make up the Jewish moral laws?
- What do these relate to?

THINK IT THROUGH
- Why is the relationship between Christians and Jews significant?

SUMMARY
- The Hebrews first lived in a place called Ur.
- Abraham made a covenant with God that he would move his family to Canaan and in return was promised the Holy Land and many descendants.
- Canaan has been known by a number of different names such as the Promised Land, the Holy Land, Palestine and Israel.
- In the Jewish tradition, moral laws are understood as part of a covenant between God and God's people.

Ancient Byzantine mosaic depicting Abraham offering the sacrifice of a ram in place of his son, Isaac

LESSON 34
RITUAL AND JUDAISM

Objective: This lesson will describe the role of ritual in the Jewish tradition, in particular those rituals associated with the Sabbath.

OPENING CONVERSATION
Name one thing you do every day. Why is this action part of your daily ritual? What would happen if you forgot to carry out this action? Can you think of any one thing that members of your religion do regularly? Name this action and explain why it is carried out.

Ritual in everyday life

As humans, we find ourselves constantly performing our own daily habits: the ritual of brushing our teeth every morning and evening; the ritual of eating our lunch at the same time and place each day; the ritual of watching our favourite TV programme every Saturday night. However, rituals can also be religious in nature. Religious rituals involve a deeper level of reflection. A ritual may be defined as a formal religious ceremony, approved by religious authorities, which gives a regular pattern to people's worship of God. Some religious rituals encourage us to be mindful of the death of a loved one and hence reflect upon the afterlife; some rituals remind us of our belief in God. The ritual of blessing oneself in the shape of a cross when passing a church building reminds Christians of the crucifixion of Christ. In Islam, the daily prayer ritual, Salat, is the duty of all Muslims and occurs five times during the day. Religious rituals focus our minds on a deeper level. Rituals are very much part of how Jewish people express their religion.

JUDAISM AND RITUAL
Being the oldest monotheistic religion, it is no wonder that Judaism is considered to be one of the most spiritually ritualistic religions in the world. Indeed Jewish followers have been called 'the people of the Book' because their belief is based on the Book, the Torah. These texts remind Jews of the importance of traditional rituals. As the parent religion of Christianity, a number of Christian rituals have their origins in Judaism. Despite centuries of persecution, Jewish people have passed down these religious rituals for several generations. Let's take a closer look at one important ritual in the Jewish tradition – the Sabbath.

Table ready for the traditional Seder ritual during the Jewish holiday of Passover

LESSON 34 — RITUAL AND JUDAISM

THE SABBATH (SHABBAT)

God gave the Ten Commandments, which are also known as the Decalogue, to Moses and through Moses to the people. The Ten Commandments are best understood in the context of the covenant between God and his people. In the covenant God promised to be with his people through thick and thin and to love them unfailingly. He promised to show them how to live, to protect them from harm and to deliver them from their enemies of all kinds. In return they would be God's people. How they would do this was summed up in the Ten Commandments.

The Sabbath, the weekly day of rest, is a uniquely Jewish concept in origin and is the fourth of the Ten Commandments in the Jewish tradition. The Jewish belief in the Sabbath is based on the Creation account in the Book of Genesis, which describes God creating the world and everything in it in six days and resting on the seventh day. 'So God blessed the seventh day and hallowed it, because on it God rested from all the work that he had done in creation' (Gn 2:3).

There is a famous Jewish saying that the first thing God blessed is time. He blessed it by withdrawing or resting. The Jewish Sabbath (Shabbat) begins at sunset on Friday and ends at sundown on Saturday. On the eve of Shabbat the house is made especially clean and tidy to greet the Sabbath and a special meal is cooked. The table is set with special china and silver. In the Book of Deuteronomy, we read:

> Six days you shall labour and do all your work. But the seventh day is a sabbath to the Lord your God; you shall not do any work – you, or your son, or your daughter, or your male or female slave, or your ox or your donkey, or any of your livestock, or the resident alien in your towns, so that your male and female slave may rest as well as you. Remember that you were a slave in the land of Egypt, and the Lord your God brought you out of there with a mighty hand ... therefore the Lord your God has commanded you to keep the sabbath day.
> (Deut 5:13-15)

So the Sabbath is equally for all of God's creation without difference or privilege. Work is seen as the productive work which is carried out during the week, by human beings as co-workers with God in creation. But one day each week the Jews are reminded that there is a limit to human striving. Ultimately creation belongs to God.

In all there are thirty-nine different types of work forbidden on the Sabbath. Thirty-nine is a symbolic number – it recalls the thirty-nine types of work that were performed in building the Temple in Jerusalem. In contemporary times, strict Jewish laws would consider as 'work' switching on or off an electrical appliance or light, or driving a motor vehicle, but technological devices such as timers and the automatic operating of lights are permitted under Jewish law, provided they are set prior to the Sabbath.

The Sabbath for Jews is not just a day off work. It is seen as a foretaste of what life will be like in the Kingdom of God. According to the Bible, even when the Israelites arrived in the Sinai desert, God provided the Israelites with manna that could be cooked and eaten like bread. Every day the Israelites gathered bread but on the sixth day they would collect enough for the sixth and for the seventh so that the seventh day would be a day for the Lord – a day of rest.

THE SABBATH MEAL

Two loaves of bread symbolise the two portions of manna or miraculous food that was provided for the Israelites in the desert during the Exodus. A goblet of wine is placed upon the table for the *Kiddush*, a traditional blessing said by the parents over their children:

> The Lord bless you and keep you, the Lord make his face shine upon you and be gracious to you; the Lord lift his face upon you and give you in peace.

The *Kiddush* recalls how God created the earth and the heavens in six days but on the seventh day he rested and made it holy. A blessing is made over the wine, the symbol of Sabbath joy. The Kiddush continues in celebration of the Sabbath. The cup of wine is then passed around the table.

A blessing is made over the two loaves of bread. A portion of bread is then handed to each of those present. During the festive meal traditional Sabbath songs are sung. In the Jewish mystical tradition, the Sabbath is considered a bride and the meal a bridegroom. The Sabbath day begins with synagogue and is then devoted to religious study, to rest, to family and friends.

As the Sabbath draws to a close on Saturday, another ceremony, that of Havdalah, literally 'separation' in Hebrew, marks the end of the Sabbath and the passage back to regular weekdays. The ceremony commences with a blessing over a full cup of wine. A spice box is passed amongst those present in order that the sweet fragrance of the Sabbath may pass on and into the forthcoming week. A blessing praising God, the creator of fire, is made over the flame of the multi-wicked havdalah candle.

The ceremony of Havdalah celebrates the separation of the holy from the profane. Sabbath prohibitions such as lighting the fire are no longer in force. After drinking the wine, the candle is then extinguished.

The singing of *Shavua tov*, 'a good week', begins, in hope of a peaceful and fruitful week until the next Sabbath.

THINK IT THROUGH
- Write down any similarities or differences between the celebration of the Jewish Sabbath and the Sunday celebration of the Eucharist for Christians.

OVER TO YOU
- How would you feel if for one day each week you were unable to turn on a light switch, watch TV, use your mobile phone or play your computer games? Write out a list of words that describe how you would feel.
- Do you have any rituals that help you to turn off or rest in your weekly routine?
- What religious rituals are important to you?

SUMMARY

- Judaism is one of the most ritualistic religions in the world.
- The Sabbath is the Jewish day of rest.
- The Sabbath meal is full of rituals and symbolism.
- Havdalah, literally 'separation' in Hebrew, marks the end of the Sabbath and the passage back to regular weekday.

LESSON 35
CELEBRATIONS AND THE LIFE CYCLE IN JUDAISM

Objective: This lesson will describe how the Jewish tradition celebrates key moments in Jewish life and times of significance throughout the year.

OPENING CONVERSATION
What is your favourite time of the year? With a partner, discuss how your family celebrate it. Do you have any rituals as part of this celebration? What times or events in the life of your family are remembered and celebrated?

Religious celebrations and rituals

Most religions celebrate special events in the life cycle, and Judaism is no exception. Birth, passage to adulthood, marriage and death are all celebrated with religious rituals and are given religious meaning. The history of their relationship with God is particularly important to the Jewish people and the main events in that story are also celebrated each year. Rituals, customs and traditions have been passed down through the centuries and give Jewish people a sense of continuation with the past and of purpose for the future.

The Jewish calendar is based on the appearance of the new moon every twenty-nine to thirty days. Jewish liturgical celebrations operate on three levels: *hallowing of* (blessing or making holy) *the human life cycle*; *hallowing of the year*; *hallowing of the week*. In the previous lesson we explored the celebration of the Jewish Sabbath, which is the principal ritual celebrating the hallowing of the week. In this lesson we look at some of the Jewish rituals to celebrate the life cycle and the year.

Interior of a synagogue in Sofia, Bulgaria

SECTION C: FAITH IN IRELAND

Rituals for the life cycle

CIRCUMCISION

For Jews, children are regarded as a gift, and deprivation of children is seen as a grave misfortune. This belief is expressed in the ceremony of circumcision, which is carried out on all male children on the eighth day after their birth. The term *brit milah* means covenant of circumcision and refers to the covenant between God and Abraham referred to in Genesis 17:9-14. Relatives and friends usually gather in the family home for the ceremony, which is performed by an expert called a *mohel*. At this time the child is also named. In the case of a girl, the father is called up for the reading of the Torah in the synagogue, thanks is given for the new birth and the baby is given her name.

BAR-MITZVAH/ BAT-MITZVAH

When a Jewish boy turns thirteen he is regarded as a 'son of the commandments' and it is marked by a joyous ceremony in the synagogue, called the *Bar-mitzvah*, during which the boy reads a section of the Torah. There is much variety within Jewish traditions. Girls become *Bat-mitzvah*, 'daughter of the commandments', at the age of twelve. In Reform and Liberal communities, this usually includes participating in the synagogue service and reading from the Torah, but in Orthodox communities girls are not allowed to do this. The occasion is marked in other ways. It is not uncommon to hear of adults celebrating the *Bar-* and *Bat-mitzvah* – they may not have been able to mark this milestone in their faith when they actually reached the age of twelve or thirteen. They see it as a way of renewing Jewish faith. Many travel to Jerusalem for this and the rituals take place at the Wailing Wall or at the ruins of Masada, an ancient fortification where the last Jewish stronghold against Roman invasion stood.

KIDDUSHIN (MARRIAGE)

Kiddushin, the Hebrew word for marriage and meaning 'sanctification', expresses how Jews view marriage. It is the sacred relationship in which God is seen as the third partner. The ceremony takes place under a canopy, a *huppah*. This *huppah* can be a simple as a *tallit*, a prayer shawl, held over the couple's heads by four friends of the groom, or it can be a more elaborate affair. It symbolises the sacred space of the family home. The ceremony usually takes the following form: first, blessings are recited over wine and both partners drink from a cup as a symbol of shared joy; second, the ring is given to the bride by the groom; third the *Ketubah*, a special type of Jewish prenuptial agreement, is read and given by the groom to the bride. It is for her to keep. While Jewish marriage is sacred, it is also a legal contract. The *Ketubah* expresses this. According to Jewish law, it spells out the responsibilities of the husband to his wife. It is prepared before the wedding, signed by the future husband and two witnesses. It has become customary to present the *Ketubah* as a beautifully designed document that the couple can display in their home.

OVER TO YOU

▶ Compare the rituals for the life cycle in Judaism to Christianity. What are the similarities? What are the differences?

Celebrations of holydays and festivals during the year

There are both major and minor festivals during the Jewish year. Here we examine two of the major festivals.

FESTIVAL OF PASSOVER

Passover is one of the three pilgrim festivals, so called because three times a year every Jew was to make pilgrimage to the Temple in Jerusalem. It commemorates the Exodus from Egypt and occurs in the spring. The fullest biblical account of Passover is found in Exodus 12:1-14.

The Passover was originally celebrated by individual families. By the seventh century it was permitted only in the Temple in Jerusalem. This explains why Jesus travelled to Jerusalem with Mary and Joseph to offer sacrifice and eat the Passover meal. After the destruction of the Temple in 70 CE, Passover once again became a home-based celebration.

Great time is put into the preparation for Passover. The house is spring-cleaned to ensure the removal of every trace of leaven, as stated in the Torah. Exodus 12:7 calls Passover the Feast of Unleavened Bread. *Matzah*, a bread that is kept especially dry by not giving it time to rise, is the central symbol in the Passover Meal. This is the bread that the Jews ate at the time of the Exodus. Leaving in a hurry, there was no time for the bread to leaven (rise), so it remained unleaven.

The Passover Meal is known as the *Seder*, which means 'order', meaning that it progresses according to the order in the Jewish text, the *Haggadah*. *Haggadah* means 'narrative' and the book contains prayers, blessings, psalms, songs and legends relating to the Exodus from Egypt that are read at the Seder meal.

The foods eaten at Passover have symbolic value. The main symbols are placed in the centre of the table on the *seder* plate. They include *matzah*; bitter herbs, usually represented by horseradish which is a reminder of slavery; green herbs, lettuce or parsley, dipped in salt water, a reminder of the tears shed by the Israelites during the slavery in Egypt; *haroset*, a mixture of nuts, spices and wine to represent the mortar with which the slaves had to make bricks, and when eaten gives a 'sweet taste of freedom'; a roasted shank bone, symbolic of the Passover lamb that was offered in the Temple (cf. Exodus 12:8); a hardboiled egg, a symbol of fertility and new life, also representing the *Chagiga* – festive offering; wine, the symbol of joy, drunk four times during the *seder*; and the cup of Elijah, a decorative goblet or glass which is set for the prophet Elijah who, according to popular belief, was expected to return at Passover to announce the coming of the Messiah.

Everyone present takes part in a discussion usually focused on where the lessons of Haggadah apply to present-day issues. Jews see in their children the future of Judaism and so the youngest child has a special role, asking the Four Questions about why this night is different from all other nights:

− Why on this night do we eat unleavened bread?
− Why on this night do we eat bitter herbs?
− Why on this night do we dip our herbs?
− Why on this night do we recline?

For many Jews, the memory of the celebration of Passover as a child with their families stays with them all their lives and nurtures their adult faith.

FESTIVAL OF WEEKS (PENTECOST)

Shavuot, the Jewish Pentecost and the second of the pilgrim festivals, is celebrated seven weeks after the Passover festival. It is the festival of the giving of the law on Mount Sinai and is celebrated by reading the section of the Torah about the giving of the Ten Commandments. It is also customary to eat dairy foods at the festive meals. Confirmation ceremonies often take place in both Reform and Orthodox synagogues since this is seen to be an appropriate time for the *Bar-* and *Bat-mitzvah* rituals of commitment to the Torah. (The third of the pilgrim festivals, Tabernacles, occurs in the autumn.)

OVER TO YOU
- Look up Exodus 12:15 and see why the removal of leaven was important.

THINK IT THROUGH
- Many of the Jewish rituals described are closely based on the Torah. Which Catholic liturgies and rituals are based on the Bible?

JOURNAL
Reflect on one time of significance in your life or the liturgical year where ritual played a part in the celebrations. What rituals were carried out on this occasion? What do these rituals mean? Describe what happened and what it meant to you.

SUMMARY
- Jewish rituals celebrate the life cycle, the year and the week. Many have their origin in the Torah.
- Circumcision takes place eight days after the birth of the male child.
- When a Jewish boy turns thirteen he celebrates his *Bar-mitzvah* and is considered a 'son of the commandments'. Jewish girls celebrate their *Bat-mitzvah*, and are regarded as 'daughter of the commandments'.
- *Kiddushin* is the Hebrew word for marriage. Jewish marriage is sacred and also a legal contract. The *Ketubah* expresses the responsibilities of the husband to his wife.
- Once a year, the Jews celebrate Pesach (Passover), where they give thanks to God for their escape from Egypt. They do this with a Passover meal or Seder meal.
- Shavuot marks the time that the Jewish people were given the Torah on Mount Sinai. Shavuot is sometimes called the Jewish Pentecost.

LESSON 35 – CELEBRATIONS AND THE LIFE CYCLE IN JUDAISM

LESSON 36
JUDAISM AT A LOCAL LEVEL

Objective: This lesson will give an account of how the Jewish community is organised at a local level in Ireland today.

OPENING ACTIVITY
Imagine someone wanted to interview you about what it is like to be a member of your faith community in Ireland today. What are the main points you would share with them?

The life of a Jew in Ireland today
The following is an interview with a member of the Orthodox Jewish community in Dublin.

How many Jews are currently living in Ireland?

At the last census there were 1,984 who named themselves as Jews. However, many of these do not affiliate themselves actively with the community or are only spending a short time working or studying here in Ireland. The number that may be counted as active members of the community is probably less than one thousand persons.

For how many years have Jews been living in Ireland?

The first record of Jews in Ireland dates back to the Annals of Innisfallen [a chronicle of the medieval history of Ireland, believed to have been written between the twelfth and fifteenth centuries] and there was a Jewish mayor of Youghal in the twelfth century, so there have been Jews in Ireland at various times since then, fluctuating in size over the centuries. The current community was enlarged during the last century when many Jews moved to Ireland from mainland Europe because of the impact of the Holocaust. In more recent times many of the community, particularly the young, have moved away from Ireland to larger communities elsewhere.

How would you describe a typical day in the life of an observant Jew?

The Jewish day commences with a short prayer thanking G-d for allowing us to wake for another day. Orthodox male members will attend the three daily services in the synagogue, one in the morning, one in the afternoon and a third in the evening. Before retiring at night, a short prayer is also recited during which we ask G-d to ensure that we wake again next day 'lest we sleep the sleep of death'. Men will don their *tzitzit* (a fringed four-cornered garment which serves to remind

A tzitzit

them of the commandments) as they dress. The *Shema*, or declaration of faith and belief, is recited both in the morning and again in the evening as part of the prayers. In between, the day will continue in a normal fashion, going about work or other necessary deeds as everybody else. On a Friday, however, work will end early so that members can return home in time to prepare for the Sabbath, which commences at sunset.

The women will pray at home in private, except on the Sabbath and holidays, and may well work outside the home too. They are, however, responsible for the maintenance of a kosher home and the early education of the children.

Who is the religious leader in your community and what is their role?

The religious leader is the Rabbi, which literally means 'teacher'. He is responsible for all affairs of a religious nature and will answer all questions on matters pertaining to Jewish laws and customs. He is also responsible for ensuring that there is adequate education in the Jewish faith in the community, both for youngsters and adults. There are some occasions when it is necessary to have a panel of rabbis to make decisions – this panel is called a *Bet Din* (House of Judgment/Law) and at least three rabbis are required for this. As we have only one rabbi here in Ireland, matters that require a *Bet Din* such as divorce, adoption and conversion will be referred elsewhere.

What is your particular role in the synagogue?

As a female lay member I personally do not have any particular role in the synagogue. There is a democratically elected synagogue council that deals with all matters pertaining to the synagogue. Men and some women may serve on this committee but it is only men who organise and assist in conducting the services in the Orthodox communities. From this committee an executive is elected, each of whom takes on certain responsibilities regarding the running of the synagogue and the services.

How would you describe the synagogue in Dublin?

There are certain basic features that are shared by all synagogues. All the features are related to the original Temple:
» They all face towards Jerusalem.
» There is a separate area for women to sit – either a gallery, as in Dublin, or else a thinly curtained-off area at the same

The synagogue in Terenure, Dublin

LESSON 36 – JUDAISM AT A LOCAL LEVEL

- level as the body of the synagogue. In the Temple there was a special courtyard for the women.
» The Ark, which is always at the eastern end of the synagogue, contains the Scrolls of the Torah – the Five Books of Moses, which are handwritten on parchment by a specially trained scribe. These are removed every Sabbath and holyday and carried around the synagogue before being placed on the reading desk for the weekly portion to be read. These scrolls are treated with the greatest respect. All stand when the Ark is opened and the scrolls are removed. We never handle the actual parchment – usually a silver pointer is used to indicate the relevant part of the text by the person reading the weekly portion. If a scroll is dropped, everyone present must fast.
» Above the Ark, the Ten Commandments, as listed in the Torah, are usually displayed in two adjacent columns of five each. One column lists the five commandments between man and G-d, and the second column lists the five commandments between man and man.
» Ner Tamid – the continuous light. Just in front of the Ark, hanging from the ceiling is a light that always burns. This represents the seven-branched candelabra – the Menorah – that stood in the Temple and was re-lit daily by the priests.
» The Bimah – a raised platform in the centre of the synagogue where the Torah is read from and from where the person leading the service may conduct the prayers. In some synagogues this is done from a reading desk at the front near the Ark. Only the Torah reading is carried out on the Bimah.

What kind of work do the members of your synagogue carry out?

The members of the community carry out all the same varieties of work as the general population of the country. We have lawyers, accountants, doctors, businessmen, nurses, teachers, artists, shop keepers …

Many are also involved in voluntary work, both within the Jewish community and in the local community.

What is it like being a Jew in Ireland today?

Ireland as a democratic state respects the religious freedom of its citizens. The Jews, like all Irish citizens, are free to practice their religion and secure their religious needs. As we are a small community we rely on the cooperation of one single shop that has a special section for the sale of kosher meat, poultry and other food items. This is

Detail of the antique Holy Ark in Nechalim synagogue, Israel

Bat-mitzvah – reading from the Torah in a Reform/Liberal synagogue

overseen by the Rabbi and a member of the community to ensure that only acceptable items – that is, those that are under rabbinic supervision – are included.

There is a school that has a Jewish ethos, Stratford College in Rathgar, where Jewish studies and Hebrew, the language of the prayer and the Torah, are taught.

Due to the small size of the Jewish community, a large number of the pupils there are not Jewish.

Jewish people play a large part in the general community and we have often had and have members of the Dáil (Alan Shatter, Mervyn Taylor), Lord Mayors (Robert Briscoe and more recently his son Ben Briscoe in Dublin; Gerald Goldberg in Cork), as well as members playing an important part in other disciplines such as law (Judge Henry Barron, Justice Hubert Wine), medicine (Professor Gerald Tomkin, Professor Abrahamson) and the arts (Gerald Davis) to name a few.

Tell us about the Jewish Museum in Dublin

Situated on Walworth Road, Dublin 8, in the centre of what has been called Little Jerusalem, the Jewish Museum has a wide variety of exhibits. The upper floor is actually an old synagogue and all the features previously described can be seen there. To the rear there are displays of Torah covers and Ark curtains (*parochet*) as well as a section on circumcision. An open Torah scroll can also be seen, as well as the charred remains of another one retrieved from the Holocaust and recently contributed to the museum. Downstairs there are sections dealing with the Holocaust, famous personages from the community, past chief rabbis, Chaim Herzog (former president of Israel), and various features of life in the community over the years. This includes sections on youth groups. A small kitchen with the table prepared in readiness for the Sabbath with candles, wine and two covered loaves of bread demonstrates an important feature of Jewish life. Various documents and paintings by Jewish artists can be seen on the walls in the stairway.

What do you think are the challenges that face Judaism in today's world?

The same challenges are faced by Judaism as by all other faiths in our ever-changing world. Judaism aims to maintain its standards and ensure that our youngsters are educated so that they can continue the practice of their faith in the same way as has been done over the centuries. It is said that 'It is not the Jews that have kept the Torah but the Torah that has kept the Jews'.

Our laws all emanating from the Five Books of Moses and their interpretation by the rabbis of old have remained unchanged over the centuries, and it is this constancy which has enabled Judaism to survive two exiles, the Crusades, the Inquisition and the Holocaust.

What does Judaism mean to you?

Judaism is a complete way of life. It governs what you do from the moment you wake in the morning until you go to sleep again at night. It covers the cycle of life from birth to death with various significant stages:

- Naming of a female child
- Circumcision and naming of a male child on the eighth day of life
- Redemption of the male firstborn on the thirty-first day of life
- *Bar-/Bat-mitzvah* – the transition from child to adult in a religious sense at the age of twelve for a girl and thirteen for a boy
- Weddings
- Death and burial.

Each of these is accompanied by its own ritual and ceremony, which has remained unchanged over the centuries.

The laws of the Bible also instruct us on how to behave towards our fellow man, showing care for the less fortunate and respecting our fellow man, being honest in business etc. All this shows us how to conduct ourselves and therefore governs the way we carry out our daily tasks. In everything that we do, we are aware of our Maker and bless and thank him for everything in the wonderful world that he has created. To me, being a Jew means trying to carry out all these duties and responsibilities and to conduct myself in a way that will be an example to others. Also I have tried to ensure that my children are taught so that they too can continue to carry on this way of life and pass it on to their children.

> ‘ *The laws of the Bible instruct us on how to behave towards our fellow man …*

OVER TO YOU

- Look up what it means to keep a kosher home.
- Who is the current Rabbi in Ireland?
- Look up Orthodox and Reform Judaism and note some of the main differences between them.

Comparative Religious Studies

Conduct a similar interview with a member of a different faith community and present a comparison with the Jewish faith.

YOU WILL FIND ADDITIONAL INFORMATION ON WWW.SEEKANDFIND.IE

SUMMARY

- The daily life of an observant Jew is centred around prayer.
- The religious leader is the rabbi, which means 'teacher'.
- There is a synagogue, a kosher shop and a school with a Jewish ethos in Ireland which helps the Jewish community practice their faith.

LESSON 37
ORIGINS AND RITUALS OF ISLAM

Objective: This lesson will explore the beliefs, rituals and traditions of the followers of Islam.

OPENING ACTIVITY
With a partner, write out all the Muslim practices and beliefs that you are aware of. Keep the record of what you have written so that you can refer to it at the end of the lesson.

Origins

Islam is the second largest world religion. The majority of Muslims live in North Africa in countries such as Algeria, Libya and Egypt and throughout the Middle East in Saudi Arabia, Iran and Iraq. Like Christianity and Judaism, Islam belongs to the monotheistic family of religions and is a prophetic religion: a religion of the prophets including Abraham, Moses, Elisha, Jonah and Jesus. The last and greatest of the prophets of Islam is the Prophet Muhammad.

The word Islam is derived from the verb 'slm' which means to resign, submit to, or surrender oneself, and Islam means the act of submitting oneself to Allah (God).

The Qur'an

The Qur'an is the 'holy book' of Islam. *Qur'an* in Arabic means recital and it come from the first words of the revelation received by the Prophet Muhammad from the Angel Gabriel. Over a period of twenty-three years until he died at Medina, the prophet continued to receive words of revelation. The Prophet Muhammad could neither read nor write and the words were recorded by scribes on whatever was at hand – dried-out palm leaves, bits of leather, white stones. Within twenty years, the Qur'an was established in its present form with numbering, titling and ordering of the chapters added.

For Muslims the Qur'an is God's presence in the form of the written word. The physical presence of the Qur'an alone is a source of grace and blessing (*barakah*). Muslims throughout the world must memorise the Qur'an, at least those parts of it that are used in worship. The Qur'an can never be translated, and the Arabic language of the text is considered to be chosen by God. Recitation of the Qur'an is very important to Muslims – for them it is the sound of God speaking.

God caused the sounds to be made in the first instance, so the very act of repeating them links the believer to God and hence to the original revelation.

Muslim artists have decorated their mosques with verses from the Qur'an, and verses are sometimes encased in an amulet and hung around the neck as a protection against evil.

The Qur'an

LESSON 37 – ORIGINS AND RITUALS OF ISLAM

Pilgrimage to Mecca

The Five Pillars of Islam

The five main religious duties or obligations of Muslims are called the Five Pillars:

THE DECLARATION OF FAITH: SHAHADA

The first duty of a Muslim is to declare the belief that 'there is only one God – Allah – and Muhammad is the Prophet of God'. To affirm this belief in front of witnesses is to declare oneself as a member of the community of believers. These words are said fourteen times a day if a Muslim says all the daily prayers that are required. They are heard at every significant occasion from birth to death and several times in between.

RITUAL PRAYER: SALAT

Prayer is central to the daily life of Muslims and must be preceded by ritual washing. There are five compulsory prayer times: at dawn, noon, mid-afternoon, sunset and late evening. A set cycle of words is used along with ritual movements and gestures. Each cycle is called a *raka'ah*, and the prayers are said in Arabic. Muslims are required to pray in the direction of Mecca. This is known as the *qibla* and is marked in the mosque by a niche called the *mihrab*. Today the *mihrab* is a symbol of the Islamic community united worldwide in prayer. The Friday *Salat* is observed by a congregation in the mosque, yet *Salat* can be observed anywhere. According to Islam, there are no sacred persons, no mediators between the believer and God. Every place is a mosque – all that matters is that the place should be clean, and to ensure that, Muslims use prayer mats.

ALMSGIVING: ZAKAT

Muslims believe that they do not own natural riches permanently but only that they have been given to them by means of trust. *Zakat* is compulsory. Muslims are expected to give two and a half per cent of their annual savings to their right benefactors. An early Islamic spiritual writer observed how prayer, fasting and almsgiving are relayed: 'Prayer carries us halfway to God; fasting brings us to the door of his praises; almsgiving procures for us admission.'

FASTING: SAWN

A compulsory fast is prescribes for all adults who are capable of it during the lunar month of Ramadan. It was during that month that the Prophet first received the revelation of the Qur'an. From dawn to sunset, Muslims fast from all food and drink. Ramadan is a reminder that the duty of the flesh is to serve the spirit rather than to engross the spirit. The ideal goal of Ramadan is for one to stand before God in one's original nature and to remove anything that might separate one from God. The rigours of the fasting also help to remind people of their dependence on God. Fasting also helps with an identification with the poor.

Ramadan is not a sad or sombre time. At the end of the day when the fast is finished, people gather with friends and family for food and simple entertainment. The first day of the month following Ramadan is a celebration of release and a time of family reunions and gift-giving. It is called *Eid al Fitr*, the Festival of the Breaking of the Fast.

PILGRIMAGE: HAJJ

The last Pillar of Islam, pilgrimage to Mecca, is the crowning glory of a Muslim's life. Every adult who is physically and financially capable is required to make the pilgrimage to Mecca once in a lifetime. Like all pilgrimage, the *Hajj* is about moving out of the ordinary, leaving family and friends, and for many it involves travelling long distances. In the past, because of the difficulties and dangers of travel, there was always a possibility that one might not return from the *Hajj*.

As the pilgrims approach Mecca, the *Hajj* opens with the cry, 'Here I am, Lord, here I am'. Male pilgrims wear a seamless garment made of two unstitched sheets of cloth, the *ihram*, while women are permitted to wear their normal dress. Distinctions of rank are removed and all stand before God in their common humanity. The *kaaba*, a cube-shaped structure in the middle of the mosque court, is circled seven times. Between the eight and the tenth day of the pilgrimage the climax is reached on the plain of Arafat. After a night's journey, the pilgrims stand from dawn to near sunset in recalling how Abraham 'stood' against idolatry. Near the plain of Arafat on the tenth day animals are sacrificed in commemoration of Abraham who, in obedience to God, was prepared to sacrifice his son.

Muslims celebrating the Mawlid-al-Nabi festival in Agra, India

Muslim festivals

The Muslim word for festival is *id* or *eid*, taken from an Arabic word meaning returning at regular intervals.

Muslims observe a number of religious festivals and also celebrate life in all its stages in the family and in the community. A number of minor festivals are celebrated annually.

Mawlid-al-Nabi remembers the birthday of the Prophet Muhammad. This date is especially important to Muslims because the birth of the prophet is regarded as a great blessing for the whole of creation.

Laylat-al-Qadr or Night of Power celebrates the first revelation Muhammad received from the Angel Gabriel. Muslims regard this as the most important event in history. It is celebrated by

Thousands of people gathered in front of the mosque at the Taj Mahal to celebrate the Muslim festival of Eid ul-Fitr

praying and reciting the Qur'an. Many Muslims spend the entire night reciting the Qur'an.

Lailat-ul-Miraj commemorates the ascension of the Prophet. The festival is celebrated by telling the story of how the Prophet Muhammad travelled in a single night from Mecca to Jerusalem and from there ascended into heaven.

There are two major festivals which are celebrated by Muslims worldwide. *Eid-ul-Adha* marks the climax of the *Hajj* pilgrimage and is also the climax of the Islamic year. It commemorates Abraham's complete submission to God, which is the ideal for every Muslim. Anyone who can afford to do so sacrifices an animal as a symbol of Abraham's sacrifice.

Eid-ul-Fitr is the Festival of the Breaking of the Fast which marks the end of Ramadan. This feast not only celebrates the end of fasting but gives thanks for the self-control needed to participate in the fast. The festival begins when the new moon is first sighted. Everyone wears best or new clothes, and attend celebrations out of doors and in mosques.

Celebration and Ritual

Within the family and local community there are rituals to mark birth, marriage and death.

BIRTH

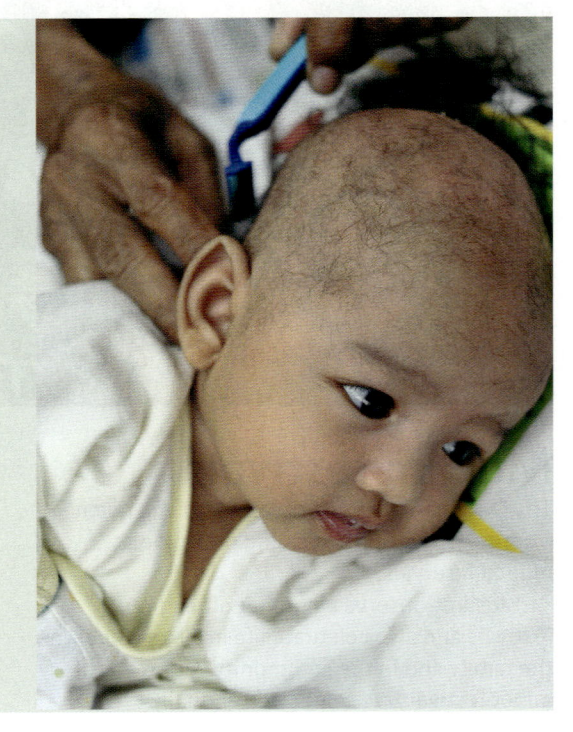

At the birth, after the baby is washed, the *adhan* (call to prayer) is recited into the baby's right ear and the *iqamah* (declaration of starting prayer) into the left ear. A tiny piece of sweet food is placed in the baby's mouth by the baby's father. This symbolises the baby being made sweet, obedient and kind. Seven days later is the ceremony of naming (*Aqiqah*) and circumcision in the case of a boy. The baby's head is shaved according to Islamic tradition, and the same weight as the hair in gold or silver is given to the poor. For Muslims, as for religious people everywhere, a new life is a gift from God and so thanks is given to God. A feast is prepared and usually some food is set aside for the poor.

MARRIAGE

Although in the west marriages are often conducted in the mosque, this is not strictly required. The ceremony is a simple one and may take only a few minutes. The bride need not attend but can send two witnesses to attest to her agreement. Any faithful member of the community can officiate at weddings and funerals as there is no priesthood in Islam.

DEATH AND BURIAL

When a Muslim dies, prompt burial follows the washing of the body and the recitation of prayers. All Muslims are laid to rest on their right side facing Mecca. Men and women are buried separately. Because of their belief in the resurrection of the body, cremation is not practiced.

The mosque in Clonskeagh, Dublin

Beliefs

There are six articles of Muslim faith:

» Belief in One God
» Belief in Angels
» Belief in the Prophets
» Belief in Revelation
» Belief in the Last Things
» Belief in the Measuring Out (that everything comes from God)

BELIEF IN ONE GOD

The first line of the creed (*Kalima*) that is recited five times daily by prayer callers is 'There is only one God – Allah'. Muslims believe that there is one God. He is absolute and real, omniscient and omnipotent. All that is depends on him for existence. The universe and all humankind are his creations. Traditionally Muslims have ascribed ninety-nine 'beautiful names' to God. The most important of these assert that God is compassionate and merciful.

BELIEF IN ANGELS

Angels are frequently mentioned in the Qur'an where they are described as 'messengers of Allah'. They have specific functions given to them by Allah. They watch over humans and guard them against harm. Two 'recording' angels are assigned to every human, one on the right who records all good deeds, and one on the left who records all bad or evil deeds. Angels are neither male nor female. They do not have free will; their defining characteristic is complete obedience to God.

BELIEF IN THE PROPHETS

Allah communicates with human beings through the prophets. They instruct the people on how to live and worship. The Qur'an refers to twenty-five prophets by name, most of whom are also mentioned in the Judeo-Christian Scriptures. The message of the prophets is that God is one and should be obeyed.

BELIEF IN REVELATION

Muslims believe that Allah revealed the Divine Books to his messengers in order for their message to be conveyed to all humankind. Some of these books are as follows:

- The Torah: The Torah is the Sacred Book which was revealed to Prophet Moses.
- The Zaboor (Psalms): The Zaboor is the Sacred Book which was revealed to Prophet David.
- The Injeel (Gospel): The Injeel is the Sacred Book which was revealed to Prophet Jesus.
- The Qur'an: The Qur'an is a record of the actual words of God which the Angel Gabriel brought to the Prophet Muhammad and which is the last of the Divine Books to be revealed.

BELIEF IN THE LAST THINGS

The Qur'an teaches that life on earth is temporary and is a preparation for the life to come. There will be a final judgement when Allah will judge the dead according to their deeds during life on earth. The good, those whose good deeds outweigh the bad, will gain admittance to Paradise while the evil, those whose bad deeds outweigh the good, will be cast into hell.

BELIEF IN THE MEASURING OUT (THAT EVERYTHING COMES FROM GOD)

Muslims frequently use the phrase 'God willing' just as Christians do. This indicates their belief that God created and oversees all creation. They believe that God has absolute knowledge of everything in the past, in the present and in the future. This is balanced by their belief that human beings are responsible for their own behaviour and for requesting forgiveness.

OVER TO YOU

- Recall the Muslim practices and beliefs that you wrote out at the start of the lesson.
- Add to this list any new beliefs and practices you have come across in this lesson.
- Write a paragraph comparing the beliefs and practices of Muslims to another world religion you have studied. Mention at least five features in your comparison.

SUMMARY

- The Qur'an is the sacred text of the followers of Islam.
- The five Pillars of Islam are: The Declaration of Faith, Ritual Prayer, Almsgiving, Fasting, and Pilgrimage.
- The six articles of faith of followers of Islam are: Belief in One God, Belief in Angels, Belief in the Prophets, Belief in Revelation, Belief in the Last Things, Belief in the Measuring Out.

LESSON 38
LIVING AS A FOLLOWER OF ISLAM

Objective: This lesson will focus on how Muslims live out their faith in their daily lives.

OPENING CONVERSATION
Discuss what you think are the main advantages of being a member of a faith community for a young person in Ireland today.

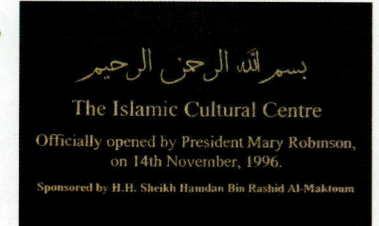

The Islamic Cultural Centre
Officially opened by President Mary Robinson, on 14th November, 1996.
Sponsored by H.H. Sheikh Hamdan Bin Rashid Al-Maktoum

The life of a Muslim in Ireland today

The following is an interview with Dr Ali Selim, who works in the Islamic Cultural Centre in Dublin.

How many Muslims are currently living in Ireland?

In the last census, in 2011, there were approximately 50,000 Muslims living in Ireland. I would expect the Muslim community to be between 60,000 and 65,000 today.

Describe the prayer life of a devout Muslim.

One understanding of prayer in the Islamic tradition is what Muslims call *salat*. The word *salat* refers to the five obligatory daily prayers that Muslims perform in a prescribed way at specific times of the day. The first prayer is offered at dawn time, and consists of two *raka'ahs*. The *raka'ah* is a unit of prayer which involves standing up straight, reciting parts of the Qur'an, bowing down, raising up again, and making two prostrations. The second prayer is at noon time and is made of four *raka'ahs*. The third prayer is afternoon time and is made of four *raka'ahs*, and the fourth prayer is after sunset and is made of three *raka'ahs*. The last prayer is night prayer and it is made of four *raka'ahs*. The timing of the prayers makes us conscious of the existence of God throughout the day.

Who is the religious leader of your Muslim community?

In Islam, we do not have a hierarchical system. We do not have priests. However, we do have Imams. An Imam is similar to a priest in many ways, but is very different in others. First, we don't ordain our Imams. One can become an Imam provided that he has Islamic knowledge; that is the

LESSON 38 – LIVING AS A FOLLOWER OF ISLAM

The interior of a Dublin mosque

The pulpit in a Dublin mosque

criteria. Second, Imams do not claim they are mediators between the people and God. Every Muslim's relationship with God is a direct relationship. Third, we do not refer to our Imams as holy people. However, Imams are highly respected in their community because of their religious knowledge. People listen to them and respect them. Imams, like all Muslims, are encouraged to marry. Being an Imam is usually a full-time and paid job, but an Imam could also be doing something else at the same time.

How would you describe the mosque in Dublin?

Inside the mosque, we don't have benches or chairs. That is because people do not pray while seated. Prayer is made of bowing down, prostration and standing up. However, you will find a few chairs in the mosque. These are to be used by people who cannot offer their prayers in the stated positions. If you go inside a mosque, you will see that it is very simply decorated. This is intentional, to help people concentrate on their prayers. We do not have stained-glass windows, but we do have a pulpit. This is used by the Imam, who gives the sermon. In every mosque there is a sign called the *mihrab*, which tells people what direction they should face when they are praying. When Muslims pray, they face the *kabba* in Mecca.

What is it like being a Muslim in Ireland today?

Whether a Muslim lives in a Muslim country or a non-Muslim country, he or she will be confronted with challenges. However, the type of challenges a Muslim faces in a Muslim country will be different to the challenges he or she faces in a place like Ireland. For instance, there are a lot of pubs in Ireland. Almost 95% of Muslims do not drink, but here it is the norm for people to go to bars and to drink, and that is accepted, it is the culture. That is the difference.

Tell us about the Islamic Cultural Centre in Dublin. What do you do there?

My job is to go out and give talks on behalf of the Islamic Cultural Centre. I take part in conferences representing the organisation, and I also facilitate guided tours of the mosque and of the centre. We welcome two groups of visitors every day. This is very important because it gives people the opportunity to hear first-hand information about Islam.

There are a number of schools on the grounds of the Islamic Cultural Centre. One is the Muslim National School, which is just like any other Irish primary school. The only difference is that the children study Arabic and Islam in that school. Other than that they study the same subjects as other children in other schools. We also have the Qur'anic school. It is attended by 650 children, who go there to learn the Qur'an by heart. The Qur'anic school operates at weekends, in the early morning and in the evenings. Children go there before or after their regular school day. Another school that we have is the Arabic school. It is a weekend school where students study Arabic. All of the students who attend the Arabic school also attend other schools, but here they study science, history and geography in Arabic. This helps them to keep their two native languages and mother tongues. Finally, we have an adult education centre. Here, students who are doing Arabic as part of the Leaving Certificate can come once a week to study that subject. We also have evening courses for non-native speakers who want to learn Arabic.

What does the Islam faith mean to you?

For me, Islam means everything. It means my entire life. I am not the best Muslim and no Muslim can claim themselves to be. I have to admit my shortcomings. However, I am exerting serious efforts to be as good a Muslim as I can be.

School on the grounds of the Islamic Cultural Centre, Dublin

LESSON 38 – LIVING AS A FOLLOWER OF ISLAM

145

OVER TO YOU

- Who officially opened the Islamic Cultural Centre on 14th November, 1996?
- Describe the role of the Imam in the Muslim community.
- Write a paragraph comparing the mosque in Dublin to other places of worship you have studied. Mention at least five features in your comparison.

THINK IT THROUGH

- With a partner, come up with some suggestions as to how relations with Muslims can be fostered within your own age-group.
- Name two similarities and two differences between the beliefs and practices of Catholics and those of Muslims.

SUMMARY

- A Muslim observes five obligatory prayer times each day.
- Religious leaders in Islam are Imams. They do not claim to be mediators between God and humankind.
- For Muslims, their faith is central to their entire life.

LESSON 39
CULTS, SECTS AND NEW RELIGIOUS MOVEMENTS

Objective: This lesson will define the terms 'cult', 'sect' and 'new religious movements'.

OPENING CONVERSATION
What are the first words and thoughts that come to mind when you hear the words 'cult' or 'sect'?

What's in a name?

Although a relatively new term, 'New Religious Movements' (or NRMs) is the term used to describe faiths that have arisen worldwide over the past several centuries. Some examples of NRMs include:

» Those of Christian Origin, e.g. Jehovah Witnesses, Mormons
» Those of Eastern Origin, e.g. Hare Krishna, The Unification Church (Moonies)
» Human Potential Movements, e.g. Scientology, the New Age Movement.

They are a very complex and diverse phenomenon. The terms 'cult' and 'sect' are other terms often used to describe these groups but this can cause difficulty as these terms often have negative connotations.

The word 'cult' comes from the French *culte*, and is rooted in the Latin *cultus*, which means 'worship' or 'devotion to a person or thing'. 'Cult' is an ambiguous term due to the fact that there is no universal definition of a cult and there are differing opinions as to its meaning. In some respects it has become a catch-all term for any group, religion or lifestyle that people don't understand, or with which they disagree. No one ever considers their own religion to be a cult because of the negative connotations associated with the term.

The term 'sect', sometimes used instead of 'cult', is similarly ambiguous. It comes from the Latin *secta*, which means an 'organised church body'. Therefore a sect can refer to:

» A religious denomination
» A dissenting religious group, formed as the result of schism (division; separation)
» A group adhering to a distinctive doctrine or leader.

Theologically, the term 'sect' is used of a group that has divided from a larger body or movement – generally over minor differences in doctrine and/or practice – but whose teachings and practices are generally not considered unorthodox.

'New Religious Movement' is a term that is considered more acceptable than 'cult' or 'sect'. These groups are 'new' in that they present themselves as alternatives to official institutional religion. They are 'religious' in that they claim to offer a religious vision of the world and respond to the fundamental questions of life; and they are a 'movement' as they are structured and often focus on spreading their message. NRMs vary in terms of leadership, authority, ideas about the individual person, family, gender, teachings and organisational structures. Hence, it has become quite difficult to compile a clear set of criteria to describe NRMs.

Sociologists tend to divide NRMs into two groups:

» World-affirming NRMs – These tend to be individualistic with an emphasis on how each member can release his or her human potential. Members usually participate actively in the secular world. These NRMs are often more like a therapeutic movement than a formal religious community.
» World-rejecting NRMs – These groups are more like existing conventional religions. Membership involves prayer, studying a sacred text and living by a moral code. These groups are more likely to be highly critical of secular society.

The Scientology Testing Center, located in Hollywood

CONTROVERSIAL CHARACTERISTICS OF NRMS

Distinctions must be made between different types of New Religious Movements as they do not all share the same characteristics. There are three distinct groups:

» Benign – NRMs that are relatively harmless even though their teachings and practices may be out of step with societal and/or theological norms. They meet the need for a sense of belonging of some people and seem to enhance their personal sense of self-worth.
» Commercial – NRMs that exploit their members for financial gain.
» Destructive – NRMs that preach apocalyptic prophesies and prepare members for the end of time. Examples include doomsday religious groups whose members have been murdered or committed suicide, e.g. the Order of the Solar Temple, Peoples Temple and the Heaven's Gate group.

Media attention tends to focus on the more controversial characteristics of commercial and destructive NRMs, which may include:

- A founder/leader who is a self-appointed, dogmatic, charismatic and authoritarian individual (or a small but powerful leadership group), who maintains control of the group's teachings and practices.
- A focus being placed more on the leader than God. Sometimes the leader claims to have special abilities.
- A consideration that their theology alone possesses the complete truth to salvation.
- The use of mind-control and other forms of manipulation to recruit, indoctrinate and retain its members.
- Secret initiation rites.
- New members experiencing love bombing – a tactic whereby potential recruits are given unconditional acceptance and constant reassurance to help them feel totally loved.
- Members being isolated from their friends and family so that easier control can be exercised over the members physically, intellectually, financially and emotionally. These groups often make great demands on the loyalty and commitment of their followers.
- A belief that 'the end justifies the means' in order to solicit funds and recruit people.
- Members experiencing threats, intimidation and violence when they try to leave.

Jim Jones, founder and leader of Peoples Temple

LESSON 39 – CULTS, SECTS AND NEW RELIGIOUS MOVEMENTS

POTENTIAL RECRUITS

New Religious Movements attract a wide variety of people – rich, poor, educated, un-educated, old, young, religious and atheist. Among the people most likely to join are those who are:

» 'In transit' – between school and university/work, between adolescence and adulthood, between relationships, between jobs, or just in a general stage of searching, feeling lost, alone or seeking meaning.

» 'In difficulty' – hurt because of failed romance/family rows/unemployment or under pressure to decide on career/future/marriage/goals or general difficulties with self-esteem and confidence.

» 'In ignorance' – unaware of their own religious tradition or the traditions of major world religions. Also unaware of the NRM itself, except very superficially, as full knowledge is often not allowed to new members.

THINK IT THROUGH
► What advice would you give to someone who is worried about a friend or family member in a NRM?

RESEARCH PROJECT
Find out more about one NRM and create a profile of it, outlining the key beliefs, characteristics, leadership and lifestyle of members.

YOU WILL FIND ADDITIONAL INFORMATION ON
WWW.SEEKANDFIND.IE

SUMMARY
- Cults are widely interpreted to refer to a group whose beliefs or practices were considered different to mainstream religions.
- A sect is a branch of an established religious group. A sect usually holds a similar worldview to its parent religion.
- 'New Religious Movement' is a term that has been applied to new faiths that have arisen worldwide over the past several centuries.
- There are benign, commercial and destructive NRMs.
- While there is no one reason as to why someone joins a NRM, a general profile type is evident.

SECTION D

MORALITY IN ACTION

LESSON 40
GROWING IN MORALITY

Objective: This lesson will introduce morality and identify the different stages in a person's moral development.

OPENING CONVERSATION

The term 'morality' can be defined in many different ways, some of which are simpler than others. However, even when one uses a relatively simple definition (e.g. morality is concerned with what is right and wrong, or good and evil), a deeper analysis of the definition inevitably reveals more complex questions.

Try to answer the questions below and come up with a class definition for morality:

- How does one know what is right and wrong?
- How do we know that something is good?
- Is morality about actions or character?
- How do we become good people?
- Do we need religion to be moral?
- What is the relationship between what is good for me and what is good for others?

Why be moral?

Can you imagine a world without any sense of morality, where it would be acceptable to kill or steal, where bullying would thrive and the weak and vulnerable of society would be considered worthless? Fortunately, most people have an inbuilt sense of morality, or knowledge of right and wrong, even if it is sometimes underdeveloped. The necessity of cooperating together for the sake of survival or the common good can motivate better behaviour, but morality is not just about this; ultimately it is a matter of love – the responsibility, care and concern we have for other people. Being moral is about doing the right thing, being responsible, loving others, taking their needs into account, taking care of them. For religious believers, this love spreads out from God, who, we are told by the evangelist John, *is* Love.

> Beloved, let us love one another, because love is from God; everyone who loves is born of God and knows God. Whoever does not love does not know God, for God is love. (1 Jn 4:7-8)

OVER TO YOU

- Why is it important to be a moral person?
- Write down five good reasons for being moral and discuss your answers with the class.
- Write down your own definition of morality.

STAGES OF MORAL DEVELOPMENT

As we grow up, our sense of morality should also grow and develop. Various theorists have researched and written extensively about the stages of moral development. From their observations they devise a scheme or model of how morality should develop in individuals, but it is not considered abnormal if we don't follow what they find to be the general pattern. Apart from anything else, people develop at different rates. You could have a very young person who is morally mature, while you could have an older person who is morally immature. There are people who are morally mature in some aspects of their lives (e.g. doing work for social justice) and yet morally immature in other aspects (e.g. cheating on their spouse).

One of the most famous and influential thinkers in this area was Lawrence Kohlberg (1927–87). Based on his research he described three broad levels of moral development, each with two stages.

LEVEL 1: PRE-CONVENTIONAL

Judgement tends to be based just on a person's own needs.

Stage 1: Punishment–obedience – the person obeys rules handed down from authority in order to avoid punishment. The rightness or wrongness of an action is often judged by what consequences it has for the person doing the action. This attitude is seen in very young children, but the stage can persist into adulthood.

Stage 2: Personal reward – actions are done for personal gain and reward. The person's own needs are taken into account when determining right from wrong and there is no great sense of a larger society. Self-interest is a strong feature at this stage.

LEVEL 2: CONVENTIONAL

The expectations that society's laws or conventions have for people are important here.

Stage 3: What's right and wrong can be judged by what pleases others. Approval from the outside is important. There's a growing awareness of a community outside the person. Personal relationships are a strong influence.

Stage 4: Law and order and a sense of society as a whole grows important. Observing laws is important. Social order must be maintained. There are punishments for lawbreaking.

LEVEL 3: POST-CONVENTIONAL

This is the level of abstract and more personal moral principles.

Stage 5: Individual rights are important, and it's good when they are part of some agreed social contract, e.g. The Universal Declaration of Human Rights. People ask about the way society *should* be. There is a commitment to democratic processes.

Stage 6: Individual conscience is important here, along with abstract ideas and principles such as justice and human dignity. People are more able and willing to see the viewpoint of another person. Laws may allow activities that cause, for example, environmental destruction, but the principled person will still challenge that.

LESSON 40 – GROWING IN MORALITY

THINK IT THROUGH
- Do you find this outline of moral development convincing?
- Which moral stage most closely matches your own at the moment (e.g. think of key decisions you might have made)?

REFLECT AND DISCUSS
In Shakespeare's play *Macbeth*, the character Macbeth is ambitious and is tempted to kill the king to steal his crown. Before the proposed murder he has a talk with himself, wondering about the morality of his proposed actions.

MACBETH

If it were done when 'tis done, then 'twere well
It were done quickly: if the assassination
Could trammel up the consequence, and catch
With his surcease success; that but this blow
Might be the be-all and the end-all here,
But here, upon this bank and shoal of time,
We'd jump the life to come. But in these cases
We still have judgment here; that we but teach
Bloody instructions, which, being taught, return
To plague the inventor: this even-handed justice
Commends the ingredients of our poison'd chalice
To our own lips. He's here in double trust;
First, as I am his kinsman and his subject,
Strong both against the deed; then, as his host,
Who should against his murderer shut the door,
Not bear the knife myself. Besides, this Duncan
Hath borne his faculties so meek, hath been
So clear in his great office, that his virtues
Will plead like angels, trumpet-tongued, against
The deep damnation of his taking-off;
And pity, like a naked new-born babe,
Striding the blast, or heaven's cherubim, horsed
Upon the sightless couriers of the air,
Shall blow the horrid deed in every eye,
That tears shall drown the wind.

If you find the language difficult, here it is paraphrased:

If only I could do the murder and get it all over with quickly. If only there were no consequences for murdering the king. If I could get away with it on earth, I'd take my chances on the next life. But our actions are judged here on earth, maybe in our hearts through guilt, or in the law courts. When people do bloody deeds, those actions usually come back to haunt them in some way, like a poisoner who ends up drinking his own poison by some mistake – a kind of poetic justice.

There are many good reasons not to kill the king: he trusts me, I'm his cousin, he's my king. Further I'm his host for the night, and it's not very hospitable to kill your guests. My duty is to protect him, not kill him. Anyway, he has been a very good king, so it will be an even greater injustice. The very heavens will cry out against it.

154 SECTION D: MORALITY IN ACTION

equality · judgement · actions · virtue · working · conscience · right · honour · honesty · conduct · rituals · viewpoint · growth · beliefs · etiquette · values · good · wrong · morality · standards · belief · morals · school · society · conduct · ethics · motives · honesty · integrity · behaviour · philosophy · develop · people · decency

In this speech Macbeth manages to convince himself not to do the murder. But later he is pressurised by his ambitious wife into carrying out the evil deed.

- Consider what stage or stages of moral development the character of Macbeth is at.
- Which of his arguments are most mature? Which arguments are more selfish and immature?

SUMMARY

- Morality is concerned with what is right and wrong.
- People's ideas and motives relating to morality change and develop as they get older.
- These changes and developments can follow certain common patterns that can be observed.
- Each person's moral development is individual to themselves.

LESSON 41
MORAL INFLUENCES

Objective: This lesson will examine the influence of family, friends and school on ideas of morality.

OPENING ACTIVITY
Draw a spider diagram to show all the influences in your life. Who or what has had the most influence on your idea of what is right and wrong?

'EASY EDDIE'
In the 1920s, Al Capone virtually owned Chicago. He was a notorious gangster and mob leader who was involved in numerous illegal activities including smuggling, prostitution and murder. Capone had a lawyer nicknamed 'Easy Eddie' O'Hare. He was very good at his job and his skill at legal manoeuvring kept 'Big Al' out of jail for a long time. To show his appreciation, Capone paid him very well. Eddie lived the high life and gave little consideration to the atrocities that were committed around him. He did, however, have one soft spot – his son whom he loved dearly. Eddie saw to it that his young son had the best of everything: clothes, cars and a good education. Nothing was withheld. And, despite his involvement with organised crime, Eddie even tried to teach him right from wrong. Eddie wanted his son to be a better man than he was. Yet, with all his wealth and influence, there were two things he couldn't give his son while he worked for Capone – a good name and a good example.

One day, Easy Eddie reached a difficult decision. He wanted to rectify wrongs he had done. He decided he would go to the authorities and tell the truth about Al 'Scarface' Capone, clean up his tarnished name and offer his son some semblance of integrity. To do this, he had to testify against the mob, and he knew that the cost would be great. Within a year, Easy Eddie's life was ended in a blaze of gunfire on a lonely Chicago street. But in his eyes, he had given his son the greatest gift he had to offer, at the greatest price he would ever pay.

Al Capone

REFLECT AND DISCUSS
- Do you think Easy Eddie did the right thing?
- What do you think helped him to make his decision?

Moral influences

When faced with moral dilemmas, we all need guidance. Our families can help us decide what is good and worthwhile, what is right and wrong. We are also guided by our schools, our friends, popular culture, our religious traditions and many other influences. At different times in our life certain influences may have a greater impact than others. Let's look at three major influences, family, friends and school, in more detail.

FAMILY

Parents and guardians are probably the most important influences in our moral upbringing. From an early age they teach us about what is right and wrong – 'Don't tease your sister!', 'Don't throw stones at the neighbour's dog!', 'Be nice to Auntie Mary!'. And it is not just what they say – what they do is crucial as well. If they didn't practice what they preached, the impact of their words might not have been as strong. For example, if a parent tells their child not to smoke, but they themselves smoke, they are sending a mixed message.

Of course, parents and guardians are not perfect and will sometimes fall short of the standards they would like to reach. So it is not always the case that the moral guidance of parents will be reliable. For example, a child brought up in a criminal family might not receive good moral guidance in relation to stealing. A child brought up in a racist family may absorb the prejudices and bigotry of their parents. Sometimes parents themselves are not in agreement and a child then has two opposing influences in their life.

Easy Eddie wanted to teach his son right from wrong but knew that his immoral actions were speaking louder than his words. Luckily his decision to change his life had the positive impact he wished on his son: Edward 'Butch' O'Hare became the American Navy's first naval aviator to win the Congressional Medal of Honour. In fact, Chicago's O'Hare International Airport is named after him.

' Show me your friends and I'll tell you who you are.

FRIENDS

You can tell a lot about a person by the company they keep, or as the saying goes, 'Show me your friends and I'll tell you who you are'. Few would deny that our friends have an influence on our moral thinking and behaviour. Theoretically it is possible for us to be friends with criminals and be good, or be friends with saints and be evil, but realistically that's not likely to happen because we tend to be influenced by those with whom we spend the most time. So we do need to choose our friends carefully, and sometimes have to make tough choices in that regard.

A PARENT'S PERSPECTIVE ON PEER PRESSURE

As my children were growing up things went fine – we got along really well, doing all the fun stuff you do with your children. We heard a lot about 'peer pressure' in the media but it never really meant much until our eldest got into her middle teens. After the Junior Cert her best friends went to a different school and that's when the trouble started. It was small stuff at first – staying out much later than we'd agreed on, apologising for it and then doing it again the next night. Then the smell of alcohol and smoke became rather obvious, despite her efforts to hide it. Notes started arriving home from school about missed homework and then missed days. When we talked about it she tended to agree that things were not going well, but as soon as she went out with the new 'friends', the negative behaviour would start again, and indeed got worse. Trying to separate her from these people was hopeless, and made her more defensive if anything. We could admire her loyalty to her friends, but still worried about the effect they were having on her. 'Peer pressure' was now a very real and even threatening presence in our lives.

THINK IT THROUGH
- What evidence of negative moral influences is there in this young girl's life?
- Write your own perspective on peer pressure, either from personal experience or from what you see around you.

SCHOOL

We learn a lot about morality in school. Some of this involves the influence of our friends, which we have just looked at. Then there is what we learn in the formal curriculum. This is true particularly in Religious Education, but moral issues are also dealt with in CSPE (e.g. racism) and SPHE (e.g. bullying). History can provide lots of evidence regarding the impact of moral or immoral actions. In English, novels, films, plays and poetry sometimes deal with moral issues and dilemmas. While these texts may not necessarily set out to teach morality, they do give an opportunity to learn about and reflect upon these issues. More broadly than what you study in class, the school ethos, mission statement and discipline code – all of which seek to teach about appropriate behaviour – also influence our understanding of morality.

GROUP WORK

Working in small groups, choose one of the texts on your Leaving Cert English course and outline the moral issues raised in the text. What in your opinion is the author's 'vision and viewpoint' on these issues? Use the following guide/template for your answer:

- Give the name of the text and author.
- Name a moral issue and give a brief summary of how it is presented in the text.
- How does it conclude? What does this suggest about the author's viewpoint on the issue?
- Do you agree or disagree with the author's position? Give a reason for your answer.

JOURNAL

List all the influences on your moral outlook. Which ones are the most important at this time in your life?

SUMMARY

- Parents have a strong influence on the moral upbringing of children. This influence is usually good, but in certain circumstances can be deficient or even harmful.
- In our moral life we can be heavily influenced by friends because we spend so much time with them and want to have things in common with them.
- In school we learn about morality through those we encounter as well as what we learn in class.
- Hopefully, most of the moral lessons we learn from friends and in school are good, but this may not always be the case.

LESSON 42
MORALITY AND THE LAW

Objective: This lesson will look at whether the State is a good guide when it comes to morality.

OPENING CONVERSATION
Can you think of any actions or activities that are or were legal but not moral? Name as many examples as you can.

The laws of the state

The law can educate and shape people's behaviour. If something is made legal or illegal it sends out a message to people. This arises, for example, in debates about whether drugs should be legalised. Some argue that this would give the state more control and regulation over them, but others would say that making drugs legal would send out the wrong message, and young people especially would begin to accept the idea that there is no problem with using drugs. In Ireland, when smoking was legally banned in pubs, restaurants and other public places, people's behaviour with regard to smoking changed and people became more aware of the harmful effects of smoking.

At its best, state law can be a guarantor of rights, an agent of change for the better, a means of settling disputes – personal, national and international. In general, a moral person will obey the law; however, this is not always the case.

Sometimes people assume without thinking that what is legal is moral – if the law says it's okay, then it must be okay. In many instances what is regarded as immoral, like murder and stealing for example, is also illegal. However, there have been many examples where state law itself has been immoral, and where it was dangerous to assume that what was legal was also moral. Let's take a look at some examples from history.

The Four Courts, Dublin

THE PENAL LAWS IN IRELAND

In eighteenth-century Ireland, the Penal Laws allowed for legal discrimination against Catholics. The following account is from a writer in the nineteenth century:

> After the surrender of Limerick in 1691, the treaty which promised religious freedom to the Catholics was grossly violated, and they were made subject to the action of severe 'Penal Laws', passed in the Irish parliament, an assembly composed of Protestant lords and of members returned for boroughs controlled by the crown or by patrons or by close corporations, and for counties dominated in election affairs by great proprietors of land. Catholics were not permitted to keep school; to go beyond seas, or to send others thither for education in the Romish religion. Intermarriage with Protestants was disallowed, in case of the possessior of an estate in Ireland. Children of mixed marriages were always to be brought up in the Protestant faith.
>
> A 'Papist' could not be guardian to any child, nor hold land, nor possess arms. He could not hold a commission in the army or navy, or be a private soldier. No Catholic could hold any office of honour or emolument [which means for a salary, a fee or profit of any kind] in the State, or be a member of any corporation, or vote for members of the Commons, or, if he were a peer, sit or vote in the Lords. Almost all these personal disabilities were equally enforced by law against any Protestant who married a Catholic wife. It was a felony, with transportation, to teach the Catholic religion, and treason, as a capital offence, to convert a Protestant to the Catholic faith. The legislation devised for the Irish Catholics in that time was described by Burke, a famous historian, as 'a machine as well fitted for the oppression, impoverishment and degradation of a people, and the debasement in them of human nature itself, as ever proceeded from the perverted ingenuity of man'.
>
> (From *The British Empire in the Nineteenth Century* by Edgar Sanderson, 1898)

THE NUREMBERG LAWS

The Nuremberg Laws enacted in Nazi Germany in 1935 made various acts of discrimination against Jewish people legal.

Some examples included:

» A Jewish person cannot be a citizen, cannot exercise the right to vote, cannot hold public office
» There can be no marriages between Jewish persons and non-Jewish Germans
» All Jewish officials are to lose their jobs.

Later measures included enforcing Jews to have the letter 'J' noted on their passports and making them wear the Yellow Star, the Star of David, to identify themselves as being Jewish. Jewish doctors were forbidden to treat non-Jews, Jewish lawyers were not allowed to practice, Jews were kept out of public schools and universities, and then even cinemas and theatres. After the war, the judges who enforced these laws were tried in the very same place that the laws were enacted, Nuremberg, and while some admitted their guilt, others used the 'legality' of these measures as their excuse.

A Yellow Star, which the Jewish people were forced to wear in the ghettos and concentration camps

THINK IT THROUGH

▶ Which of the Penal Laws and/or the Nuremberg Laws do you find most offensive? Explain your answer.

LESSON 42 — MORALITY AND THE LAW

Controversial issues

Problems arise when people who think it is important to be moral do not agree on what is moral or immoral. There is a certain level of agreement, e.g. most people would admire someone who saves another person's life. Likewise, there are some actions that most people regard as morally wrong, e.g. murder. However, even among people who try to be moral, there is disagreement on some issues. For example, those who support capital punishment and those who oppose it often come from the same starting point, that human life is sacred and that it is a terrible thing to kill another. Supporters say that those who murder must get the ultimate penalty and in this way society can be protected. Others argue that it is wrong to kill anyone, even those guilty of horrible crimes, and that society can be adequately protected by putting murderers in jail.

Some issues are controversial, and in some cases complicated. However, there is still a 'right answer' though it may be more difficult to find. For example, there was a time when slavery was merely controversial, but thanks to courageous campaigners it is generally accepted nowadays that slavery is immoral, and that it always was. The same applies to corporal punishment in schools and women not being allowed to vote – once upon a time these were accepted; later campaigners drew attention to them; then society came to accept that corporal punishment and women being disallowed the vote were wrong.

Ron Kovic, an American anti-war activist who was paralysed in the Vietnam War. His story was depicted in the movie, Born on the 4th of July, *starring Tom Cruise*

MORAL COURAGE

Sometimes those in authority will order a person to do something immoral, something that is against the person's conscience. An employer might order his workers to dump toxic waste illegally; a team captain might order a player to cheat or foul; parents might order their children to steal; an army commander might order his soldiers to shoot prisoners or civilians. If we recognise that the person in authority over us is asking us to do something immoral, we are under no obligation to follow the voice of authority; in fact, the right thing to do is to resist such orders and even report the matter to a higher authority. This can be very difficult because such action requires much moral courage.

SECTION D: MORALITY IN ACTION

Entrance to Robben Island Prison, where Nelson Mandela was held for eighteen years of the twenty-seven he spent incarcerated as a political prisoner

OVER TO YOU
▶ Make a list of controversial issues in the world today. These are issues that even people of high moral standard can't agree on.

RESEARCH PROJECT
Research any other examples you can think of where the state law is or was immoral in Ireland and elsewhere. Some suggestions are the unjust Apartheid laws that applied in South Africa until the mid-1990s; or various forms of discrimination against women in twentieth-century Ireland, e.g. the marriage bar in the civil service. Present your findings to the class. This can be done individually, in pairs or in groups.

SUMMARY

- At its best, state law can serve the common good of all citizens.
- Some people wrongly assume that if something is legal it must also be moral.
- There are many examples from history and modern times that show how the law itself can be immoral.
- It takes moral courage to stand up and do the right thing.
- Most people agree that some actions are moral and some immoral.
- There are controversial moral issues on which people disagree.

LESSON 42 – MORALITY AND THE LAW

LESSON 43
NATURAL MORAL LAW

Objective: This lesson will explain the meaning of 'Natural Moral Law'.

OPENING ACTIVITY

We all experience wants, needs and desires. Take a few moments to think about what are some of your wants, your needs and your desires. Try to decide what the difference is between these three.

The desire for happiness

More than likely, when we really think about it, the wish for happiness is at the very centre of all our wants and desires. Many people spend a lot of time thinking about things that might make them happy – they think, 'If only I had this or that, or could do this or that, I would be happy'. And very often, if it happens that they achieve what they wished for, they find that in fact it does not make them happy, and so the search goes on!

God also has a desire for you. Take a moment to think about and to articulate what God's desire for you might be.

The extraordinary thing is that God also wants for us to be truly happy. We read in the Book of Genesis that God created us in his own image and likeness. The German theologian Karl Rahner wrote, 'God has planted a God-seed in each of us, it is to grow and blossom throughout life.' This is God's desire for us: that we grow to become the people God intended us to be. We believe that it is this alone that will bring us true happiness, a life lived to bring goodness, truth and beauty to all around us.

To enable us to achieve this, God has implanted in every human heart the natural law.

INTRODUCTION TO THE NATURAL LAW

'Natural law' is an ambiguous term. In one sense, it is neither 'natural' nor is it a 'law', at least not in the way these words are commonly understood. First, God is its author, implanting this law within us; so it is more divine than 'natural'. It is a moral capacity that God has given us.

It is 'natural' in the sense that it is accessible to all and arises from the very nature that God has designed for us. God created us in his own image. We are created for goodness, truth and beauty.

It is a 'law' in the sense that its moral force comes from its reasonableness; to act contrary to the natural law is foolish for ourselves and for others. It envisages a way of being that respects the fundamental dignity and nature of every human being.

The natural law is not the same as physical, biological or chemical laws of nature. For example, if an apple comes loose from its branch it will fall to the ground – a law of nature. The natural law, on the other hand, is only fulfilled when we make good moral choices to live alongside others with dignity and in a way that leads to wholeness and fullness of life for all.

The natural law means that we can appeal to our shared human nature and moral instinct as a source of moral enlightenment to guide our own lives and our common life in society. In fact, much of the explicit law of God that we learn from the Bible simply enhances and clarifies this natural law. For example, the Wisdom books in the Old Testament constantly encourage people to reflect on their own human experience and to discover moral values by which to live. Many of the parables of Jesus also appeal to the natural law, what people can know by listening with good reason to their own hearts. Jesus often encouraged people to look at their ordinary human experiences to recognise basic values by which to live. Recall the story of the Good Samaritan (cf. Luke 10:25-37). This parable illustrates that basic values such as respect, equality and compassion can be known by everyone, even the outsider (here the Samaritan). We refer to such values as 'universal' principles or norms because they can be recognised and shared by all humankind.

So, the natural law tradition means that when people use human reason to reflect on human nature and experience, they can arrive at moral norms and know what it means to live a good life. This is not only true for Christians but for all people. All people possess this natural law within; through reason they can come to know what is right and just.

Saint Thomas Aquinas

SAINT THOMAS AQUINAS

While the natural law tradition is reflected in the Bible and in many philosophies of life, it became central to Catholic moral teaching through the work of St Thomas Aquinas (1225–74). For Aquinas, the natural law refers to the participation of the human person in the eternal law of God. He believed that human beings, unlike animals, can come by reason to know and understand something of God's own divine providential plan for the world. For him, God is the ultimate source of all moral values and obligations. The use of reason and reflection on human experience can give a person the sense of what is good, what is right and what is just. For Aquinas, reason in this context is not just an intellectual pursuit; it also includes such things as intuition, affection, common sense and one's aesthetic sense of what is fitting – whatever it takes to come to understand human reality. Aquinas says that the most fundamental principle of natural law is to do good and avoid evil. However, such a norm might not actually tell us how to act in a given situation in a particular place where we might grapple with competing choices. The natural law is more of a tendency or direction in which we must move, as opposed to a detailed code of action that we must follow.

THINK IT THROUGH
▶ Do you think that broad, overarching principles like 'do good and avoid evil' are any help in dealing with the everyday difficulties of life? Why/why not?

NATURAL AND DIVINE LAW

What then is the relationship of the natural law to the explicit law of God that we find revealed in the Bible? First, God is the author of both and the two must work hand in hand. The Bible constantly echoes the great moral principles and precepts that we can know from natural law. For example, like the natural law, the Bible condemns murder. However, it is more accurate to think that murder is wrong not just because the Bible condemns it, but that murder is wrong and that's *why* the Bible condemns it.

On the other hand, the Scriptures and Christian Tradition deepen and clarify the natural law and lend motivation and clear guidelines to help us to follow it. For example, the Bible makes it very clear that all people of God must do the works of justice, opposing injustice of every kind and helping to see to it that all can have what they need to live with dignity. The Bible brings an added motivation to obey this law because the Bible reveals to us God's steadfast love for us and God's dream for us and for all of creation. Made in God's image and likeness, we must love our neighbours as ourselves because we are made in the image of God who *is* love.

OVER TO YOU

- Make a list of those actions that are generally regarded, by the vast majority of people, as moral or good acts, that could be seen as part of the natural law.
- Make a list of actions that are generally regarded as being immoral – actions that the vast majority of people would regard as going against the natural law.

SUMMARY

- The natural law means that we can appeal to our shared human nature and use our reason to know right from wrong.
- All people possess this natural law.
- Aquinas says that the most fundamental principle of natural law is to do good and avoid evil.
- The Scriptures and Christian Tradition deepen and clarify the natural law, lending motivation and clear guidelines to help us to follow it.

LESSON 44
CONSCIENCE

Objective: This lesson will examine the meaning of conscience.

OPENING CONVERSATION

Read these quotations about conscience. What do you think each quotation means? Which is your favourite?

Never do anything against conscience, even if the state demands it
— Albert Einstein, scientist

The human voice can never reach the distance that is covered by the still small voice of conscience
— Mahatma Gandhi, Indian philosopher and activist

Conscience is a man's compass
— Vincent van Gogh, artist

Labour to keep alive in your breast that little spark of celestial fire, called conscience
— George Washington, first president of the United States of America

Conscience is God present in man
— Victor Hugo, French author

A conscience without God is like a court without a judge
— Alphonse de Lamartine, French poet

So what is our conscience?

Consider how the word 'conscience' is used. When they don't want to do something wrong, people might say, 'My conscience wouldn't allow it'. Someone critical of another person doing wrong might say, 'Has she no conscience?' In wartime, a person might think it is wrong to fight – they become 'a conscientious objector'. In some countries, a person who criticises the government might be locked up even though they haven't done anything criminally wrong – they become 'prisoners of conscience'. Nowadays there is much talk of people having 'a social conscience', for example human rights activists campaigning for 'freedom of conscience'.

Conscience is present at the heart of every person. It is the basic capacity that God has given every person to know good from evil. Our conscience informs our choices and helps us to do what is good and avoid what is evil. So, another way of thinking of conscience is that it is a law inscribed by God on our hearts. Our conscience doesn't only help us to decide what to do, it shapes us into the kind of person we become. Our conscience is not just something we have, it is part of who we are. So conscience cannot be determined by the opinion of the majority, because large groups of people can and have been wrong. Conscience cannot be determined by feelings, because feelings change, while what is morally right or wrong stays the same. It is our duty to inform our conscience according to the natural law that God has implanted in our hearts and the law that God has revealed to us in the Bible. In order for our conscience to have the capacity to direct our actions, we need to be sufficiently present to ourselves and to what is stirring within us to hear what our conscience is prompting us to do. When we follow our conscience, we are acting out of freedom rather than under the pressure of following the crowd or deciding we must do something just because everybody else is doing it.

Over the next few lessons we will look at how conscience can be approached – we can follow it (doing what our conscience tells us – recommended!), ignore it (doing the wrong thing despite what conscience tells us), inform it (finding out more about what's right and wrong – recommended!) or twist it (arguing with conscience, rationalising until we hardly know what's right or wrong anymore). Conscience is a powerful force in human life and a great gift when used wisely.

REFLECT AND DISCUSS

This is a poem about someone who didn't want to listen to their conscience and turned it into a prisoner. Read this poem and answer the questions that follow.

> *Conscience is a man's compass.*
>
> Vincent van Gogh

'DISSIDENT VOICE'

I lived at peace with my conscience
Until it became
A dissident voice in my conversation.
It was an undesirable element
In my otherwise peaceful regime,
An enemy of my state
Of independence,
Its activities destabilised
My whole economy,
And it was clearly a threat
To my rational security.

At first I simply banned it
From appearing in public;
I put it under house arrest
And allowed it no visitors.
But it would not desist
From its self-appointed role
As watch-dog to my thinking and behaviour.
So I did as any autocrat would do,
I locked it up
And threw away the key.
I sentenced it to life
In solitary confinement
And put it in a place
Where even foreign journalists
Wouldn't think to look.

But the horrors of the world
Have increasingly been lobbying my senses
Petitions of hungry children
Have been delivered to my eyes
Compassion and responsibility
Have been dripping
Through the growing hole
In my ozone layer
I am under mounting pressure
For an amnesty.

Consciences
Like prisoners
Are never quite forgotten.

(Gerard Kelly)

- What is the poet trying to say about conscience?
- He compares stifling one's conscience to the way a government might try to silence a political opponent – is this a useful comparison?
- What signs are there that, despite his efforts, his conscience is still getting through to him?
- Do you think that 'watch-dog' is a suitable image for conscience?

OVER TO YOU

- Write down your own definition of conscience.
- Give an example of a situation where you followed your conscience.
- Can you think of another suitable metaphor for conscience? Write about your choice and/or draw a symbol to illustrate it.

SUMMARY

- Conscience is an inner guide, given to us by God, to what's morally right or wrong.
- We should follow our conscience, but sometimes there's a danger we could ignore or stifle it.

LESSON 45
DISTORTIONS OF CONSCIENCE

Objective: This lesson will describe some of the ways in which conscience can become distorted and identify ways in which this can be overcome.

OPENING CONVERSATION
Can you think of examples of people carrying out immoral actions that they believed to be morally right?

When conscience becomes distorted

While it is very important to follow one's conscience, we must also be aware that conscience can become distorted. This can be very dangerous. The men who flew the planes into the World Trade Center towers in New York on that tragic day in 2001 felt they were following their consciences, even doing their duty. Yet we can safely say that they were doing a seriously immoral act, no matter how they personally felt about it. In fact, a lot of harm has been done in the world by people who thought that what they were doing was the right thing.

On a smaller scale, we could see this happening in a family – with the best of intentions a parent or guardian might give a child everything they wanted, which might then lead to the child being 'spoiled' or overly demanding, making future relationships difficult.

MORAL BLIND SPOTS
Moral blind spots exist when people find ways of protecting themselves from the truth that they are engaging in immoral activity. Our inbuilt attitudes of greed and selfishness enable us to persuade ourselves that an immoral action is in fact acceptable because we perceive it as being 'good' for us. If we buy into an attitude that is promoted by a group or society that we belong to, such as sexism or racism, it can block our ability to recognise something as immoral. Read the following story to help you to reflect on what it might mean to say that someone has a moral blind spot:

> There once was a successful businessman. He prided himself on his success and his charity work. He was always generous with sponsorship for various worthy causes and even had a scholarship in his name so that students who couldn't otherwise afford it could attend university. Everyone in town, perhaps even himself, was surprised when he was found guilty of serious tax evasion and jailed for a short time.

THINK IT THROUGH
- Why do you think people were surprised when the businessman was found guilty of tax evasion?
- Why do you think he was surprised himself?
- Can you think of any other examples of moral blind spots?

RATIONALISING

Rationalising is a vital tool for us as we try to work out what's right and wrong. It is, however, also possible to use our rational powers to avoid taking on board the reality that something we really want to do is morally wrong. Imagine that you are tempted to do something that you know in conscience is wrong. Being a generally good person, you don't want to go against your conscience. However, the temptation to do the immoral thing is great, so you start arguing with your conscience and coming up with excuses – it's not so bad, everybody's doing it, it won't do any harm. Finally you manage to convince yourself that what you are doing is acceptable and you give in to temptation, imagining that it's not bad after all.

If you fool yourself into thinking that what is actually wrong is right, that doesn't excuse guilt or responsibility – you have to take responsibility for refusing to listen to your conscience in the first place. Somewhere deep down you knew the action was wrong and you still did it.

There are many common phrases used by those that rationalise in this way:

» 'I had no choice' – beware of this one! It usually means the person had a choice but opted for a particular action they now feel bad about. Remember that conscience acts before and after an event – before to warn you against a certain action, afterwards to make you feel guilty for doing wrong. Denying choice is usually a way of avoiding responsibility. There are very few situations where we don't have choices.

» 'Everybody is doing it' – it is highly unlikely to be true, and even if it were, that would not make the immoral action right.

» 'No one will notice' – even if no one notices your wrongdoing, it doesn't make it right.

» 'It's just the way I am' – an excuse used by people who do wrong (e.g. act rudely to others) but are too lazy or unwilling to change and improve themselves.

OVER TO YOU

▶ How do you think someone who in general wants to do what is good, manages at times to persuade themselves that it is acceptable to do something that is morally wrong?
▶ Has this ever happened to you?

EXAMINATION OF CONSCIENCE

In the Catholic Tradition, before a person goes to Confession (Sacrament of Reconciliation), an 'examination of conscience' is always recommended. It is also recommended that we examine our conscience at the end of each day. Those who pray regularly probably do this naturally. One way to examine our conscience is to go through the commandments and ask ourselves if we broke any of them.

There is also an opportunity at the beginning of each Mass during the Penitential Rite, when the priest asks us to call to mind our sins, to remember the times we failed to live up to our best selves.

CHOOSING ACCORDING TO OUR CONSCIENCE

It can sometimes be difficult to decide what is right and what is wrong, even when we make our best effort. The *Catechism of the Catholic Church* gives us a number of guidelines to help us:

- » You may never do evil so that good may result from it
- » Follow the golden rule: Treat others as you would like them to treat you
- » Respect other peoples' conscience. Never do anything to entice another person to go against his or her conscience.

We must also be careful to be at least as aware of our own failings as we are of the failings of others. It is not our role to judge others. Jesus said to his followers:

> Why do you see the speck in your neighbour's eye, but do not notice the log in your own eye? Or how can you say to your neighbour, 'Let me take the speck out of your eye,' while the log is in your own eye? You hypocrite, first take the log out of your own eye, and then you will see clearly to take the speck out of your neighbour's eye. (Mt 7:3-5)

JOURNAL

Consider the following scenarios. In each case, think about what you should do and what you think you would do:

- You accidentally break something in a large department store – you look around and no one seems to have noticed …
- You find an iPod on the corridor in school …
- The Luas arrives while you are queuing for a ticket. You know if you wait to get a ticket, you will miss it. You are already late …
- You get more change than you should have in the local shop …

Think of any excuses you've ever made to convince yourself that what you felt was wrong was really not that bad, or even good.

SUMMARY

- ⊙ Sometimes we can distort the message conscience gives us.
- ⊙ Having a 'moral blind spot' and 'rationalising' are two examples of this.
- ⊙ In the Catholic Tradition, before a person goes to Confession (Sacrament of Reconciliation), an 'examination of conscience' is always recommended.
- ⊙ During the Penitential Rite at Mass we are asked to call to mind the times we have sinned.

LESSON 45 – DISTORTIONS OF CONSCIENCE

LESSON 46
INFORMED CONSCIENCE

Objective: This lesson will identify ways in which people can inform their conscience.

OPENING CONVERSATION
Can you think of any situation where a person would have to seek guidance in order to know whether a certain action is right or wrong?

Informing our conscience

As we have seen, it is important to follow conscience, but conscience can be distorted or misinformed. We have recognised how lots of damage can be done by people who sincerely think that what they are doing is right. So, we need to know that we are not just sincere in our actions, but that we are morally right. For this to work, our consciences must be well-informed. As we have also seen in earlier lessons, we have a certain sense of right and wrong built in (e.g. in relation to obvious wrong acts like murder), but there are other matters that are more complicated, so we need to inform our consciences if we are to be confident about doing the right thing.

It is a bit like getting a new computer – a certain amount of basic software comes built in or pre-loaded. But we're never going to be happy or even effective if we leave it at that. We'll want to add more programmes, like anti-virus and anti-spyware software, an office suite, a better media player, a web browser. And this will go on for the lifetime of the computer. It is similar in the case of conscience. To help us make right decisions we need to keep our consciences well-informed.

SECTION D: MORALITY IN ACTION

HOW CAN WE INFORM OUR CONSCIENCE?

Conscience formation is a lifelong task. We can inform our conscience by talking to our families, through RE classes, listening to homilies on Sundays, consulting with trusted friends, following the good example of other well-informed people, and so on. Our families and teachers might try to pass on this teaching, but ultimately, as we grow older, we must take personal responsibility for it. Having an ill-informed conscience is not an excuse for doing something that is immoral. Sacred Scripture and the teachings of the Church are the sure ways to inform our conscience. In the Bible we find the story of God's dealings with his people down through history. This reveals God's Law, telling us what is right and what is wrong. In the New Testament Jesus, in his life and in his teachings, shows us how to live and how to treat other people. When it comes to more complex matters, especially those thrown up by modern technology (e.g. genetic engineering, nuclear weaponry), we are not going to find any account in the Bible of Jesus speaking of these things. This is why we need the Church to continue in its teaching role, reacting to new developments that have moral implications. For Catholicism, one source of such information is the *Catechism of the Catholic Church* (there's also a young people's version called *YOUCAT*). These teachings are also conveyed through the pastoral letters of the bishops, the encyclicals of the popes and official documents of important Church councils (e.g. the Second Vatican Council of the early 1960s). With the development of the internet, these sources of moral guidance are more readily available than ever.

RESEARCH PROJECT

Select one of the papal encyclicals as follows and choose three quotations from it that, in your opinion, say something important to the world today. Explain your choices.

» *Evangelium Vitae* (1995)
Pope John Paul II's landmark teachings on right to life issues like capital punishment, abortion and euthanasia.

» *Veritatis Splendor* (1993)
Pope John Paul II's teaching about the nature of truth and morality.

» *Deus Caritas Est* (2005)
Pope Benedict XVI's encyclical on how God is love, and on many other aspects of love.

» *Caritas in Veritate* (2009)
Pope Benedict XVI's reflection on the Church's social teaching and human development issues.

YOU WILL FIND ADDITIONAL INFORMATION ON WWW.SEEKANDFIND.IE

> A well-formed conscience is upright and truthful. It formulates its judgements according to reason, in conformity with the true good willed by the wisdom of the Creator. Everyone must avail himself [herself] of the means to form his [her] conscience. (CCC, 1798)

HOW DO WE DECIDE IF AN ACTION IS MORALLY WRONG?

Every act has three elements:

- What we do
- Why we do the act
- The circumstances and consequences of the act.

For an act to be morally good, what we do must be good in itself. In other words, it must be objectively good. Some acts are always wrong because they go against a fundamental human good, for instance direct killing of the innocent, torture, rape. They are wrong in themselves and are always wrong irrespective of the reason they are done or the circumstances around them.

The 'why' or the intention comes from within the person doing the act. It is the subjective part of the act. For an act to be morally good, the intention must be good. If we are motivated to do something by a bad intention, even something that is objectively good in itself, the action is morally evil. On the other hand, a good intention cannot make a bad action good. We can never do something wrong or evil even to bring about a good ending. This is what is meant by saying 'the end does not justify the means'.

Finally, the circumstances and consequences of the act are secondary when it comes to judging whether it is moral or not. They simply add to the goodness or badness of the act. For example, doing something immoral out of fear of death, e.g. in self-defence, does not make the act good but it does lessen the guilt of the person who did it.

All three of the above must be good in order for an act to be morally good.

> Love toward oneself remains a fundamental principle of morality. Therefore it is legitimate to insist on respect for one's own right to life. Someone who defends his life is not guilty of murder even if he is forced to deal his aggressor a lethal blow.
>
> (CCC, 2264)

OVER TO YOU

- What if a driver was up in court for going through a red light, and claimed in his defence that he didn't realise red meant stop. What do you think the judge would say?
- What if a driver went over the speed limit in the main street of a small town and claimed she didn't know there was a limit, or thought it was a higher limit? What would the judge say? Would it be different if that driver was speeding outside of town?
- Can you describe or outline a situation where a person's failure to inform their conscience might lead to harm?

JOURNAL

Is there an issue that you need to inform your conscience about? Pick one issue and find out what the Church teaches. Try to draw on Church teaching, Scripture and what your family and friends think. Write up your reflection after investigating the issue.

SUMMARY

- One should follow conscience, but conscience must be well-informed.
- Catholics can read the *Catechism of the Catholic Church* and papal encyclicals to inform themselves about Church teaching.
- Every act has three elements:
  - What we do
  - Why we do the act
  - The circumstances and consequences of the act.

LESSON 47
THE TEN COMMANDMENTS

Objective: This lesson will look at the shared ethical vision of the Jewish and Christian faith traditions as seen in the Ten Commandments.

OPENING ACTIVITY

Imagine that you are setting up a new country. There are no laws, rules or regulations yet. Your task is to set up a society that will allow humans to live to their best potential, in love, justice and peace.

In groups of three or four, list the five best guidelines needed for people in this society to flourish – very general rules for the best way to live.

Now share your rules with the class. Were there any rules/guidelines that every/most groups had listed? Write these on a large poster and hang it in a central place.

'JUDEO-CHRISTIAN' ETHICAL VISION

Christianity's ethical vision – i.e. an outlook or viewpoint on what is moral – grew from Judaism. Our religious values are often called 'Judeo-Christian' in acknowledgement of this. This shared tradition is most obvious when we look at the Ten Commandments from the Old Testament. They are also known as the Decalogue, meaning 'ten words', and they appear in the books of Exodus and Deuteronomy. The Ten Commandments were given to the people by God through Moses as part of the covenant between God and his people. God reached out in love to the people who had been in slavery. He promised that he would be their God and would love them unfailingly. God offered them freedom from slavery and protection from harm in all its forms. The Ten Commandments articulate how they would live as God's people.

Then God spoke all these words: I am the Lord your God, who brought you out of the land of Egypt, out of the house of slavery …
(Ex 20:1-2)

1. I am the Lord your God: you shall not have strange gods before me.
2. You shall not take the name of the Lord your God in vain.
3. Remember to keep holy the Lord's day (Sabbath).
4. Honour your father and your mother.
5. You shall not kill.
6. You shall not commit adultery.
7. You shall not steal.
8. You shall not bear false witness against your neighbour.
9. You shall not covet your neighbour's wife or husband.
10. You shall not covet your neighbour's goods.

The Ten Commandments today

Sometimes people only speak about the sins involved in breaking the commandments. However, that's only part of the story. A more positive approach would be to consider not only the sins, but also the values behind each commandment. As a bigger challenge, we could ask what we could actually do to show our commitment to each commandment.

FIRST, SECOND AND THIRD: WORK ON YOUR RELATIONSHIP WITH GOD

The first three commandments are all about our relationship with God. They call on us to put God first in our lives, to make God the centre of what we believe in and hope for before anything or anyone else. Money, celebrities, our image or popularity are all examples of things to which we can give greater importance in life than we give to God. We are also called to have reverence for God's name and we can affirm this value by not using God's name casually. For example, we should avoid saying 'Oh my God' or 'Jesus' as exclamations. For Jews, the Lord's Day – the Sabbath – is Saturday, for Christians the Lord's Day is Sunday. This is a day to set aside for rest. It has its origins in the fact that God created the world and everything in it in six days, resting on the seventh day. By resting on the Sabbath we create space and time to worship God, to acknowledge God's place in our lives and to give God thanks for all his gifts. Catholics honour the Lord's Day by going to Mass.

The rest of the commandments are a guide to our relationships with others.

FOURTH: HONOUR YOUR PARENTS (AND RESPECT AUTHORITY)

Unlike those that follow, this commandment is expressed in a positive way. Values here include respect for parents, guardians and the broader family. The family has a central place in God's plan for humanity. It is the first place where we learn how to love and live with others. The attitudes children owe to their parents are respect, gratitude, obedience and assistance. Traditionally the fourth commandment has also been seen as endorsing respect for all other legitimate authority – guards/police in relation to state law, teachers in relation to school, and employers in relation to work. However, if someone in authority tells us to do something that we know to be wrong, there is no obligation to obey; in fact there is an obligation not to obey, and maybe even to protest and/or expose the wrongdoing. In Nazi times, during World War II, those who refused to follow the immoral laws and orders of the Nazi government are now admired.

FIFTH: PROMOTE THE CULTURE OF LIFE

Human life is God's greatest gift to us. Respect for life is at the heart of this commandment, life from conception to natural death. If we are supporting this commandment we will oppose all direct killing (including abortion and euthanasia). We will also work for peace, social justice and the alleviation of poverty. In fact, we will oppose anything that degrades life in any way. On a personal level, we will try to lead a healthy life and always respect the lives and health of others. We are made in the image of God, so how we treat our bodies is important. We are called to care for our own bodies and those of others. We are called to practice the virtue of temperance, which challenges us to avoid the abuse of food, alcohol or the use of tobacco. The use of illegal drugs or the misuse of legal drugs can put our lives and the lives of others at risk. Taking care of our mental health is also an important aspect of 'choosing life'.

SIXTH AND NINTH: BE FAITHFUL AND PRACTICE PURITY OF HEART

Closely connected to God's gift of life is the gift of sexuality. It is the gift of our human sexuality that enables us to bring new life into the world. God created us male and female, different and complementarily suited to loving each other intimately.

For those called to marriage, we are called to always be faithful and loving to our spouse, working to keep our marriage healthy by seeking advice and counselling if necessary. But this commandment doesn't just apply to married couples. It is about affirming the value and dignity of human sexuality. We are called to show respect to people we are dating, never using the other person for our own gratification, and always thinking about their best interests. We also should avoid anything (pornography, for example) that will make it harder for us to respect sex and keep it in its rightful place in marriage. People often don't associate their sexuality with their spirituality. In fact, many people see these as opposite forces in their lives. However, the commandments remind us that they belong together. Our relationship with God should permeate all of our human relationships, and vice versa. The key to their integration is to see all of our desires as having the potential to lead us to God.

SEVENTH AND TENTH: ACT JUSTLY

Here we are called to show respect for the property of others, and indeed public property. If we are keeping this commandment we will never steal, will return borrowed items in good condition, will not vandalise and will offer to compensate if we damage the property of others. People who keep this commandment need to act justly in all areas of their lives. For example, someone in business living out this commandment would pay their taxes, pay their employees a just wage and maintain safe and ethical working conditions. The tenth commandment warns against envy and greed. If we covet for ourselves things that rightfully belong to another, we are not acting in accordance with the tenth commandment. At the root of the seventh and tenth commandments is the truth that God created the universe and everything in it for the whole human race to care for and enjoy — those who will come after us as well as those who have gone before us. The Catholic Church teaches that this also includes care for the environment and animals. We need to act justly by sharing the natural resources in our world, protecting animals from cruelty and preventing the destruction of the environment as it is only on loan to us and we need to be accountable for its treatment in our lifetime.

EIGHTH: TELL THE TRUTH

Our commitment here is to live and speak truthfully. Words are powerful weapons that can be used constructively or destructively. The words we speak, whether they are gossip, rumours, truth or lies, all have the power to destroy another, and therefore we need to be careful about what we say and how we say it. Of course, we don't just need to use caution with words we speak but also with anything we write down or post online. Lying means consciously and intentionally speaking or acting against the truth and misleading others who have the right to know the truth. We can also lie by omission, by letting others believe something we know to be untrue by not saying anything. In our everyday lives, telling the truth also requires discretion. Sometimes people can speak the truth to be cruel or spiteful and it can be hurtful rather than helpful. If we want to live out this commandment, a good rule to follow is to think before you speak:

T – is it true?
H – is it helpful?
I – is it inspiring?
N – is it necessary?
K – is it kind?

Mount Sinai in Egypt, where Moses received the Ten Commandments

OVER TO YOU
▶ Look back at the list of rules/guidelines that your group assembled in the opening activity. How many are similar to the Ten Commandments? Which ones are different? Explain the differences if you can.

GROUP WORK
Gather some magazines and newspapers. Cut out some images that reflect people keeping the commandments. Now cut out some contrary images – of people breaking the commandments. On a large poster, make a collage of these conflicting images. Highlight the injustice, sadness and exploitation that results from breaking the commandments. Use the first set of images to show how living the commandments can push back against such injustice, sadness and exploitation.

JOURNAL
Reflect on the Ten Commandments and write a journal entry called 'Why the Commandments are still important for today'.

SUMMARY

- The Ten Commandments started life as part of the Jewish Tradition and are still valued in that tradition today.
- The commandments are also valued by the Christian Tradition.
- There are sins that can be made against each commandment, but each commandment also supports important values.
- There are positive actions we can do to show our commitment to the commandments.

LESSON 48
JESUS' ETHICAL VISION OF RIGHT RELATIONSHIP

Objective: This lesson will summarise the idea of 'right relationship', in the life of Jesus and in people's lives today.

OPENING ACTIVITY

Write a brief summary of your favourite story about Jesus or told by Jesus, then note briefly what relationships are involved. What did Jesus teach about right relationship? Read Mark 12:28-34, 'The First Commandment'.

The golden rule

When the scribe asks Jesus which commandment is the greatest, Jesus answered:

> The first is 'Hear, O Israel: the Lord our God, the Lord is one; you shall love the Lord your God with all your heart, and with all your soul, and with all your mind, and with all your strength.' The second is this, 'You shall love your neighbour as yourself.' There is no other commandment greater than these. (Mk 12:29-31)

If we love God, love ourselves and love our neighbours as ourselves we will be living out all of the commandments. While Jesus identified two great commandments, he ends with the singular 'commandment' as if all are one. This is known as the 'great commandment' or the golden rule. This is the basis for the teachings of Jesus for living a moral and ethical life. Jesus didn't just preach about loving one another, he lead by example. It is noticeable that most stories about Jesus and told by Jesus involve relationships, and most teach a moral lesson about what makes for a right relationship. It is clear that relationships are not about vague feelings but essentially about who we are and what we do.

ZACCHAEUS

Read the story of Zacchaeus in Luke 19:1-10
Zacchaeus was a dishonest tax collector and an unpopular man in his community. When he heard Jesus was coming to town he wanted to see him and hear what he had to say. Being small, he climbs a tree to get a better view – perhaps a symbol of his efforts to reach a higher standard in his life or to get a better view of where his life is heading. Jesus could have ignored him, scolded him for his dishonest practices as a tax collector. Perhaps this is the approach we might have taken. But Jesus sees the spark of good in Zacchaeus and fans it to a flame, even before Zacchaeus himself was ready to acknowledge his wrongdoing and his willingness to change. Jesus sees the possibilities of spiritual growth and of building better relationships. For his part, Zacchaeus shows in the first instance an openness to listening, a welcoming spirit, leading to an awareness that he needs to change and a willingness to change his ways.

THE WOMAN CAUGHT IN ADULTERY

Read the story of the woman caught in adultery in John 8:3-11

In line with the culture of the time, the woman in this story was about to be stoned to death for her adultery. There is no sign of the man with whom she had the relationship. The onlookers and accusers are all set to condemn her and start throwing the stones. Jesus' ethical vision calls for a different approach – we see how reflective he is, as he patiently writes in the dust. One theory is that he was writing out the sins of those who were planning to throw the stones. Whatever the case, he said that memorable line: 'Let anyone among you who is without sin be the first to throw a stone at her' (Lk 8:7). The people walk away. We could learn from this story that we should be slow to judge others, that in our relationships we should be respectful and thoughtful, and that we should never be judgemental. But we can challenge others – notice that Jesus tells her not to sin any more. We can love the sinner, but we can disapprove of the sin.

THE PRODIGAL SON

Read the parable of the Prodigal Son in Luke 15:11-32

In this story, the main relationship is that between father and son. It is a difficult relationship. The son wishes to grab his inheritance and go, which upsets the father. However, the father still generously allows the son his freedom. When the son finally decides to return, the father is delighted, runs out to greet him and throws him a party. As we saw Jesus doing in the story of Zacchaeus, the father did not wait for his son to apologise, he ran out immediately to greet him and to welcome him back. The other son, however, is rather annoyed – he has stayed behind and served the father and is now jealous of the attention the prodigal son is getting. This is understandable, but his reaction is self-focused and lacking in any of the generosity exhibited by his father, or by God. The story is telling us something about the fatherly attitude of God – he allows us to move away but is always overjoyed to have us back.

THINK IT THROUGH

- For each of the above stories, write one statement about the relationships between Jesus and the various characters.

OVER TO YOU

- Jesus of Nazareth spent his adult life sharing a vision for ethical living. You have been asked to write an article for a teenage magazine in which you are to describe these ethical teachings. Write the article suitable for your age group and include in it the following ideas:

  – Jesus' moral vision
  – Jesus' understanding of right relationship
  – An example from the life of Jesus.

JOURNAL

For one or more of the stories mentioned, consider and write about what lessons of the story might apply in some way to your own life.

COMPARATIVE RELIGIOUS STUDIES

Research the ethical vision of one major religion other than Christianity.

YOU WILL FIND ADDITIONAL INFORMATION ON WWW.SEEKANDFIND.IE

SUMMARY

- Jesus summed up the greatest commandment by saying: 'You shall love the Lord your God with all your heart, and with all your soul, and with all your mind, and with all your strength', and 'You shall love your neighbour as yourself'.
- Jesus' vision of ethical relationship involves challenging and engaging with people, relating to people individually and respectfully, and seeing the good in people.
- In Jesus' vision, forgiveness and love are central.

LESSON 49
THE REALITY OF SIN

Objective: This lesson will define sin, different types of sin and reconciliation.

OPENING ACTIVITY
Write down your own definition of sin, then share it with the class and compare it to a dictionary definition.

What does sin mean?

When people speak of sin they usually think in terms of doing something wrong, something immoral or something unethical. For those who belong to a religious tradition, this wrongdoing is seen as an offence against God as well as against people. It is the result of human beings living in ways that are not in keeping with the fact that they are created in the image of God and called by God to live in accordance with that. Non-believers may speak in terms of 'ethical' or 'unethical' behaviour. Going deeper, it can be seen as something that causes damage or breakdown in relationships — between ourselves and others and/or between ourselves and God. Many people throughout history have pondered the issue of sin and come up with some words of wisdom:

Sin is not hurtful because it is forbidden, it is forbidden because it is hurtful
— Benjamin Franklin, American writer, scientist and politician

We are punished by our sins, not for them
— Elbert Hubbard, American writer and philosopher

I could not live in peace if I put the shadow of a wilful sin between myself and God
— George Eliot, English novelist

Compassion will cure more sins than condemnation
— Henry Ward Beecher, anti-slavery campaigner

LESSON 49 — THE REALITY OF SIN

SIN AS AN OFFENCE AGAINST GOD

Sin is an offence against reason, truth and right conscience; it is failure in genuine love for God and neighbour caused by a perverse attachment to certain goods. ...

Sin is an offence against God. ... Sin sets itself against God's love for us and turns our hearts away from it. Like the first sin, it is disobedience, a revolt against God through the will to become 'like gods', knowing and determining good and evil. Sin is thus 'love of oneself even to contempt of God'. In this proud self-exaltation, sin is diametrically opposed to the obedience of Jesus, which achieves our salvation.

(CCC, 1849, 1850)

The many faces of sin

We can encounter sin in many forms. Being aware of the many faces of sin can help us recognise sin in our personal lives as well as in the social structures and policies of the communities to which we belong.

MORTAL SIN

Mortal sin is a very serious or grave sin, causing a major breakdown in our relationship with God, and with the person who has been offended. There are three conditions for a sin to be mortal: 1. the action must be serious (grave matter); 2. the person must know that it is seriously wrong (full knowledge); 3. the person must freely want to do it (full consent). Mortal sin destroys our loving relationship with God. The Catholic Church teaches that to gain forgiveness from such a sin a person must repent, be truly sorry, and go to Confession. Certain actions can objectively be described as seriously wrong and therefore fit into this category (e.g. murder, child abuse), but for the person to be personally and *subjectively* guilty of mortal sin, the action itself must be seriously wrong and the person must do it deliberately, freely and knowingly.

VENIAL SIN

This is usually a sin that is not so serious or that a person doesn't do deliberately or knowingly. Venial sin does not cause a major breakdown in our relationship with God but can damage it, especially if it becomes a regular pattern. Neither does venial sin cause our relationship with another person to be completely destroyed but most likely it causes personal hurt, so we shouldn't take venial sin too lightly. Of course all sin is serious and it is not advisable to casually think that it is 'only' a venial sin. If we get careless and thoughtless about our venial sins, we more easily drift into sins that are more serious. For example, it would be no great surprise if a person who developed a pattern of stealing small amounts of money from the workplace drifted towards stealing large amounts when they had an opportunity. The Church encourages us to confess these sins in the Sacrament of Reconciliation, where we get an opportunity to confront such behaviour in our lives and where we get graces to help us avoid these in the future.

SIN OF COMMISSION AND SIN OF OMISSION

A person who knowingly and freely chooses to do or say something that is contrary to God's law and will commits a sin of commission. Sins of commission may be of thought, of word or of deed. A person can also sin by failing to do or say something good. A person who knowingly and freely chooses not to do something good that they have the responsibility to do and can do, commits a sin of omission. It might be when as students or teachers we don't do our work as well as we might. On a more serious level it might be, for example, a safety officer on a ship deliberately not checking all the safety equipment on a regular basis – something that could obviously have very serious consequences.

PERSONAL SIN AND SOCIAL SIN

Personal sin refers to sins of commission or omission committed by an individual person. We can also contribute to a group or a society developing a sinful attitude that infects its very structure. We can do so by supporting one another in sinful actions or by taking part in the sin of a group or by not speaking out against sin. When we act or fail to act in this way, we bear some 'responsibility for the sins committed by others' (CCC, 1868).

THE SEVEN DEADLY SINS

The Church names seven sins 'Deadly Sins', which are also called 'Capital Sins'. They are anger, avarice (greed), envy, gluttony, lust, pride and sloth. These are sins that lead us into other more serious sins and vices. A vice is 'the habitual practice of repeated sin'.

Anger: The passion that leads a person either to harm or want to harm another person or group of people because of a desire for vengeance.

Avarice (greed): The excessive attachment to the goods of creation, frequently expressed in the pursuit of money or other symbols of wealth, which leads to sins of injustice and other evils.

Envy: The excessive desire to want the possessions of another person, even to the point of wishing harm on them or rejoicing in their misfortune; envy includes resentment or sadness at another's good fortune.

Gluttony: Excessive eating and drinking.

Lust: The excessive desire for earthly pleasures, particularly sexual pleasures.

Pride: Excessive self-esteem or self-love; pride includes a strong desire to be noticed and honoured by others, and sets one in opposition to and competition with God.

Sloth (Acedia): A culpable lack of physical or spiritual effort in meeting one's obligations to God, to others, and to oneself.

lust **gluttony** **envy** **pride**
sloth **anger** **greed**

OVER TO YOU
- Review the three conditions for a sin to be mortal. Give some examples of all three being met.
- If someone commits a mortal sin, what should they do as soon as possible?
- Explain the difference between a sin of commission and a sin of omission and give an example of each.
- Name some examples of social sin in our society.

THINK IT THROUGH
- Why are the seven deadly sins likely to lead people into other more dangerous sins?
- How do personal sins contribute to social sins?
- How are you working against social sin?

SUMMARY
- Sin is an offence against God.
- Mortal sin is a very serious or grave sin, causing a major breakdown in our relationship with God, and with the person who has been offended.
- Venial sin does not cause a major breakdown in our relationship with God but can damage it, especially if it becomes a regular pattern.
- Personal sin refers to sins of commission or omission committed by an individual person.
- Social sin is when a group or a society develop a sinful attitude that infects its very structure.
- The seven deadly sins can lead us into other more serious sins and vices.

LESSON 50
FORGIVENESS AND RECONCILIATION

Objective: This lesson will look at forgiveness and reconciliation as a response to sin.

OPENING CONVERSATION
Can you think of any popular or current examples from music, TV, film or literature that deal with the issue of forgiveness and reconciliation? How is the topic dealt with?

Forgiveness and reconciliation

The themes of forgiveness and reconciliation have such an impact that artists, musicians, writers and filmmakers have turned to them for inspiration, and have conveyed their insights in their creative works. In the film biography of Pope John Paul II, *Karol: A Man Who Became Pope*, there's a moving scene where Karol forgives a tearful young man who has been spying on him for the communist authorities in Poland. This is followed by a similar scene where this man is forgiven by his girlfriend – he had initially used her to get close to Karol (she was one of Karol's students), but fell in love not only with her but with the Christian philosophy of life that Karol spoke so much about.

In the song 'Forgiveness', Peter Katz pays tribute to Michael and Nicholas Berg. Nicholas was kidnapped and murdered in Iraq, but his father Michael found it in himself to opt for forgiveness instead of continuing with the cycle of hatred and revenge. 'I won't participate, in spreading all this hate/So I guess I'm going to have to try forgiveness.' In the video, songwriter Katz uses a red bucket as a rather unlikely symbol for forgiveness – it turns out to be a bucket of paste for his posters designed to promote forgiveness.

REFLECT AND DISCUSS

Read the lyrics to the song and reflect on the questions that follow.

'FORGIVENESS'

You ask me to explain it
Well there's everything and nothing to say
Some things they happen
And once they do they never go away

They tell you that this life is eye for eye
Well man you know I think that's all a lie
Oh I will not stoke the fire of this fight, when I know it isn't right

So I guess I'm going to have to try forgiveness
'Cause man you know that's all that I've got left
My boy did not deserve this, but neither do the rest
I guess I'm going to have to try forgiveness

You can call me a coward
Call me whatever you choose
Once you could have hurt me
But now, I've nothing left to lose

Go on and spite me 'cause I will not curse his name
Tell me though I'm broken, I am to blame
Well go on, but I won't participate, in spreading all this hate

So I guess I'm going to have to try forgiveness
'Cause man you know that's all that I've got left
My boy did not deserve this, but neither do the rest
I guess I'm going to have to try forgiveness

They shot at me for speaking out against this tired war
Said 'How can you lose one life and not demand one more?'
Well what good will it do us in the end?
There's nothing that should justify revenge

And I stand now here before you
Living out the hardest test
And still I swear the only answer is …
Forgiveness
Forgiveness
Forgiveness

Oh you know we've got to try forgiveness
'Cause man you know it's all that we've got left
Our boys and girls are watching and they've put us to the test
Come let's show them forgiveness
Forgiveness

(Peter Katz)

▶ How are other people expecting the person in the song to react in this situation?
▶ How do they treat him when he chooses to forgive?
▶ Why does he claim the only answer is forgiveness?

FORGIVENESS AS THE PATH TO RECONCILIATION

It is possible to repair the damage caused by wrong, sinful actions. Obviously the immediate or direct harm resulting from certain actions can't be undone (e.g. in the case of murder), but there are ways of remedying terrible situations. Through forgiveness and reconciliation, our relationship with God and others can be mended and people's lives can get back on track.

> During his public life Jesus not only forgave sins, but also made plain the effect of this forgiveness: he reintegrated forgiven sinners into the community of the People of God from which sin had alienated or even excluded them. A remarkable sign of this is the fact that Jesus receives sinners at his table, a gesture that expresses in an astonishing way both God's forgiveness and the return to the bosom of the People of God. (CCC, 1443)

Forgiveness is the path to reconciliation – it is hard to see how individuals in a severely damaged relationship can possibly be reconciled without the offender being sorry and the offended person being forgiving. For Christians this forgiveness is not an optional extra – in the Our Father, people pray: 'Forgive us our trespasses as we forgive those who trespass against us' – a dangerous prayer to say if we are not inclined to be forgiving. Here we are asking God to forgive us in the same way that we forgive others. This is also clear in the biblical story of the unforgiving servant (cf. Matthew 18:23-35). A servant owed his master a large sum of money but couldn't pay, so the master took pity on him, let him off the hook and forgave him. And what did the ungrateful servant do? He, in turn, was unmerciful to all the people who owed him small amounts of money. The biblical account leaves us in no doubt as to God's message – God will forgive us great wrongs, but we must practice the same level of forgiveness towards others.

Bear in mind that God requires us to be forgiving so that we can be reconciled, but he doesn't ask us necessarily to feel forgiving – we may feel the need for revenge against the person who has already hurt us, but we can overcome that and do the right thing regardless. Above all, we must resist any temptation to hurt the person who has hurt us. We may feel forgiving eventually but the only thing we might be able to do in the short term is to choose to forgive as best we can.

Jesus doesn't just talk about forgiveness and urge others to practice it. He showed the way, by example, at the time of his crucifixion when he prayed to his Father for those who had conspired to put him to death: 'Father, forgive them; for they do not know what they are doing' (Lk 23:34).

THE SACRAMENT OF RECONCILIATION

In the Catholic Church, reconciliation is regarded as being so important that it has the status of being a sacrament. The Sacrament of Reconciliation is that graced moment, event or process when we mend the breakdown of our relationship with God and other people. God knows that deep down we need this reconciliation and provides us with the means to do it. When we celebrate the Sacrament of Reconciliation, we take the opportunity to identify, name and admit to our sin and take responsibility for it, in a context where we can get advice, and where the sin can be seen not just as a personal matter, but as something that has a negative effect on others in our community. In the Sacrament of Reconciliation we come face to face with the wrong we have done but we also come face to face with the unending love and forgiveness of God. This is the God whose qualities are shown in the story of the prodigal son. God's forgiveness, as was the case with the father of the prodigal son, is always available to us.

THINK IT THROUGH
▶ How do we know that forgiveness and reconciliation are essential in Christian teaching? In your answer you may use evidence from the Gospels and Church teaching.

JOURNAL
Forgiveness is not easy. Recall a time you struggled to forgive someone. What helped you forgive them? How did you feel afterwards? Is there anybody in your life that needs your forgiveness now? Reflect on the lyrics of the song to try and help you reach out and forgive.

Forgiveness doesn't mean that what was done was okay and it doesn't mean that you will forget what happened, but it can be the end of a cycle of anger and the start of a new chapter in your own life.

SUMMARY
- Forgiveness can lead to reconciliation.
- Forgiveness and reconciliation are positive responses to sin.
- Forgiveness and reconciliation are essential for Christians.
- The Sacrament of Reconciliation is that graced moment, event or process when we mend the breakdown of our relationship with God and other people.

LESSON 51
MORAL DECISION-MAKING

Objective: This lesson will explain one process for moral decision-making.

OPENING CONVERSATION
'A good decision should involve ...'
How would you finish this statement?

> *'God calls us to grow in a relationship of love with him and with others.*

What we consider before we do something

When we consider whether we should carry out a certain action or not, we could bring various factors to mind:

- Is it right or wrong?
- Is it against State law?
- Is it against God's law (e.g. the Ten Commandments)
- Is it against Church law?
- What consequences will it have for others?
- What consequences will it have for me?
- Will I feel guilty after it?
- What are my real motives?
- What will it cost me?
- Is it against my conscience?
- Does this action make me feel uncomfortable?
- Does this action feel right?
- What are the facts of the situation?
- What are the alternatives?

Moral theorists and philosophers stress that there is no magic formula involved in making moral decisions. Sometimes we have to make quick decisions – if someone is drowning in a river we can't dally about on the riverbank pondering our next move, we must act fast. Fortunately, when we come to make important moral decisions, we often have time to consider our proposed action carefully.

Although some exercises of our freedom are way more significant than others, it can be argued that there are no morally neutral decisions. Every choice we make is either a reasonable one, a good and responsible use of the freedom that God has given us, or it is not a good use of that freedom.

Through the choices we make and especially through the pattern of behaviour we create for ourselves, we are choosing the kind of person we want to be and the kind of person we want to become in the future. Are we going to become the person God has created us to be, or will we settle for something less? By choosing to be generous, we become generous. By telling lies, we become dishonest. In building relationships with others, we choose either to honour the dignity and equality of all those whose lives we touch, or we relate to people in such a way as to serve our own selfish purposes.

In the wider society in which we live, do we treat its structures in a way that acknowledges that they are for the benefit and wellbeing of every citizen, or do we use them for our own benefit regardless of how that impacts upon others? Are we fully aware of the issues and questions behind political decisions that affect the lives of every citizen? Do we try to ensure that laws and policies and structures strengthen rather than weaken the possibility that every human being in society will flourish?

We live in a world where resources are limited and are currently being used at an unsustainable rate. We must not use the earth's resources as if they are unlimited and determined for our personal use. Even at a time of recession in Ireland, our lifestyle would seem extraordinarily comfortable in comparison to the living standards of many others around the world, our brothers and sisters. Will we choose to think twice about how we use the earth's resources and to make decisions that favour the needs of others, especially the poor, rather than our own needs.

Freedom is not just a matter of 'doing our own thing'. We must be open to learn from the wisdom of others before making our decisions. Added to this, a person who is trying their best to live a Christian life will be guided by Scripture, especially by the Ten Commandments, by the Law of Love which Jesus gave us and showed us how to live, and by the teachings of the Church. It is through these that our conscience is informed. Any choices or actions which are not in keeping with these are sinful.

We are created in the image and likeness of God. We are called by God to grow in a relationship of love with him, with one another and with the world in which we live. It is only in growing to become the people God has made us to be that we will be fulfilled as human beings. To do other than this is to diminish ourselves as human beings and to lessen the possibility of reaching our full potential. So as to understand how we must live in order for this to become a reality, we need to take our example from Jesus who showed us how to live and how to love.

Christian life is not about 'an ethical choice or a lofty idea, but the encounter with an event, a person, which gives life a new horizon and a decisive direction' (Benedict XVI, *Deus Caritas Est*, 1). That person is, of course, Jesus Christ.

A CASE STUDY

Let's say you're a passenger in a car driven by a friend. The driver is going too fast and you're getting worried about your safety. What do you do? You don't want to seem like a coward, you don't want to appear foolish in front of your other friends who are in the car and you don't want to offend your friend who is driving.

You have to think fast as the situation is getting more dangerous. It's clearly against state law, clearly against God's law as respect is not being shown to other road users, and the results may be fatal, so it is a very serious matter. You ponder the possible consequences – death, injury, mutilation, paralysis for you, your friends, the driver, passengers in oncoming cars. Even if no one is hurt, the cost could be huge financially if there is an accident. You feel you ought to do something, time is running out. Is there any argument in favour of doing nothing?

OVER TO YOU
▶ What would you do in this situation?
▶ List two other moral dilemmas that young people today might have to face, and try to decide what is the appropriate course of action.

A PROCESS FOR MATURE DECISION-MAKING

When we have to make a decision, sometimes, like in the case study, we have to react fairly quickly. On other occasions we will have time to think about our options more carefully. In these situations it helps to have a process to work through. One helpful approach is the LISTEN process:

L – Learn the facts
I – Imagine the outcome
S – Seek insight from elsewhere
T – Turn inward
E – Expect God's help
N – Name your decision

Let's look at each step more closely with a practical example:

Hugh knows that Tricia is not being totally honest with her boyfriend, Tom, Hugh's friend. She has been seeing someone else lately. Now Tom is going to ask Tricia to marry him. What action, if any, should Hugh take?

L – LEARN THE FACTS

So often people do not know the full story before jumping in and making a decision. Be totally aware of the full facts of a situation. Know all sides of a situation or argument as best you can. Hugh must be absolutely sure of his facts before he makes any accusation.

I – IMAGINE THE OUTCOME

What are the likely consequences of this decision: for me and for others? Is this going to lead to a good outcome?

Hugh must imagine a number of scenarios: if he chooses not to tell, then he must consider what implications this has for his relationship with Tom, or for a marriage between Tom and Tricia. If he does tell Tom, he must try to imagine Tom's reaction, the effect on Tom's relationship with Tricia and on his own friendship with Tom. Another possible course of action would be to confront Tricia with knowledge of her deceit.

S – SEEK INSIGHT FROM ELSEWHERE

When looking for advice, it is important to choose people whom you can trust, people who will be totally honest with you and not just tell you what you want to hear. For help with particular moral dilemmas there are professional counsellors and helplines available. Take on board what others view to be right and wrong. For the religious person, the insight of their sacred text and faith community will be important.

Hugh might turn to another friend who knows the couple well to get a different perspective, or he might ask someone who professionally

LESSON 51 – MORAL DECISION-MAKING

counsels couples and married people for their advice.

T – TURN INWARD

This means reflecting on one's own gut feeling, listening to one's own conscience. Which decision sits well with me? What is my experience of life, my sense of right and wrong telling me to do?

For Hugh, this means thinking about the decisions he might have to make and seeing which sits most easily with his own principles: to tell the truth to a friend, or not get involved and let them work things out themselves. His own moral development, his own values of friendship, honesty and so on will come into play.

E – EXPECT GOD'S HELP

Drawing strength from God in prayer and reflection is important when making a Christian moral decision. This means allowing what the Bible says about the issue, or what one's faith community teaches about the issue, to shape the decision. It also means taking some time in quiet prayer with the living God, presenting the issue to God, who knows the reality of what is within us.

Hugh might think about honesty and truthfulness. He might take some time to pray for both Tom and Tricia, and this time of prayer might help him to see the situation from a wider perspective.

N – NAME YOUR DECISION

This means coming to a clear decision after reflection. Even if it means taking no action, or postponing action, at least you have reflected and come to a thought-out position. You are not drifting along wondering what to do.

Hugh has a deadline: Tom is going to ask Tricia to marry him. Either Hugh is going to act or he is not.

THINK IT THROUGH
- Does the LISTEN process make sense to you?
- Is there anything you would add or change in the process?
- What would you do in Hugh's situation?

RESEARCH PROJECT
Research one topical moral dilemma and apply this process and all that you have learned in this section to provide an overview of the facts, Church teaching and the insight you would share with someone facing this moral dilemma.

YOU WILL FIND ADDITIONAL INFORMATION ON WWW.SEEKANDFIND.IE

JOURNAL
Write a prayer that a person could say while trying to make a moral decision.

SUMMARY
- Moral theorists and philosophers stress that there is no magic formula involved in making moral decisions.
- When faced with a tough moral dilemma we can use a process like LISTEN to help us discern what we should do.

SECTION E

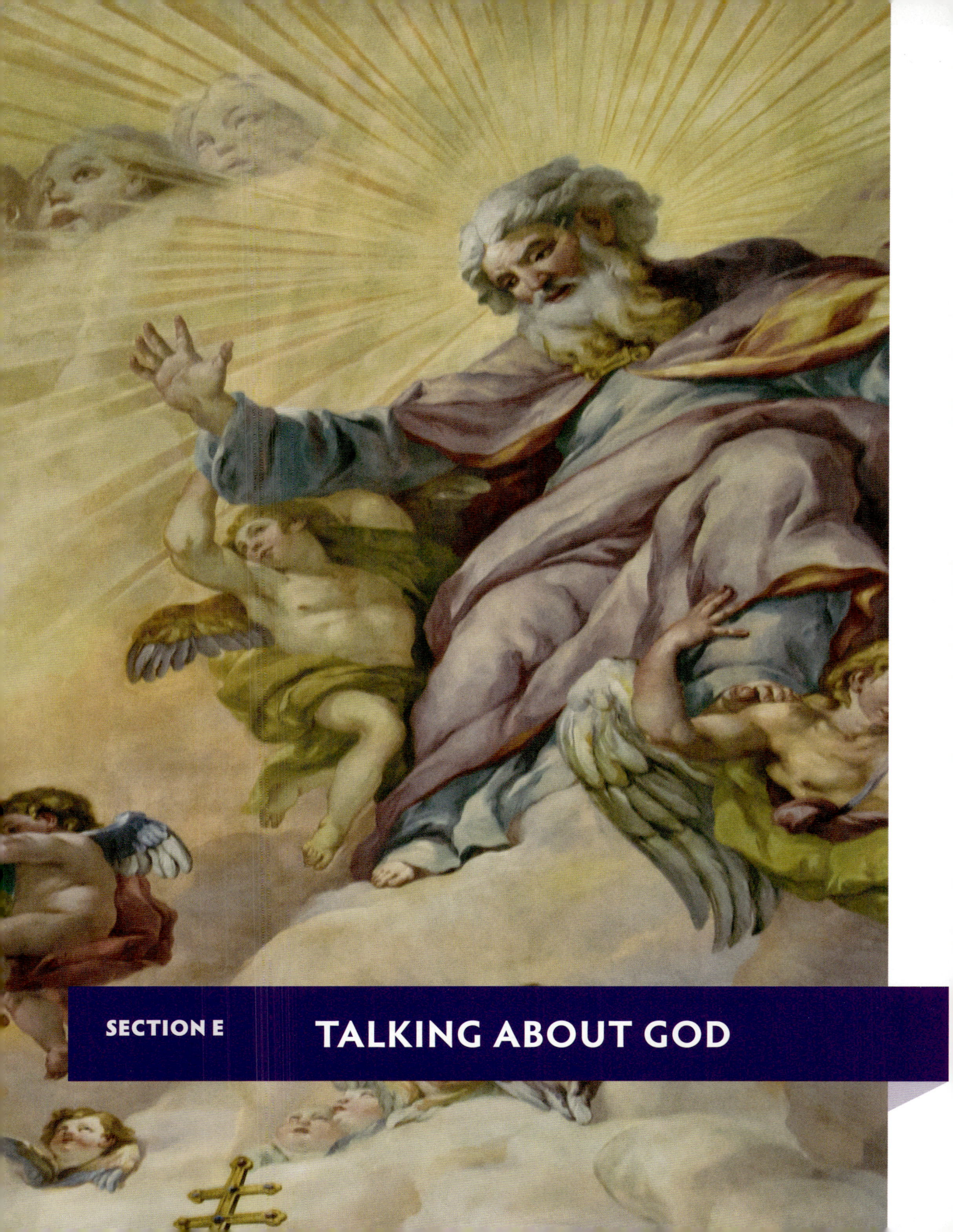

TALKING ABOUT GOD

LESSON 52
IMAGES OF GOD

Objective: This lesson will analyse various images of God and examine what the Church says about images of God.

OPENING CONVERSATION

Read the following descriptions of images of God and discuss the questions that follow:

> I think God looks like a normal human except he would probably have a beard and a moustache and dark brown hair and a holy medal. He would have a long cloak – black on the inside and red on the outside. He would be about five foot six inches and he would be smiling. He makes good things. But sometimes when he is angry, he punishes people for doing bad. He lets things happen. I think he wears brown sandals. Derek, 9

> I think God is a huge man who can do anything. He shines brightly, has a kindly face and loves everybody. His clothes are white and have lots of holy designs on them. His eyes can see anything and his ears can hear anything. His hair is grey and his hands are all wrinkled. Andrew, 12

> The image I have of God is of a guide, because I know that he'll be there whenever I need him. Sometimes when I pray I'm kind of frightened because I can't see him and I feel silly talking to someone who's in mid-air. Jacqueline, 16

' [God's] eyes can see anything and his ears can hear anything ...

> I believe God is a supreme force that we don't really understand. He is close. If I try to picture him, I see him in human form because we were told we have been created in his image. Nora, teacher

> I believe good is God, and evil is the absence of God. If I try to describe my image I think of blinding lights and booming voices sometimes. On the other hand, I think of God as nature unspoilt by man. Frank, parent

> I don't believe for one minute that God is a man. I believe in a being that isn't man or woman, but both. I find God frightening because sometimes God is close and other times so remote it's hard to believe God exists. I believe in God but sometimes believe God hasn't got much to do with the Church. I prefer talking to God rather than formal prayer. Nancy, parent

– What do these images of God tell you about the person's belief in God?
– Where do you think their image came from?
– What is your image of God?
– Where does it come from?
– Does your image of God change as you get older?

Images of God

Artists and filmmakers offer us a variety of images of God. One of the most common images of God is that of the 'bearded old man in the sky', similar to how Michelangelo portrayed God on the ceiling of the Sistine Chapel. Some religions do not allow living or human images of God – Islam, for example. Instead Islam has specific names or titles for God. There are 'Ninety-Nine Beautiful Names', such as the Merciful, the Creator, Lord of Worlds and Ever-Forgiving. These names often adorn the interior of mosques. Protestant Reformers also objected to the way in which the Catholic Church displayed images of God on the basis that such images could lead to idolatry.

Christian artists who seek to come up with images of God realise that their images are incomplete and inadequate. An image might reflect *some* aspect of God – e.g. God's power, love, creativity or forgiving nature – but it is unlikely that any artist would assume that their image presents the full story of God.

> The Christian veneration of images is not contrary to the first commandment, which proscribes idols. Indeed, 'the honour rendered to an image passes to its prototype', and 'whoever venerates an image venerates the person portrayed in it.' The honour paid to sacred images is a 'respectful veneration', not the adoration due to God alone ... (CCC, 2132)

In other words, Christians are clearly told in the Commandments that they must only worship the one true God. So when they use a sacred image they do not honour the image itself because the image is not God, but the image can help people to direct their minds and hearts to God. There is only one perfect 'image of God' and that is Jesus the incarnate Son of God, the second person of the Blessed Trinity, who came on earth to show us, in his own person, who God is and what God is like. Human beings are made in the image of God and the challenge for each of us is to become more and more authentic as an image of God in the world. All other artistic 'images of God' seek to capture some aspect of what God has revealed to us about himself. Such images together with the words of Sacred Scripture help us to come to know God and can enrich our relationship with God.

St Thomas Aquinas said:

> Religious worship is not directed to images in themselves, considered as mere things, but under their distinctive aspect as images leading us on to God incarnate. The movement toward the image does not terminate in it as image, but tends toward that whose image it is.

Pope John Paul II in his Letter to Artists in 1999 confirms the importance of the work of artists in helping us to come to know and understand God more deeply:

> In order to communicate the message entrusted to her by Christ, the Church needs art. Art must make perceptible, and as far as possible attractive, the world of the spirit, of the invisible, of God ... Art has a unique capacity to take one or other facet of the message and translate it into colours, shapes and sounds which nourish the intuition of those who look or listen. It does so without emptying the message itself of its transcendent value and its aura of mystery. The Church has need especially of those who can do this on the literary and figurative level, using the endless possibilities of images and their symbolic force. Christ himself made extensive use of images in his preaching, fully in keeping with his willingness to become, in the Incarnation, the icon of the unseen God.

Interior of the Hagia Sophia in Istanbul, Turkey, a former Eastern Orthodox basilica, then a mosque, and now a museum

OVER TO YOU
- Why do some religions object to images of God?
- What does the Catholic Church say about images of God?
- According to the Church, what is the one perfect image of God?
- Why did John Paul II say the work of artists was important?

REFLECT AND DISCUSS
Read the following quote about the difference between a 'picture of God' and an 'image of God':

> Talking about a 'picture of God', for example, strikes us as naïve or blasphemous, while the notion of an 'image of God', though it may be controversial, is taken seriously. The key lies in the use or function: a picture reproduces; an image exemplifies. An image is a picture in which nonessential features have been suppressed and essential ones highlighted. A picture, we might say, represents features indiscriminately; an image, by contrast, represents selectively. An image is both more and less than a picture: more insofar as it makes a claim about what is definitive or essential to the object; less insofar as it may be less complete or 'literal'. A picture shows us something; an image seeks to show us what that something really is.
> (From *Imagining God: Theology and the Religious Imagination* by Garrett Green)

- What point do you think the author is making?

JOURNAL
Draw or write a description of your image of God, and explain why you have this image of God. How do you see God in relation to yourself and to the world? Do you think it is any different from the way you would have described God in primary school?

SUMMARY
- There is only one perfect 'image of God' and that is Jesus.
- All other artistic 'images of God' seek to capture some aspect of what God has revealed to us about himself.
- Pope John Paul II confirmed the importance of the work of artists in helping us to come to know and understand God more deeply.

Holy Trinity and Coronation of Holy Mary – fresco from main apsis of Saint Simpliciano Church, Milan

LESSON 53
THE TRINITY

Objective: This lesson will summarise Christian teaching on the Trinity and describe various images of the Trinity.

OPENING ACTIVITY

Take some time to reflect on the relationships in your life. Draw a large spider diagram and put your name in the middle of it. Then, through words and images, represent the different relationships in your life. Be sure to include any groups to which you belong.

The Trinity – A loving relationship

Belief in the Trinity, the teaching that there is one God, and that there are three persons in that one God, is essential to Christianity. The doctrine of the Trinity teaches that at the heart of God there is a loving relationship – Father, Son and Holy Spirit in relationship with each other. In fact the Trinity shows that God *is* a loving relationship. God is a community of persons who desires to be in relationship with humanity. God desires to be in a relationship with us not simply because God created us and loved us into being, but because that's who, and how, God is: a relationship. As we are created in the image of God, we are created in the image of a relational God. We are therefore created to be in relationship with others and with God.

Experience shows that human beings do not always live up to their true selves, their true identity as images of God. The media, each and every day, reminds us of what happens when we fail to do this. The Christian life is modelled on the Trinity. A Trinitarian spirituality invites us to broaden our awareness of the presence and action of God in us and in the world around us. God is the connection, the shared relationship, who binds us together. This faith, this reality, invites us to recognise that God calls us to work for justice and peace, to strive to build communities founded on dignity and respect, friendship and love. It is in and through such work – such holy relationships – that we will grow in our relationship with God and others and all of God's creation.

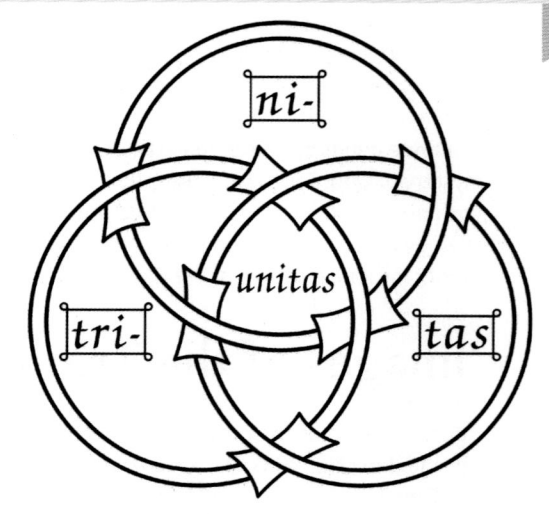

THINK IT THROUGH
- Where do you see the results of people living as images of God?
- Where do you see the results of people not living as images of God?
- When we see God as Trinity, how might this affect how we relate to God?

THE MYSTERY OF THE TRINITY

The mystery of the Most Holy Trinity is the foundation that shapes and influences *everything* Christians believe. The Trinity is 'the source of all the other mysteries of faith, the light that enlightens them' (CCC, 234). It is the mystery that explains everything: who God is, who we are, and how we are to live as the People of God. No one has ever completely understood the great mystery of the Trinity and no one ever will – in this life or the next. Why? Because we are talking about God – the Ultimate, Infinite Mystery, who is far beyond the reach of human reason and language. The attempts at explanation have varied from St Patrick's famous analogy of the shamrock – three leaves, one stem, yet all one shamrock – to St Augustine's elegant 'The Lover, the Beloved, and the Love Between'.

CONSIDER THIS ANALOGY

An 'analogy' is a comparison that uses something familiar, something we know well from experience, to try to explain something that is difficult to grasp. We have seen that the Holy Trinity is a mystery of faith which is so much deeper than our human capacity, that we could never have even imagined it on our own and that we can never fully understand. Our finite minds can never grasp the infinite mystery of God. Saint Augustine put it this way: 'If you understood him, it would not be God.' We use analogy in speaking of God to help us gain some insight into the meaning of the Divine Mystery.

In science, the substance we know as water is referred to as H_2O. This is because water consists of tiny H_2O molecules, each of which is made up of two even smaller atoms of hydrogen joined to a single atom of oxygen. Water, or H_2O, can take three forms: a liquid form (water), a solid form (ice) and a gas form (steam). However, it remains H_2O no matter what form it takes. Using this analogy gives us some insight into the truth that God is one God whether we speak of God the Father, God the Son or God the Holy Spirit.

Images of the Trinity

An artist or filmmaker who shows God as one person, which is the most common approach in the depiction of God, captures the one-ness of God, but misses out on the three-ness. An artist or filmmaker who portrays God as three persons might be in danger of losing the one-ness of God. Again it is important to realise that no one image can capture the fullness of God.

FOUR DEPICTIONS OF THE TRINITY

1. The image of the Trinity by modern English artist Elizabeth Wang shows God as Trinity reaching out to humanity. Suitably it is Jesus in particular who reaches out – we can recognise him by the scars on his hands. The surrounding circle shows the unity of God. The figure on top may be the Holy Spirit warmly embracing the other persons. The Holy Spirit is often described as the Love between the Father and the Son. The Father holds people in his hands.
2. This is the famous Trinity icon from the fifteenth-century artist, Andrei Rublev. The three persons are seen in a moment of table fellowship. The three faces are identical, suggesting the one-ness of God. Their blue garments symbolise transcendence. On the right, the Holy Spirit's green cloak suggests growth and new life. In the middle, Christ wears a brown garment, suggesting his closeness to the earth. On the left is the Father in shimmering golden clothes, emphasising his divinity.
3. This is a very traditional image of the Trinity. It is very easy to see who is who: the Father is like the common image of God we saw in the last lesson; the Son is obviously Jesus, again showing the wounds in his hands; and the Holy Spirit is represented here as a dove, quite a common image for the Spirit.
4. This is a painting from the eighteenth century of the Holy Family and the Trinity by Dutch artist Jacob de Wit. Note how the human family is in the foreground, while the Father and Holy Spirit watch from the background. Jesus, the son, is common to both the human family and the Trinity. It is one of the few paintings of the Trinity where Jesus, the second person of the Trinity, is portrayed as a child.

REFLECT AND DISCUSS

Reflect on the images of the Trinity on the opposite page. In each case, write your own opinion of the portrayals. Which is your favourite portrayal? Explain your answer.

SUMMARY

- The Church teaches that there is one God in three divine Persons.
- The Trinity is a core teaching of Christianity, emphasising the loving nature of God and the importance of relationship.
- It is the mystery that explains everything: who God is, who we are, and how we are to live as the People of God.

1. The Trinity *by Elizabeth Wang*

2. Holy Trinity Icon *by Andrei Rublev*

3. Statue of Holy Trinity *from side altar, Almudena Cathedral, Madrid*

4. Holy Family and the Trinity *by Jacob de Wit*

LESSON 53 — THE TRINITY

LESSON 54
IMAGES OF GOD IN POETRY

Objective: This lesson will look at how various writers have described God in their poetry.

OPENING CONVERSATION
Can you think of any poems that mention God? If so, what kind of image of God is presented?

Poems about God

Being made in the image of God, we share to an extent in God's creativity. Some poets turn their creativity to coming up with thought-provoking images of God.

JOHN MILTON

In the poem, 'When I Consider', seventeenth-century English poet John Milton portrays God as a hard taskmaster – one who will be cross if we don't do the jobs he has set us: 'To serve therewith my Maker, and present/My true account, lest he returning chide'. Milton wants to serve his maker, God, by writing his poetry, but fears he cannot do it because he has gone blind: '"Doth God exact day-labour, light denied?"' His image of God softens towards the end – this time God is like a king, who has plenty of people to do his work. Milton realises, in the last line, that it is enough to be *available* for service.

'WHEN I CONSIDER'

When I consider how my light is spent,
Ere half my days in this dark world and wide,
And that one talent which is death to hide
Lodged with me useless, though my soul more bent
To serve therewith my Maker, and present
My true account, lest he returning chide;
'Doth God exact day-labour, light denied?'
I fondly ask. But Patience, to prevent
That murmur, soon replies: 'God doth not need
Either man's work or his own gifts. Who best
Bear his mild yoke, they serve him best. His state
Is kingly: thousands at his bidding speed,
And post o'er land and ocean without rest;
They also serve who only stand and wait'.

SECTION E: TALKING ABOUT GOD

GEORGE HERBERT

Another seventeenth-century English poet, George Herbert creates a much softer image of God in his poem 'Love'. He sees God as a kind host, welcoming the soul to the banquet of heaven. But the soul feels guilty and therefore reluctant to enter. Love/God has to gently persuade the soul of its worthiness.

'LOVE'

> Love bade me welcome; yet my soul drew
>   back,
> Guilty of dust and sin.
> But quick-eyed Love, observing me grow
>   slack
> From my first entrance in,
> Drew nearer to me, sweetly questioning
> If I lack'd anything.
>
> 'A guest,' I answer'd, 'worthy to be here:'
> Love said, 'You shall be he.'
> 'I, the unkind, ungrateful? Ah, my dear,
> I cannot look on Thee.'
> Love took my hand and smiling did reply,
> 'Who made the eyes but I?'
>
> 'Truth, Lord; but I have marr'd them: let my
>   shame
> Go where it doth deserve.'
> 'And know you not,' says Love, 'Who bore
>   the blame?'
> 'My dear, then I will serve.'
> 'You must sit down,' says Love, 'and taste my
>   meat.'
> So I did sit and eat.

Patrick Kavanagh sculpture, located on the banks of the Grand Canal in Dublin

PATRICK KAVANAGH

Irish poet Patrick Kavanagh often reflected on God in nature, for example in his poem 'The One':

> God is down in the swamps and marshes […]
>   that beautiful, beautiful, beautiful God
> was breathing His love by a cut-away bog.

He pictures the Trinity in 'The Great Hunger':

> Yet sometimes when the sun comes through
>   a gap
> These men know God the Father in a tree:
> The Holy Spirit is the rising sap,
>   And Christ will be the green leaves that
>   will come
> At Easter from the sealed and guarded tomb.

LESSON 54 – IMAGES OF GOD IN POETRY

GERARD KELLY

A more modern poet, Gerard Kelly, tries out a variety of positive God images in his poem 'This God'. He sees God as artist, lover, creator, parent, playwright. Another of Kelly's poems, 'Rob's God', describes 'a glowing God of graceful inclination', a God, who is 'a poet,/ painting people as his poems', and a God who is a 'furnace of forgiveness'.

'ROB'S GOD'

I want to follow Rob's God;
God the goal of my soul's education.
Rob's God is approachable, articulate and
    artful,
a glowing God
of graceful inclination.

Rob's God snowboards cloudscapes
and paints daisies on his toes
while watching Chaplin re-runs
on his iPod.
He smiles at cats and children,
jumps in puddles
with his shoes on;
he is a 'where's the fun in
    fundamentalism?' God.

Rob's God doesn't shoot
his wounded
or blame the poor for failing
at prosperity.
He doesn't beat the broken
with bruised reeds from their garden
or tell the sick that healing's
their responsibility.

Rob's God is a poet,
painting people as his poems;
a sculptor shaping symphonies from
    stone;
a maker of mosaics,
curator of collages
woven from the wounds and wonders
we have known

A furnace of forgiveness,
Rob's God radiates reunion,
pouring oil on every fight
we've ever started;
a living lover
loving laughter,
lending light
to the helpless and the harmed and
    heavyhearted

Other Gods may claim more crowded
    churches,
higher profiles,
better ratings,
fuller phone-ins,
but in the contest for commitment,
in the battle for belief,
in the war to woo my worship,
Rob's God wins.
In the fight for my faith's fervour,
in the struggle for my soul,
in the race for my respect,
Rob's God wins.

Absolutely.

OVER TO YOU
- Which of these images of God do you prefer? Explain your answer.
- Which of the poets' images of God is most likely to draw people to God?
- Pick one or more of the images from these poems and illustrate it/them in a drawing or collage.

JOURNAL
Write a poem featuring your image of God.

SUMMARY
- Many poets, both old and modern, have written about God and presented a variety of images.
- Reaction to such images will vary according to personal taste – some might find these images appealing, some might not.

LESSON 55
IMAGES OF GOD IN SONGS

Objective: This lesson will identify some images of God in songs.

OPENING CONVERSATION
Can you think of any songs that mention God? What image of God comes through?

‘ *My stronghold, my saviour, I shall not be afraid at all.*

Songs about God

There are many examples of images of God in songs. Some are biblical images – e.g. the well-known hymn 'The Lord is My Shepherd' (from Psalm 23). John Michael Talbot is a contemporary Catholic songwriter and performer of reflective spiritual music, and often uses the Bible for inspiration. In his song 'Only in God' (based on Psalm 62), God is seen as 'saviour' and 'stronghold': 'My stronghold, my saviour, I shall not be afraid at all'. In another of his songs, 'The Empty Canvas', Talbot writes of God as a painter – 'The empty canvas waits before the Painter' – an image in which the creative songwriter captures the creativity of God.

Composer Carey Landry has two powerful images in one of his best-known songs, 'Abba Father'. As the title suggests, God is 'father', but also in the song he is imagined as a 'potter'. Like Talbot's painter image, Landry also sees God as being creative and artistic.

Singer-songwriter Charlie Landsborough conveys a simple yet appealing idea in 'My Forever Friend': 'He's my forever friend/My leave-me-never friend/From darkest night to rainbow's end/He's my forever friend.'

Others take a more unusual line. In singer-songwriter Julie Miller's song 'My Psychiatrist', she sees God as just that – a kindly psychiatrist: 'If you've got problems, small or large, /his therapy is free of charge,/For mental health, just take a look,/He wrote it all down in a best selling book'.

More peculiarly, in the song 'UFO', Christian rocker Larry Norman sees God as an unidentified flying object: 'He's an unidentified flying object/You will see Him in the air/He's an unidentified flying object/You will drop your hands and stare'.

Joan Osborne had a Grammy award-nominated hit, 'What If God Was One of Us?' which, though the imagery might be controversial or daring, challenges us to reflect on what it would be like if God was living among us: 'What if God was one of us/Just a slob like one of us/Just a stranger on the bus/Trying to make his way home.'

OVER TO YOU
- Which of these images of God in music do you find most appealing and why?
- Which of these images of God in music do you find least appealing and why?
- What characteristics of God do these lyrics speak of?
- How do these characteristics compare to those that God revealed himself to have?

REFLECT AND DISCUSS
Read and reflect on these lyrics from the song 'God Is' by Danielle Rose and answer the questions that follow. The songwriter describes this song as 'a meditation on the infinite nature of God, who cannot be summarised with mortal words, yet whose presence is revealed through truth and beauty in the Body of Christ.'

'GOD IS'

You want to know me?
You want to see my face?
I do not age with time
I do not fit into a space
I transcend the capacity of your eye, so who am I?
It is the question of the moment
It is the question for all time
I am you, and you are mine

I am the beginning in the end
I am the faith in your believing
I am the colour of truth
I am the dreamer of your dreams
I am the falling in your love
I am the words of a prayer
I am the silence in the music
I am the music in the silence

I'm the cross you carry again
I'm all you have forgotten
I am all that you have not been
I am in you – all of this is within you
Let the journey begin, Amen
I am in you, Amen.

(Danielle Rose)

- Which line stands out for you and why?
- Which line most closely captures your image of God?
- Is there a line that challenges your image of God?
- If you had to add one more image to this song, what would you add?

SUMMARY
- Many songwriters have included images of God in their work.
- Sometimes these images are traditional, sometimes biblical, and sometimes they are very modern and unusual.

LESSON 56
IMAGES OF GOD IN FILM

Objective: This lesson will describe how God is portrayed in the film Bruce Almighty.

OPENING CONVERSATION
If you had God's power for a day, what would you do and why?

Images of God in film

Filmmakers, like other artists, have turned their creative minds to coming up with images of God. One of the best known and most popular is the portrayal of God in the film *Bruce Almighty*.

BRUCE ALMIGHTY

In this film God is nothing like the stereotypical image of God as an old man wearing a cloak. Instead he is portrayed by Morgan Freeman who, when he first appears, is dressed as a janitor cleaning the floors, then an electrician, and then later wearing a smart white suit.

In the movie, Jim Carrey plays a reporter named Bruce Nolan who longs to do serious news features. He wants to be more than the guy that everyone laughs at. He wants to be the news anchor on the station's nightly broadcast. When he doesn't get this position, he reacts as if his life has no meaning. God has tried everything to help Bruce see the meaning in his life and becomes tired of Bruce's constant negative attitude towards life. So he decides to let Bruce take over as God for a few days to show him that what he does isn't so easy.

When God hands over the power to run the world to Bruce, he does not set his sights on fixing world poverty or establishing peace for all people. The first thing Bruce does as God is see to his own needs. He uses his power to create big news events so he is able to provide exclusive coverage. In the process, though, his personal life starts to fall apart and the rest of the world is in chaos. Bruce is not doing a good job as God. It seems the job is much more difficult that he ever imagined.

Once Bruce takes over the universe's greatest responsibility, his limited, selfish human agenda nearly ruins his life and the lives of those who care for him. While the power may have gone to Bruce's head and he tries to manipulate people, God is portrayed as being powerful but committed to free will, giving people the choice to accept or reject him. God is portrayed as being interested in people and totally selfless. One of the most powerful images of God comes when Bruce asks God, 'How do you make someone love you without affecting free will?' and God replies, 'Welcome to my world son'.

Bruce then wants to give back to God the power that has been bestowed upon him because it has become too much for him. In his distress Bruce kneels on a highway and begins to pray, then ends up in heaven.

Morgan Freeman portraying God in the film Bruce Almighty

Bruce: Am I ...?
God: Can't kneel down in the middle of a highway and live to talk about it son.
Bruce: But why, why now?
God: Bruce, you have the divine spark, you have the gift for bringing joy and laughter to the world.
I know.
I created you.
Bruce: Quit bragging.
God: You see, that's what I'm talking about, that's the spark.

God gives Bruce a prayer bracelet.

Bruce: What do you want me to do?
God: I want you to pray son, go ahead, use them.
Bruce: Ahm, Lord, feed the hungry and bring peace to all of mankind. How's that?
God: Great, if you want to be Miss America. Now come on, what do you really care about?
Bruce: Grace. *(Grace is the woman with whom Bruce is very much in love.)*
God: Grace, you want her back?
Bruce: No, I want her to be happy, no matter what that means. I want her to find someone who will treat her with all the love she deserved from me. I want her to meet someone who will see her always as I do now, through your eyes.
God: Now that's a prayer.
Bruce: Yeah.
God: Yeah, it's good.
Bruce: It's good.
Together: It's good.
God: I'm going to get right on it.

This film portrays the idea that less is more where God's intervention is concerned. God also displays infinite patience with Bruce. The film also tries to show us that human suffering and the pain and tragedy so prevalent in our world does not occur because God doesn't care, but rather because, in our sin and confusion, we ignore God and try to find happiness and fulfilment in all the wrong places. Yet God still treats us with goodness and loving kindness. The message is that God desires a relationship with all of humanity. The film portrays God's love, wisdom and mercy. God also challenges people to grow and he wants people to learn to be less selfish and more loving and respectful. We see Bruce's transformation from beginning to end and how encountering God changed him.

OVER TO YOU
- Why do you think God appears in the film dressed as a janitor, an electrician and in a smart white suit?
- What characteristics of God are portrayed in the film?
- Do you find this image of God appealing? Why or why not?
- How does the portrayal of God in *Bruce Almighty* compare to your own image of God?

THINK IT THROUGH
- Can you think of any other images of God in film, TV or literature?
- What are the most common characteristics of God portrayed in these?
- Why do you think this is?

GROUP WORK
Working in small groups, imagine you have been asked to produce a new film featuring God. Who would you choose to play the part? Explain your answer. What characteristics of God would you include in the film? Why?

SUMMARY
- *Bruce Almighty* shows human suffering and how the pain and tragedy so prevalent in our world does not occur because God doesn't care, but rather because, in our sin and confusion, we ignore God and try to find happiness in all the wrong places.
- The film portrays God's love, wisdom, patience and mercy, but also a God that can be challenging.
- We see Bruce's transformation from beginning to end and how encountering God changed him.
- The portrayal of God in this film promotes the idea that less is more where God's intervention is concerned.

LESSON 57
IMAGES OF GOD IN THE OLD TESTAMENT

Objective: This lesson will examine various images of God in the Old Testament.

OPENING ACTIVITY
Briefly write about any image of God you can remember from the Old Testament.

The God of Scripture

While it is interesting to see how poets, songwriters, filmmakers and artists use their imaginations to convey images of God, the Bible is the essential source for developing and maturing our own image of God. After all, Scripture is the inspired Word of God. We find many metaphors to speak the truth about God and his revelation in Scripture. God is described as a king, judge, rock, fresh water, mother, gardener, lover, friend, breadmaker, washerwoman, lion, shepherd, midwife, and more.

The Old Testament God is sometimes seen as very stern (e.g. the plagues sent on the Egyptians for keeping the Jewish people in slavery) but there are many appealing images. In Deuteronomy we find this striking image:

> As an eagle stirs up its nest,
> and hovers over its young;
> as it spreads its wings, takes them up,
> and bears them aloft on its pinions ... (32:11)

In the Book of Wisdom, the inspired writer sees that God can be a friend. Depicting 'Wisdom' as a person, the writer says:

> I do not hide her wealth, for it is an unfailing treasure for mortals; those who get it obtain friendship with God, commended for the gifts that come from instruction (7:13-14)

God is often portrayed as a loving parent. The Book of Hosea speaks of the Israelites: 'It shall be said to them [you are] "Children of the living God"' (1:10).

GOD AS MOTHER

The *Catechism* reminds us: 'God's parental tenderness can also be expressed by the image of motherhood' (CCC, 239). The *Catechism* refers to two biblical passages from the Old Testament. The first is from the writings of Isaiah: 'As a mother comforts her child, so I will comfort you' (66:13). In Isaiah we also read, 'Can a woman forget her nursing child ...? Even these may forget, yet I will not forget you' (49:15). The second is from the Book of Psalms: 'But I have calmed and quieted my soul, like a weaned child with its mother' (131:2).

GOD AS CREATOR

In Genesis, the first book of the Bible, we see God as Creator: 'In the beginning ... God created the heavens and the earth' (1:1). God is portrayed as a careful, imaginative and loving creator. The account stresses how happy God was with creation: 'God saw everything that he had made, and indeed, it was very good' (1:31). But God is the creator not just of things, but of people, the high point of creation. And from the beginning this creator wants people to be in community: 'It is not good that the man should be alone' (2:18). In Genesis we see a relaxed God 'walking in the garden at the time of the evening breeze' (3:8), but also one who confronts Adam and Eve for their wrongdoing, making them face up to the consequences of their actions.

GOD AS SHEPHERD

One image very familiar to us is the image of God as a caring shepherd: 'He will feed his flock like a shepherd; he will gather the lambs in his arms, and carry them in his bosom' (Is 40:11). This image is also seen in Psalms: 'The Lord is my shepherd, I shall not want. He makes me lie down in green pastures; he leads me beside still waters; he restores my soul' (23:1-3). In Ezekiel, it says:

> For thus says the Lord God: I myself will search for my sheep, and will seek them out. As shepherds seek out their flocks when they are among their scattered sheep, so I will seek out my sheep. I will rescue them from all the places to which they have been scattered on a day of clouds and thick darkness. (34:11-12)

IMAGES OF GOD IN THE PSALMS

The Psalms are filled with beautiful imagery about God. God is described as laughing: 'He who sits in the heavens laughs' (2:4). On numerous occasions in the Bible, God is compared to a host – as if God is throwing a party and inviting us all: 'You prepare a table before me in the presence of my enemies; you anoint my head with oil; my cup overflows' (23:5). At times the Psalm writer wants to emphasise the strength and power of God: 'Who is the King of glory? The Lord, strong and mighty, the Lord, mighty in battle' (24:8).

THINK IT THROUGH
- Which Old Testament images of God are most appealing to you? Explain your answer.
- Which are least appealing? Explain your answer.
- What does each of these images tell us about God?

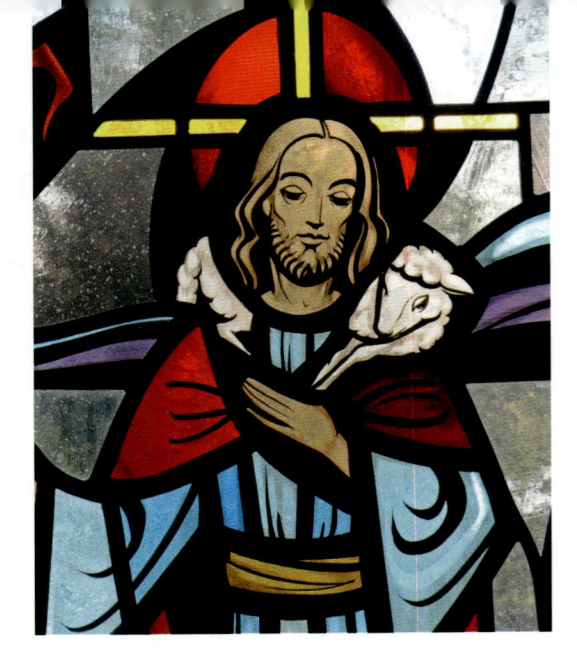

OVER TO YOU
Read this second verse of Psalm 18:

> The LORD is my rock, my fortress, and my deliverer,
> my God, my rock in whom I take refuge,
> my shield, and the horn of my salvation,
> my stronghold.

- Name the different metaphors for God in this verse.
- What attribute, or quality, of God do you think the psalmist was trying to communicate through each of these metaphors?

SUMMARY
- The Bible is the essential source for developing and maturing our own image of God because Scripture is the inspired Word of God.
- The Old Testament features a variety of images of God, some stern but many gentle and caring.
- Popular images describe God as a loving parent, a host and a shepherd.

LESSON 58
IMAGES OF GOD IN THE NEW TESTAMENT

Objective: This lesson will look at images of God in the New Testament, in the person of Jesus and the stories he told.

OPENING ACTIVITY
Write a brief account of any New Testament story that tells us something about what God is like.

Powerful images

Of all the sources of God imagery, for a Christian the New Testament is the most important because in it God, in the person of Jesus, reveals what he is like. Christians believe that Jesus himself is the ultimate image or face of God. This is made clear in John's Gospel: 'Whoever has seen me has seen the Father' (14:9).

> '*Whoever has seen me has seen the Father.*'
>
> Jn 14:9

We don't know for sure what Jesus looked like, though artists have been very influential in offering pictures of Jesus. We look instead to what Jesus said or did, the stories he told, to his *personality*.

GOD AS FATHER
One of the most influential images of God is that of the Father in Jesus' parable of the Prodigal Son:

> So he set off and went to his father. But while he was still far off, his father saw him and was filled with compassion; he ran and put his arms around him and kissed him. Then the son said to him, 'Father, I have sinned against heaven and before you; I am no longer worthy to be called your son.' But the father said to his slaves, 'Quickly, bring out a robe – the best one – and put it on him; put a ring on his finger and sandals on his feet. (Lk 15:20-22)

God is portrayed here as a loving, forgiving father. When the son came back after wasting his inheritance money, the father could have made him grovel, could have banished him from the house – but instead he ran down the road to greet him as soon as he saw him coming home, and even threw a party for him. Note that the son was repentant: 'Father, I have sinned against heaven and before you; I am no longer worthy to be called your son.'

The Return of the Prodigal Son by Rembrandt van Rijn (1661–1669)

It wasn't the only time Jesus spoke of God as Father. When teaching his followers how to pray, he suggested they start with 'Our Father …'. The word he used for father, 'Abba', is more like the familiar 'Dad', a powerful lesson for how we can relate to God.

GOD AS HOST

Jesus told a number of stories that described God as a host – someone throwing a great party. The idea of the Kingdom of Heaven being like a banquet is a common biblical image:

> The kingdom of heaven may be compared to a king who gave a wedding banquet for his son. He sent his slaves to call those who had been invited to the wedding banquet, but they would not come. Again he sent other slaves, saying, 'Tell those who have been invited: 'Look, I have prepared my dinner, my oxen and fat calves have been slaughtered, and everything is ready; come to the wedding banquet.' But they made light of it and went away, one to his farm, another to his business, while the rest seized his slaves, mistreated them, and killed them. The king was enraged. He sent his troops, destroyed those murderers, and burned their city. Then he said to his slaves, 'The wedding is ready, but those invited were not worthy. Go therefore into the main streets, and invite everyone you find to the wedding banquet.' Those slaves went out into the streets and gathered all whom they found, both good and bad; so the wedding hall was filled with guests.
>
> But when the king came in to see the guests, he noticed a man there who was not wearing a wedding robe, and he said to him, 'Friend, how did you get in here without a wedding robe?' And he was speechless. Then the king said to the attendants, 'Bind him hand and foot, and throw him into the outer darkness, where there will be weeping and gnashing of teeth.' For many are called, but few are chosen. (Mt 22:1-14)

GOD AS SOWER

On a number of occasions God is compared to a sower – one who sows seeds and hopes they will grow well. The seeds are the Word of God, as Jesus himself explains:

> A sower went out to sow his seed; and as he sowed, some fell on the path and was trampled on, and the birds of the air ate it up. Some fell on the rock; and as it grew up, it withered for lack of moisture. Some fell among thorns, and the thorns grew with it and choked it. Some fell into good soil, and when it grew, it produced a hundredfold. (Lk 8:5-8)

God sows the seeds of his word in us. God's word reveals to us who we are as sons and daughters of God, made in God's own image and likeness.

Fresco of the Holy Trinity from side nave in the Church of the Gesu, Palermo, Italy

THINK IT THROUGH
- Which New Testament image appeals to you most? Explain why.
- Which New Testament image appeals to you least? Explain why.
- Can you remember any other New Testament images of God?
- Compare these images of God with the images of God from the Old Testament, examined in the previous lesson.

JOURNAL
Write and/or illustrate your favourite New Testament image of God.

Comparative Religious Studies
Research images of God in another major world religion and compare it to the Christian images of God.

YOU WILL FIND ADDITIONAL INFORMATION ON
WWW.SEEKANDFIND.IE

> **SUMMARY**
> - The best way to know what God is like is to look at the person of Jesus as depicted in the Four Gospels.
> - In what he said and did, Jesus reveals many aspects of what God is like.

LESSON 59
INADEQUATE IMAGES OF GOD

Objective: This lesson will examine distorted images of God and the implications these can have.

OPENING CONVERSATION

Here's what one person remembers about her image of God when she was young:

> My image of God as a child was that of a film director sitting in his director's booth with hundreds of screens in front of him. It originated from my parents who informed me that 'no matter what you do, we may not see you, but God will see you'. The image was my attempt at rationalising how he could see us at all times. I figured that he must have invisible cameramen peering around corners trying to get the best shot.

Briefly give your opinion of this person's image of God. What does this image of God tell us about this person's relationship with God?

Inadequate images

God transcends all creatures. We must therefore continually purify our language of everything in it that is limited, image-bound or imperfect, if we are not to confuse our image of God – 'the inexpressible, the incomprehensible, the invisible, the ungraspable' – with our human representations. Our human words always fall short of the mystery of God. (CCC, 42)

As we have already said, every image of God is to some extent a problem image. No image can capture the fullness of God, and so every image is inadequate. The Bible, as we saw, has many different images of God, so we know there is no one definitive image. We can have a few favourite images that help us to develop a healthy image of God.

There are, however, some images of God that might be negative, distorted or downright harmful, to the extent that they may even cause people to turn away from God. One of the documents of Vatican II says: 'Some form for themselves such a fallacious idea of God that when they repudiate this figment they are by no means rejecting the God of the Gospel' (*Gaudium et Spes*, 19). In other words, people say they don't believe in God, but the idea of God that they are rejecting to begin with is nothing like how God revealed himself to be. Sometimes people hang on to an image of God from childhood – appropriate to the child but failing to develop as the person grows toward adulthood. Many people develop professionally, move on to interesting careers, but their image of God can remain immature.

'SANTA GOD'

In this impression, God is seen as a kindly old man in the sky, bearded like Santa Claus, cuddly and unchallenging. Young children often have this image of God. However, as we get older, our image of God needs to develop. Adults who continue to see God in this way will struggle to have a meaningful relationship with God. They could find themselves leaving this God behind, along with Santa, the Tooth Fairy and the Easter Bunny.

SECTION E: TALKING ABOUT GOD

'GOD OF THE GAPS'

This is where God becomes the explanation for everything and anything we don't understand. God is seen as filling 'the gaps' in our knowledge. This idea developed out of the idea that gaps in our scientific knowledge is evidence for God. The problem with this version is that the need for God might dwindle or even disappear as science explains things that at one time we didn't understand. As our knowledge grows this distorted image of God becomes redundant.

'FATHER GOD'

Jesus called God 'Abba' and taught us to pray the Our Father. For many people who have a good relationship with their own father, the image of God as father works well. However, if someone has a difficult or no relationship with their own father, the image of God as father could be a negative image for them.

'MAN GOD'

Some people wrongly assume that God is a man as God is more often than not referred to as 'he' or 'him'. There is a danger that this can lead to women being seen as less important than men. The issue shows up a difficulty in language – God is a person we can relate to, and we think of people as being either male or female. So for convenience, God is generally, and traditionally, referred to as 'he'. Calling God 'it' would sound too impersonal, while constantly avoiding the pronoun and using the term 'God' all the time would lead to awkward syntax. Further, the Bible usually speaks of God in masculine terms. The Church clarifies this by saying:

> In no way is God in man's image. He is neither man nor woman. God is pure spirit in which there is no place for the difference between the sexes. But the respective 'perfections' of man and woman reflect something of the infinite perfection of God: those of a mother and those of a father and husband. (CCC, 370)

Referring to this passage from the *Catechism*, Pope John Paul II said:

> We find in these passages an indirect confirmation of the truth that both man and woman were created in the image and likeness of God. If there is a likeness between Creator and creatures, it is understandable that the Bible would refer to God using expressions that attribute to him both 'masculine' and 'feminine' qualities. (*Mulieris Dignitatem*, 8)

THINK IT THROUGH
- Which of these images, in your opinion, is likely to cause the most problems?

LESSON 59 – INADEQUATE IMAGES OF GOD

Images and relationships

Our image of God will affect our relationship with God, the way we pray to God and the way we relate to other people. We can see this in human relationships. For example, if we think that a friend has really let us down, we will find it hard to maintain a relationship with that person. If we believe that a person is generous and supportive, we will be more inclined to want to develop a close relationship with that person. In the same way, if we see God as an uncaring, harsh God, it will be hard to have a close, loving relationship with him – at best we'll do what's right because we're scared; at worse we'll turn away from God altogether. On the other hand, if we see God as a caring person, concerned about us and loving us, it will be easier to develop a good relationship.

Let's say we believe that God is forgiving, that he will forgive our sins if we repent, but also expects us to forgive others. How will our behaviour be influenced? First, we might have a sense of relief and confidence – knowing that if we slip up and sin, and then regret it, God will be willing to forgive us. However, we won't become presumptuous or arrogant and assume we can do whatever evil we like because God will forgive us. We'll also realise that we must make our best effort to forgive others when they offend us, as some of them surely will. This may be hard on an emotional level, we may not feel forgiving, but we'll still try to do the right thing. In our prayers we'll be particularly conscious of the lines of the Our Father – 'Forgive us our trespasses as we forgive those who trespass against us'.

To consider a more negative example, let's say we think that God is tough, harsh, unforgiving. Then in our relationship with God we'll probably be fearful. Our prayers will be overloaded with begging for forgiveness. In our human relationships, we might pass on this harshness to others – always looking to blame someone for everything, constantly stressing other people's guilt to avoid admitting our own.

However, if we believe that God is loving, forgiving and merciful and wants us to treat others the same way, then this will have a very positive impact on our relationship with God and others.

OVER TO YOU

► For each of the descriptions of God below, write about how a person influenced by the image would be likely to behave in their life – e.g. how would they relate to God? What kind of prayer would they say? How would they relate to other people?

- God is challenging. He wants to bring out the best in me.
- God is deadly serious. He has no time for humour.
- God loves me dearly, and hopes that I will love others.
- God is peaceful, serene, calming.
- God interferes all the time – he is like a puppeteer, always pulling our strings.

SUMMARY

- Some images of God are not helpful in bringing us closer to him.
- Some images of God are distorted and misleading.
- The images people have of God can affect the way they relate to God and to other people.
- This can work in a positive way or in a negative way.

LESSON 60
MEETING GOD IN ORDINARY LIFE

Objective: This lesson will consider how people can meet God in their ordinary, everyday life.

OPENING ACTIVITY
Imagine meeting God now. What would you say? What would God say? Write a short dialogue.

Where is God?

We have looked at how our images of God affect how we relate to God and others. Let's assume for the moment that we have some sort of a positive image of God, or at least not a negative one. How then do we meet God in everyday life?

Some meet God in places that are special to them. For example, it might be a particular church they attend.

> When I was in college there was a little oratory. It was always quiet, calm and cool there. I really felt a strong sense of the presence of God. Things did not always go smoothly in college, and this oratory was a place I could go to talk things over with God, a place where I could leave my troubles at the door, and pick them up on the way out, and I always did so with a better outlook on them. Even after leaving college I would sometimes go back for a visit, and even after a long absence there was still that same feeling of meeting God.

Nature provides beautiful settings for people to feel the presence of God. It might be on a starry night when you can have an intimate conversation with God as you look skywards and contemplate the mysteries of the universe. It might be on a sunny day in lush countryside, or even in a park in the city.

> When I spent a year backpacking around the world I felt the presence of God in nature. I remember one particular occasion when I was scuba-diving off the Great Barrier Reef. I was mesmerised by all the colourful fish and beautiful coral. It was a whole other world that I had never

LESSON 60 – MEETING GOD IN ORDINARY LIFE

215

seen before. And then it hit me, I just knew this world could not have been an accident. It had to be created by God. I felt very close to God as I got a glimpse of the miracle of creation.

We can also meet God in other people. It might be a special person that helped us out when we were in trouble – e.g. a teacher who helped us through a difficult time in school, a priest who helped us through a bereavement, a friend who stayed with us in times of illness.

> It's a long time ago now, but my father's death was a hard shock to me. Yet strangely, I felt God was near – in the comforting I got from others at the time. It was like it was God who was giving me a comforting hug.

We can feel a strong presence of God at special times in our lives. This elderly person remembers two such experiences:

> When asked about special times that I have felt that God was close, two events come to mind. I can remember my wedding day clearly. Perhaps it was the presence of such love that made me feel God's closeness so vividly. And the birth of my children. When I looked at their beautiful faces and held them in my arms for the first time and just fell in love with them, I better understood the idea of the unconditional love that God has for me.

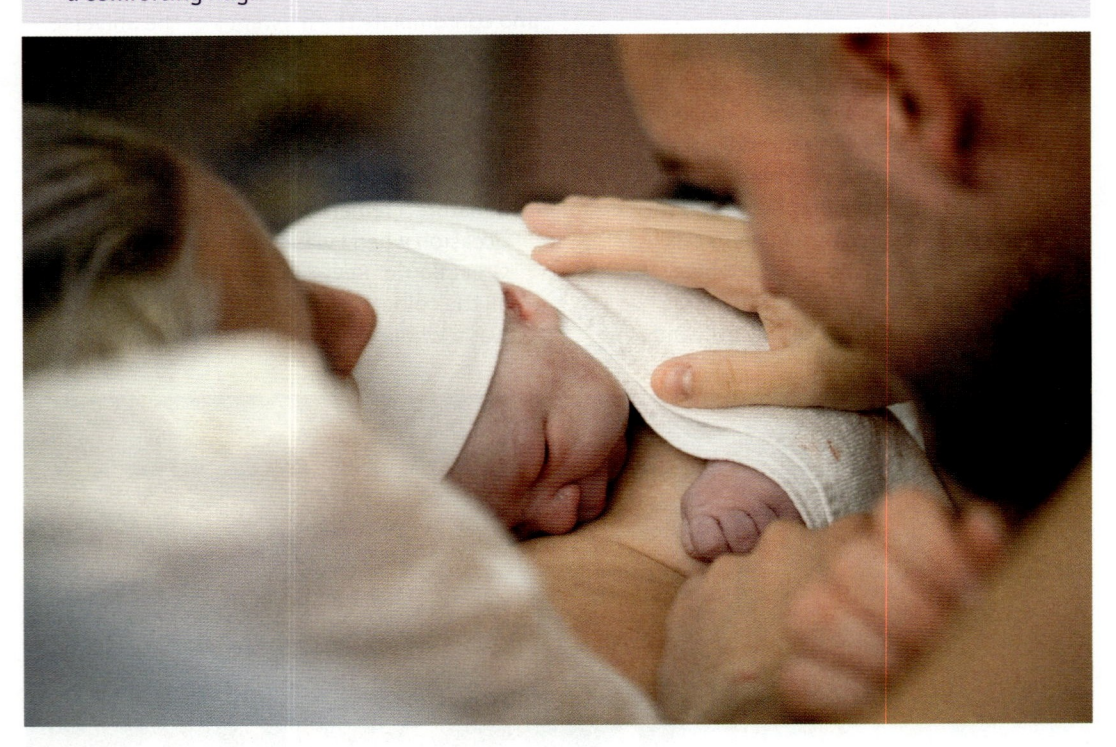

OVER TO YOU
- Which of the four ways of meeting God described above – in a special place, through nature, through other people or at special times in life – appeals to you the most?
- Have you ever experienced God in any of these ways?
- What do you consider to be an ideal location for experiencing the presence of God.

MEETING GOD IN DIFFICULT TIMES

Sometimes we can meet God in difficult times. We may feel broken, confused, even angry. We may have sinned and not be sure how to get back to God. We may be upset over a tragedy and be frustrated with God, finding it hard to see God's plan in the mess we feel our lives have become. The poet Gerard Manley Hopkins was also a priest. In his poem 'Thou Art Indeed Just, Lord', he respectfully questioned God:

> [...] why must
> Disappointment all I endeavour end?
>
> Wert thou my enemy, O thou my friend,
> How wouldst thou worse, I wonder, than
>   thou dost
> Defeat, thwart me?

Yet in the end he figures that God is also the only source of help:

> Mine, O thou lord of life, send my roots rain.

The attitude of Jesus in similar situations shows that in his humanness he can share our difficult times – for example in the Garden of Gethsemane on the night before he died, or on the cross when he cried out, 'My God, my God, why have you forsaken me?' (Mk 15:34).

THINK IT THROUGH
▶ How can a belief in God's presence during the most difficult times in life help people?

JOURNAL
When have you felt closest to God? Are there certain times or places where you feel closer to God. Describe and reflect on these times.

SUMMARY
- It is possible to experience God in ordinary life – for example, in special places, at special times, in nature and in other people.
- Some of our meetings with God can be at difficult times in our lives.

LESSON 60 – MEETING GOD IN ORDINARY LIFE

LESSON 61
MEETING GOD IN THE SACRAMENTS

Objective: This lesson will look at how God can be met in a special way in the sacraments.

OPENING CONVERSATION

Recall one sacrament that your received or attended. What made the ceremony special? Reflect on how the sacrament was celebrated.

Were you aware of this occasion as a special encounter with God?

Meeting God

Sacraments are special meeting points with God, accompanied by a particular ritual or ceremony. We can meet God in a very special way in the sacraments. God, who loves us, wants to be with us at the special and significant times in our lives, as a parent would want to be with their children at their special occasions, like birthdays, graduations, wedding.

IN BAPTISM

God wants to be there for us at the start of our lives, especially as we are brought to church for the first time to become part of the Christian community. You can imagine God's joy at new life, smiling on the occasion with loving approval – as indeed family, friends and community do. In many countries adult baptisms are also common – in this case God is present and active at the beginning of a person's *new* life as a Christian.

IN RECONCILIATION

God knows we sin sometimes and wants to offer us a chance to be forgiven, to know we're forgiven and to move on. Even if we go off the rails in a serious way, God still loves us and is always ready to welcome us back when we are sorry. The story of the Prodigal Son that we looked at in a previous lesson illustrates this. The father rushes out to meet the son, even before the son said he was sorry – he might have shunned his son or made him beg for forgiveness. So, if we sin, God is available for this special healing meeting in the Sacrament of Reconciliation – a meeting that can change our lives for the better from that moment on.

IN THE EUCHARIST

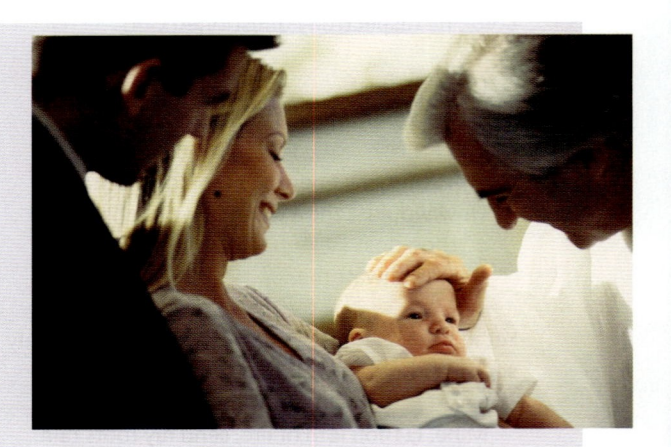

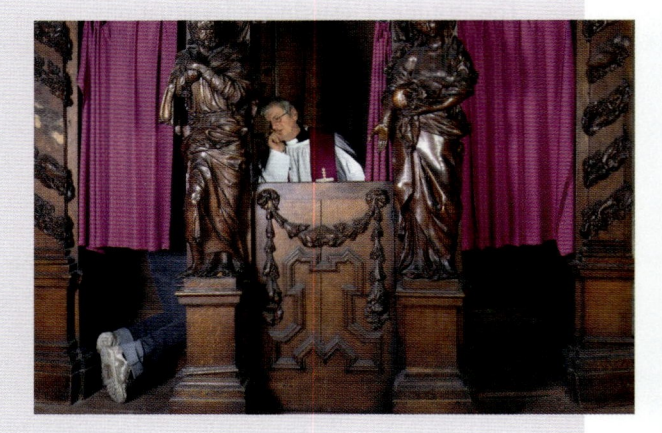

God, who loves us so much, wants to be close to us physically. This is a very special meeting point with God. It is no wonder we refer to it as the 'celebration' of the Eucharist. The word Eucharist comes from the Greek *eukaristos*, and means thanksgiving. It is the Church's great prayer of thanks to God. We can make being at Mass a time to recall all the blessings we have received from God and to give thanks for them. Yet some call it 'boring', as if it were meant to be entertainment. The best way to ensure that we are not bored at Mass is to become involved, for example by reading, singing hymns or being involved in altar serving. Most particularly we can join in the Mass by offering ourselves – our joys, our sorrows, our achievements and our disappointments to God, so that our offering shares in this offering which Jesus made of his Body, his Blood, and his whole self. The Father is always waiting to receive our gifts of ourselves. In this way, we can become more aware of how God meets us in this sacrament. Further, the moment of receiving communion is not the end of it. We go from Mass 'to love and serve the Lord'. As we receive the Body of Christ in Holy Communion we are empowered to *be* the Body of Christ for others in the world.

IN CONFIRMATION

Here we meet God as we become more mature about our faith, more willing to take personal responsibility for it. Naturally God wants to meet us in this special moment when the relationship moves to a new and higher level. Confirmation is one of the three sacraments through which we become members of the Church. The others are Baptism and Eucharist. They are called Sacraments of Initiation. We receive the gifts and fruits of the Holy Spirit, which will inspire, guide and support us through the rest of our lives.

IN MARRIAGE

God is love, and we are made in the image and likeness of God. So is it any wonder that when we come to share love in a special way with another human being in marriage, God wants to be there to share the moment. Marriage is quite a challenge – commitment for life to one other person isn't always encouraged by our culture, so God wants to be there right through the marriage, not just at the wedding, to give us special help, the assistance (also known as 'graces') that will support us throughout married life. The word 'grace' comes from the Latin word *gracia* and means 'free'. Grace is the free and undeserved gift of God's love to us. God's grace is ever at work in our lives helping us to live as children of God and as disciples of Jesus.

IN HOLY ORDERS

If we want to offer ourselves to work as a priest, it is no surprise that God would want to mark that occasion with his presence. This life is also hugely challenging in modern times. Accepting this vocation, with all its joys and frustrations, is a brave step, so it makes sense that God would want to walk with us on this road. That road

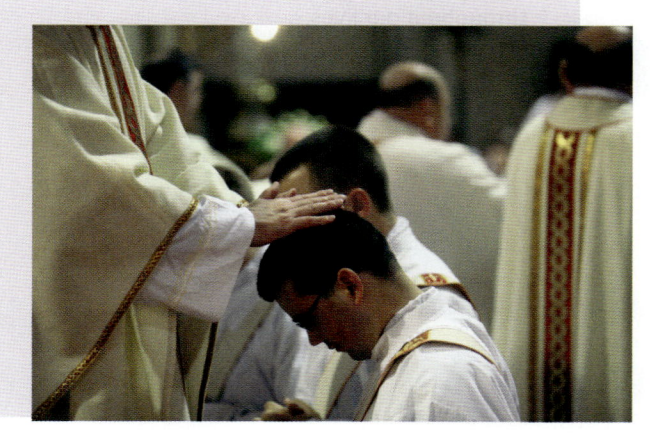

LESSON 61 – MEETING GOD IN THE SACRAMENTS

has its challenges, and God wants to give the newly ordained priest the graces to meet those challenges. Priests are ordained to preach the word, to guide, inspire, encourage the people they serve and to gather and lead the members of Christ's Body in the celebration of the Eucharist. In the Sacrament of Holy Orders, priests receive the graces they need to enable them to fulfil this role in the service of God's people.

IN THE ANOINTING OF THE SICK

When we are sick and weak, God reaches out to us in the Sacrament of Anointing of the Sick, offering us the graces we need to deal with our illness. Jesus healed many people while he was on earth and he told his disciples to continue to 'cure the sick' (Mt 10:8). In the past this sacrament was known as Extreme Unction and people received the sacrament only when they were near death. As the hour of death comes near, the anointing helps to remind us of God's touch and supporting presence at this time. Some of those anointed may receive a physical healing; many receive a calmness to help them in the face of their impending death. During the celebration of the Sacrament of Anointing of the Sick, we receive Holy Communion. In the case of those close to death, Holy Communion is called Viaticum, a Latin word which means 'food for the journey'. However, since Vatican II all those who are seriously ill are encouraged to receive the sacrament. The Rite of Anointing tells us there is no need to wait until a person is at the point of death to receive the sacrament. The sacrament may be repeated if the sick person recovers after the anointing but becomes ill once again, or if, during the same illness, the person's condition becomes more serious. Our experience of the revised Sacrament of the Anointing has brought about a change in the way we think about the sacrament. For example, this sacrament (like all sacraments) can be a community celebration and we acknowledge that sickness involves more than bodily illness. More and more parishes today are scheduling celebrations of the Sacrament of the Anointing of the Sick within the community Eucharist.

OVER TO YOU

▶ Why are the sacraments a special time for people to meet God?

RESEARCH PROJECT

What are the seven gifts of the Holy Spirit? For each one, write a brief note on how it can help us throughout our lives.

SUMMARY

- We can meet God in a special way in the sacraments.
- In the sacraments, God meets us at important moments in our lives.

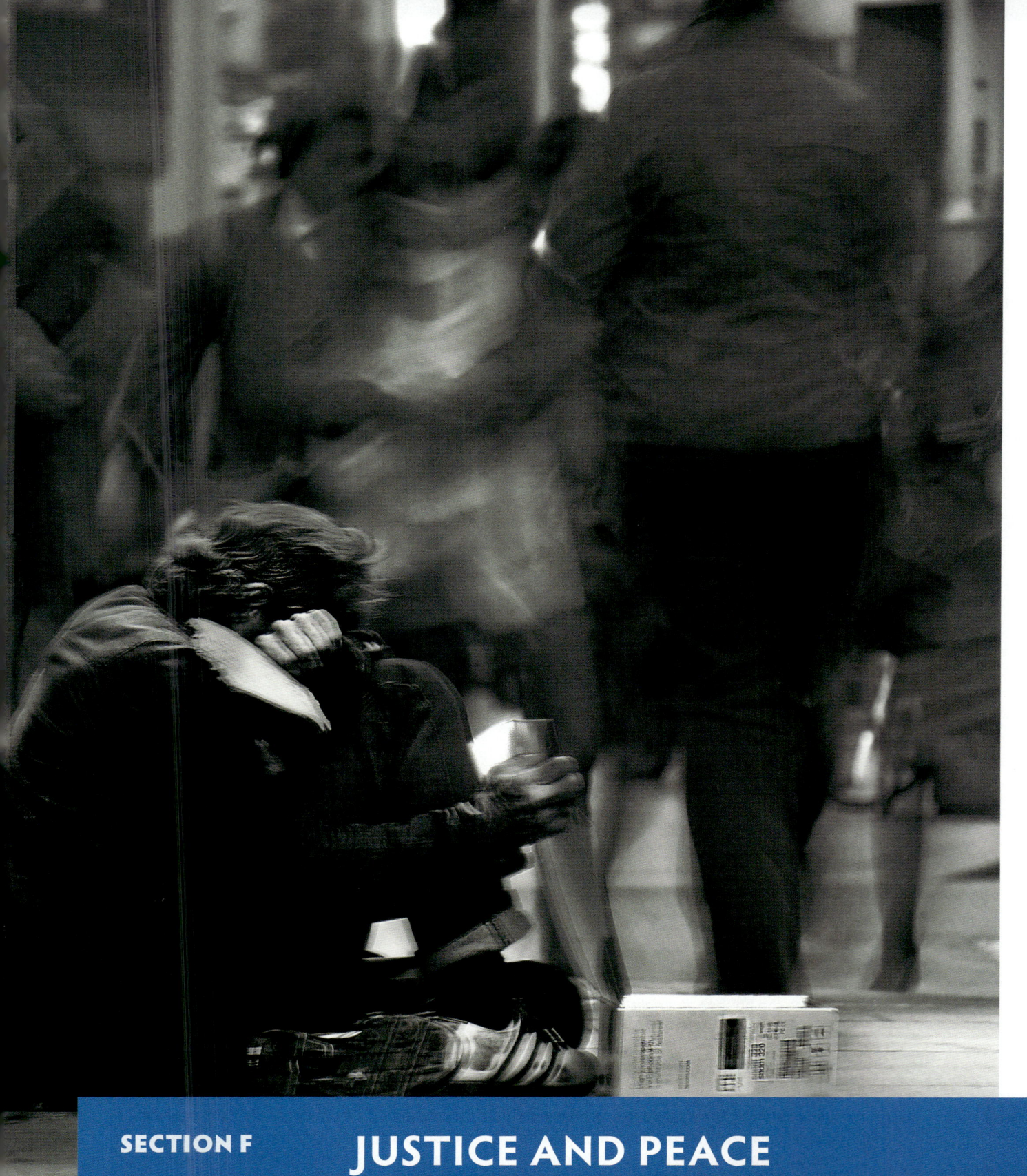

SECTION F — **JUSTICE AND PEACE**

LESSON 62
UNDERSTANDING JUSTICE

Objective: This lesson will explore different understandings of justice.

OPENING CONVERSATION

It is in justice that the ordering of society is centred
— Aristotle (384–322 BCE)

Injustice anywhere is a threat to justice everywhere
— Martin Luther King Jr. (1929–68)

Justice ... consists in the constant and firm will to give their due to God and neighbour
— *Catechism of the Catholic Church*, 1807

Discuss the relevance of each quote to the contemporary world.

Understandings of justice

There are a number of understandings of justice and its influence on society. No one meaning or understanding can comprehensively describe justice but the many and varied descriptions can lead to a broader understanding. The following are some of the common understandings of justice:

» Justice as Holding Right Relationships
» Justice as Fair Play
» Justice as Retribution
» Justice as the Upholding of Human Rights.

Justice can be seen as a *right relationship* between people, between people and the world in which we live, and with God. This understanding encourages us to act with a sense of the interdependence between people, between people and creation and between God and all creation. It demands commitment to the sacredness of all creation. The model for justice in this understanding is the relationship that God has with humanity and with all creation, highlighting the social nature of justice. The weakness of this understanding of justice is that it is idealistic and open to confusion because of different understandings and different standards throughout history of what 'right relationship' actually constitutes. In a world where many are denied the basic necessities of life because of unjust structures, it is clear that there is a need for more than right relationships in order to create a just world for all.

Justice is also seen as *fair play* and acting fairly. This, at first glance, is a simpler, more straightforward understanding of justice. We have experience of fair play in games and in rules at home and at school. In fact, even very young children have the capacity to recognise lack of fairness. The golden rule of doing unto others as you would have them do unto you is the norm. This understanding of justice has its origins in a legalistic view of justice. This idea of justice originated with Aristotle and his belief that those who harm others should in turn face physical punishment.

It is closely linked to an understanding of justice as *retribution* or punishment. This is where society attempts to balance the wrongs committed with punishment for those wrongs. Its purpose is the protection of the community from the convicted criminal. The punishment is therefore seen as a deterrent and the desired outcome is the restoration of moral order.

Justice can also be seen as the upholding of *human rights*. This understanding of justice is based upon an understanding of basic human rights: the right to adequate housing, nourishment, standard of living etc. These rights are due to people simply because they are human beings. The focus is on society and the onus is on society to provide structures which respect each individual's human rights. Justice is denied when fundamental human rights are prohibited or unrecognised. How social structures are put in place and how wealth is distributed are of paramount importance in this understanding of justice. This definition of justice respects the fundamental rights of all and sees the provision of basic needs and self-esteem as crucial. The strength of this model of justice is that it works towards a just society. A weakness of this understanding is that it can be seen to place greater emphasis on a very individualistic and selfish concept of rights, rather than on the individual's responsibility to the development of society. Advocates of this understanding of justice can also often place more emphasis on civil and political rights and less on social and economic rights. This in turn can be seen as protecting the rights of the 'haves', while not devoting similar attention to the rights of the 'have-nots'.

THINK IT THROUGH
- Which understanding of justice do you think has the most influence on Irish society?
- Which understanding of justice appeals to you the most?
- Which understanding of justice appeals to you the least?

JOURNAL
Write about an event in your life in which you experienced injustice. What was the outcome of this injustice? How do you know that what you experienced was an example of injustice?

SUMMARY
- Justice is often understood under the following headings:
  » Holding Right Relationships
  » Fair Play
  » Retribution
  » The Upholding of Human Rights.

LESSON 63
JUSTICE IN THE BIBLE

Objective: This lesson will examine the religious vision of justice.

OPENING ACTIVITY
For each of the following statements, select a number on the scale representing your view, and in pairs discuss your answers.

> *Compassion calls for us to look upon other people as 'another self'.*
> — CCC, 1944

1 = completely disagree; 2 = disagree; 3 = neither disagree nor agree; 4 = agree; 5 = completely agree

The world would be a better place if more people read the Bible.
1 ☐   2 ☐   3 ☐   4 ☐   5 ☐

We cannot provide for everyone in the world; some, unfortunately, have to suffer.
1 ☐   2 ☐   3 ☐   4 ☐   5 ☐

Care of the less well-off should be the responsibility of the State.
1 ☐   2 ☐   3 ☐   4 ☐   5 ☐

Greed is a contributing factor to world hunger.
1 ☐   2 ☐   3 ☐   4 ☐   5 ☐

It is important to show concern for others in our own communities.
1 ☐   2 ☐   3 ☐   4 ☐   5 ☐

The world's major religions teach that their followers should try to make the world a better place for everyone.
1 ☐   2 ☐   3 ☐   4 ☐   5 ☐

Committed to justice from the beginning

Most basically, and going back to Aristotle, justice means giving everyone their due. Almost any person will agree on this much, but God has always demanded a higher standard. Jesus taught us that we must treat others with love and compassion, which are over and above their due. The word compassion comes from a Latin word that means 'suffering together'. Compassion calls for us to look upon other people as 'another self' (CCC, 1944), sharing their joys and lamenting their suffering.

From the beginning, the Catholic Church has been committed to compassion as well as justice and mercy. In fact, its care for the poor and needy was a feature that attracted converts to the first Christian communities. Of course, they were following Jesus' example of radical compassion for all in need which he reflected in his life. Jesus inherited this legacy from the writings of the Old Testament prophets.

JUSTICE IN THE OLD TESTAMENT

In the Old Testament, the prophets tell us that we do not love God unless we also love our fellow human beings, that worship of God is fake unless we respect others, especially those less well-off than us. In Old Testament times, as is the case in the contemporary world, people frequently overlooked and mistreated those whom they considered to be the outcasts of society: the widow, the orphan and the stranger. The prophets would remind God's people repeatedly that they should not draw any such distinction between themselves and others. Isaiah, Jeremiah, Amos and Micah in particular stand out as prophets who spoke courageously against injustices in their society, often at great personal cost. The prophet Isaiah preached: 'Learn to do good; seek justice, rescue the oppressed, defend the orphan, plead for the widow' (1:17). The prophet Jeremiah urged people to:

> Act with justice and righteousness, and deliver from the hand of the oppressor anyone who has been robbed. And do no wrong or violence to the alien, the orphan, and the widow, or shed innocent blood in this place. (22:3)

The prophet Amos saw that prosperity was limited to the wealthy, and that it fed on injustice and oppression of the poor. He denounced the use of cheating, price rigging and short-changing. He said:

> Therefore because you trample on the poor and take from them levies of grain, you have built houses of hewn stone, but you shall not live in them; you have planted pleasant vineyards, but you shall not drink their wine. (5:11)

The devotions of those who cheat will never be pleasing to God unless they 'let justice roll down like waters, and righteousness like an ever-flowing stream' (Am 5:24). Micah summarised what God requires of people by asking, 'What does the Lord require of you but to do justice, and to love kindness, and to walk humbly with your God?' (6:8).

THINK IT THROUGH

▶ How do the messages of the Old Testament prophets speak to our world today?
▶ Who are the vulnerable in our society that we need to defend?
▶ What is one change you could make right now to make the world a better place?

JUSTICE IN THE NEW TESTAMENT

In the New Testament, Jesus introduced himself at the beginning of his public mission by saying:

> The Spirit of the Lord is upon me, because he has anointed me to bring good news to the poor. He has sent me to proclaim release to the captives and recovery of sight to the blind, to let the oppressed go free. (Lk 4:18)

Jesus went further still. He gave us the new commandment, the golden rule of Christianity:

> 'You shall love the Lord your God with all your heart, and with all your soul, and with all your mind.' This is the greatest and first commandment. And a second is like it: 'You shall love your neighbour as yourself.' (Mt 22:37-40)

Sometimes Jesus' view of justice seems very radical. He tells us to love our enemies. He reached out to the outcasts in society and showed compassion to everyone he met. In his parables he described how God's idea of justice might be different to what we would expect. In the parable of the Labourers in the Vineyard we see that God treats us in a way that is different from the world's standards.

THE LABOURERS IN THE VINEYARD

> For the kingdom of heaven is like a landowner who went out early in the morning to hire labourers for his vineyard. After agreeing with the labourers for the usual daily wage, he sent them into his vineyard. When he went out about nine o'clock, he saw others standing idle in the market-place; and he said to them, 'You also go into the vineyard, and I will pay you whatever is right.' So they went. When he went out again about noon and about three o'clock, he did the same. And about five o'clock he went out and found others standing around; and he said to them, 'Why are you standing here idle all day?' They said to him, 'Because no one has hired us.' He said to them, 'You also go into the vineyard.' When evening came, the owner of the vineyard said to his manager, 'Call the labourers and give them their pay, beginning with the last and then going to the first.' When those hired about five o'clock came, each of them received the usual daily wage. Now when the first came, they thought they would receive more; but each of them also received the usual daily wage. And when they received it, they grumbled against the landowner, saying, 'These last worked only one hour, and you have made them equal to us who have borne the burden of the day and the scorching heat.' But he replied to one of them, 'Friend, I am doing you no wrong; did you not agree with me for the usual daily wage? Take what belongs to you and go; I choose to give to this last the same as I give to you. Am I not allowed to do what I choose with what belongs to me? Or are you envious because I am generous? So the last will be the first, and the first will be last.' (Mt 20:1-16)

The landowner represents God whose grace and mercy are shed abundantly. The landowner's decision to pay all the workers the same was an act of mercy, not injustice The workers are not paid strictly according to the hours they work but according to the generosity of God. The owner's decision might seem illogical according to our understanding of justice but it shows that God values everyone equally and is generous to all and that all have equal rights in the kingdom of heaven.

OVER TO YOU
- How would you feel if you were the worker who worked all day and got the same pay as the one who worked less?
- How would you feel if you were the worker who worked less and got the same pay as the worker who worked all day?
- 'So the last will be first, and the first will be last.' What do you think Jesus meant when he said this?

REFLECT AND DISCUSS

Another of the great examples of mercy in action in the Gospel is in the story of the Prodigal Son (Lk 15:11-32). Read or recall the story, and then read as follows what Pope John Paul II says about it in his Apostolic Letter, *Dives in Misericordia*:

> When he decides to return to his father's house, to ask his father to be received – no longer by virtue of his right as a son, but as an employee – at first sight he seems to be acting by reason of the hunger and poverty that he had fallen into; this motive, however, is permeated by an awareness of a deeper loss: to be a hired servant in his own father's house is certainly a great humiliation and source of shame. Nevertheless, the prodigal son is ready to undergo that humiliation and shame. He realises that he no longer has any right except to be an employee in his father's house. His decision is taken in full consciousness of what he has deserved and of what he can still have a right to in accordance with the norms of justice. Precisely this reasoning demonstrates that, at the centre of the prodigal son's consciousness, the sense of lost dignity is emerging, the sense of that dignity that springs from the relationship of the son with the father. And it is with this decision that he sets out. The prodigal son, having wasted the property he received from his father, deserves – after his return – to earn his living by working in his father's house as a hired servant and possibly, little by little, to build up a certain provision of material goods, though perhaps never as much as the amount he had squandered. This would be demanded by the order of justice, especially as the son had not only squandered the part of the inheritance belonging to him but had also hurt and offended his father by his whole conduct … And yet, after all, it was his own son who was involved, and such a relationship could never be altered or destroyed by any sort of behaviour. The prodigal son is aware of this and it is precisely this awareness that shows him clearly the dignity which he has lost and which makes him honestly evaluate the position that he could still expect in his father's house. (*Dives in Misericordia*, 6)

▶ According to Pope John Paul II, how is the son aware of his lost dignity?
▶ The person who receives mercy is not humiliated but, as Pope John Paul II says, is 'restored to value'. How does this parable show this to be true?

Vatican II teaches:

> God destined the earth and all it contains for all people and nations so that all things created would be shared fairly by all humankind under the guidance of justice tempered by charity … Therefore everyone has the right to possess a sufficient amount of the earth's goods for themselves and their family … Persons in extreme need are entitled to take what they need from the riches of others.
> (*Gaudium et Spes*, 69)

OVER TO YOU

▶ If everyone took this teaching seriously, what would change in the world?
▶ How might this affect you personally?

JOURNAL

Reflect on the Scripture quotes in this lesson. Write out the one that you like the most and explain why this quote appeals to you. How can these words influence people to work for justice? What words motivate you to work for a fairer world?

SUMMARY

- From the beginning, the Catholic Church has been committed to compassion as well as justice and mercy.
- In the Old Testament, the prophets tell us that we do not love God unless we also love our fellow human beings.
- In the New Testament, Jesus' parables teach us that God values everyone equally and is generous to all.
- Jesus' view of justice may seem very radical but we are called to do the same.

LESSON 64
DO WE LIVE IN A JUST SOCIETY?

Objective: This lesson will analyse the society in which we live.

OPENING ACTIVITY
Conduct a class vote asking the question: Do we live in a just society? Yes or no?

Analysing our society

Justice is the act of being just and/or fair. The struggle for justice is at the heart of Christianity. The Church asks us to follow the teachings of Jesus Christ and to act justly towards our neighbour. However, the struggle for justice is not exclusive to Christianity. It is shared by all who work continually to bring about a world that is in line with the demands of the great commandment, 'Love one another as I have loved you'.

Social analysis is a useful device in religious and secular teaching. Communities of faith use social analysis in addressing contemporary justice issues. Ireland is a very different place today to the one that existed a few years ago. The economic boom and the subsequent bust have left a deep impact upon our society. Irish people today are well-educated and well-travelled compared to previous generations. However, many Irish people are now forced to emigrate to find work, repeating experiences of the past. Irish people are renowned all over the world for our generosity of spirit. Yet Ireland has a serious problem with homelessness. Poverty is also on the increase, with the phrase 'the working poor' having recently been coined. Families are struggling to stay above the poverty threshold, with many mortgages in negative equity and the threat of repossession looming large for some.

Similar conditions exist in many countries in Europe where the recent economic boom has also ended, resulting in widespread poverty. Many people from Eastern European countries travelled here during the late 1990s and early part of the century to escape poverty in their own countries, but now find themselves struggling to survive here.

It is only when we take time to reflect and really study the society in which we live that we can assess whether we live in a just world or not. People in a just society find themselves asking the following questions:

- Who has power in our society?
- Is everyone treated equally?
- Are men and women treated equally?
- Is everyone included in our society?
- Does the colour of skin matter in our society?

A number of factors or structures determine whether a society is considered just or not. Society can be analysed under any of the following four headings: economic, political, social and cultural.

ECONOMIC STRUCTURES

When analysing the society one lives in, in terms of whether it is just or not, one must first observe the workings of its economy. How do the business and commercial institutions distribute resources and wealth? Are the industrial and agricultural sectors working to spread the wealth fairly? Does the society depend on multinational companies, and if so, do these companies treat their workers fairly?

POLITICAL STRUCTURES

When analysing a society it is also essential to study the workings of power. One can analyse any society, whether it is through a commercial company, a club or a church, by observing how the power structures on which it is built function. Who has power and are they using their power in a just manner? Do political parties work to ensure that all members of their society have an equal say? Does the legal system of the society work justly? Is the police force working without bias? Do the trade unions serve the interests of their members?

SOCIAL STRUCTURES

Social analysis also requires a study of the various relationships that function within any society in order to determine whether that same society is just or not. Are various class groupings evident in the society? Does the society segregate races? Does the society ensure that both sexes, male and female, are treated equally? How a society takes care of its younger and older members can be an indicator of whether it is just or not. Does the society give their older members the respect they deserve? Do children have a voice in the society? Does the society discriminate against people because of their sexual orientation? Does the society discriminate against people because of their religious belief, or is it a pluralistic culture allowing people of all faiths and none to coexist peacefully? Are resources such as healthcare, education, etc. equally spread countrywide or localised in certain areas?

CULTURAL STRUCTURES

A just society is one in which the expression of various cultural customs and practices is promoted. Free speech is vital to any just society once it does not impede upon the freedom of others. Does the society allow free speech? Does the society contain members of various ethnicities? Are cultural traditions valued in the society and, if so, in what way? A society can be assessed according to the manner in which it allows its members to own and express their own values and beliefs. While various cultural practices might be promoted within the society, are they all promoted equally?

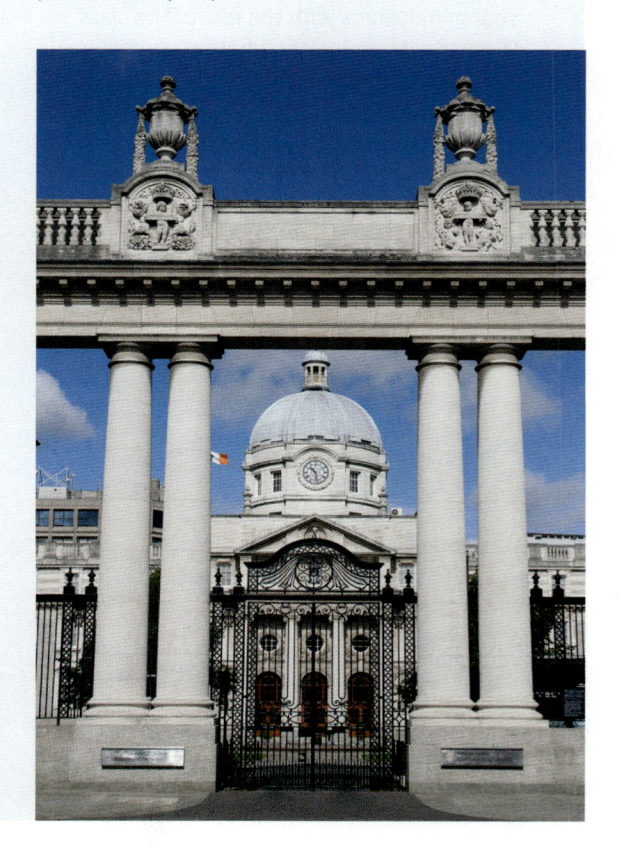

abuse homelessness help rights world poverty generosity safety share economical rituals good dignity choice judge poor humanity wrong respect belief education political social bad conduct money behaviour support cultural respect justice power freedom decency

GROUP WORK
Divide into four groups, each one taking one of the four categories – economic, political, social and cultural. As a group, discuss and try to answer the questions asked in your category. Does everybody agree on the answers? Share your conclusions with the rest of the class. Discuss with your class whether you believe we live in a just society.

THINK IT THROUGH
- What is a just society?
- Describe what such a society would be like.
- What behaviour would not be tolerated?
- What can be done to address issues of injustice in our society?

SUMMARY
- The struggle for justice is at the heart of Christianity.
- People of all religions and none share in the work for justice.
- Society can be analysed under any of the following four headings: economic, political, social and cultural structures.

LESSON 65
JUSTICE BEGINS AT HOME

Objective: This lesson will look at the issue of homelessness in Ireland today and the work of those following the example of Jesus to address this issue.

OPENING CONVERSATION
In one sentence, say what in your opinion makes a home.

'Home is _____,'

What would you miss most if you were put out of your home? What do you know about homelessness in Ireland? What is your image of a homeless person?

Why does homelessness occur?

There are a number of underlying causes of homelessness. Particularly, in the current economic circumstances, some people find themselves homeless because of an inability to pay the rent or mortgage. But for many the reasons are much more complex. Focus Ireland, an organisation that works to reduce homelessness, has identified some of the more common reasons. They include:

- A young person leaving the parental home after continuous arguments
- Marital breakdown
- The death of a spouse
- Leaving prison without somewhere to live
- A deterioration of a mental health problem
- Drug or alcohol addiction
- Financial crisis, caused by circumstances such as job loss
- Eviction

It is obvious from this list that prevention of homelessness is about much more than providing housing and shelter. It also requires resources for healthcare, education, training and support to help people who are out of home to reintegrate back into society as well as to prevent others from becoming homeless.

In a world where there is so much wealth, so many resources to feed everyone, it's incomprehensible how there can be so many hungry children, so many children without an education, so many poor.

– Pope Francis

LESSON 65 – JUSTICE BEGINS AT HOME

231

WORKING WITH THE HOMELESS

There are a number of individuals and groups in Ireland who do a lot of work to counter homelessness and its causes. One of them is Fr Peter McVerry. As a young Jesuit priest, Peter McVerry began a journey that would take him into the heart of disadvantaged communities. He has stated that this journey has helped him to find a deeper connection to the life, death and Resurrection of Jesus. His work with those who have been excluded by our society has shown him the true meaning of being Christian.

In 1979 he set up a hostel for homeless boys. Four years later he established the Arrupe Society, now known as the Peter McVerry Trust, which is committed to reducing homelessness, drug misuse and social disadvantage through its provision of housing and support services. Father McVerry reminds us that in post-Celtic Tiger Ireland, one in nine children live in consistent poverty without proper food or clothing. There are more homeless people, more on social housing waiting lists and longer queues for vital services for vulnerable people, especially children with special needs. In all this, he believes that our Christian faith needs to inform and challenge our attitudes and actions. His call is for each of us to hear the Gospel message, which requests that we live in solidarity with those on the margins.

The Irish Government made a pledge in 2013 to end long-term homelessness by 2016. While organisations that work with the homeless welcomed this, they also pointed out that similar targets were set before and were never reached. Unfortunately, only too frequently we see people, male and female, young and old, in need of the basics in life. Whatever our current economic difficulties, we as a people must not abandon that pledge to those in grave need. As a society, we have a duty to fulfil our pledge.

JESUS: SOCIAL REVOLUTIONARY?

Jesus saw people around him who had been rejected by the rest of society – the sick, the poor and the sinners. Jesus reached out to these people; he shared meals with them. At the time of Jesus, eating with someone was a sign of respect: sharing a meal was more than just about food, it was a form of social inclusion, while refusing to share a meal was a form of social exclusion.

In his book, *Jesus: Social Revolutionary?* Fr McVerry opens a debate about the meaning of our faith and the obligations that belonging to the Christian community imposes on us. Father McVerry believes that Jesus gave us a clear example of how we should relate to those who are marginalised in our society by treating them in a respectful and dignified way. It is this message of solidarity and compassion for the most vulnerable in our society that is the central message of the Gospels.

> We are sometimes told that religion and politics should be kept apart, but that was not Jesus' way. His caring and insistence on the dignity of every person as a child of God had political implications for the ordering of his own society – and still has today for the ordering of our own society. It also had personal implications for himself and his life, turning many of his contemporaries against him and mobilising the authorities to get rid of him. So, too, our caring may demand political changes in our own society and may also have personal implications for our own lives.
> (From *Jesus: Social Revolutionary?* by Fr Peter McVerry)

Father Peter McVerry

THINK IT THROUGH
- How does Fr Peter McVerry express the Christian message of a just and inclusive society?
- What can you do to raise awareness of the homeless in your community?
- Suggest ways in which the issue could be challenged and addressed today.
- How can the problem of homelessness be prevented?

OVER TO YOU
- Read the following Scripture passages and answer the questions that follow:
  Matthew 11:18-19; Mark 1:21-34; 2:13-17; Luke 7:36-50; 13:10-16; 19:1-10.
  - Who were the outcasts at the time of Jesus?
  - How did Jesus relate to these people?
  - How did Jesus challenge the authorities of his time?

SUMMARY
- There are a number of underlying causes of homelessness.
- Prevention of homelessness is about much more than providing housing and shelter.
- Father Peter McVerry has campaigned tirelessly for the rights of homeless people in Ireland.
- Jesus gave us a clear example of how we should relate to those who are marginalised in our society by treating them in a respectful and dignified way.

LESSON 66
CATHOLIC SOCIAL TEACHING

Objective: This lesson will identify some of the main beliefs and principles found in Catholic Social Teaching.

OPENING CONVERSATION
Where does your understanding of justice come from? Do Scripture, Church teaching, reason and experience play a role in your understanding of these justice issues? Explain your answer.

What is Catholic Social Teaching?

Catholic Social Teaching sums up the teachings of the Church on issues of justice. It seeks to bring the Gospel message to bear on the social justice issues that arise in the society in which we live. Catholic Social Teaching provides principles for reflection and guidelines for our actions and behaviours. These guidelines are most often expressed in encyclicals or 'circulating letters'. Catholic Social Teaching offers guidelines on the promotion of social justice and gives direction about making choices in relation to key justice issues. There are seven key themes that are covered in Catholic Social Teaching:

LIFE AND DIGNITY OF THE HUMAN PERSON

The Catholic Church proclaims that human life is sacred and that the dignity of the human person is the foundation of a moral vision for society. Our belief in the sanctity of human life from the moment of conception to natural death and the inherent dignity of the human person is the foundation of all the principles of our social teaching. The Church teaches that every person is precious, that people are more important than things, and that the measure of society is whether it threatens or enhances the life and dignity of the human person.

CALL TO FAMILY, COMMUNITY AND PARTICIPATION

The person is not only sacred but social. How we organise our society in economics and politics, in law and policy directly affects human dignity and the capacity of individuals to grow in community. The family is the central social institution and must be supported and strengthened, not undermined. We believe people have a right and a duty to participate in society, seeking together the common good and wellbeing of all, especially those who are poor and vulnerable.

RIGHTS AND RESPONSIBILITIES

The Catholic Tradition teaches that human dignity can be protected and a healthy community can be achieved only if human rights are protected and responsibilities are met. Therefore, every person has a fundamental right to life and a right to those things required for human decency.

Corresponding to these rights are duties and responsibilities to one another, to our families and to the larger society.

OPTION FOR THE POOR AND VULNERABLE

A basic moral test is to look at how the most vulnerable members of a society are faring. In a society marred by deepening divisions between rich and poor, Catholic Social Teaching instructs us to put the needs of those who are poor and vulnerable first.

THE DIGNITY OF WORK AND THE RIGHTS OF WORKERS

The economy must serve people, not the other way around. Work is more than a way to make a living; it is a form of continuing participation in God's creation. If the dignity of work is to be protected, then the basic rights of workers must be respected: the right to productive work, to decent and fair wages, to organisation and membership of unions, to private property, and to economic initiative.

SOLIDARITY

We are our brothers' and sisters' keepers, wherever they live. We are one human family, whatever our national, racial, ethnic, economic and ideological differences. Learning to practice the virtue of solidarity means learning that 'loving our neighbour' has global dimensions in an interdependent world.

CARE FOR GOD'S CREATION

We show our respect for the Creator by our stewardship of creation. Care for the earth is a requirement of our faith. We are called to protect people and the planet, living our faith in relationship with all of God's creation. This environmental challenge has fundamental moral and ethical dimensions that cannot be ignored.

OVER TO YOU

▶ Read each of the following extracts from Church teaching and match them to the key principles of Catholic Social Teaching. (Some may correspond to the same theme, some may correspond to more than one theme.)

	CHURCH TEACHING	KEY PRINCIPLE
1	'… there is a growing awareness of the sublime dignity of human persons, who stand above all things and whose rights and duties are universal and inviolable. They ought, therefore, to have ready access to all that is necessary for living a genuinely human life: for example, food, clothing, housing, the right freely to choose their state of life and set up a family, the right to education, work, to their good name, to respect, to proper knowledge, the right to act according to the dictates of conscience and to safeguard their privacy, and rightful freedom, including freedom of religion.' *Gaudium et Spes*, Second Vatican Council, 1965, 26	
2	'Profound and rapid changes make it more necessary that no one ignoring the trend of events or drugged by laziness, content himself with a merely individualistic morality. It grows increasingly true that the obligations of justice and love are fulfilled only if each person, contributing to the common good, according to his own abilities and the needs of others, also promotes and assists the public and private institutions dedicated to bettering the conditions of human life.' *Gaudium et Spes*, 30	
3	'The dignity of the human person involves the right to take an active part in public affairs and to contribute one's part to the common good of the citizens.' *Pacem in Terris*, John XXIII, 1963, 26	
4	'Therefore political leaders, and citizens of rich countries considered as individuals, especially if they are Christians, have the moral obligation, according to the degree of each one's responsibility, to take into consideration, in personal decisions and decisions of government, this relationship of universality, this interdependence which exists between their conduct and the poverty and underdevelopment of so many millions of people.' *Sollicitudo Rei Socialis*, Pope John Paul II, 1987, 9	
5	'Solidarity helps us to see the "other" – whether a person, people, or nation – not just as some kind of instrument, with a work capacity and physical strength to be exploited at low cost and then discarded when no longer useful, but as our neighbour, a helper (cf. Gn 2:18-20), to be a sharer, on a par with ourselves, in the banquet of life to which all are equally invited by God.' *Sollicitudo Rei Socialis*, 39	
6	'The risk for our time is that the *de facto* interdependence of people and nations is not matched by ethical interactions of consciences and minds that would give rise to truly human development.' *Caritas in Veritate*, Benedict XVI, 2009, 9	
7	'God destined the earth and all it contains for all people and nations so that all created things would be shared fairly by all humankind under the guidance of justice tempered by charity. No matter how property is structured in different countries, adapted to their lawful institutions according to various and changing circumstances, we must never lose sight of this universal destination of earthly goods.' *Gaudium et Spes*, 69	

Grand procession of the Council Fathers at St Peter's Basilica, Rome, during Vatican II

GROUP WORK

Working in groups, choose one of the seven key themes outlined in this chapter. Identify examples from our world today that show this theme in action. Identify situations from the world today where this theme should be applied. Search through newspapers and magazines for photographs and/or headlines which you could use to present the responses from your group to the class. Present to the rest of the class one aspect of Catholic Social Teaching that addresses the issue you have identified.

SUMMARY

- Catholic Social Teaching offers guidelines on the promotion of social justice.
- The key themes of Catholic Social Teaching are:
  » Life and Dignity of the Human Person
  » Call to Family, Community and Participation
  » Rights and Responsibilities
  » Option for the Poor and Vulnerable
  » The Dignity of Work and the Rights of Workers
  » Solidarity
  » Care for God's Creation.

> ❛ *God destined the earth and all it contains for all people and nations ...*
>
> Gaudium et Spes, 69

LESSON 66 – CATHOLIC SOCIAL TEACHING

LESSON 67
WAR AND PEACE

Objective: This lesson will outline the Just War theory and examine the conditions for a just war.

OPENING ACTIVITY
Write the word 'War' in the centre of a blank piece of paper. What thoughts come to mind when you think about war? Write these thoughts around the word 'War'. Discuss what you have written with the person sitting beside you. Then share your ideas with the class.

What does the Bible say about war?

Warfare was part of life in the Old Testament. At times God commanded Israel to go to war. However, there is also a profound respect for God's creation evident in the Old Testament. The Book of Genesis teaches us to respect the value of every human life, as God created people in his image and likeness. The fifth commandment, which prohibits killing, is also found in the Old Testament.

In the New Testament, Jesus is loud in his condemnation of killing and violence. In the Sermon on the Mount he tells the crowds:

> You have heard that it was said 'An eye for an eye and a tooth for a tooth.' But I say to you, Do not resist an evildoer. But if anyone strikes you on the right cheek, turn the other also; and if anyone wants to sue you and take your coat, give your cloak as well.

Jesus also told his followers:

> You have heard that it was said, 'you shall love your neighbour and hate your enemy.' But I say to you, Love your enemies and pray for those who persecute you. (Mt 5:43-44)

CAN WAR EVER BE JUSTIFIED?
For Christians, this issue is set against the backdrop of a profound respect for the value of human life. However, it is recognised that war can sometimes be an unavoidable reality in our world. Therefore we need to establish why and under what circumstances war might be considered tolerable.

THE JUST WAR THEORY
The Just War theory attempts to address this very question. Although it was originally developed by Christian theologians, it can be used by people of every faith and none. Both Augustine of Hippo and Thomas Aquinas were key figures in shaping the Just War tradition. Augustine saw war as both a result of sin and as a tragic remedy for sin in the life of political societies. The theory is not intended to justify wars but to prevent them. By emphasising that going to war, except in certain very limited circumstances, is wrong, it motivates countries to find other ways of resolving conflicts. It only applies to countries, and not to individuals (although an individual can use the theory to help them decide whether it is morally right to take part in a particular war).

Church teaching on the Just War theory provides a number of criteria, all of which must be present before a government can declare war.

ELEMENTS OF THE JUST WAR THEORY

There are two parts to the Just War theory, both with Latin names:

» *Jus ad bellum* ('right to war'):
The conditions under which the use of military force is justified.

» *Jus in bello* ('justice/laws of war'):
How to conduct a war in an ethical manner.

A war is only a Just War if it is both justified and carried out in the right way. Some wars fought for noble causes have been rendered unjust because of the way in which they were fought.

There are six criteria under *jus ad bellum*, all of which have to be satisfied:

Just Cause: There must be a proper reason for going to war, such as protecting the innocent, restoring rights wrongfully denied or re-establishing order. Revenge or upholding a ruler's prestige is never just reason for going to war. If lives of innocent citizens are threatened, if basic human rights are being violated, if there is a real need for self-defence, then there would be just cause.

Proportionate Cause: Besides being just, the reasons for going to war must be weighty enough to warrant the massive step of engaging in war, with all of its certain and possible evils. The damage to be expected must be weighed against the good that is expected.

Right Intention: A war must be waged for the right intentions and a process for reconciliation must be implemented post-war. Needless destruction or cruelty to prisoners cannot be tolerated. The aim must be to create a better, more just society and a more lasting subsequent peace than there would have been had war not been embarked upon. The achievement of peace and justice must be the only reason for the use of arms.

Right Authority: The right to declare war belongs to those who have legitimate authority and responsibility for the common good. Even just causes cannot be served by actions taken by individuals or groups who do not constitute an authority sanctioned by whatever the society and independent observers deem legitimate.

Reasonable Prospect of Success: A war can only be just if it is fought with a reasonable chance of success. Deaths and injury incurred in a hopeless cause are not morally justifiable.

Last Resort: A just war can only be waged as a last resort. All non-violent options must be exhausted before the use of force can be justified.

Anti-war protest in Dublin, September 2004

LESSON 67 – WAR AND PEACE

World War II ruins, Hiroshima, Japan

There are two criteria under *jus in bello*, both of which have to be satisfied:

Discrimination: The weapons used in war must discriminate between soldiers and civilians. Civilians are never permissible targets of war and every effort must be taken to avoid killing civilians. The deaths of civilians are justified only if they are unavoidable victims of an attack directed at a military target.

Proportionality: The violence used in the war must be proportional to the injury suffered. Countries are prohibited from using unnecessary force to attain the limited objective of addressing the injury suffered. The lives of military personnel on both sides need to be taken into account.

The phrase 'Just War', though traditionally used, might be misunderstood as suggesting that a war might be good and just in itself. It is virtually impossible to envisage a case where war could be just on both sides. Many, maybe most, wars are unjust on both sides. Some wars can appear to meet all of these conditions.

For example, World War II (1939–1945) would appear to have been a Just War:

- It was fought by countries who were legal authorities
- Nazi Germany was being attacked for invading other countries
- The intention was to stop the evil that Hitler and Nazi Germany were responsible for
- The Allies felt that they had a reasonable chance of success
- Negotiation was tried first but had failed so this was a last resort
- Most of the fighting was limited to the armies concerned.

This looks as though it was a 'properly constituted' Just War, but some actions during the war, for example the Allied bombing of Dresden, a two-day raid by over 1,000 bombers that destroyed the city and killed approximately 25,000 civilians for virtually no military purpose, broke the conditions.

Building in the centre of Dresden, Germany, destroyed during World War II

Pacifism

There are several different sorts of pacifism, but they all include the idea that war and violence are unjustifiable, and that conflicts should be settled in a peaceful way. Some people are pacifists because of their religious faith; others regardless of their religion are opposed to war and violence because of their belief in the sanctity of life or because of the practical belief that war is wasteful and ineffective. Many believe that pacifism is more than opposition to war. They argue that it must include action to promote justice and human rights. Some Christians are pacifists and are totally opposed to violence and refuse to fight in war, even if it meets the criteria of the Just War theory. They take a public stance against conflict as conscientious objectors.

Mohandas 'Mahatma' Gandhi

REFLECT AND DISCUSS

> War may sometimes be a necessary evil. But no matter how necessary, it is always an evil, never a good. We will not learn how to live together in peace by killing each other's children.
> — Jimmy Carter, 39th president of the United States

> What difference does it make to the dead, the orphans and the homeless, whether the mad destruction is wrought under the name of totalitarianism or the holy name of liberty or democracy?
> — Mahatma Gandhi, civil rights activist

Reflect on the above quotes and write your own quote about war.

THINK IT THROUGH

- How is war portrayed in the media?
- How is war portrayed in the arts – for example, poems, novels, songs, TV shows or films?

Comparative Religious Studies
Research the teaching about war and peace in one other major world religion.

YOU WILL FIND ADDITIONAL INFORMATION ON WWW.SEEKANDFIND.IE

SUMMARY

- The aim of the Just War theory is to provide a guide to the right way for countries to act in potential conflict situations.
- There are two parts to the Just War theory:
  - *Jus ad bellum*
  - *Jus in bello*
- The following criteria apply in the Just War theory:
  - Just Cause
  - Proportionate Cause
  - Right Intention
  - Right Authority
  - Reasonable Prospect of Success
  - Last Resort
  - Discrimination
  - Proportionality.

LESSON 68
CAPITAL PUNISHMENT

Objective: This lesson will identify arguments for and against capital punishment and examine the Catholic Church teaching on this issue.

OPENING ACTIVITY

Consider the statement 'Killing is always wrong'. Stand at the top of the room if you agree, stand at the bottom of the room if you disagree and stand in the middle if you are undecided. In turn, share the reason for your position and, working one on one, try to convince others to join you. Change location only if you really change your mind.

The Catholic Church and capital punishment

Catholic teaching on crime and punishment begins with the recognition that the dignity of the human person applies to both victims and offenders. Catholic teaching is rooted in the belief that all life is a gift from God that must be respected and defended from conception to natural death. It affirms our commitment to comfort and support victims and their families, while acknowledging the God-given dignity of every human life, even those who do great harm. Trying to follow the example of Jesus, the Church has always favoured mercy and forgiveness for sinners and criminals. Yet for a long time it also made exceptions, allowing capital punishment for certain crimes. It even pursued and promoted the death penalty for people considered heretics to its faith. The Church's teaching, however, has evolved to a current position which essentially opposes the death penalty. Some of this development is because circumstances change from era to era. For example, a traditional reason for the death penalty for convicted murderers was to protect society from them committing murder again. But this can be achieved now by sentencing them to life in prison. The Church agrees that every state has in principle the right to punish crime but teaches that punishment, as far as possible, should contribute to the rehabilitation of the offender. Clearly the death penalty does not meet that criterion.

Protesters at an Anti-Death Penalty rally

SECTION F: JUSTICE AND PEACE

DEAD MAN WALKING

In the highly acclaimed film *Dead Man Walking*, Susan Sarandon plays Sr Helen Prejean, a nun whose experiences of ministering to men facing execution, and later to the families of murder victims, are based on a true story. The movie allows audiences to see the reality of murder and punishment from the viewpoints of death row inmates, their families, the families of the victims, and prison officials. Here is an extract:

Prison guard: Tell me something sister, what's a nun doing in a place like this? Shouldn't you be teaching children? Didn't you know what this man has done? How he killed them kids?

Sister Helen: What he was involved with was evil. I don't condone it. I just don't see the sense of killing people to say that killing people's wrong.

Prison guard: You know what the Bible says, 'An eye for an eye'.

The prison guard is right. The Bible does say 'an eye for eye', but Jesus elaborated on this, saying, 'You have heard that it was said, "An eye for an eye and a tooth for a tooth." But I say to you, Do not resist an evildoer. But if anyone strikes you on the right cheek, turn the other also' (Mt 5:38-39).

We are called to always to try to follow the radical demands of the preaching of Jesus. Everything we find in the Bible must be interpreted through Jesus' teaching.

Later in the film, the father of one of the victims becomes angry when he sees Sr Helen with the man who murdered his child:

Clyde Percy: How can you stand next to him?

Sister Helen: Mr Percy, I'm just trying to follow the example of Jesus, who said that a person is not as bad as his worst deed.

THINK IT THROUGH
- Do you agree that Sr Helen is following the example of Jesus? Why or why not?
- Do you agree that a person is not as bad as their worst deed? Explain your answer.

LESSON 68 — CAPITAL PUNISHMENT

ARGUMENTS FOR AND AGAINST CAPITAL PUNISHMENT

Arguments for

- People committing the most heinous crimes have forfeited the right to life.
- The death penalty shows the greatest respect for the victim.
- It makes the world a safer place, as among prisoners and ex-prisoners there are many who relapse into crime.
- It provides peace of mind for the families of victims of crime.
- It says in the Bible 'an eye for an eye'.
- It recognises humankind's natural sense of justice.
- It is less cruel than prolonged sentences of imprisonment.
- It shows how seriously society looks upon the most heinous crimes.
- It enjoys the democratic support of citizens in some US states and other countries where it is legal.
- It may deter violent crime and murder.

Arguments against

- The death penalty is murder. Christian moral values instruct that while accidental killing, killing in self-defence and killing in a Just War are not wrong, all deliberate, direct killing is wrong, therefore the death penalty is wrong.
- The death penalty is a human rights violation.
- Torture and cruelty are immoral. Some executions have been botched, with the executed suffering extended pain. Even those who die instantly suffer mental anguish leading up to the execution.
- Criminal proceedings are fallible, i.e. not always correct. There have been cases where people facing the death penalty have been exonerated. Someone falsely convicted to life in jail can be released if his or her innocence is proven. Nothing can be done for someone who has been executed and is later found to be innocent.
- People from disadvantaged backgrounds with no money for hiring the best defence are more likely to end up on death row.
- Racial bias has always been a significant issue in death penalty debates. For example, in the US there have been many careful statistical studies indicating that prosecutors are more likely to seek the death penalty when the victim is white and less likely when the victim is black.
- It can encourage police misconduct, as in the incident described in the documentary film *The Thin Blue Line*. In the late 1970s, an innocent man named Randall Adams was framed by the Dallas County police department in Texas for a notorious murder of a police officer because they knew the more likely suspect, David Harris, who had accused Adams of being the murderer, was still a minor and thus ineligible for the death penalty, so Adams was 'chosen' in his place to be executed.
- Some people argue that the death penalty brutalises society, by sending out the message that killing people is the right thing to do in some circumstances.
- It is argued that it is not a deterrent, because anyone who would be deterred by the death penalty would have already been deterred by life in prison.
- It is more expensive than sentencing the convicted criminal to life in jail. In the USA, with mandatory appeals and other procedural requirements for capital punishment cases, the cost of a death penalty case far exceeds the cost of a trial and life imprisonment.

(From www.deathpenaltyinfo.org/)

OVER TO YOU

- Which of the arguments for or against the death penalty are the most convincing?
- Are there any arguments that you think are weak or unconvincing?
- Are there any other arguments you would add to the lists?

REFLECT AND DISCUSS

Read the following account about Troy Davis and answer the questions that follow.

An innocent man sentenced to death?

The high profile case of Troy Davis, convicted in 1991 of killing an off-duty police officer, Mark MacPhail, came to an end when he was executed on Wednesday, 21 September 2011, despite an international outcry over executing a man amid such overwhelming doubt. Eyewitness testimony was primarily the deciding factor in convicting him, but that evidence was called into question over the years after seven of nine key witnesses recanted their statements. Davis had eleven court hearings after the guilty verdict. Attorneys representing Davis maintain that the case surrounding his death sentence was full of holes. Despite public scepticism, then prosecutor Spencer Lawton has stood behind his case. So have the MacPhails. Mark MacPhail Jr. told reporters that he's certain Davis is 'the man who killed my father'. He was only two months old when his father died.

Church leaders called for clemency. Pope Benedict XVI was among the nearly one million supporters rallying to get Davis off death row. A group of US Catholic bishops wrote a letter to the state board which said, 'The Gospel that Christians proclaim is a gospel of mercy, love and forgiveness .. We believe that the death penalty is not compatible with the Gospel ... The common good and public security can be achieved in other ways ... The Gospel calls us to proclaim the sacredness of human life under all circumstances.' Davis, forty-two, was described by family pastor Rev. Raphael Warnock as a 'man of deep faith' who considered his decades-long fight a 'spiritual journey'.

For twenty years, Troy Davis maintained that he was innocent. 'The incident that night was not my fault. I did not have a gun,' Davis said in the death chamber. He urged his family to keep praying and 'Look deeper in this case so that you can really find the truth. [To the MacPhails] I did not personally kill your son, father and brother. I am innocent.' He then turned to those about to take his life saying, 'May God have mercy on your souls.'

▶ Why do people believe Troy Davis was innocent?
▶ Why do you think he was still executed in spite of this?
▶ What argument did the US bishops make on his behalf?

San Quentin State Prison, which houses California's death row inmates

RESEARCH PROJECT

Find current statistics about the death penalty in the US:

- How many states have the death penalty? Which states do not?
- Who was the last person executed in the US?
- How many inmates are currently on death row?
- What are the profiles of inmates (age, race, economic background, etc.)?
- What is the cost of the death penalty compared to keeping inmates in prison?

Find out about organisations working to end the death penalty.

YOU WILL FIND ADDITIONAL INFORMATION ON WWW.SEEKANDFIND.IE

JOURNAL

We have only one incident in the Gospels where Jesus was faced with a decision about the death penalty. Read John 8:1-11 and write your response to Jesus' actions.

SUMMARY

- Catholic teaching on crime and punishment begins with the recognition that the dignity of the human person applies to both victims and offenders.
- A traditional reason for the death penalty for convicted murderers was to protect society from them committing murder again. But this can be achieved now by sentencing them to life in prison.
- Punishment, as far as possible, should contribute to the rehabilitation of the offender. Clearly the death penalty does not meet that criterion.

LESSON 69
STEWARDSHIP: JUSTICE FOR THE PLANET

Objective: This lesson will explore the concept of stewardship and caring for the earth and explain how this is linked to religious faith.

OPENING CONVERSATION
How aware are you of environmental issues?
What issues are you most concerned about?
Do you actively do anything to care for the environment?

Religion and Ecology

Stewardship is a theological belief that humans are responsible for the world and should take care of it. To be a steward is to look after and protect all of creation. It involves responsible planning and management of resources. However, every day our planet is being destroyed: oil spills polluting our seas; the white rhino in South Africa being poached to the point of extinction; the destruction of rainforests; the impact of climate change. It is estimated that a quarter of the earth's mammals now face extinction. Justice demands that we fulfil our stewardship responsibility by living our lives in a way that creates a sustainable world for the sake of people all over the world, today, and for future generations.

THE CRY OF THE EARTH

The Cry of the Earth is a pastoral reflection on climate change from the Irish Catholic Bishops' Conference. At its launch in 2009, Archbishop Dermot Clifford said that the bishops of Ireland wished to raise awareness of our vital responsibility toward sustaining the environment.

The pastoral reflection has two parts. The first outlines the scientific evidence for global warming. The bishops looked to the scientists for assistance in this area. The document leaves us in no doubt that the temperature of the earth has been on the rise since the beginning of the Industrial Revolution 250 years ago. The average global temperature had risen in 2008 by 0.7°C since the late nineteenth century, yet the consequences of this small change have already been considerable. The vast majority of climate scientists put the rise in temperature down mainly to carbon emissions caused by the burning of fossil fuels.

If the present upward trend continues to 2°C and beyond, climate scientists tell us we are likely to have more heat waves, floods, storms, fires, droughts and famines. These will cause death or displacement for millions of people. Environmental refugees will run into millions because the places where they live will no longer be habitable. A rise of 1°C–2°C could see the extinction of one-third of the species of the world.

In the second part of the reflection, the bishops situate the subject of the environment in Scripture and theology and they suggest a Christian response. The Creation account in the Book of Genesis states that on the fifth day, 'God saw all he had created and it was good'. God then instructed Adam and Eve to care for his creation.

The message of the accounts of Creation in the Book of Genesis were written to convey that God created the universe and everything in it, that human beings are the high point of God's creation and that we have a responsibility to care for the whole of creation.

How has the human race exercised its stewardship down through the millennia? Archbishop Clifford summed up his response with two quotes. The first came from a participant at the 1997 Kyoto Conference on climate change:

> Nearly half of the earth's rain forests are gone ... water tables are dropping rapidly ... farmland, rivers and costal waters are saturated with nitrates and phosphates ... one in four of Europe's trees are dying due to acid rain ... up to 10 per cent of the earth's species of plants and animals have been made extinct. Fourteen of the world's seventeen major fishing grounds are either fished out or seriously depleted.

The second is from Pope John Paul II who during a General Audience held in 2001 said:

> Unfortunately, when we scan the regions of our planet, we immediately see that humanity has disappointed God's expectations.

WHAT CAN BE DONE?

Every action taken in favour of a more sustainable environment, no matter how small, has an immense value. Pope Benedict's encyclical, *Caritas in Veritate*, invites contemporary society:

> ... to a serious review of its lifestyle, which, in many parts of the world, is prone to hedonism and consumerism, regardless of their harmful consequences. What is needed is an effective shift in mentality which can lead to the adoption of new lifestyles in which the quest for truth, beauty, goodness and communion with others for the sake of common growth are the factors which determine consumer choices, savings and investments. (51)

A modern theologian, Fr John Fuellenbach, said:

> The earth is the first sacrament of God's love for its inhabitants; it is the world that gives life and nurtures it, it is a partner in the journey of humanity toward the Kingdom. The earth can no longer be considered as an object to be controlled and dominated or as a means to be used or misused as one pleases. The earth is part of humanity and humans are part of the earth: they have a

common destiny. To abuse the earth is to threaten life; to respect the earth, to treasure it as one of God's greatest gifts, is to ensure life. (From *Church: Community for the Kingdom* by Fr John Fuellenbach)

Is there hope for halting global warming? A joint declaration of Pope John Paul II and Patriarch Bartholomew of the Orthodox Church stated that:

> It is not too late. God's world has incredible healing powers. Within a generation, we could steer the earth towards our children's future. Let this generation start now with God's hope and blessing.

OVER TO YOU
- What does the scientific evidence presented in *The Cry of the Earth* tell us about climate change?
- What does Scripture and theology tell us about the environment?

THINK IT THROUGH
- How, in your opinion, has the human race exercised its stewardship?
- Are you hopeful for the future of the planet? Explain your answer.
- What practical actions can individuals, parishes and schools take to reduce the impact of their day-to-day activities on the environment?
- What action can you do now to help make a positive difference?

REFLECT AND DISCUSS
Pope John Paul II in 1979 proclaimed St Francis as heavenly patron of those who promote ecology, due to his love for the Creator, for animals and birds. Saint Francis extended the concept of neighbour to all living creatures. The main sources of energy and life were what he termed Brother Sun and Sister Water. Saint Francis expressed his beliefs in his prayer 'The Canticle of the Sun'.

> *' The earth is the first sacrament of God's love for its inhabitants ...*
>
> Fr John Fuellenbach

LESSON 69 — STEWARDSHIP: JUSTICE FOR THE PLANET

THE CANTICLE OF THE SUN BY FRANCIS OF ASSISI

Most high, all powerful, all good Lord! All praise is yours, all glory, all honour, and all blessing. To you, alone, Most High, do they belong. No mortal lips are worthy to pronounce your name.

Be praised, my Lord, through all your creatures, especially through, my Lord, Brother Sun, who brings the day; and you give light through him. And he is beautiful and radiant in all his splendour! Of you, Most High, he bears the likeness.

Be praised, my Lord, through Sister Moon and the stars; in the heavens you have made them, precious and beautiful.

Be praised, my Lord, through Brothers Wind and Air, and clouds and storms, and all the weather, through which you give your creatures sustenance.

Be praised, my Lord, through Sister Water; she is very useful, and humble, and precious, and pure.

Be praised, my Lord, through Brother Fire, through whom you brighten the night. He is beautiful and cheerful, and powerful and strong.

Be praised, my Lord, through our sister Mother Earth, who feeds us and rules us, and produces various fruits with coloured flowers and herbs.

Be praised, my Lord, through those who forgive for love of you; through those who endure sickness and trial. Happy those who endure in peace, for by you, Most High, they will be crowned.

Be praised, my Lord, through our Sister Bodily Death, from whose embrace no living person can escape. Woe to those who die in mortal sin! Happy those she finds doing your most holy will. The second death can do no harm to them.

Praise and bless my Lord, and give thanks, and serve him with great humility.

▶ How does this poem convey a love of creation?
▶ Which line of the poem appeals to you the most? Explain your answer?

JOURNAL
Write and design your own creation prayer.

St Francis of Assisi

SUMMARY

- Stewardship is a theological belief that humans are responsible for the world and should take care of it.
- The objective of stewardship is to pass on the earth to our descendents in the same condition or better condition as we were given it.
- *The Cry of the Earth* is a pastoral reflection on climate change from the Irish Catholic Bishops' Conference that outlines the scientific evidence for global warming and situates the subject of the environment in Scripture and theology.
- Christians are called to care for the environment and to have hope that their actions, no matter how small, can make a big difference.

LESSON 70
JUSTICE IN ACTION

Objective: This lesson will describe the lives of people known for their work for peace and justice.

OPENING ACTIVITY
Write down the name of a leader you admire. It could be a local, national or world leader, either living or historical. Write down three reasons why you admire this leader.

AUNG SAN SUU KYI

Aung San Suu Kyi, Burma's pro-democracy leader and Nobel Peace Prize winner, has come to symbolise the struggle of Burma's people to be free from the Burmese military-backed dictatorial government. Following a military coup in September 1988 a new pro-democracy party, the National League for Democracy (NLD), was formed. Aung San Suu Kyi was appointed general secretary. She gave numerous speeches calling for freedom and democracy. In May 1990, the government held free elections for the first time in almost thirty years. Suu Kyi's party overwhelmingly won, but was never allowed to take power. The 67-year-old had spent most of the last twenty years in some form of detention but the majority of it under house arrest, because of her efforts to bring democracy to military-ruled Burma. She was released from her most recent period of detention on 13 November 2010. In February 2012, Suu Kyi was given permission to run in the following April's parliamentary by-elections. In the election, she emerged victorious, with her NLD party winning forty-three of the forty-four contested seats.

In June 2012, Suu Kyi travelled first to Norway, where she collected the Nobel Peace Prize she was awarded in 1991, and then came to Dublin, where she accepted the Freedom of the City, which she was awarded in 2000. She also received the prestigious Amnesty Ambassador of Conscience award, and in her acceptance speech Suu Kyi said: 'To receive this award is to remind me that twenty-four years ago, I took on duties from which I have never been relieved.'

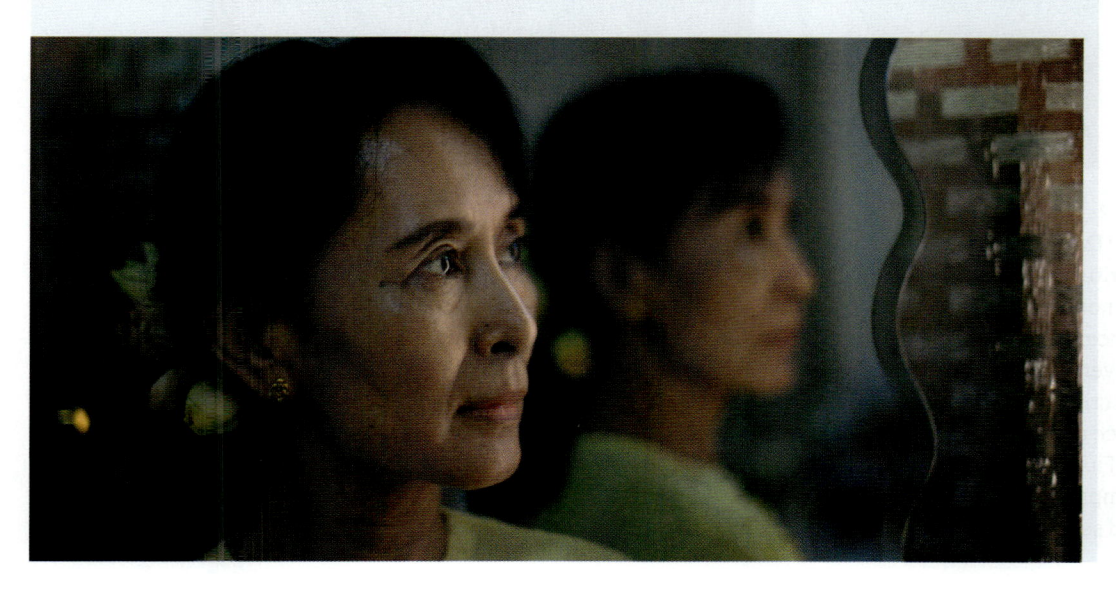

NELSON MANDELA

Nelson Mandela serves as a symbol for peace, unity and change for the people of South Africa. South Africa is now a democratic country with a constitution that guarantees rights for all its people. Mandela was the recipient, along with F. W. de Klerk, of the 1993 Nobel Peace Prize. Like many great leaders of the twentieth century, Nelson Mandela had an unwavering commitment to his belief in justice for all. His fight for justice for the people of South Africa guided all his actions, and he stayed true to his vision in spite of enormous obstacles and personal sacrifices that he was required to make.

HIS HOLINESS THE 14TH DALAI LAMA

The Dalai Lama is both the head of state and the spiritual leader of Tibet. Since 1959, he has received numerous awards in recognition of his message of peace, non-violence, interreligious understanding, universal responsibility and compassion. He describes himself as a simple Buddhist monk with three main commitments in life.

First, the promotion of human values such as compassion, forgiveness, tolerance, contentment and self-discipline.

Second, the promotion of religious harmony and understanding among the world's major religious traditions. It is important for all religious traditions to respect one another and recognise the value of each other's respective traditions.

Third, as a Tibetan who carries the name of the 'Dalai Lama', to act as the free spokesperson of the Tibetans in their struggle for justice.

REFLECT AND DISCUSS
Read the following quotes and share your responses:

- Suu Kyi wrote to those outside of Burma: 'Please use your liberty to promote ours.' What do you think she meant by this?
- President Barack Obama praised Suu Kyi's 'determination, courage and personal sacrifice in working for human rights and democratic change in Burma which inspire all of us who stand for freedom and justice'. How can Suu Kyi inspire us to stand for freedom and justice?
- Archbishop Desmond Tutu said in relation to what Nelson Mandela did to fight for justice and what any individual can do in the face of injustice: 'If an elephant is standing on the tail of a mouse and you say you are neutral, the mouse will not appreciate your neutrality.' Explain, in your own words, what Bishop Tutu meant.
- When the Dalai Lama visited Derry in 2013, he told the crowds gathered to see him: 'This century should be a century of dialogue – last century was a century of violence … If that amount of global violence really brought a better world, a happier world, then some people may justify it but that's not the case … peace does not mean there are no longer any problems. The problems remain. The creation of a peaceful world means when we face problems, try to solve that problem through dialogue, through talk.' How can we develop a world of dialogue as opposed to violence?

Young people working for justice – A story of action

A teacher of religious education once asked a group of fifth year students, 'What are you doing for your community and what are you doing to show love to your neighbour?' One student in the class replied, 'Give us an opportunity to do something and we'll do it.' From that initial discussion, a vibrant group of students worked with their teacher to establish the Social Action Group in Rathmore, Co. Kerry. The group was formed in 1975 and is still running today. Initially the young people set about organising a laundry service for the elderly and disadvantaged of their community. They also decided to raise money to build a day care centre and a headquarters for the group. Thirty-five years later, the Social Action Group has over 1,500 past and present members, has built a day care centre for the elderly and a youth centre which houses a playgroup, canteen, games room, hall and several meetings rooms. The philosophy of the Social Action Group is to provide young people with an organisation through which they can make a difference in their local community and beyond.

Jeremiah O'Donoghue, the teacher who inspired the group, went on to become the school principal, and although now retired from that position, he continues to work with the Social Action Group. He never ceases to challenge young people to make sacrifices to improve the lot of others. He says, 'What's making the headlines are the bad things that young people get up to, but the vast majority of young people are exactly the same as they always were – they want fun, they want enjoyment, they want education. They have a tremendous amount to offer in idealism and energy and it's a question of older people tapping into that idealism and that energy and turning it into something good.'

DOES GOD LISTEN?

When people pray, they often want something so badly that they expect an immediate response from God, a response that meets that specific request. It is almost telling God what he is to do for them. Very often the request is not granted. Christians believe that while God will answer prayers, his answer may not always be 'yes'. How often have we considered that a 'no' or 'later' might have been the answer to the prayer?

There are times when it is necessary to trust that God knows best. There are times when a request can be left with God. Such trust acts as a reminder of Jesus on the cross, suffering yet trusting that God was with him. His prayer 'Father, into your hands I commend my spirit' (Lk 23:46) offers us the greatest example of complete faith in the love of God. It shows us that even in the deepest despair, when God seems to be at a distance, one should not give up hope.

ASK, SEARCH, KNOCK

Ask, and it will be given you; search, and you will find; knock, and the door will be opened for you. For everyone who asks receives, and everyone who searches finds, and for everyone who knocks, the door will be opened. Is there anyone among you who, if your child asks for bread, will give a stone? Or if the child asks for a fish, will give a snake? If you then, who are evil, know how to give good gifts to your children, how much more will your Father in heaven give good things to those who ask him! (Mt 7:7-11)

THINK IT THROUGH

- What does this scripture passage suggest about God's response to prayers?
- What would happen if a parent always said yes to everything a child asked for?
- Can you think of a situation that you have heard of or from your own experience where it seemed that a prayer was not answered? Has your opinion of the answer to the prayer changed as time passed?
- On what occasions can unanswered prayers be a gift? Have you ever experienced this?

LESSON 74 — OVERCOMING OBSTACLES TO PRAYER

PRAYING REGULARLY

The best way to overcome obstacles to prayer is to keep on praying.

> Pray as you can and do not try to pray as you can't. Take yourself as you find yourself; start from that.
>
> — Dom John Chapman (1865–1933)

Saint Paul wrote, 'Pray without ceasing' (1 Th 5:17). Psalm 131 says that even resting can be prayer. The Church believes that prayer and Christian life are inseparable. When life and prayer are integrated, then it is possible to 'pray without ceasing'. When everything we do, whether it be prayer, work or recreation, is done with love for others and for God and when we offer all that we do to God, then it is as if it is all a prayer and so it is possible to pray without ceasing. Those who pray regularly will say that it has an effect on their everyday life. They say it helps them have clarity in making decisions; they are less likely to get angry at simple things; and they have a general ability to appreciate and listen to others.

Sometimes we tend to turn to God only when we 'need' something. The truth is that we need God more than we need 'something' from him. Just as breathing is vital to our physical life, praying is vital to our spiritual life. We need to 'pray without ceasing' just as we need to breathe without ceasing. We need to keep in touch with God on a regular basis – even more than we text our closest friend. Remember, God is always in touch with us. The reality is that prayer requires time, attention and effort.

JOURNAL

Reflect on these questions:

- Do you trust God with your prayers?
- What makes it easy or difficult for you to trust?
- Are there any prayers that you are waiting on an answer to? Consider that the answer might not be what you want, perhaps the answer is 'no' or 'later'.

SUMMARY

- Everyone can face obstacles throughout their prayer life.
- Christians have faith that God hears their prayers.
- The answer to a prayer is not always what we want or expect.
- Prayer requires trust in God, time, attention and effort.
- Prayer is vital to our spiritual life.

LESSON 75
SILENCE AND REFLECTION

Objective: This lesson will examine the value of silence and reflection in our lives today.

OPENING ACTIVITY

Stillness and silence are rarely part of the average person's day and certainly not part of the average student's day. Create a table like the one opposite to help you analyse how your average day is spent. Begin and end your day at midnight, rounding off your time to the nearest quarter. Choose a weekday rather than a weekend. Remember to count the times you do two things at once, for example texting a friend while watching TV. And be honest with what you put down!

- Did any of the results surprise you?
- What would you like to change about your time allocation?
- What value do you think some quiet time might offer you?

ACTIVITY	TIME in hours/minutes
SLEEPING	
SCHOOL	
HOMEWORK	
EATING	
TRAVELLING	
USING SOCIAL MEDIA	
TEXTING OR ON PHONE TO FRIENDS	
SPORTS	
WATCHING TV	
WITH FRIENDS	
LISTENING TO OR PLAYING MUSIC	
WORKING	
WITH FAMILY	
QUIET TIME/PRAYER	
OTHER	
TOTAL	

STILLNESS AND REFLECTION

Sister Stanislaus Kennedy, or Sr Stan as she is affectionately known, promotes the importance of stillness, silence and reflection in life. She founded a beautiful place of stillness in the heart of Dublin city called the Sanctuary, which offers quiet space where people of all ages can attend a variety of programmes and workshops. Helping people to be still and live in the present moment is key to the programmes and workshops offered by the Sanctuary. Sister Stan practices what she preaches by making time for stillness and reflection in the midst of a very busy life.

REFLECT AND DISCUSS

Read the following extract from Sr Stan's book, *Now is the Time,* and discuss the questions that follow:

> As a child I didn't know why my father always stopped before he started anything, but looking back on it now, I realise that he was assessing the land, thinking about it, weighing up the possibilities, but I also think his stopping and looking at it was a sort of prayer, a blessing on the work he was about to undertake.
>
> My life is not like that. I live an urban life and a frantic one, far removed from the steady, reflective life on the farm. I am one of those people who is always busy, always rushing around, making phone calls, taking calls, going to meetings, making things happen, writing things in my diary, talking to people, making plans, making appointments, keeping appointments, thinking up schemes, driving to Cork or Limerick or Waterford and driving home again the same day, giving talks, catching planes to far-off places like Venezuela or Nigeria or San Francisco, getting my passport renewed, getting visas sorted out, remembering to get vaccinations, forgetting to get vaccinations, visiting family, visiting sick and dying people, the homeless people who have for many years been the centre of my work, going to weddings and funerals, celebrations and parties, writing newspaper articles, writing books.
>
> I love my way of life, but I fear it too, because I know how easily all the traffic and the movement and the coming and going can prevent me from taking root, from settling down and taking time to do the really important things like being still and calm and keeping in touch with my inner being.
>
> I often think of my father when I start work each day or when I start into anything new, a meeting, an exchange, an interview or a phone call. Sometimes I can go into my office and before I know it I have a pen in hand and I am lost in what I do.
>
> This is not the way my father went about his work of sowing the seed, beginning by being still, standing in his field in respect for the soil. When I think about him doing that, it reminds me to make time and take the trouble to stop for reflection or a little prayer before starting on a job or an enterprise or making a call.
>
> If I don't make a conscious effort to do this, I find myself skating on the surface of what I am doing. I feel ungrounded and I become easily agitated when things don't go smoothly. I know that I need to take time to centre my breathing, to pray or perform a ritual that is meaningful to me. That makes me present to myself and to the task before me and brings a new balance as I start into any situation, reconnecting me with the deep creative, divine currents within and around me.
>
> (From *Now is the Time: Spiritual Reflections* by Sr Stanislaus Kennedy)

- What benefits does Sr Stanislaus identify from moments of reflection?
- How does she fit in these reflective moments in her day?
- How does the image of her father at work speak to her?
- How could you set about organising more quiet time for yourself each day?

GOD IS WAITING IN THE SILENCE

In his book, *The Hope Prayer*, Fr Liam Lawton shares his insights into prayer:

> To find stillness is not easy, as to find stillness one must also find silence. One is necessary for the other, I believe, but both are difficult to sustain. Silence can be frightening and almost threatening, for when we journey into it, we can be left feeling vulnerable. We are so used to noise, to the constant stream of other sounds, that to be alone with nothing can be ominous. It is interesting that in life today, silence is seen as a disturbance. Even in recreation time, people find silence very difficult and constantly need to listen to something or someone else. We are left feeling very exposed when everything stops and we are faced with simple silence.
>
> However, it is only when we do stop and move into the silence that we can become aware of what is happening internally for us. Silence puts us in touch with all the chaos within ... What many of us don't realise is that God is already there, waiting for us. The time of silence is God's gift to us.
>
> (From *The Hope Prayer* by Fr Liam Lawton)

THINK IT THROUGH

Consider the fast-paced world in which we live and discuss the following:

- Where are our quiet spaces today?
- What is their function?
- Where do you go to find peace and quiet in your life?
- Are you comfortable with spending time in silence? Why or why not?

JOURNAL

Spend some time in silence and reflect on this quiet time as God's gift to you. Write down the thoughts and feelings you had during this experience. Did you find it difficult or easy? Did you get distracted? Did anything about the experience surprise you?

SUMMARY

- Finding silence and stillness in our world can be very difficult.
- Time spent in reflection and contemplation helps us to be rooted in our own lives.
- Stillness and silence are necessary to connect to the voice of God within us.

LESSON 75 – SILENCE AND REFLECTION

LESSON 76
MEDITATION IN THE CHRISTIAN TRADITION

Objective: This lesson will explore the place of meditation in the Christian Tradition.

OPENING ACTIVITY

Take a few minutes to try a meditation that focuses on the breath, and then answer the questions that follow:

» Sit comfortably with your back straight
» Close your eyes lightly
» Sit as still as possible
» Breathe deeply, staying both relaxed and alert
» Stay focused on your breath; when thoughts enter your mind, acknowledge them and let them pass
» If possible, remain in this position for three minutes
» Slowly open your eyes and bring your attention back to the class.

- What was the exercise like?
- What did you find worked well for you?
- Would you be able to improve this exercise with practice?

What is meditation?

Meditation is a universal tradition found in all the great religions. It is open to all, whether a person belongs to a particular church or not. Meditation is simple and practical. It is about experience rather than theory: a way of being rather than thinking. It involves the physical body in prayer. Western people are often described as 'head' people because of an overemphasis on thinking and intellectualising. Meditation connects one's physical body with the mind. As a tradition from Eastern cultures, Western people have gained much insight into the benefits of this form of prayer. According to one Christian who meditates:

When we meditate, we place ourselves in the presence of God and let go of our cares and worries. Through relaxing our bodies, we begin to become aware of our breathing and gradually travel into our hearts. It is at this point that we can experience the presence of God.

THE REVIVAL OF CHRISTIAN MEDITATION

Over thirty years ago, John Main was working as a diplomat in Asia, and while he was there he met an Indian monk who became his spiritual teacher and guide. They got to talking about prayer:

Main: How do you pray?
Monk: We pray slightly differently. We don't think, we come to an inner silence.
Main: How do you come to this inner silence?
Monk: It is difficult, there are distractions. The mind is like a tree full of chattering monkeys. To clear a way through the jungle we take a single word, a mantra, and repeat it ceaselessly in our mind and heart, giving it our full attention.
Main: How long will this take?
Monk: As long as it takes you to say the mantra.
Main: What about posture? What about distractions? What about insights?
Monk: Sit still. Sit upright (there is no need to sit cross-legged!). Say the mantra. Listen to it as a sound within you. Give it your full attention. Let everything else go. It will lead you into the silence of oneness with God.

Main believed so strongly in the value of this form of prayer that when he returned to Europe he established small meditation groups and began to teach Christian meditation. These were the origin of the ecumenical network of Christian meditation groups that have become the World Community for Christian Meditation. Main later went on to become a Benedictine monk and continued to spread the teaching of this ancient tradition of prayer that has its origins in the Indian tradition and parallels in the Christian monastic tradition and Irish Christian settlements. He realised that this very simple and ancient Christian form of prayer could lead people of all walks of life to a spiritual experience that was both practical and meaningful for them.

> Because of the profound effect meditation has on one's life, it is even more than a method of prayer; it is a way of life, a way of living from the deep centre of one's being in every situation.
>
> John Main OSB (1926–1982)

THINK IT THROUGH
- Why do you think meditation is a universal form of prayer?
- How can meditation have an impact on a person's life?

> ' *Lord Jesus, Son of God, have mercy on me.*

WHAT IS A MANTRA?

The mantra is used in many faith traditions. A mantra is a word or phrase that is repeated. The aim of the repetition is to release the mind from distractions and allow it to focus on God. The Jesus Prayer, 'Lord Jesus, Son of God, have mercy on me', is a very popular mantra for Christians. Some even say the prayer with the ancient custom of breathing in for the first part, 'Lord Jesus Christ, Son of God', and on the out breath 'have mercy on me'. The prayer follows the advice of a seventh-century mystic who wrote:

> If many words are used in prayer, all sorts of distracting pictures hover in the mind, but worship is lost. If little is said ... the mind remains concentrated.

LESSON 76 – MEDITATION IN THE CHRISTIAN TRADITION

REFLECT AND DISCUSS

For the past few years, Philip has been interested in contemplative Christianity, and particularly the practice of Christian meditation. He is part of a group that organises regular meditation events and retreats, and has edited a collection of articles called *Young and Contemplative*, written by 18–25-year-olds on the topic of prayer and the importance of stillness and silence. Read this extract about his experience and answer the questions that follow:

> I came across the practice of Christian meditation when I was seventeen. Since then I have tried to keep up a regular practice, sitting for about half an hour every morning and evening. I would be lying if I said that my times of meditation were always filled with peacefulness and insight. I am rarely the serene, Buddha-like caricature contemplating the depths of beauty and truth that many people imagine when thinking about meditation. The reality of the practice is normally something quite different for me when I sit on my meditation cushion in my room at university. Sometimes I don't seem to get that much out of it. Sometimes meditation feels easy, but still doesn't give me the profound insights I might have hoped for. And sometimes meditation is difficult, even painful, touching emotional and spiritual places within that I would rather not face up to.
>
> It's like training your body to run efficiently: sometimes boring, sometimes hard work, and sometimes extremely difficult. Yet there are also rewards to the practice. When you keep up a discipline of running, your body becomes healthier and more mobile as your muscles strengthen. Meditation, too, changes the practitioner. Meditation might not seem to help the body in the way that running does, but it certainly has an effect on the mind, and also on the spirit. On the one hand it is hard to say exactly what has changed in me over the past four years of meditation practice, because meditation does not make me visibly stronger in the way running would. On the other hand, I do think that meditation can help us to keep spiritually 'fit', whatever that might mean.
>
> One of the main tasks of meditation practice is to let go of thought, or at least to try to let go of thought. Much of the time all sorts of analysis is going on in the complex landscape of our brains. If I close my eyes and just watch what is going on in my head, I soon realise how busy and hard-working my mind is. Meditation is about watching that busyness, allowing it to settle, to calm down, to be still. If we watch, wait and listen sometimes,

rather than always talking and moving and analysing, the brain is given a rest.

At that point, I believe the spiritual dimension is given a chance to speak, not necessarily in language or words, but in a deeper kind of communication, beyond our thoughts, beyond what we can describe. Perhaps we get spiritually fit by getting to know ourselves, and by being honest with ourselves about who we really are. In meditation I find that I can listen more and more to myself and to what is going on deep down, where I believe God's presence dwells, giving me life and purpose.

Meditation does not make me better as a person, but it does help me to see what kind of person I am. When you are young, this is crucial, because young people have so much to deal with – falling in love, growing up, thinking about what we want to do with our lives, learning what sort of a friend we want to be to others, discovering what sort of creative life we have inside ourselves, and so on.

When I was seventeen I wouldn't have thought much of an explanation of meditation as an abstract concept. What really got me interested was that I could sit down and do meditation. I could simply get on with it by sitting on a cushion for twenty minutes or half an hour and seeing for myself whether all the talking about spiritual fitness was true for me, in my own world. You don't get fit by reading about running, and the same is true of meditation. You have to get on with it and try it for yourself.

All I can really say is that meditation takes me to a place that words can't touch, and changes me in a way that can't fully be put down on paper. A short testimony about meditation is only a very small part of the story. The real way to learn about it is to try it for yourself.

– Philip Seal

- What are the rewards that Philip sees to the practice of meditation?
- How does he describe the main task of meditation?
- What advice does he give for those interested in meditation?

OVER TO YOU

- Repeat the exercise of meditation you tried at the beginning of the lesson. This time try using a mantra. Listen to the mantra as you say it and give it your full attention. Say it in rhythm with your breathing. The mantra helps focus attention in prayer and helps us remain in the present moment. When thoughts or images distract you, simply let them go by saying the mantra.

SUMMARY

- Meditation is a universal tradition found in all the great religions.
- A mantra is a prayer word repeated. The aim of the repetition is to release the mind from distractions and allow it to focus on God.
- The Jesus Prayer, 'Lord Jesus, Son of God, have mercy on me', is a very popular mantra for Christians.
- Meditation can help us to keep spiritually 'fit'.
- Meditation increases our sense of wellbeing and deepens our personal relationship with God.
- Meditation requires practice.

LESSON 77
PRAYER AND IMAGINATION

Objective: This lesson will examine another form of meditative prayer which was developed by St Ignatius of Loyola – prayer using imagination.

OPENING ACTIVITY
Examine the pictures. Choose one and answer the questions opposite:

- Use your imagination to give a brief outline of his/her story (life situation).
- Write one prayer/request which you think he/she may have at this time.
- Find others in your class who chose this picture and compare your results.

Human imagination

From the invention of the wheel to Einstein's Theory of Relativity to the innovation of technology, the power of the human imagination is what separates us from the rest of the animal kingdom. Imagination is a powerful way of seeing the world in a new way. What a wealth of poems and songs have been written because people have entered into the realm of their imagination.

Imagination is the ability to form mental images, sensations and concepts, in a moment when they are not perceived through sight, hearing or other senses. Imagination helps provide meaning to experience and understanding to knowledge; it is a fundamental facility through which people make sense of the world.

Saint Ignatius of Loyola recognised the wonder of the imagination and developed a prayer form which has great appeal for many people today. This method of prayer requires the person who is praying to think of and imagine a scripture passage. As the passage is read, the person is drawn to a more personal experience of it and then to a heightened awareness of its meaning and a real encounter with Jesus and his message.

SECTION G: PRAYER AND WORSHIP

IGNATIUS OF LOYOLA

Ignatius of Loyola is the founder of the Jesuit order. As a young adult, his goal and purpose in life was to achieve fame and fortune. He entered the army, and at the age of thirty was badly wounded in battle. During this period of severe suffering, he read books on the life of Christ and on legends of the saints. He read them over and over again as he was so impressed by the lives of St Dominic and the heroic deeds of Francis of Assisi and other great monastic leaders.

This experience led him to change his goal of a life of fame and worldly pleasure to a life in the service of God. He developed spiritual exercises to guide people who wanted to live a truly Christian life and shared these with his companions, whom he called 'the company of Jesus', better known today as the Jesuits.

This method of prayer is still used today. Often those who practice this prayer say they notice elements in the Gospel story that they had not noticed before. Remember that each of us will respond to the text in a different way.

Read the following passage from Matthew 8:23-27:

> And when he got into the boat, his disciples followed him. A windstorm arose on the sea, so great that the boat was being swamped by the waves; but he was asleep. And they went and woke him up, saying, 'Lord, save us! We are perishing!' And he said to them, 'Why are you afraid, you of little faith?' Then he got up and rebuked the winds and the sea; and there was a dead calm. They were amazed, saying, 'What sort of man is this, that even the winds and the sea obey him?'

OVER TO YOU

- Assume a comfortable position. Become silent. Close your eyes. Notice the gentle rhythm of your breath. Do not change the rhythm of your breathing; just be aware of it.
- Imagine you are in that boat. Feel the gentle rocking of the boat as you set out. Listen to the sounds of the gulls calling. Feel the warmth of the afternoon sun on your face. Listen to the gentle chat of the others on the boat with you, the easy conversation and the occasional laughter. You are sitting comfortably and feel relaxed.
- Suddenly the wind changes and you feel the boat rock with the strength of the waves. A feeling of tension comes over you. Your nervousness and that of the others builds up. The swells of the waves continue to grow higher and stronger. Notice the change in the dialogue as the anxiety of the others becomes apparent. You are soaking wet as the waves crash over and into the boat. You take a tight hold of the side of the boat, and as you look at the worried faces of the others who are trying to keep the boat under control, you notice that Jesus is asleep ...

> *Why are you afraid, you of little faith?*
>
> Mt 8:26

LESSON 77 – PRAYER AND IMAGINATION

THINK IT THROUGH
- Who wakes Jesus?
- What is your reaction when he asks, 'Why are you afraid, you of little faith?'
- What feelings do these words rouse in you?
- Watch as Jesus calms the storm. Note your disbelief.
- Think back on the doubts you held just a short time ago. How do you feel about them now?
- Notice the reactions of the others; observe their facial expressions.
- Go over to Jesus and tell him what you feel. Be honest; share your doubts and fears.
- How does he respond to you? Listen to his words; repeat them to yourself.
- Recall the events of the afternoon and gratefully remember the conversation you had with Jesus.
- Notice your breath; breathe in deeply and slowly. When you are ready, slowly open your eyes.

JOURNAL

Reflect on the experience for yourself. You can use the questions below to help you:

- What did it feel like to be in the midst of a storm?
- How did I feel when Jesus asked, 'Why are you afraid?'
- Did I trust I would be saved? Why? Why not?
- What was my reaction when I noticed the wind and waves had died down?
- What did I want to say to Jesus then?
- What message or image will I remember from this prayer experience?

SUMMARY

- Another form of meditative prayer invites the use of one's imagination to experience a sacred text.
- Ignatius of Loyola is credited with introducing this form of prayer.
- People respond differently to the text when they engage in this prayer.

LESSON 78
LECTIO DIVINA

Objective: This lesson will look at Lectio divina and examine it as a form of prayer.

OPENING CONVERSATION
Have you ever read the same book more than once? Did you notice anything different about it the second time? Why would someone re-read a book or a passage from a book a number of times? What are your favourite books or passages to re-read?

What is *Lectio divina*?

Lectio divina is a very ancient method of prayer from the monastic tradition of Christianity. It is also said to be adaptable for people of other faiths in reading their sacred texts. The actual practice of *Lectio divina* begins with a time of relaxation, making one comfortable and clearing the mind of mundane thoughts and cares. Some *Lectio* practitioners find it helpful to concentrate by beginning with deep, cleansing breaths and reciting a chosen phrase or word (like a mantra) over and over to help free the mind. Then they begin with the following steps:

» *Lectio* – this Latin word means 'reading'. The passage of scripture is read slowly to allow the words to be heard and appreciated. Sometimes the passage can be re-read to allow the reader focus on a particular word or phrase. Any passage of Scripture can be used for this way of prayer but the passage should not be too long.
» *Meditatio* – this word means 'meditation' and is where the reader tries to understand what God is saying in the text. To do this, the reader often asks questions like 'What does this passage/phrase mean for me?', 'How does it relate to my life at this time?'
» *Oratio* – this is Latin for 'prayer'. In this step the reader responds to what has been read and makes a prayer of thanksgiving, repentance and petition.
» *Contemplatio* – this means 'contemplate' or rest quietly in the presence of God, listening to God.
» *Actio* – this means 'action'. This reminds the reader that time in prayer should affect one's life. At this point the reader will often ask questions such as 'How has my prayer today affected the way I live my life? Is there any action that I will make part of my life?'

These stages of *Lectio divina* are not fixed rules of procedure but simply guidelines as to how the prayer normally develops. Its movement is towards greater simplicity and silence, with less and less talking and more listening. Gradually the words of Scripture are revealed to the reader. How much time should be given to each stage depends very much on whether it is used individually or in a group. If *Lectio divina* is used for group prayer, obviously more structure is needed than for individual use.

OVER TO YOU
▶ Take a moment to prepare yourself for this time of prayer.

LECTIO – READING THE TEXT

Let us read the text of the Gospel of John 4:5-42, Jesus and the Woman of Samaria/the Woman at the Well, slowly and reverently in the knowledge that God is speaking to each one of us in a very special way.

Narrator:	Jesus came to a city of Samaria, called Sychar, near the field that Jacob gave to his son Joseph. Jacob's well was there. So Jesus, tired from the journey, sat down beside the well. It was about the sixth hour. There came a woman of Samaria to draw water. Jesus said to her,
Jesus:	Give me a drink.
N:	For his disciples had gone away into the city to buy provisions. The Samaritan woman said to him,
Woman:	How is it that you, a Jew, ask a drink of me, a woman of Samaria?
J:	If you knew the gift of God, and who it is that is saying to you, 'Give me a drink', you would have asked him, and he would have given you living water.
N:	The woman said to him,
W:	Sir, you have no bucket, and the well is deep; where do you get that living water? Are you greater than our father Jacob, who gave us the well, and drank from it himself, and his sons, and his cattle?
N:	Jesus said to her,
J:	Everyone who drinks of this water will thirst again, but whoever drinks of the water that I shall give him will never thirst; the water that I shall give him will become in him a spring of water welling up to eternal life.
N:	The woman said to him,
W:	Sir, give me this water, that I may not thirst, nor come here to draw.
J:	Go and call your husband and come back here.
N:	The woman answered,
W:	I have no husband.
N:	Jesus said to her,
J:	You are right in saying, 'I have no husband'; for you have had five husbands, and he whom you now have is not your husband; you spoke the truth there.
N:	The woman said to him,
W:	Sir, I see that you are a prophet. Our fathers worshipped on this mountain; and you say that Jerusalem is the place where one ought to worship.
N:	Jesus said to her,
J:	Believe me, woman, the hour is coming when neither on this mountain nor in Jerusalem will you worship the Father. You worship what you do not know; we worship what we know, for salvation comes from the Jews. But the hour is coming, and now is here when true worshippers will worship the Father in spirit and truth, for such the Father seeks to worship him. God is spirit, and those who worship him must worship in spirit and truth.
N:	The woman said to him,
W:	I know that the Messiah is coming – he who is called Christ – when he comes, he will show us all things.
N:	Jesus said to her,
J:	I who speak to you am he.
N:	Just then his disciples returned. They were surprised that he was talking with a woman, but none said, 'What do you want?' or, 'Why are you

278

SECTION G: PRAYER AND WORSHIP

N:	talking with her?' So the woman left her water jar, and went away into the city, and said to the people,
W:	Come, see a man who told me all that I ever did. Can this be the Christ?
N:	They went out of the city and were coming to him. Meanwhile the disciples were urging him saying,
Disciples:	Rabbi, eat.
N:	But he said to them,
J:	I have food to eat of which you do not know.
N:	So the disciples said to one another,
D:	Has someone brought him food?
N:	Jesus said to them,
J:	My food is to do the will of him who sent me, and to accomplish his work. Do you not say, 'There are yet four months, then comes the harvest?' I tell you, lift up your eyes, and see how the fields are already white for harvest. He who reaps receives wages and gathers fruit for eternal life, so that sower and reaper may rejoice together. For here the saying holds true, 'One sows and another reaps'. I sent you to reap that for which you did not labour; others have laboured, and you have entered into their labour.
N:	Many Samaritans from that city believed in him because of the woman's testimony, 'He told me all that I ever did'. So when the Samaritans came to him, they asked him to stay with them; and he stayed there two days. And many more believed because of his word. They said to the woman,
People:	It is no longer because of your words that we believe, for we have heard for ourselves, and we know that this is indeed the Saviour of the world.

The Word of the Lord.

Each person now re-reads the Gospel quietly to themselves, noting a word or phrase which has special meaning for them.

MEDITATIO – REFLECTION

'What does this passage/phrase mean for me?' 'How does it relate to my life at this time?' Some of the following prompts might help:

– John's story of Jesus meeting the Samaritan woman uses metaphors to talk about spiritual things. The important metaphors here are thirst and water. What do I thirst for? Where will I find the water to quench my thirst?

– Jesus reaches out to someone others reject and ignore. Who are the people I know who always make time to reach out to others? Who do I ignore? Who do I need to reach out to?

– The woman leaving down the water jar is leaving everything behind to announce what she has heard from Jesus. She is the bearer of good news and she will proclaim it. Who are the people in the world today who are furthering God's kingdom of justice and love? How can I do this?

ORATIO – PRAYER

Lord, we thank you for the great people of faith we have known and for all who nurture our faith, our parents, grandparents, teachers and faith community.

May we in these times continue to discover the 'spring of water' deep within us so that our lives will encourage all those we meet every day. We make this prayer through Christ our Lord. Amen.

CONTEMPLATIO – CONTEMPLATE

With eyes closed for a few minutes, rest quietly in the presence of God, listening to God. Call to mind a word or phrase you will remember today as you leave this room.

ACTIO – ACTION

How has my prayer today affected the way I live my life? Is there any action that I will hope to make part of my life from now on?

SUMMARY

- *Lectio divina* is a very ancient method of prayer from the monastic tradition of Christianity.
- There are five stages:
  - » *Lectio* – reading
  - » *Meditatio* – meditation
  - » *Oratio* – prayer
  - » *Contemplatio* – contemplate, or rest quietly in the presence of God
  - » *Actio* – action.

LESSON 79
THE CONTEMPLATIVE TRADITION

Objective: This lesson will examine the origins and development of the contemplative tradition and describe how the tradition continues to have appeal.

OPENING CONVERSATION
Name some rules that you follow in your daily life at home, in school and in society. Who makes these rules? What is the benefit of keeping them?

Saint Benedict

It might surprise you to learn that rules written over 1,500 years ago by St Benedict are still in existence for those living in a monastic community today.

Legend holds that St Benedict was born in the mountains north-east of Rome. His parents were Christian and sent him to study law in Rome when he was about sixteen years of age. However, the atmosphere of the great city shocked and depressed him to the extent that he fled the city to become a hermit. Benedict went on to found monasteries and wrote rules for the monks to live by, known as the Rule of St Benedict.

Indeed, the real influence of St Benedict down the centuries was not so much due to the monasteries he founded as to the Rule he wrote for monks. It is flexible enough to allow other monastic communities to adapt it for themselves, which is why it has lasted for over 1,500 years. Saint Benedict is one of the patron saints of Europe and students, and his feast day is 11 July.

RULE OF SAINT BENEDICT – *LABORARE EST ORARE* – A LIFE OF WORK AND PRAYER

Saint Benedict's model for the monastic life was the family, with the abbot as father and all the monks as brothers. Priesthood was not initially an important part of Benedictine monasticism – monks used the services of their local priest. There are also Benedictine communities of women under the authority of an abbess.

Saint Benedict's Rule organises the monastic day into regular periods of communal and private prayer, sleep, spiritual reading and manual labour – *ut in omnibus glorificetur Deus*, 'that in all [things] God may be glorified' (cf. Rule, ch. 57.9). In later centuries, intellectual work and teaching took the place of farming, crafts or other forms of manual labour for many – if not most – Benedictines.

It is a day-to-day prescription for those interested in living with and in God. Those following the rule have enough in food, drink and clothing but own little in terms of personal possessions. Saint Benedict wanted his monks to imitate the Apostles who supported themselves with their work, more often than not the work of their hands.

Second, he insisted that his monks would spend some time each day doing *Lectio divina*. Benedict set out a certain time each day for study and reflective reading, and his love and knowledge of the Scriptures shaped his Rule.

Third, Benedict emphasised the importance of both the human person and relationships between persons living together. His rule contains directions for all aspects of community life. A large focus of the rule of St Benedict is to show compassion and hospitality towards strangers, the young, the old and the sick.

The Rule of St Benedict promotes the belief that God is present everywhere and the 'eyes of the Lord in every place behold the good and the evil'.

THINK IT THROUGH
- Which rule would you consider to be the hardest to live by?
- Why do you think these rules have survived for so long?

An Irish Benedictine monastery

The Abbey of Saints Joseph and Columba at Glenstal (Glenstal Abbey) is a Benedictine monastery in County Limerick, founded in 1927. The monks at Glenstal Abbey live out the rule of St Benedict in this peaceful place.

LIFE IN GLENSTAL ABBEY

Having recently completed his one-year novitiate, one man who is now a simply professed monk of the monastery at Glenstal Abbey answers some questions about his life and explains what it is about contemplative life that appeals to him.

How long does it take to become a monk?
I am often asked how long it takes to become a monk and the simple answer is 'a lifetime', which started the day I arrived, though in reality it had been going on for years. However, as in any journey into relationship, there are key ritual moments along the way (Simple Profession and Solemn Profession). After spending time among the community and living the life, I requested to continue my journey here. I made my wish known, and after a number of discussions the community made its decision known. This process of mutual discernment I am convinced is absolutely directed by the Holy Spirit.

How would you describe life in Glenstal?
The monastery is located on five hundred acres of farmland, forest, gardens, rivers and lakes and is a beautiful location. This alone could make living here worthwhile; but Glenstal can likewise at times be cold, grey and damp. A word that comes to mind most often is 'real'. Though away from many of the concerns of daily living, a monk is faced with the reality of his own being at all times. This can be very sobering, challenging and at times even wonderful. I would also describe it as a balanced life. For the most part our way of living is pretty simple.

What drew you to it?
I came here at age forty-three after working at many jobs, playing many roles, but still with the question 'Who am I?' At a very human level, I knew that this particularly structured way of life was good for me. Some immediately ask

Glenstal Abbey

if it is not limiting since you have little freedom. This is true; for example, I no longer have my own money or car – in the past these were great symbols of freedom for me. However, I have freedom to go to university in Limerick, which I enjoy a lot. The ultimate question here of course is, what is freedom? I sometimes liken myself and this journey to a rose bush. Standard roses, once planted, with a little care and attention just grow and do what they are meant to do – produce flowers. Treat a climbing rose in the same way and the result is not so good. A trellis is needed. With this support the climber can flourish and blossom. In simple terms, I liken myself to the climbing rose and monastic life to the trellis. Its structure, apparently limiting, is rather a support that allows me freedom to grow and blossom. It is good for me!

Give a brief outline of your average day.

Every day has one beginning and one end – God; and the day is structured around 'strong' moments of encounter – the liturgy. We rise about 6 a.m. for prayer at 6.35 a.m., followed by a period of silence which continues through breakfast. By 9 a.m. most are beavering away at a variety of jobs – the farm, garden, library, hospitality, guests, teaching, a variety of domestic and administrative duties, many areas of study and academic research. Community Mass is at 12.10 p.m., followed by lunch, after which many take a short nap, and by 2 p.m. we are engaged in all sorts of things again. Lest one thinks it's all work, there is plenty of time for leisurely walks, reading and things like that. The activity of the day begins to wind down for Vespers (evening prayer) at 6 p.m. and a more silent air returns. For supper at 7.15 p.m., which is in silence, the guests join the monks in the monastery refectory. Night prayer is at 8.35 p.m. and most people have pretty much turned in by 10 p.m.

Saint Benedict said that a monk is a man who is searching for God. In your opinion, what is the role of a monk in today's world?

The search for meaning, relevance, God, has gone on among people for thousands of years. It still does, and the monk's role is still the same – one who seeks God. I think more than ever the monastery has the responsibility to be that space where God is breathed in and out in the daily round of work and prayer that has gone on since Benedict's day. In this, the monk is called to be firm in this commitment so that through him and the monastery, God's presence is almost Everpresent!

What does prayer mean for you?

In essence prayer for me is part of the dialogue of my relationship with God. But it is becoming the part of the conversation where I am learning more and more to shut my mouth, silence the mind and listen – a real challenge! Each morning of a monk's life, the words, 'O that today you would listen to his voice, harden not your hearts' (Ps 95:8) are heard. This act of listening permeates all of the Rule of Benedict. So in all the events of the day – reflection, reading, conversation, work, encounter with people, amazement at nature, liturgy – the eyes of the mind and the ears of the heart are attuned to the promptings of God nudging, luring and directing.

OVER TO YOU
- Design a poster to encourage people to consider the monastic way of life.
- Highlight what you think are the most important and/or appealing aspects of contemplative life.

> ❛ *O that today you would listen to his voice ...*
>
> Ps 95:8

SUMMARY

- The Rule of St Benedict is used in monastic communities all around the world.
- Saint Benedict's Rule organises the monastic day into regular periods of communal and private prayer, sleep, spiritual reading and manual labour.
- Key ritual moments in becoming a Benedictine monk include Simple Profession and Solemn Profession.
- A monk is someone who searches for God and spreads God's love to the world.
- Each morning of a monk's life, the words, 'O that today you would listen to his voice, harden not your hearts' (Ps 95:8) are heard.

LESSON 80
MODERN EXPRESSIONS OF A CONTEMPLATIVE TRADITION

Objective: This lesson will describe a contemporary contemplative community in Ireland.

OPENING CONVERSATION
What is your understanding of a hermit? What do you think is the appeal in living such a life?

A contemplative outlook

We have been sent into the world to be people who live life to the full, to be 'people for life'. Our lives must translate into action what the Gospel says in words. In order to achieve this, we need to foster in ourselves and others a contemplative outlook, which can come through spending time getting to know the mind of God so that we can see reality as God sees it. This comes from faith in the God of life who created every individual as a wonder: 'I praise you, for I am fearfully and wonderfully made' (Ps 139:14). It is the outlook of those who see the deeper meaning of life, its beauty and the fact that it is a totally free gift of God. It leads people to recognise that being alive is in itself an invitation to freedom and responsibility. People who cultivate a contemplative outlook are more likely to discover in others the image of God who created them and in all of creation a reflection of the beauty and wonder of God the Creator. A contemplative outlook enables us not to give in to discouragement even in the face of suffering or death, but challenges us to search for God who is present to us in all of life's situations. Read the following description of life in a hermitage.

THE SPIRITUAL LIFE INSTITUTE

The Spiritual Life Institute is an example of a contemporary contemplative community in Ireland. This is how one member of the community describes the community:

> The Spiritual Life Institute is a small community of men and women hermits who take vows of poverty, chastity and obedience. We have two hermitages, Holy Hill Hermitage in Skreen, County Sligo, and Nada Hermitage in the Rocky Mountains near Crestone, Colorado.
> Our primary job is prayer. We each live in a separate house, and spend one week a month and two days a week completely alone. On other days we pray and work together, and on Sundays we have a meal

Rocky Mountains, Colorado

together and enjoy some recreation. We have two historical models for our lives as hermits. The first Carmelites were hermits who lived on the side of Mount Carmel. They were men who had come to the Holy Land in the twelfth century as pilgrims or 'crusaders', and decided to stay and devote their lives to God. They had a simple rule, which included the important line: 'Stay in your cell day and night meditating on the law of the Lord, unless otherwise engaged in a just occupation.' They would sometimes leave the hermitage in order to help other people to find God, and Carmelites have been both contemplative and apostolic ever since. We are strongly influenced by two Carmelites who lived in Spain during the sixteenth century: St Teresa of Jesus, also known as St Teresa of Ávila, and St John of the Cross. They both wrote books on prayer that we use as basic texts. We are also influenced by the early Celtic monks, who lived as hermits in stone huts on remote islands and in places like Glendalough and Clonmacnoise. Like them, we find God in the beauty of nature and both of our hermitages are surrounded with wonderful scenery.

At both places, we have hermitages that are available for anyone who would like to come for a retreat. We believe that all people are meant to find union with God, and we try to create an atmosphere where that will be easy for them to do. We have a large library with books, taped talks and music, and retreatants are invited to join us for prayer. However, everyone is free to do as they want, and some people come to spend time writing or painting, and spend all of their time alone. People of all faiths, or no faith, are welcome.

In the spring, we have a programme for people under thirty-five years of age who come and live as a 'community within the community'. They pray and work with us, have discussion groups and meals together, and go on outings together.

We do occasional retreats for secondary school or confirmation classes, and on the first Sunday of every month we have an open Sunday. Anyone is welcome to join us for Mass at noon and to stay for tea and a tour of Holy Hill.

One of the students who came for a retreat wrote a one-word response in our guest book: 'Savage'! A retreatant, Marian Sorensen, who came later noticed that response and wrote a poem about Holy Hill based on it.

'HERMITAGE'

'Savage'? I'll say!
And more as I pray
To thank the One
Who inspired this common, solitary cell,
This happy, holy well.
This house of refuge
Where weary guests
And questers,
Pilgrims on the open road,
Stop awhile ...
S L O W the pace
Find His face
Are embraced
In rhythm and round
Of work and play.
Share in prayer
Chant and song
Meditation gong
ALL belong
In the CENTRE OF ONE VAST HEART
Be still and know ... be known ...
    and K N O W.
'Savage'? I'll say!
And pray one day
I can return
To feast again on beauty
The Beauty of Holiness
Of hearts devoted, hands outstretched,
Silence, stillness,
S P A C E to dream.
Springing up and rooting down
On this Holy Hill.

(Marian Sorensen)

THINK IT THROUGH
- What memories does the writer of the poem have of the hermitage?
- Read the poem again and identify key words that you think explain what the life of a hermit involves.
- Would life in a contemplative community appeal to you? Why or why not?

RESEARCH PROJECT
Research either St Teresa of Ávila or St John of the Cross, outlining the life story and understanding of prayer of your chosen saint.

SUMMARY
- The community at Holy Hill Hermitage are influenced by St Teresa of Ávila and St John of the Cross as well as by the early Celtic monks.
- Prayer is the primary function of the life of those in the community.
- People of all faiths and none are welcome to spend time in the hermitage.

LESSON 81
MASS ATTENDANCE AND PARTICIPATION

Objective: This lesson will examine Mass attendance and participation.

OPENING CONVERSATION
How often do you attend religious services? How do you participate in these services?

Mass attendance

In previous lessons we looked at personal prayer. In many religious traditions prayer is both personal and communal. In the Christian Tradition, communal celebrations of prayer are centred mainly on the sacraments. The Mass (Eucharist) is the central prayer of the Church.

In recent years much notice has been drawn to the numbers attending Mass in this country. A poll taken in 2009 on Mass attendance found that 44% of Catholics attend Mass weekly or more often. Two-thirds of Irish people go to church at least once a month. Almost a third of 18–24 year olds go to Mass weekly (31%) and another 22% go monthly or more. Contrary to popular opinion, these statistics show that over 50% of 18–24 year olds attend Mass at least once a month. Church attendance also varies by region. In rural areas, 56% of respondents said they go weekly compared with 38% in Dublin. Among those aged over 65, the weekly attendance rate is 70%.

(RedC on behalf of the Iona Institute, 21/10/09)

THINK IT THROUGH
- Do these figures surprise you?
- How good an indicator of a person's faith is Mass attendance?

A PRIEST'S PERSPECTIVE
The above statistics give a very positive overview of Mass attendance in Ireland today. However, sometimes the view on the ground can be slightly different. The following is one priest's response to the question of how Mass attendance in Ireland has changed since he was ordained thirty years ago:

> Thirty years ago almost everyone went to Mass every weekend in Ireland. It was easier to go than it might have been to stay away. Today things are different, and in some parts of Ireland going to Mass on Sunday is going against the trend. The regularity that was there is gone from people's lives. People come to the church at festival times, at funeral Masses and at special events, but every weekend the majority of people that are regular are all greying and ageing like myself. Yet at the local level, I feel supported, welcomed and valued in my ministry by young and old, and community lives on, inspired by the life and ministry of Jesus.
>
> — Fr Pat Moore, Diocese of Kerry

OVER TO YOU
- What changes has this priest noticed in Mass attendance in the last thirty years?
- How does he understand the role of church attendance now?
- Do you think the survey results reflect this priest's experience of Mass attendance? Explain your answer.

PARTICIPATION

A key Vatican document called *The Constitution on the Sacred Liturgy* states: 'The Church earnestly desires that all the faithful be led to the full, conscious and active participation in liturgical celebrations' (14). The Church calls on each member of the community to take part in the celebration, as it is their right through baptism. For centuries there has been more passive than active participation at Mass. People sometimes claim they are bored at Mass and simply don't find anything in it, but if one doesn't fully understand it or make any effort to take part, how can they expect to get much out of it? How often would someone go to a concert but not get into the spirit of it? Imagine how different the whole experience would be if no one sang along. Inevitably there will be days where people will not fully engage with Mass – sometimes they may have too many things on their minds and not be able to concentrate on the prayers and readings; there may be distractions in the church, or the priest may simply not connect with the congregation. However, 'full, conscious and active participation' goes beyond being a spectator at Mass. We have to make an effort.

This does not necessarily mean having to do certain things like reading or bringing up gifts. Participation is really about one's awareness of what is being celebrated. Some people who appear to be 'doing' very little may in fact be participating most intensely. Active participation calls on those attending to understand what they are doing and grow in their appreciation of the sacrament. Sharing in the Eucharist means trying to see the whole of our life, all of our relationships, and indeed the whole of creation as our offering to God along with the offering of Christ: 'With humble spirit and contrite heart may we be accepted by you, O Lord.' It would be a mistake to see the Eucharist as simply an abstract ritual.

When there is an awareness of the real significance of the liturgy, it becomes an encounter with Christ. For Catholics, belief in the presence of Christ in the Eucharist is as real today as it was in first-century Palestine. We will look more closely at this in the next lesson.

GROUP WORK
Think of the more positive experiences people have had at a religious service and discuss what it was that enhanced those liturgies. As a group, compile a list of ways religious services can appeal to young people.

SUMMARY
- 'The Church earnestly desires that all the faithful be led to the full, conscious and active participation in liturgical celebrations.'
- The more one engages in the Mass, the more one will get from it.
- Active participation calls on those attending to understand what they are doing and grow in their appreciation of the sacrament.

LESSON 81 – MASS ATTENDANCE AND PARTICIPATION

LESSON 82
THE EUCHARIST

Objective: This lesson will look at the meaning of the Eucharist.

OPENING CONVERSATION
Think of a particular meal you shared with family and friends to celebrate a special occasion. What was it about that meal that made it enjoyable for you? How did you participate in this meal? Was it for a special occasion? How did you prepare for it? How did you feel after it?

The real meaning of Mass

'Celebration' is a word we tend to associate with 'big' occasions in our lives. Mass is a weekly celebration for the Christian community; for some it is a daily celebration. The word 'eucharist' comes from the Greek *eukaristos*, and means 'thanksgiving'. As the faith community gathers to celebrate the Eucharist, they express appreciation and thanks to God. In the words of the Gloria: 'We praise you, we bless you, we adore you, we glorify you, we give you thanks for your great glory …' Yet how many people attending the liturgy have any real sense of what it is they are celebrating?

THE LAST SUPPER
The night before he died, Jesus assembled with his disciples for the Passover meal. There, anticipating his death the next day, Jesus instituted the Eucharist. In this sacrament he gave and gives us his own body and blood, to be constantly celebrated and received as 'a living sacrifice of praise' to God. Sacrifice is a free offering, a gift, made by a person for the welfare of others. The word comes from two Latin words meaning 'to make sacred'. The greatest sacrifice of all is to give one's life for another. Christ's sacrifice fulfils and surpasses all other sacrifices. It is the source of salvation for all. We are made sharers in this sacrifice through our participation in the Eucharist. The Mass calls us to become 'a living sacrifice of praise' to God – by how we live our lives in the world now.

At the Last Supper, Jesus took a loaf of bread, and after blessing it he broke it, gave it to his disciples and said, 'Take, eat; this is my body'. Then he took a cup of wine and after giving thanks he gave it to his disciples and said, 'Drink from it, all of you; for this is my blood of the covenant, which is poured out for many for the forgiveness of sins' (Mt 26 26-28). His actions expressed the meaning of his death, which would follow shortly – it would be a sacrifice, the giving of his life in a cruel execution whereby his body was given up and his blood poured out for our salvation, redemption, liberation, reconciliation and the forgiveness of sins. It would advance the coming of God's kingdom of love and freedom, goodness and holiness, justice and peace for all.

Jesus asked his followers to do as he had done, and promised that he would be with them when they did.

From her very beginning, the Church has fulfilled Jesus' command and continued to do as Jesus instructed – to celebrate this sacrament, the Eucharist, in his memory. The first Christians gathered in their own houses and brought bread that they had made, blessed it and shared it amongst each other as Jesus had done. It is difficult for us today to understand the image of a meal for the Eucharist, as many of our churches are built for and hold large numbers. Jesus' earthly life was marked by many significant meals. Sharing a meal was significant as it showed that those Jesus chose to eat with were valued and loved. This was particularly noteworthy when Jesus shared a meal with the outcasts of society.

❛ Take, eat; this is my body.

The members of the early Church firmly believed, as we do today, that the bread and wine become the body and blood of Jesus; that the Risen Christ is truly and really present under the appearances of bread and wine to be received in the Eucharist. This belief is known as transubstantiation. Receiving this body and blood of Christ not only bonds us more closely to Christ but also to the body of Christ in the world, the Church, and gives us the grace to live faithfully as his disciples, becoming sharers in his death and in his rising to the new life of the New Creation. The celebration of the Eucharist is the summit of the Church's life. In a very special way, the celebration of Sunday Mass is at the heart of our worship of God. This is where we fulfil the mandate of Jesus from the Last Supper to 'do this in memory of me'.

THE WASHING OF THE FEET

Unlike the Synoptic Gospels, the Gospel according to John does not give an account of the institution of the Eucharist at Jesus' final Passover meal with the disciples. Instead, it tells the story of Jesus washing the disciples' feet before the meal and his final discourse with his disciples. The washing of the feet sets the context for Jesus' teaching on the true meaning of being his disciple. It was an amazing and most symbolic act by Jesus. He, their leader, was performing a task for them that not even a slave was required to perform. When he had finished, Jesus said to them, 'So if I, your Lord and Teacher, have washed your feet, you also ought to wash one another's feet. For I have set you an example, that you also should do as I have done to you' (Jn 13:14-15).

THINK IT THROUGH
- What do you think Jesus was teaching all disciples – including us – through this action?

GO IN PEACE

All Christian prayer, even when a person prays alone, is made as a member of the community to Our Father. 'The summit and source of Christian prayer and life is when the community gathers to celebrate the Eucharist' (*Constitution on the Sacred Liturgy*, 10). The Eucharist is about a community gathering for prayer. The Eucharist is a liturgy. The word 'liturgy' comes from a Greek word that means 'the work of the people'. It is the term given to the public rites of the Church, in which people gather together as a community to worship God and remember what God has done for them, so that when the liturgy is completed they will go out of the church to live fully Christian lives. 'Mass' comes from the Latin word *Mitto/Missum,* which means sending/mission. Mass ends with the words, 'Go in peace, glorifying the Lord by your life': when the service is over the real service begins! The sharing of the bread of life at the Lord's table is an empty celebration if those who participate are unconcerned about sharing with those in need in the world.

Blessed John Paul II in his message to the Eucharistic Congress in London in 1981 said:

> The Congress has taught you to live the breaking of bread as Church, according to its demands: welcoming, exchanging, sharing, going beyond barriers, being concerned for the conversion of people, the renunciation of prejudices, the transformation of our social milieu in structure and spirit. You have understood that to be true and logical; your meeting at the Eucharist table must have practical consequences.

REFLECT AND DISCUSS

Read the following prayer written by Henri Nouwen and answer the questions that follow:

> Dear Lord ... I think of the thousands of people suffering from lack of food and of the millions suffering from lack of love ... Isn't my faith in your presence in the breaking of the bread meant to reach out beyond the small circle of my brothers to the larger circle of humanity and to alleviate suffering as much as possible?
>
> If I can recognise you in the sacrament of the Eucharist, I must also be able to recognise you in the many hungry men, women and children. If I cannot translate my faith in your presence under the appearance of bread and wine into action for the world, I am an unbeliever.
> (From *A Cry for Mercy* by Henri J. M. Nouwen)

- What is the main point that Henri Nouwen is making?
- Do you think many people attending Mass understand the significance of the final blessing?

RESEARCH PROJECT

Research one Catholic organisation that takes action for the world. Outline the work that they do. How does the Catholic faith shape their vision and work?

SUMMARY

- When people come together to celebrate the Eucharist, they remember how and why Jesus gave his life for them.
- Transubstantiation is the belief in Christ's Real presence in the Eucharist.
- 'Mass' comes from the Latin word *Mitto/Missum* which means sending/mission.
- When the Mass ends, people are sent out of the church to live fully Christian lives.

LESSON 83
SACRED SPACES

Objective: This lesson will examine the importance of sacred spaces and church buildings.

OPENING ACTIVITY

Read this extract from the poem 'Church Going' by Philip Larkin and answer the questions that follow:

'CHURCH GOING'

Once I am sure there's nothing going on
I step inside, letting the door thud shut.
Another church: matting seats and stone,
And little books, sprawling of flowers, cut
For Sunday, brownish now; some brass stuff
Up at the holy end; the small neat organ;
And a tense, musty, unignorable silence,
Brewed God knows how long. Hatless, I take off
My cycle clips in awkward reverence.

– What sort of atmosphere does the poet suggest one finds in a church?
– How is a sense of the sacredness of the place conveyed?
– How does he show respect for the building he has entered?
– What do you think prompted him to go in?

CHURCH BUILDINGS

Eucharistic celebrations began in the homes of Christian families. However, since the beginning of Christianity, church art and architecture has sought to provide an appropriate setting to worship God. From the solemn basilicas of the early centuries to the imposing cathedrals of the Middle Ages, to the churches, large and small, which gradually sprang up throughout the world, all give witness to people's attempts to express the mystery of God and to provide spaces where people can most easily experience the presence of God in their lives.

Sometimes people make a habit of visiting the church. Often when passing, they stop in for a few minutes of silence or to light a candle and offer a prayer.

REFLECT AND DISCUSS
Read this quote and answer the questions that follow:

On holidays I often call into some of the huge cathedrals they have in the big cities. I suppose I'm a bit of a tourist and a bit of a worshipper. I take pictures rather guiltily, wondering if I'm being respectful. But I do kneel or sit down to pray, and in these beautiful places I'm filled with a sense of God's majesty. The high-domed ceilings remind me of the vastness of God, the holiness of God, and yet it doesn't prevent me from praying with a sense of closeness to this Supreme Being that has inspired human beings to build such a place. The beauty of the wonderful artwork reminds me of the creativity of God, and I imagine God admiring the work as well, just as loving parents smile approvingly at the artwork of their children.

▶ What draws this person in to sacred buildings?
▶ Have you ever found yourself drawn to visit a cathedral when visiting a new town or city?
▶ Name a church or cathedral that you were impressed by and say why it impressed you.
▶ In the first letter to the Corinthians, St Paul says '… you are God's temple' (3:16). What do you think St Paul meant?

The interior of St Mel's Cathedral, Longford before the fire that destroyed it in 2009

SAINT MEL'S CATHEDRAL

On Christmas Day 2009, one of the finest Catholic churches in Ireland, St Mel's Cathedral in Longford, was destroyed by a fire. Remarkably, with the fire taking place on the feast of the Nativity, a painting of the Holy Family in the side chapel escaped damage. The cathedral was a neo-classical stone building designed by Joseph B. Keane and built between 1840 and 1889. It displayed many outstanding features, including twenty-four limestone columns, a belfry and portico. The cathedral was dedicated to St Mel, whom it is believed came to Ireland with St Patrick and was Bishop of Ardagh. Restoration of the cathedral is underway. Bishop Colm O'Reilly, speaking about the planned restoration of the cathedral, said:

A cathedral is a lot more than an elegant and beautiful building. Always remember, I tell people, that any church, large or small, is first and foremost a place for prayer and for worship of God. A sacred place to be in the presence of Our Lord. The beauty of every church and every fine cathedral is for a purpose, to lift our minds to what transcends the material world to the world of the spirit. Saint Mel's Cathedral needs to be a cathedral for the future as well as for the present. It must be a place where people long after our time will continue to worship in spirit and in truth, as Jesus told the Samaritan woman at the well.

OTHER SACRED PLACES

We can create sacred places in our own homes by making a space where we can sit quietly, meditate and get in touch with God who is always present in our lives but whose presence we sometimes miss amid all the noise and activity. A candle, a picture or icon, a plant or other symbol of nature, or background music can all help to create a space in which the normal activities and noises of our daily lives make way for us to experience God with us.

Throughout the world there are many places of pilgrimage that because of the events that took place in them and the stories behind them are known and experienced as sacred places. People who visit these sites experience themselves in the presence of God, find it easier to pray, and come away renewed to return to their daily lives. We will look at some of these in the next lesson

OVER TO YOU
- Create a design for the restoration of St Mel's Cathedral.
- In words or drawings, highlight the key features you would include in this building.
- What items would you use to create a sacred space in your home or school?

GROUP WORK
Working in groups, find out more about a church in your locality. Use the following questions to guide you:

- What shape or design does it have?
- When was it built?
- Who designed it?
- What changes, if any, to the design has it undergone in recent years? Why?
- To whom is the church dedicated? Why?

SUMMARY
- From earliest times people have built sacred places to gather to celebrate the Eucharist.
- Sacred buildings, whether of the most simplistic form or of the most sophisticated design, can point to the mystery, wonder and awe of God.

LESSON 84
SACRED PLACES

Objective: This lesson will examine what it means to be a pilgrim and explores some places of pilgrimage.

OPENING ACTIVITY
In pairs, look at the images below and answer the questions:

- Can you identify the location in each of the pictures?
- What action/event is associated with each of the locations depicted?
- What draws Christians to these places?

A pilgrim's journey

Making a journey or pilgrimage to a holy place in order to obtain God's help or as an act of penance or thanksgiving has long been part of world religions. A pilgrimage is a journey undertaken for a religious motive; often it is a journey to a shrine of importance to a person's beliefs and faith. The journey is as important as the arrival and time spent at the place of pilgrimage. A person who makes such a journey is called a pilgrim.

Sacred places, such as Knock, Lourdes and the Holy Land as depicted in the images, continue to attract people of all ages and from different backgrounds and experiences. The characteristics of a particular pilgrimage, its traditions, the rituals associated with it, all offer something which is deeply inspiring. Even in the advanced world we live in today, the pilgrimage with its simple practices is still popular.

People go on pilgrimage for all sorts of reasons. There may be just a simple curiosity about the place involved, or they might seek a deeper understanding of their faith. For others, pilgrimage is about thanksgiving or may be a journey where healing, understanding or a special favour is sought. To be a pilgrim is different from being a tourist or any other kind of traveller. Pilgrims set off on a sacred journey with a definite goal.

ASPECTS OF A PILGRIMAGE

» Those who travel as pilgrims come close to the simpler side of life. The sense of removing oneself from everyday life is essential. This is symbolised in various ways, for example in certain places of pilgrimage by removing footwear. For the pilgrim, the journey is meaningful: in climbing the mountain or walking the pilgrim route one gets a sense of being in rhythm with the order of things in nature. In ancient times, going on a pilgrimage to ancient places such as Jerusalem or Compostela usually meant travelling unfamiliar and often dangerous roads, often on foot, for many weeks or months to a place unfamiliar to the pilgrims, and finding lodging wherever possible.

» Along with travelling to a sacred place, pilgrimages frequently involve ritual movements at the site itself. Praying the Stations of the Cross (re-enacting the events of the Passion of Jesus) is a frequent ritual at Roman Catholic shrines.

» Pilgrims tend to travel with others. Meeting others on pilgrimage is enjoyable and rewarding; people share their stories and support each other. There is healing in the companionship.

» Going on a pilgrimage invites change, change in mind and soul. Those who go on pilgrimage come back with a new perspective; some say a trouble or worry has eased.

» Going on pilgrimage can lead to a deeper experience of living and prayer which brings one closer to God.

THE CAMINO – THE WAY

The Camino de Santiago de Compostela (the Way of St James) is a series of eight walks, each twenty–thirty kilometres in length. The walks begin in Portugal, Seville or the Pyrenees in France and they all end at the cathedral in Santiago de Compostela in Spain, where it is believed the relics of St James are kept. Those who walk the stages are given a 'pilgrim passport' which can be stamped at the end of each completed stage. As with all pilgrimages, people choose to walk the Camino for a variety of reasons. Many travel with a friend or in a small group, while others will make the pilgrimage on their own, often meeting up with others on the way and sharing their story. The popularity of the Camino is increasing each year, many choosing it as an alternative to the Spanish sun holiday. UNESCO made the Camino de Santiago a World Heritage site in 1993.

The film *The Way* tells the story of a father-son relationship set against the backdrop of the Camino de Santiago pilgrimage in Spain. Martin Sheen plays the father, while his son Emilio Estevez wrote and directed the film and also plays his son in the film. The film depicts the pilgrimage motif; the journey through life, the baggage we carry, the varying paths we take and the people we journey with are all discussed. The scene where they arrive at the cathedral in Santiago de Compostela captures a sense of awe and wonder that many who walk the Camino speak of as they attend Mass at the cathedral at the end of their pilgrimage.

LOUGH DERG

Lough Derg, also known as St Patrick's Purgatory, is believed to be among the oldest centres of Christian pilgrimage in Western Europe, supposedly dating back to the sixth century. Lough Derg lies about four miles north of the village of Pettigo in County Donegal. The association of the name of St Patrick with Lough Derg dates back as far as records go and the legends that link him with the place point to a tradition already firmly established by the twelfth century. Pilgrims go to Lough Derg because of the intensity of the experience. Although it is one of the most penitential of pilgrimages, many make the pilgrimage annually.

The following is one person's account of her pilgrimage to Lough Derg:

I have made the pilgrimage every year for the last eleven years. I usually go with a friend or family member. I don't know what it is – each year I say this is the last one, but as June approaches I just want to go back. I suppose I feel grateful for so many things in my life – my family and especially my health – so I go in thanks to God for that. I also dedicate prayers and aspects of the pilgrimage to those for whom I want to pray. For example, this year a friend of mine has been diagnosed with cancer so I prayed the rounds especially for her.

For me, the hardest part of the pilgrimage is the fast. From midnight prior to arriving on Lough Derg you observe a complete fast from all food and drink (water and medication excluded of course). During the three days on the island, one meal a day is allowed. This consists of dry toast with black tea or coffee. The fast ends on midnight of the third day. I really find this difficult – I just love my food!

Having arrived on the island, three stations are made before 9.20 p.m. on the first evening. Four more stations are made in the Basilica during the night vigil and one is made on the second and third days.

For some reason this year the vigil was very tough as well. The vigil involves staying awake for twenty-four hours. It begins at 10 p.m. on the first evening and ends after Benediction on the second day, when we can finally go to bed. Regarding walking barefoot, I am a fit and sporty person so I don't have a problem with it, whatever the weather! Somehow, I think walking barefoot brings the group together and builds a bond between the people on pilgrimage.

I always enjoy the quietness of Lough Derg and I find the stations and the rounds help me to focus and offer prayers for the intentions of others and for myself. I suppose it is hard to imagine it and even more difficult to explain it, but there is a huge sense of peace and everyone seems to get a lot out of the whole experience. I find it really rewarding, and while many people say they could never do it as it is so tough, I think that life's journey on a daily basis is often even harder. Lough Derg's motto is 'Bringing you the gift of hope', with a supporting message of 'With you on life's journey'. The pilgrimage reminds me that God is with me as I go through life, so each year I am glad of the opportunity to reflect on that. Maybe this is what draws me back.

THINK IT THROUGH
- Explain why people are drawn to this pilgrimage today?
- What aspect of the pilgrimage would you find difficult?
- A recent report outlined that there was between a 10% and 15% increase on numbers making the one-day pilgrimage over the previous year, with an increase in the three-day retreats also. Can you suggest possible reasons for the increase in these figures?

Comparative Religious Studies
Research a place of pilgrimage in one other major world religion.

YOU WILL FIND ADDITIONAL INFORMATION ON WWW.SEEKANDFIND.IE

SUMMARY
- Pilgrimage is a sacred journey undertaken with a definite goal.
- Motivations for pilgrimage vary, but can include thanksgiving, healing or a desire to deepen one's faith.
- In the present day, pilgrimage has maintained and even increased its appeal around the world.
- Santiago de Compostela in Spain is a popular destination for pilgrims of all ages, from all over the world.
- The Lough Derg pilgrimage is physically demanding: it involves sleep deprivation, fasting, ritual and personal sacrifice, but it is popular today and considered rewarding by those who participate.

LESSON 85
CELTIC SPIRITUALITY

Objective: This lesson will look at the traditions associated with sacred places in Ireland and give an account of a Pattern day celebration.

OPENING ACTIVITY
Below are pictures of four Celtic sites. Name the site and the saint associated with each site. The table opposite contains the answers, though not in the correct order.

Celtic Site	Saint
Ardfert Cathedral	St Ciaran
Glendalough	St Patrick
Croagh Patrick	St Kevin
Clonmacnoise	St Brendan

The Celtic Christians

After their conversion to Christianity, the Celts believed in the one God the Creator, the All-Powerful Spirit. They had a great sense of the presence of God in the world around them. The Christian Celts saw God as part of their everyday life, not someone reserved for one day in the week. They did not see separation between the 'sacred' and the 'profane'. Their every task was linked with God through simple prayers asking for blessings or protection or to offer praise for what they had.

The Celtic Christians prayed in simple ways. They were observant and appreciative of the world in which they lived and saw God in it. Therefore they sang and prayed as part of their working day. As well as a spirit of adventure, the Celtic faith fostered a love of solitude, a life set in tune with nature.

Saint Patrick's Breastplate, or the Lorica of St Patrick, is an example of a Celtic prayer. It is written in simple language and in the style of a druidic incantation, and is recited for protection on a journey. *Lorica* is a Latin word which means armour. The Celtic Christians believed God was with them in every aspect of their lives, and especially that God protected them against danger.

OVER TO YOU
- Read St Patrick's Breastplate slowly line by line. Note if any lines stand out for you.

SAINT PATRICK'S BREASTPLATE

I arise today
Through a mighty strength, the invocation of the Trinity,
Through a belief in the Threeness,
Through confession of the Oneness
Of the Creator of creation.

I arise today
Through the strength of Christ's birth and his baptism,
Through the strength of his crucifixion and his burial,
Through the strength of his resurrection and his ascension,
Through the strength of his descent for the judgement of doom.

I arise today through the strength of Heaven
the rays of the sun,
the radiance of the moon,
the splendour of fire,
the speed of lightening,
the swiftness of the wind,
the depth of the sea,
the stability of the earth,
the firmness of rock.

I arise today through the power of God:
God's might to comfort me,
God's wisdom to guide me,
God's eye to look before me,
God's ear to hear me,
God's word to speak for me,
God's hand to lead me,
God's way to lie before me,
God's shield to protect me,
God's Heavenly Host to save me
from the snares of the devil,
from temptations to sin,
from all who wish me ill,
from near and afar,
alone and with others.

May Christ shield me today
against poison and fire,
against drowning and wounding,
so that I may fulfil my mission
and bear fruit in abundance.
Christ behind and before me,
Christ behind and above me,
Christ with me and in me,
Christ around and about me,
Christ on my right and on my left,
Christ when I lie down at night,
Christ when I rise in the morning,
Christ in the heart of every man who thinks of me,
Christ in the mouth of everyone that speaks of me,
Christ in every eye that sees me,
Christ in every ear that hears me.

LESSON 85 — CELTIC SPIRITUALITY

Our Lady's Well, Ballyheigue, Co. Kerry

The Celtic tradition is still alive

In recent times, there is an increased awareness of the spiritual energy of ancient places of worship. The open-air celebration of Mass at holy wells has experienced a revival. The village of Ballyheigue, Co. Kerry, celebrates Pattern day on 8 September. The Pattern, which takes its name from the word 'patron' and honours the patron saint associated with the sacred place of an area, usually marked harvest time and was often offered as a thanksgiving for the year's work.

REFLECT AND DISCUSS

Here is an account of the Pattern day celebrations in Ballyheigue, Co. Kerry, as recounted by one of a group of Transition Year students who attended the event and interviewed a variety of people who had travelled for the celebration:

Many people from far and near travel to Ballyheigue to celebrate its annual Pattern day. Preparations were underway many days before the event. The local sergeant remarked as he oversaw the traffic arriving, 'We spent four hours preparing last night and I will be working until 6 a.m. tomorrow morning. It is my pleasure to work hard on this special day.'

The Pattern began as usual with open-air Mass, celebrated by the Bishop of Kerry, Bishop Bill Murphy, at Our Lady's Well. At all times, the well is a place of pilgrimage and hope in times of need for people in this area.

As crowds of people started to arrive, the area around the blessed well filled up, and eventually by eleven o'clock the place was packed with people. The parish priest, Fr Tom Leane, said, 'It is great to see the community spirit and we all enjoy welcoming visitors to celebrate the day with us.' As the Mass ended, Bishop Bill Murphy walked around and chatted to locals and visitors. Bishop Bill said one of the things he likes most about the Pattern day in Ballyheigue is that 'it links religion and life as people go to Mass in the morning and socialise around the village afterwards'.

After Mass, everyone headed to the village, and the Pattern day festivities were well underway. The stewards, local people and organisers were delighted with the turnout of people. Postmaster Brendan Moriarty said, 'Today is one of the days that many people look forward to, but the only problem is that it is very hard to deliver the post as there is never anyone at home!' A local, Fiona Moriarty, said, 'It is a day enjoyed by all. From generation to generation, people of all age groups in Ballyheigue look forward to this day all year long.' Now that this year is over it is time to tidy up and people are hoping that next year will be as successful as this year was!

▶ Why do you think this is such a popular event?
▶ What does Bishop Bill Murphy like about this day?
▶ Have you ever attended a similar event?

JOURNAL

What aspect of Celtic tradition appeals most to you?

RESEARCH PROJECT

Research a holy well or Celtic site. Prepare and present a report outlining the traditions and rituals associated with the place.

SUMMARY

- Celtic spirituality linked people's faith with everyday life, work with prayer, individual with communal prayer.
- Some of the Celtic sites continue to be popular places of pilgrimage in parts of Ireland today.

SECTION H

GOD'S UNFOLDING STORY

LESSON 86
STORIES AND STORYTELLERS

Objective: This lesson will explore the importance of stories in life.

OPENING CONVERSATION
Do you have a favourite story, perhaps a favourite story from childhood, or something interesting that happened to you? Share this story with a partner.

THE GOLD AND IVORY TABLECLOTH

A pastor assigned to a new ministry, to reopen an old church, arrived at his new place of work in early October. When he arrived, he saw that the church was very run-down and needed much work. He set a goal to have everything done in time to have a service on Christmas Eve. After weeks of hard work, repairs were ahead of schedule, but on 19 December a terrible storm hit the area and lasted for two days. On the 21st, the pastor went over to the church. His heart sank when he saw that the roof had leaked, causing a large area of plaster to fall off the front wall of the sanctuary just behind the pulpit.

On his way home he noticed that a local business was having a second-hand sale for charity so he stopped in. One of the items he saw was a beautiful, handmade, gold and ivory tablecloth with a cross embroidered right in the centre. It was just the right size to cover up the hole in the front wall. He bought it and headed back to the church.

An older woman coming the opposite direction was trying to catch the bus, but she missed it. The pastor invited her to wait in the warm church for the next bus. She sat in a pew and paid no attention to the pastor while he got a ladder to put up the tablecloth as a wall tapestry. The pastor could hardly believe how beautiful it looked, and it covered up the entire problem area.

Then he noticed the woman walking down the centre aisle. Her face was like a sheet. 'Pastor,' she asked, 'where did you get that tablecloth?' The pastor explained. The woman asked him to check the lower right corner to see if the initials EBG were crocheted into it there. They were. These were the initials of the woman, and she had made this tablecloth thirty-five years before, in Austria. The woman could hardly believe it as the pastor told how he had just bought the tablecloth.

The woman explained that before the war, she and her husband were well-to-do people in Austria. When the Nazis came, she was forced to leave. Her husband was going to follow her the next week. He was captured, sent to prison, and she never saw him or her home again. The pastor wanted to give her the tablecloth but she made him keep it for the church. The pastor insisted on driving her home – it was the least he could do.

On Christmas Eve the first service in the reopened church was almost full. At the end of the service, the pastor greeted everyone at the door. One older man, whom the pastor recognised from the neighbourhood, continued to sit in one of the pews and stare, and the pastor wondered why he wasn't leaving. The man asked him where he had got the tablecloth on the front wall because it was identical to one that his wife had made years ago when they lived in Austria before the war, and he wondered how could there be two tablecloths so much alike. He told the pastor how the Nazis came, how he forced his wife to flee for her safety and he was supposed to follow her, but he was arrested and put in prison. He never saw his wife or his home again.

The pastor asked him if he would allow him to take him for a little drive. They drove to the same house where the pastor had taken the woman three days earlier. He helped the man climb the three flights of stairs to the woman's apartment, knocked on the door, and he saw the greatest Christmas reunion he could ever imagine.

A COMPELLING STORY

All good stories convey truths, though not all stories are historically factual. As one old proverb says: 'All stories are true, and some of them actually happened.' True or not, this is one fantastic story, containing many of the elements that make a story compelling: A lonely couple, separated by a great evil, each unaware of the other's fate, brought together again on the holiest of holidays. The key to their reunion is an ordinary object that no one else valued, and the chain of events unfolds due to an amazingly serendipitous series of circumstances. If the storm hadn't knocked a hole in the church wall, if someone else had bought the tablecloth, if the woman hadn't happened to be standing outside the church at just the right moment, if her long-lost husband hadn't coincidentally been a member of that particular church, the couple might never have found each other again.

What do we know of this tale? It was written by the Reverend Howard C. Schade, a pastor from New York, and was first published in the December 1954 issue of *Reader's Digest*. There are a few internet-circulated versions of this tale that add some additional details not present in the original. As for verifying the truth of this remarkable tale, there's very little to go on. Its author, the Reverend Schade, passed away in 1989 and therefore can't provide additional information, and the story as presented is remarkably devoid of detail for a supposedly 'real-life' drama: it includes no dates, no names, no locations – no starting point whatsoever that would prove useful in verifying it. And perhaps the oddest factor of all is that apparently no one other than the Reverend Schade – not another writer, not the pastor who reunited the tragically separated spouses, not the couple themselves – ever chronicled this amazing story or identified its subjects.

> '*All stories are true, and some of them actually happened.*

THINK IT THROUGH
- Do you think this is a true story?
- If the Reverend Schade made up this story, what message do you think he was trying to convey?
- What in your opinion are the qualities of a compelling story?

LESSON 86 – STORIES AND STORYTELLERS

Stories in our culture

Everyone likes a good story. It would seem that the human mind and heart learn best from stories – especially in sharing wisdom for life. Right from the earliest days of human history, it appears that people loved stories – we can see this in the early cave paintings, which tell stories of, for example, a day's hunting (the cave drawing pictured comes from Lascaux near Montignac, France, which was discovered in 1941). We can imagine the early humans gathered around a fire listening to the exploits of their hunters and their chases! The stories were passed on orally when most people couldn't read or write, and even today stories are still passed on orally in families.

Styles and methods of storytelling and experiencing stories have changed but the essentials are still the same and stories are still hugely popular. We don't just listen to stories, we can watch them unfold on the big screen, on TV or on the internet.

As a nation we spend hours watching TV every week, and most of the programmes we view tell a story in some shape or form. This is obviously true in the case of soaps operas and animated series. News programmes tell the stories of the day, while documentaries often tell stories of the past.

Not all stories in our culture need to be visual. Lots of people still enjoy reading a good story. This was evident when large numbers of people queued up for the release of the *Harry Potter* books. Of course many books like *Harry Potter*, the *Twilight* series and *The Hunger Games* go on to be equally popular as films.

And we are still telling oral stories – when you go home from school today, you may tell stories about what happened, especially if it was something dramatic or unusual.

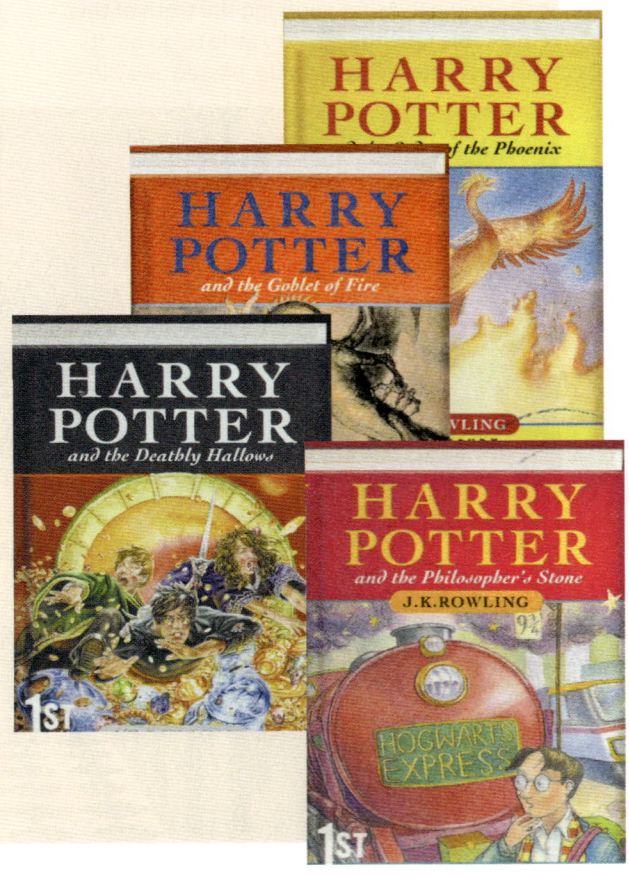

WHO TELLS THE STORIES?

Different people tell different kinds of stories. For fiction writers, their whole livelihood is based on their ability to tell compelling stories. Novelist Maeve Binchy once said that she was always telling stories to people anyway, so she might as well write them down. Songwriters tell stories in their lyrics and music. Historians tell true stories of the past as objectively as they can. Teachers, especially in primary schools, try to capture their students' attention by telling stories in class. Priests often tell stories as part of the homily. Jesus himself told stories to convey his message. It would be hard to get through life without telling stories.

In a way we are all storytellers. We share our life stories with others. On a Monday morning when we tell our friends what we did over the weekend, when we tag ourselves on Facebook, when we post images from our lives on Instagram – these are all ways that we tell our story. The media now has to keep up with Twitter as people tell the stories of what is happening in the world in real time. We are all storytellers and more people than ever before get to hear our stories.

OVER TO YOU

- Write a short account of your favourite programme on TV. What do you like about it? What do you think of the quality of the storytelling? Share your ideas with the class.
- Write a short review of a film or book that you like. What did you like about it? What made it a good story?
- Design what you would see as the cover of your autobiography and write a blurb for the book.

SUMMARY

- From the earliest days of human history people have loved stories.
- Styles and methods of storytelling and experiencing stories have changed but the essentials are still the same.
- Different people tell different kinds of stories.
- We all have stories to tell.

LESSON 87
THE BIBLE

Objective: This lesson will give a brief overview and description of the Bible.

OPENING CONVERSATION
The Bible is the most widely published and read book in the history of the world. Why do you think this is so?

Stories in the Bible

The story told in the Bible covers many centuries. The Bible is not, in fact, a single book but a library of seventy-three books – the forty-six books of the Old Testament and the twenty-seven books of the New Testament. The earliest parts of the Bible come from four thousand years ago, while the last books were written around 1,900 years ago. All the books are closely linked because, when put together, they tell a single story of God's unconditional love and plan for humankind since the beginning of time.

The first part of the Bible, the Old Testament, tells the story of God's covenantal relationship with the Israelites – now the Jewish people – before the coming of Jesus. ('Testament' means covenant, and refers to the agreement or treaty that God and the People of God have entered into.) The Old Testament also contains the Sacred Scripture of the Jewish people, though there are some books in the Old Testament that are not recognised by Jews today as part of their Scriptures. The Old Testament also contains some books which are not listed in some Protestant bibles. Jesus himself was very familiar with the books of the Old Testament. As a child and young man, he would have studied them and heard them read in the synagogue; they shaped his trust in his Father and how he fulfilled his mission on earth. As an adult, Jesus quoted from them frequently.

The second part of the Bible, the New Testament, is the story of Jesus Christ, the founder of the Church, his life and teachings, Passion, Resurrection and Ascension. It is also the story of the early Church, whose members, after Jesus' Ascension, came to be known as Christians.

LITERARY GENRES IN THE BIBLE

The biblical authors used a variety of literary genres to pass on the truth of God's Revelation. The term 'literary genre' is used to describe different kinds of writing; for example, poetry, fiction, history, parable, hymn, sermon, letter and so on. Knowing the literary genre of a particular book or passage helps us to discover the message the author intended to communicate and to interpret the meaning of God's Word, or Revelation, for us. Just as we would approach a novel with a different frame of mind than we would read a history or science book, so we read the biblical historical books in one way, and biblical poetry or parables or hymns or sermons or letters in another way. In the Bible we find stories that are factual, stories based on fact, and non-factual stories; in other words, we find a wide variety of literary genres. For example, in the Old Testament we read the books of Kings as historical accounts of the reigns of kings, while we read the books of Jonah and Job as short stories, not as factual accounts of actual happenings. We read the Song of Songs as a love poem, and the books of Wisdom, Proverbs and Sirach (Ecclesiasticus) as accounts that offer guidance and advice on how to live the covenant faithfully. In the New Testament, the story of Jesus' Death is the account of his actual, historical death on the Cross; whereas the stories of the Good Samaritan and of the Prodigal Son are not accounts of historical events. They are parables, intended to teach great truths and spiritual wisdom for life. So it is important to know the literary genre of the biblical text or passage we are reading.

Jonah and the whale

WORDS OF WISDOM IN THE BIBLE

The Bible is full of words of wisdom. These were handed down from one generation to the next primarily by word of mouth, using simple language and examples from people's own life experiences. What was important was the wisdom or meaning they contained for the people. The stories were the vehicle used to pass on this wisdom. For example, for nomadic farmers, fishing folk, shepherds or merchants, the stories were fashioned to suit their situation. While stories of lost sheep might seem irrelevant to people today, they spoke clearly to nomads, farmers and shepherds of biblical times.

Readers of the Bible today need to take this into consideration. Once we understand that such biblical stories are a vehicle for meaning, and we peel back the layers and discover that meaning, we find that their wisdom is as relevant for us today as it was for the audiences of old. This is how we must approach the Bible if we are to learn from its infinite wisdom and apply it to our lives now.

OVER TO YOU

▶ Read the following words of wisdom from the Book of Proverbs. What do these mean for your life today? Proverbs 10:12; 22:24-25; 26:20; 27:19; 28:15; 28:18; 29:11.

▶ Have a go at composing your own wise saying using images that speak to people today.

LESSON 87 — THE BIBLE

Interpreting the Bible

The Bible is a sacred and unique text. The Church teaches that the people who wrote the Bible were inspired by God and, therefore, that the Bible is the Word of God spoken through the words of human beings. In order to hear God's Word accurately we must strive to understand the cultural and historical contexts in which the sacred authors lived, the images they used and the audiences for whom they were writing. To truly understand what God is trying to teach us, we need to be open to the guidance of the Holy Spirit and the guidance of the Church. The Church guides us through the Magisterium – the living teaching office of the Church – and through the living Tradition of the Church. The Catechism states:

> The task of interpreting the Word of God authentically has been entrusted solely to the Magisterium of the Church, that is, to the Pope and to the bishops in communion with him. (CCC, 100)

There are many biblical scholars who spend years studying the Bible and deciphering its words and meaning. This includes their study of the time and the place in which the different books of the Bible were written, taking into account the culture and customs that were prevalent back then. The various translations of the Bible are constantly being updated in light of new insights from such scholars. It can be useful to take all of these things into consideration when we are trying to discover the meaning of a particular story or passage in Scripture.

We must also consider the biblical author's intention if we are to correctly interpret a biblical text. This includes identifying whom the biblical author was primarily addressing and what style of writing, or literary genre, the biblical author used. Biblical scholars help us to achieve these criteria. For example, Mark's account of the Gospel, which was the first account of the Gospel to be written, was primarily addressed to non-Jewish people who had become Christian. Because Mark's audience was not Jewish, there are very few references to the Old Testament in his Gospel. On the other hand, Matthew's Gospel, which was written about twenty years after Mark's, was addressed primarily to a Jewish audience. It is thought that Matthew was a teacher and that he worked as a rabbi for a while. This would explain why Matthew's account of the Gospel has many references to the Old Testament. He was writing for Jews who had converted to Christianity and so he used many Old Testament references to show how Jesus and his teaching brought about what had been foretold by the prophets in the Old Testament. Matthew's extensive use of the Old Testament also clearly shows the unity of the whole Scripture. So, when trying to understand correctly what is being said in Scripture, we need to take into account who the writer was and the group of people for whom he was actually writing.

The Bible is our story. It tells us where we, the Church, the new People of God, have come from. It recounts not just the actions of our ancestors and the understandings they had of the world in which they lived; more importantly, it tells the story of the action and plan of God for our

Matthew, Mark, Luke and John, the Four Evangelists

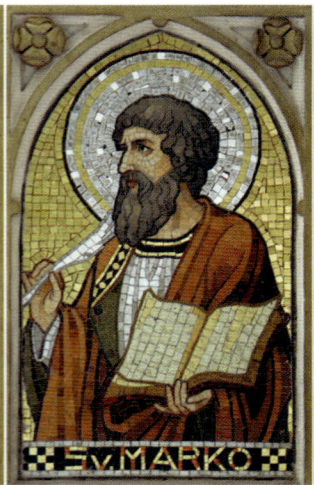

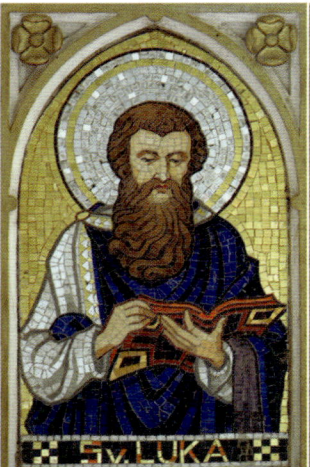

ancestors in faith and, ultimately, for us. God is the central agent in this story. This was true in biblical times and it is still true today. God is still active in our stories, in our own lives, in the Church and in our world.

THINK IT THROUGH

- How carefully do you listen to the readings from the Bible in church?
- Explain the effect, if any, that these readings have on you.
- Think of powerful words from the Bible that have influenced your life; pieces of advice, perhaps, that gave you courage or hope or direction. Share these.

> ❛ *The Bible is our story. It tells us where we, the Church, the new People of God, have come from.*

SUMMARY

- The Bible is not a single book but a library of seventy-three books.
- The first part of the Bible, the Old Testament, tells the story of God's covenantal relationship before the coming of Jesus.
- The New Testament is the story of Jesus Christ and the early Church.
- The biblical authors used a variety of literary genres to pass on the truth of God's Revelation.
- The Bible is the Word of God spoken through the words of human beings.
- To truly understand what God is trying to teach us, we need to be open to the guidance of the Holy Spirit and the guidance of the Church.

LESSON 88
CREATION STORIES

Objective: This lesson will summarise the Creation accounts in the Book of Genesis.

OPENING CONVERSATION
What are the things that make humans different from other animals?

The Book of Genesis – A faith account

The Book of Genesis is not an eyewitness account of what happened billions of years ago but a faith story written by people who wanted those who would come after them to know the truth about how the world and everything in it came to be. The stories told in the first two chapters of Genesis are not meant to teach *scientific truths* about the origins of the world and the universe, questions that scientists and others continue to explore; rather, they teach us some of the great *truths of our faith*. The task of the authors was to give people the answer to the question, 'Where did it all come from?' from a *faith* point of view rather than from a scientific perspective.

The Creation story of Genesis teaches us the truth about the world, about ourselves and about God. It teaches that God made the universe and everything in it. It tells us that God made the trees and plants and everything that grows on the earth; that he made the animals, insects and all the creatures that live upon the earth; and all creatures that live in the sea. Most importantly, it tells us that God made human beings and that he saw human beings as the pinnacle of all creation.

We read in Genesis that when God looked back at the work of Creation he found that it was good, but when God had made man and woman, he found that it was *very* good. Then God gave man and woman responsibility for all creation:

Then God said, 'Let us make humankind in our image, according to our likeness; and let them have dominion over the fish of the sea, and over the birds of the air, and over the cattle, and over all the wild animals of the earth, and over every creeping thing that creeps upon the earth.'

So God created humankind in his image, in the image of God he created them; male and female he created them.

God blessed them, and God said to them, 'Be fruitful and multiply, and fill the earth and subdue it; and have dominion over the fish of the sea and over the birds of the air and over every living thing that moves upon the earth.' ... And it was so. God saw everything that he had made, and indeed, it was very good. (Gn 1:26-28, 30-31)

312   SECTION H: GOD'S UNFOLDING STORY

OVER TO YOU

▶ Read the two creation accounts in Genesis 1–2:3 and 2:4-25. As you read them, note the following:

» God created darkness and light on the first day but the sun and moon on the fourth day. Clearly, this is not a scientific account and cannot be interpreted literally. What this story teaches from a faith point of view is that God is the living Creator and Sustainer of all that exists.
» God created man and woman 'in the image of God'. In the eyes of God, men and women are equal; both fully reflect the divine image.
» According to the first account of Creation, God gave humankind 'dominion' over the rest of creation. The second account of Creation makes it clear that God, therefore, has made us responsible for all of creation and he demands that we be good stewards of creation.
» The story tells us that God rested on the seventh day and made it holy. We, too, should remember to make the Sabbath day holy: a time to disengage from our normal daily routines, so that we have an opportunity to think about our lives, what we really want, and to ask God's help in achieving this.
» The 'person of the earth' (in Hebrew 'Adam') becomes alive by the breath of God.

THE SECOND ACCOUNT OF CREATION

At the beginning of the second chapter of Genesis, there is a second description of the creation of human beings. This parallel story is much older than that in chapter one. It imagines God as a modeller of clay. It is a very different kind of story and yet one that reaffirms and elaborates on the truths in the first account of Creation.

> ... the Lord God formed man from the dust of the ground, and breathed into his nostrils the breath of life; and the man became a living being. (Gn 2:7)

It was when God breathed life-giving breath into the man that he became a living human being. In Hebrew, the word 'breath' is the same as 'spirit', as in words like 'respiration' (which means 'breathing'). As human beings, we share in the very life of God. Not only is the breath we breathe the breath of God but we are created in the image of God. Every breath we breathe is God's own breath too. Human life is an expression of God's life.

LESSON 88 – CREATION STORIES

Then the Lord God said, 'It is not good that the man should be alone; I will make him a helper as his partner.' So out of the ground the Lord God formed every animal of the field and every bird of the air, and brought them to the man to see what he would call them; and whatever the man called every living creature, that was its name. The man gave names to all cattle, and to the birds of the air, and to every animal of the field; but for the man there was not found a helper as his partner. So the Lord God caused a deep sleep to fall upon the man, and he slept; then he took one of his ribs and closed up its place with flesh. And the rib that the Lord God had taken from the man he made into a woman and brought her to the man. Then the man said,

'This at last is bone of my bones
and flesh of my flesh;
this one shall be called Woman,
for out of Man this one was taken.'
(Gn 2:18-23)

The story now refers for the first time to 'man' and 'woman'. And, as in the first account, both are equally created in the divine image. So, we learn that human beings are specially created, individually. Each human being is unique and different. Just as each one of us has different fingerprints, so too every heart, every mind, every soul is different. 'For we are what [God] has made us' (Eph 2:10).

THINK IT THROUGH
- The Book of Genesis teaches us that our life is a share in God's own life. What conclusions does this lead you to make about your own life and about human life in general?

Comparative Religious Studies
Different religions have their own stories and myths to express their belief in how the world was created. Research a creation story from another religion or worldview.

YOU WILL FIND ADDITIONAL INFORMATION ON WWW.SEEKANDFIND.IE

JOURNAL
What do you think it is about you personally that shows you are made in the image of God?

SUMMARY
- The stories told in the first two chapters of Genesis are not meant to teach scientific truths about the origins of the world and the universe.
- The creation accounts in Genesis teach us some of the great truths of our faith.
- In the eyes of God, men and women are equal; both fully reflect the divine image.
- God has made humankind responsible for all of creation.
- The story tells us that God rested on the seventh day and made it holy.
- We, too, should remember to make the Sabbath day holy.

LESSON 89
COVENANT STORIES

Objective: This lesson will examine God's self-revelation and his covenant relationship with humankind.

OPENING ACTIVITY
Write briefly about one thing you found out because someone revealed it to you, rather than because you found it out for yourself. How did you feel in this situation?

God's self-revelation

God has created us and continuously reaches out to us, inviting us to live in a unique relationship with him. This is the core message of Divine Revelation.

The term 'Divine Revelation' describes how God, out of his love, has freely reached out to make himself and his divine plan of Creation and Salvation known to everyone gradually over time. The divine plan of Creation reveals that God has created everyone to live in relationship, or communion, with him. The divine plan of Salvation reveals that God desires to restore his original plan and to adopt every person as a son or a daughter through their relationship with his Son, Jesus Christ.

Through Revelation we experience God's loving outreach and we receive the gift of spiritual wisdom for our lives and the gift of grace that enables us to live it. Divine Revelation began through God's action at the dawn of Creation and his relationship with the first humans, and continued through his relationship with Noah, Abraham, Moses and the ancient Israelites. Jesus is the centre and fullness of all Revelation and there will be no Revelation after him (cf. John 1:14-16.) God still makes himself and his loving plan of goodness and Salvation known — it is happening now and will continue until the end of time.

God always desires that each of us would come to know him better and better. He invites each of us to live in a deeper and deeper friendship and communion with him. God gave the world the Church to pass on his Revelation and to invite us into a loving relationship and to live as his people, the People of God. We call this transmission of Divine Revelation Sacred Tradition. God extends this invitation through the Church to each person in their own particular place and time, situation and circumstance.

A Noah's ark built by Turkish and German Greenpeace volunteers, on the face of Mount Ararat in Turkey, the site where it is thought that the biblical ark landed

LESSON 89 – COVENANT STORIES

315

THE STORIES OF THE COVENANT IN THE OLD TESTAMENT

The first part of the Bible, the Old Testament, passes on the story of God's dealings with humankind and in particular with his chosen people, the Israelites. The story begins in the Book of Genesis, the first book of the Old Testament, with the story of Creation and the Fall. God revealed himself to be the Faithful One and the Keeper of Promises. He entered a covenant with his people and promised them salvation. That promise and covenant is reaffirmed in the story of Noah and the Great Flood (cf. Genesis 9:1-17). We next read about the great promise that God made to Abram, whom he later named Abraham. God chose Abram and made a covenant with him and in turn with the descendants of himself and his wife Sarai, whose name God later changed to Sarah. (In Old Testament times, the changing of a person's name often signified that the person had been chosen for a special task by God.)

God promised to be their God, to give them numerous descendants and a special land to live in and to bring blessings through them on all people. In return, God asked them to believe in his promises and to be obedient to the commands of the covenant. Biblical covenants were 'solemn' agreements, the seriousness of which was often sealed by a blood ritual (cf. Exodus 24:1-8.) These covenants were entered into freely by both parties. However, biblical covenants are not agreements between equals. Human beings have nothing to offer to God which is not in the first place God's gift to us, except their free response to God. We love God because God loved us first (cf. 1 Jn 4:19). In a covenant, it is the 'relationship' between the two parties that is central; it is the 'word' of both parties that is the sacred binding force.

The Bible (and the blessing of the water during the celebration of baptism) refers to these covenants:

» The Covenant with Noah: God made an everlasting covenant with Noah and with all living beings. When the waters of the flood had receded, God asked Noah and his people to have special care 'for human life' (Gn 9:5); God promised the people that 'never again shall there be a flood to destroy the earth' (Gn 9:11). As a sign of this covenant, God placed the rainbow in the sky. (Read the story in Genesis 9.)

» The Covenant with Abraham: Later (biblical scholars set the date around 1800 BCE), God invited Abraham and Sarah and their descendants into a covenant relationship, promising them that they would have many descendants, who would bring a blessing for all the nations on the earth. (Read about God's covenant with Abraham, Sarah and their descendants in Genesis 12:1-4, Genesis 15:1-6 and Genesis 17.)

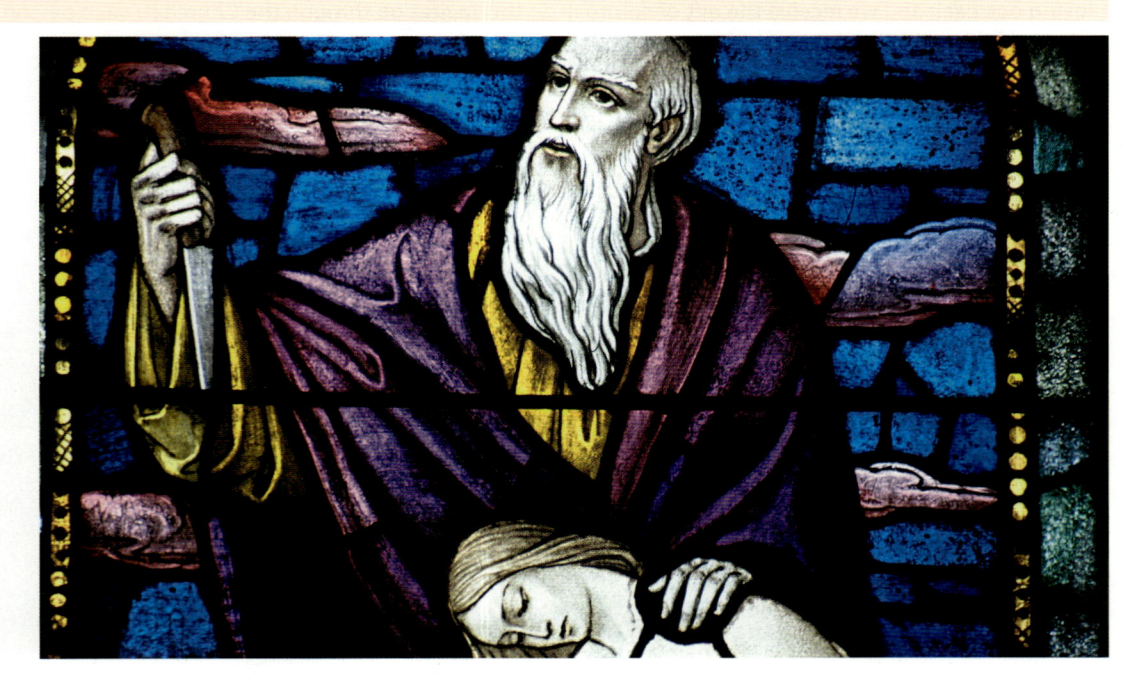

Stained-glass of Abraham and Isaac

Crossing the Red Sea by Luca Giordano (1681)

» **The Covenant at Sinai:** During the Exodus (Biblical scholars set the date around 1200 BCE), God, through Moses, led the Israelites out of slavery in Egypt and invited them into the covenant at Mount Sinai. The Israelites committed themselves to living as God's own people. They received the Ten Commandments, summarising the Law of the Covenant. (Read Deuteronomy 4–6).

The Prophets: While God was always faithful to the covenant, the Israelites often failed to keep and live faithfully by the commitment they made in the covenant. God, in his faithfulness, raised up prophets, such as Isaiah (whose name in Hebrew means 'God is salvation'), to call them back to living the covenant as they promised.

GROUP WORK

Work in groups of three. Each person looks up and reads one of the great accounts of the covenant in the Old Testament:

- The Covenant between God and Noah in Genesis 9.
- The Covenant between God and Abraham and Sarah and their descendants in Genesis 12:1-4, Genesis 15:1-6 and Genesis 17.
- The Covenant between God and the Israelites in Deuteronomy 4–6.

After reading the biblical text carefully, take turns to explain to the others in your group what you have read. Then share ideas:

- What do all these texts have in common?
- What different images of God are found in each text?
- What do these texts tell us about God's wish for humanity?

The Prophet Isaiah by Gustave Doré (1866)

LESSON 39 – COVENANT STORIES